Y0-BGV-985

★★★★SCRATCH ANKLE, U.S.A.★★★★

AMERICAN PLACE NAMES AND THEIR DERIVATION

★★★★★ SCRATCH ANKLE, U.S.A. ★★★★★

AMERICAN PLACE NAMES AND THEIR DERIVATION

By

MYRON J. QUIMBY

Illustrated by

GLORIA PERRY

South Brunswick
New York: A. S. Barnes and Company
London: Thomas Yoseloff Ltd

Library of Congress Catalogue Card Number: 68-23069

A.S. Barnes and Company., Inc.
Cranbury, New Jersey 08512

Thomas Yoseloff Ltd
108 New Bond Street
London W1Y OQX, England

First Printing, May 1969
Second Printing, May 1970

ISBN: 0 498 06638 X
Printed in the United States of America

To

the small town postmaster

who is fast vanishing

from the American scene.

★★★★PREFACE★★★★

The history of a country is the history of its cities, towns, and villages. I chose to write of the histories, legends, and stories behind American communities with unusual names, skipping intentionally over the Jonesvilles and the Smithtowns.

Screening thousands of names, I tried to choose only those with a bit of the unusual in the name, and, even more, with a story behind that name. Thousands of letters were written, and the replies came rolling in from chambers of commerce, postmasters, grocery stores, lumber companies, insurance companies, power companies, librarians, and just about every other source imaginable.

From the large cities came prepared, expensive brochures, and from the hamlets came scrawled notes on the bottom of my letters of inquiry. Who's to say which were the best stories, those written in posh, expensive surroundings, or those scribbled on the counter of a dusty little store? In my opinion, each was of equal importance for the stories related accounts of the hardships and the humor that helped to weld this gigantic land into one inseparable nation.

It would require an entire library to record each and every name that might qualify for a place in this book. I have but scratched the surface.

Much herein is based upon established and recorded history, carefully checked for accuracy; and much more was gleaned from the memories of old-timers, and from traditions and legends.

Indian legends, in particular, were a great source of information and form a unique part of our historical background as a nation.

A large part of the unrecorded history of our country is included in these pages, and the old-timers' recollections have been captured on paper, before they and their memories pass from the scene forever.

My research started a lot of digging and searching all over the country, as many communities suddenly realized that they, themselves, had no idea from whence came their names. Regrettable for some, it was much too late as there are no records. Those who could have given the history from personal experiences and recollections have passed on, and gone with them are their irreplaceable memories.

Though this book is historical in fact, it is also intended as one of humor. It is fondly hoped that these pages will not only inform and amuse, but will awaken nostalgic memories for the older generation, and for the young, stimulate an interest in, and an appreciation of, the history of these United States of America.

June 17, 1966 — Myron J. Quimby
St. Petersburg, Florida

★★★★ACKNOWLEDGMENTS★★★★

To the hundreds and hundreds of small town postmasters all over the nation goes my appreciation for helping me to write this book. Without the love they showed in writing about "their town," this book could not have been completed.

To the hundreds of chambers of commerce, staffed with dedicated people, who devoted valuable time and gave valuable assistance to my research, I express equal appreciation. It is too often that these organizations and their labors are not appreciated enough by the very people they benefit the most.

The Texas State Historical Association, Austin, Texas, long ago realized the historical value of recording the histories not only of their communities, but of their rivers, mountains, valleys, etc. In a two-volume set, their *Handbook of Texas* sets a standard for all to follow. In these volumes they have recorded the Lone Star State on paper. It is because of their generosity and foresight that you will find a preponderance of Texas names recorded in this book, as I had the history of Texas at my call.

The University of Pennsylvania Press, Philadelphia, Pennsylvania, is greatly appreciated for the wonderful material they allowed me to use from their publication *Pennsylvania,* a guide series book.

My appreciation goes to the *Arizona Republic,* Phoenix, Arizona, for the material they allowed me to use from their publication, *Arizona Days and Ways,* and its supplement *This Is Arizona,* published in February, 1962.

The Dallas *Morning News,* Dallas, Texas, for material used from their *Texas Almanac,* 1966-1967 edition.

To Mr. R. E. Barclay, Copperhill, Tennessee, for the material he so graciously furnished me from his book, *Ducktown-Back in Raht's Time* (Published by the University of North Carolina Press).

Appreciation to the Providence *Journal Evening Bulletin,* for material used from their Rhode Island *Gazetteer,* 1964.

Billy W. Jones, Historian, Ebenezer Missionary Baptist Association, Dry Branch, Georgia, for his delightful material on Dry Branch, Georgia.

J. Gordon Bryson, for material used from his book *Culture of the Shin Oak Ridge Folk,* dealing with Liberty Hill, Texas.

The Wyoming Historical Society, Cheyenne, Wyoming, for their invaluable assistance dealing with Wyoming names and histories.

The San Jacinto County Historical Association, Cold Springs, Texas, for their assistance.

Southern Nevada Historical Museum Association, Las Vegas, Nevada.

Mrs. Annie Sheldon, Eastern Shore Chamber of Commerce, Fairhope, Alabama, for her help, encouragement, and assistance.

Mr. Herman R. Kasper, Secretary-Manager, Jackson County Chamber of Commerce, Marianna, Florida, for great help and originality.

Mr. C. A. Gildersleeve, Wounded Knee Battleground Store, Wounded Knee, South Dakota, for his delightful story of the naming of Wounded Knee, and for one of the most graphic accounts of the Wounded Knee Massacre, which I used liberally, changing very little.

United States Department of the Interior, and their various departments throughout the United States, whose assistance aided in the accuracy of dates, times, and places.

★★★★SYMBOLS★★★★

To avoid endless repetition indicating credits, the figures 1 through 6 have been used, as explained below:

1. Postmasters
2. Chambers of Commerce
3. The Texas Historical Association, Austin, Texas
4. University of Pennsylvania Press, Philadelphia, Pennsylvania
5. *The Arizona Republic,* Phoenix, Arizona
6. Other

****SCRATCH ANKLE, U.S.A.****

AMERICAN PLACE NAMES AND THEIR DERIVATION

★★★★★★★★★★★★★★★★★★★★★★

ACCIDENT, Maryland

About the year 1751, a grant of land was given to a Mr. George Deakins by King George, II, of England, in payment for services rendered. Accord-

Accident, Maryland

ing to the terms Mr. Deakins was to receive 600 acres of land anywhere in western Maryland that he chose. Mr. Deakins sent out two corps of engineers, each without knowledge of the other, to survey the best land in this section that contained 600 acres.

After the survey, the engineers returned with their maps of the plots they had surveyed. To their surprise, they discovered that they had surveyed a tract of land starting at the same tall oak tree and returning to the starting point. Mr. Deakins chose this plot of land and had it patented "The Accident Tract." When a town was later established here it was, of course, named Accident, Maryland.

The early settlers were of English descent and came here from Prince George's County with the object of raising tobacco. In this project they were unsuccessful, as the tobacco they raised was of a poor quality. They continued to live here, however, until 1850, when German immigrants arrived in such numbers that the nature of the village changed from English to German and remains so to this day. (2)

ACCORD, New York

Settled in the seventeenth century, this village had trouble agreeing upon a name for its post office. One exasperated citizen finally wrote to the Post Office Department, recommending the name Discord, and the Department promptly accepted the name Accord. (6)

ACCOMAC, Virginia

In the year 1614, Governor Dale dispatched a group of men to an island at the tip of what is now the Eastern Shore Peninsula for the purpose of "kerning salt." The island, previously explored by Captain John Smith during his famous tour of the Chesapeake in 1608, now bears his name; however, in 1614, it was known as Dale's Gift. It was one of six settlements in Virginia at that time. The Salt Works, as records tell us, was soon *"gone to wrackle and lett fall,"* and thus ended the first attempt to settle in this area. In 1620 an official settlement was made in the "Kingdome of Accawmacke," as the Eastern Shore Peninsula was then called. This was the beginning of the town of Accomac, Virginia.

Located on the Eastern Shore Peninsula of Virginia, Accomac is the county seat of Accomack County, and takes its name from the Accawmacke Indians, who had occupied this peninsula peacefully for many years. The deviations in the spellings is quite common in the history of America. It was the white settlers, who, listening to what the Indian had to say, decided upon the spelling, often changing it later to suit themselves.

The early courts exercised much ingenuity in the selection of punishments—fines, stripes, duckings, stocks, the pillory, lying neck and heels together at the church door, doing penance by making confession draped in sheets, etc. In the nineteenth century there was popular use of an old English Law which imprisoned debtors for the non-payment of debt. This continued for some time under the American Code. Non-payment of debt seemed to be one of the most serious crimes, hence the need of a Debtor's Prison. (2)

ADAMANT, Vermont

Adamant was named back in 1905, according to history, for the granite that is quarried there. The name connotes the hardness of the stone. A little pond that lies in the heart of the village of Adamant, however, is still popularly known as "Sodom Pond."

In the early 1800's the New Enterprise Quarry opened here and the population soon boomed. An application for a post office was made and granted and the Sodom post office came into existence. It officially opened July 17, 1893.

A more educated class of people from Montpelier and surrounding areas later built homes and summer places in Sodom, but shuddered at the mere mention of the name of the village. One resident had his mail sent elsewhere, refusing to have it addressed to Sodom. He finally circulated a petition to have the name changed. Postal authorities agreed that he did indeed, have a relevant point, and eventually acquiesced to his outraged demands. On June 10, 1905, the Sodom post office went out of business, and Adamant, Vermont was born. (1)

ADOBE WALLS, Texas

Adobe Walls was established in the spring of 1874 in Hutchinson County near the ruins of a trading post built about 1843 by William Bent of the South Canadian River. It was given the name by traders and buffalo hunters because it was constructed of adobe with walls about nine feet high, and only one entrance. Abandoned as a trading post because of the hostility of the Comanche, Cheyenne, and Kiowa Indians, the post became a landmark on the plains.

There were two famous battles fought at the trading post of Adobe Walls. The first by the Army against the Kiowas and Comanches in 1864, and the second by hunters and other civilians against the Cheyenne, Comanche, and Kiowas. In this last battle the Indians were led by Quanah Parker and Lone Wolf. This final battle was fought in 1874. The Indians, who had been urged into the fight by a medicine man, I Satai, conducted a desultory siege for four or five days, but made no other attacks. On the second day a group of fifteen or twenty of the Cheyenne appeared on a high mesa overlooking the post. This incident formed the setting for William (Billy) Dixon's famous shot. Dixon, inside the stockade, shot one of the Indians off his horse from seven-eighths of a mile away.

Adobe Walls, Texas

Had the battle of Adobe Walls resulted in a victory for the Indians, it is possible that the settlement of the southwest would have been delayed for a decade or more.

The hamlet of Adobe Walls, Texas, takes its name from the famous trading post. Only a monument erected by the Panhandle-Plains Historical Society marks the place of its namesake. (3)

AGENCY, Iowa
Agency, a town of about seven hundred, located in southeastern Iowa, received its unusual name from the Sac-Fox Indian Agency, which was located here around 1830.

It was here on October 11, 1842, that a peace treaty was made and concluded between the Federated Sac and Fox Indians, in the Territory of Iowa, and the United States of America. An historical park, nearby, contains the graves of Chief Wapello and General Street, and their families. (1)

AGENCY, Missouri
Platted in 1863, after the Sac and Fox Indians had been driven out, the location was first settled by Robert Gilmore, who in 1839 established a ferry here. The location was originally an agency of the government to

administer to the needs of the Sac-Fox Indians, and was called Agency Ford. The name was later shortened to Agency. (2)

AGUA DULCE, Texas
Agua Dulce, in west-central Nueces County on the Texas-Mexican railroad, has a Spanish name meaning "sweet water." (3)

AGUA NUEVA, Texas
In southeastern Jim Hogg County, Agua Nueva was named for a spring found by early Spanish explorers, and was later used as a roundup point for early ranchers. The name is Spanish and means "new water." (3)

AGUILAR, Colorado
Located in the heart of the Apishapa Valley in southeastern Colorado, it was named Aguilar in 1894 for J. R. Aguilar, former statesman. It is a meaningful name, for in Spanish it is "the eagle," our national bird. (1)

AHMEEK, Michigan
Ahmeek, located in Keweenaw County, was a product of the boom days of the Copper Industry. The name is Indian and means "beaver." (6)

AHWAHNEE, California
Ahwahnee, in Madera County, is located on the old wagon road that led from Madera, on the Santa Fe and Southern Pacific Railroad, to the Yosemite Valley. The area was first settled by the Sells family, who built an Inn here in 1889 or 1890. The name Ahwahnee is Indian and applied to the entire Yosemite Valley area. The translation as given by old Indians to Edward Ballard is "beautiful valley, home of the deer." (2)

AJO, Arizona
Ajo, in southwestern Arizona and flanked on three sides by the Growler, Sauceda, and Pozo Redondo Mountains, is Papago Indian "Au-Auho," and means paint. Ajo, as it is written, is Spanish and means "garlic." (5)

ALAMOGORDO, New Mexico
It was June, 1898, when the first train of the El Paso and Northwestern Railroad puffed its way into this area and Alamogordo had its beginning. The town derived its unusual name from the cottonwood trees which lined and overlapped the streets. The name Alamogordo is Spanish, and means "fat cottonwood."

Watered by means of ditches from the "Madre Acquia," these trees grew to enormous sizes and lent a note of beauty and enchantment to the town. Alas, the cottonwoods have since been cut down and replaced. In their stead now grow Chinese and American Elms, Mimosa, and others. Fat Cottonwood, New Mexico, now short of cottonwood trees, is never-the-less three shaded, with wide streets, beautiful homes, and an unusual and interesting name. (2)

ALBUQUERQUE, New Mexico
On April 23, 1706—seventy years before the American Revolution—by decree from Santa Fe, Albuquerque was officially born. It was christened Villa de San Francisco Xavier de Albuquerque. The governor had named the village in honor of the Duque de Alburquerque, Viceroy of New Spain, as well as Francis Xavier, patron saint of the area. Upon orders from Mexico, however, the name was changed to San Felipe de Alburquerque after the king of Spain. Later the first r was dropped for convenience and the name shortened to Albuquerque. The Viceroy never set foot in the village named for him, but 250 years later (in 1956) the Duke of Alburquerque came here from Spain with his lovely Duchess to help celebrate Albuquerque's 250th anniversary. (2)

ALCOLU, South Carolina
Around 1887 Mr. Davis Wells Alderman started a lumber mill in Clarendon County. Mr. Eugene Colwell was a partner in the business. When a village grew up around the mill they named it AL, for *Al*derman, CO for *Co*lwell, and LU for *Lu*la, Mr. Alderman's eldest child. (1)

ALDER BRANCH, Texas
Alder Branch, in southern Anderson County, was named for the Alders that were growing along Box Creek. B. F. Chambers established a sawmill on the creek in the early 1880's and a community grew up around it. (3)

ALFARATA, Pennsylvania
This town was named for "Alfarata, the Maid of Juniata," as Mrs. Marie Dix Sullivan sang of her:

Wild roves an Indian Girl—
    Bright Alfarata—
Where sweep the waters of
    The Blue Juniata
Swift as an antelope, through
    The forest going;
Bright are her jetty locks,
    In wavy tresses flowing. . . . (4)

ALIQUIPPA, Pennsylvania
Near the junction of Pennsylvania, Ohio, and West Virginia, it was named for "Queen" Aliquippa, an Iroquois Indian. (4)

ALLGOOD, Alabama
Allgood was named for a family of pioneer settlers from South Carolina, who homesteaded land in the vicinity and in the community in the early 1800's. Interesting to note there is no one by the surname Allgood living in Allgood, Alabama, today. (1)

Alligator, Mississippi

ALLIGATOR, Mississippi
In northwestern Mississippi, near the Mississippi River and the Arkansas border, this town takes its name from Alligator Lake, which was once heavily infested with alligators. (6)

ALLOY, West Virginia
Formerly a coal mining camp, Alloy got its present name due to its dependence upon the plants of the Electro Metallurgical Company, which manufactures ferrochorome alloy. (1)

ALOE, Texas
Aloe, a farming community in central Victoria County, was named for the many Aloe flowers growing in the vicinity. (3)

ALTAIR, Texas
Altair, Colorado County, developed as a community with the building

of the Texas and New Orleans Railroad about 1890. Once called Stafford's Ranch, a new name was needed with the coming of the post office. Curly Jones suggested the village be named Altair, for the largest star in the constellation of Aquila. (Quite a boy, that Curly!) According to local legend, the name really came about when someone (not Curly) suggested it as an appropriate name because the cowboys were always "all-on-a-tear." (3)

ALTA LOMA, California

This town held a contest to choose a name, and appropriately selected a Spanish one meaning "high ground." The center of Alta Loma has existed since 1913, when the Pacific Railroad put in the tracks. It is principally an agricultural area. (2)

ALTA LOMA, Texas

Alta Loma, in southwestern Galveston County, on the Gulf, Colorado, and Santa Fe Railroad, was established about 1893 and named Alta Loma, Spanish for "high ground" by the development company. The altitude here is very very high–18 feet above sea level! (3)

ALTO, Texas

Alto, in southern Cherokee County, was founded about 1849 by R. F. Mitchell on land acquired in a lawsuit with John Durst and once a part of a land grant to the House of Barr and Davenport. Because of its location on the highest point between the Angelina and Neches rivers, the name Alto was bestowed upon it by Henry Berryman. (3)

ALTOGA, Texas

Altoga, in northeast Collin County, was named by Dock Owensby, an early settler who suggested the name as a motto meaning "all together." A rural post office was established in 1890. (3)

ALTUS, Arkansas

Altus is Latin for "altitude," and received its name because it was the highest point of the railroad between Little Rock and Fort Smith. It was settled during the early 1870's. (6)

AMADOR CITY, California

The smallest incorporated city in California, located in Amador County, this once lusty gold camp boasted, at one time, over 5,000 inhabitants, but has now dwindled to about 200. The city, and the county, was named for José Maria Amador, a valiant Indian fighter.

During the fall of 1849, Amador City was the home of four ministers who found gold mining more lucrative than "soul saving." But they were a hard lot, and after a back-breaking day of work at their own diggings, they would preach night sermons in the surrounding communities. The name Amador is Spanish, and appropriately enough means "love of gold." (2)

AMBIA, Texas
Ambia is a flag station on the Santa Fe, seven miles southwest of Paris. The name of the post office, established in 1886, was derived from "amber" by Justice of the Peace Minor, of Roxton, who said the men of the community were *"The Greatest Tobacco Chewers and Spitters,"* he ever saw! (3)

AMONATE, Virginia
Located about ten miles from War, West Virginia, half in West Virginia and half in Virginia, Amonate was named for the mother of Pocahontas. (1)

ANALOMINK, Pennsylvania
Originally called Spragueville for the local industry of making Spragues, it was changed to the present name, which is Indian and is believed to mean "rapid water." Probably named for the Brodheads Creek which flows through the village.

What is a sprague? It is a piece of round timber about three inches in width and sharpened on both ends, like a pencil. Spragues were used by miners to stop ore carts by throwing them into the spokes of the wheels. (1)

ANCHORAGE, Texas
Anchorage, in northwestern Atascosa County, was established and named in 1880 by a retired sea captain who "anchored" himself to the land there. (3)

ANGEL CITY, Texas
Angel City, in Goliad County, is said, by old-timers, to have been so named because of the severe fights that were wont to accompany regular Sunday night dances. (3)

ANGELS CAMP, California
It is the only incorporated city in Calaveras County, and was an 1848 trading post which grew into one of the Mother Lode's most historical towns. It was here that Mark Twain got the inspiration for his classic, "The Jumping Frog of Calaveras," for many years told in Calaveras Mining Camps. From this story comes the annual event held at Frogtown near Angels Camp, "The Jumping Frog Jubilee." Angels Camp was named for

Anchorage, Texas

a man by the name of Angel who opened a trading post here in 1848, and was probably the only angel to visit this spot for many years. A partner in the camp, James Carson, discovered the rich Carson Hill Mine, a few miles south of here. (2)

ANTELOPE, Texas
Antelope, in northwestern Jack County, was named for Antelope Springs, a favorite watering spot for antelope herds and a camp site for Kiowa Indians. A post office was established here in 1859. (3)

ANTES FORT, Pennsylvania
Derives its name from Antes Fort, erected in the late 1700's by settlers to repel Indian attacks in this section of the West Branch of the Susquehanna River, which flows near the village. It was named for its first commander, Lt. Colonel Henry Antes. The village is situated in the river valley at the foot of the Bald Eagle Mountains in north-central Pennsylvania. (1)

ANTREVILLE, South Carolina
This village was supposed to be named Centreville, but when the new

postmaster submitted the name to the Post Office Department in Washington, he either had a shaky hand, or the clerk in there couldn't read. Taking the "CE" as an "A," they accepted the name of Antreville. (6)

APACHE JUNCTION, Arizona
Named for the Old Apache Trail, which winds through the eastern and northern edges of the ruggedly impressive Superstition Mountains. It has played a major part in the history of Arizona, having developed in the early 1900's in the vicinity of the many trails of the Apaches, who once freely roamed this vast area. (2)

APALACHICOLA, Florida
Records of the Spanish Conquistadores show that they rested here on their forays into the newly found continent, e.g., Panfilo Narvaez in 1528. British adventurers used the bay during the first decades of the nineteenth century as a focal point for stirring up Indian troubles for the fledgling republic to the north. During the War of 1812, English forces occupied Apalachicola, building a fort on the east side of the river near what is now known as Fort Gadsden.

Where the Apalachicola-Chattahoochee-Flint rivers meet the Gulf, men seem to have lived here as long as people have been on the continent. Prehistoric men, the earliest of the Indians, congregated here and left broken pieces of crude pottery intermingled with the shells of oysters they ate. The Indians, Hitchiti, called it Apalachicol, which means "the land beyond the river."

A famous son of modern Apalachicola is Dr. John Gorrie, who is known as the "father" of artificial ice-making, and a pioneer of our modern air-conditioning. The town was incorporated in 1831. (2)

APOLLO, Pennsylvania
Apollo, on the banks of the Kishiminetas, was once called Warren for an Indian trader who often stopped there. It was re-named in 1848, by Dr. Robert McKisson, physician, poet, and student of the classics. (4)

APPLE RIVER, Illinois
Located in the extreme northwestern part of Illinois, on the Wisconsin border, Apple River takes its name from a nearby river. The river and Apple River Canyon were named for the many wild crab apple trees which grew along the banks of the Apple River. (1)

APPLE SPRINGS, Texas
Apple Springs was originally called May Apple Springs because of the

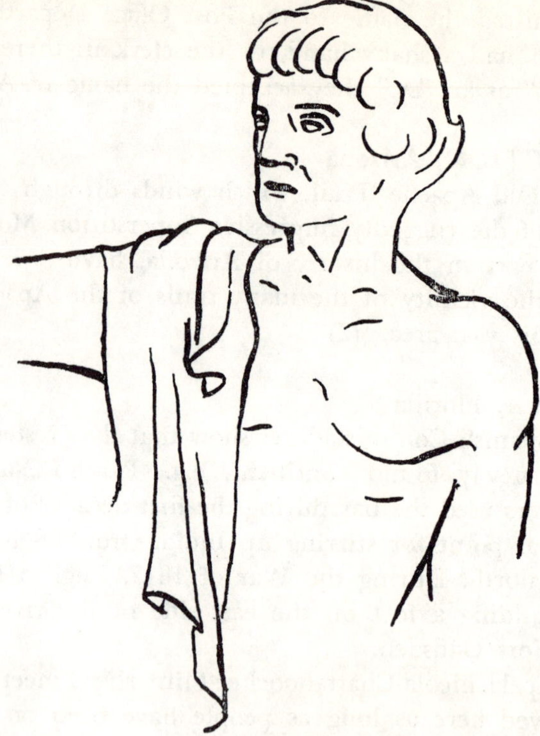

Apollo, Pennsylvania

abundance of May apples growing near the spring. The name was shortened to Apple Springs when a post office was established. (3)

AQUASHICOLA, Pennsylvania
The town takes its name from a stream flowing through the valley to the Lehigh River at Lehigh Gap. The name is Delaware Indian and is a variation of Achquoanschicola, which means "where we fish with the bush net." (Towmensing Mutual Ins. Co., Mr. John B. Helmath.)

ARAB, Alabama
First settled in 1858 on Brindlee Mountain Plateau, it wasn't until 1882 that a post office was established here. The Post Office Department asked J. A. Thompson, one of the first settlers, and the new postmaster, for three suggested names for the new post office. He submitted the names Ink, Bird, and Arad—the latter being the name of his son. As the Arab *Tribune* put it, "Perhaps the old gentleman's handwriting left something to be desired, or maybe a postal employee had smutty glasses, 'cause the Post Office Department accepted the name Arab. Nobody complained about the mistake, however, since they were very happy just to have a post office. So the next time you're ribbed about being from Arab, just think about Ink and Bird, and go smiling on your way!" (2)

Arab, Alabama

ARIZMO, Arizona

Missouri homesteaders combined Arizona and Missouri to make the unique name of their town. (5)

ARIZOLA, Arizona

The name of this hamlet is a combination of the state's name, and the name of the daughter of the founder. (5)

ARMAGH, Pennsylvania

The name of this town is Erse for "field on a hill," and was so named in 1792 by Irish immigrants who found the hillside bare except for a few scrubby oaks. In stage coach days Armagh had almost as many taverns as it has homes today. (4)

ARMOREL, Arkansas

This village took its name in a very unique way. AR is from the state of Arkansas, MO is from the state of Missouri, and REL are the initials of a man by the surname of Wilson who started this sawmill town. Located on the Arkansas-Missouri border, the name Armorel was well chosen. (1)

ARROW ROCK, Missouri

The name Arrow Rock is first mentioned by Lewis and Clark in their account of their expedition in 1808, and William Clark noted it as a good place for a fort. The name is derived of an old Indian legend.

At this point the Missouri River is very narrow, running north and south. On the Saline County side there is a high white limestone bluff; on the eastern side, opposite this bluff, was a large Indian camp. As the legend tells it an Indian chief announced that the hand of his beautiful daughter would go to the Indian brave, who, standing on the eastern

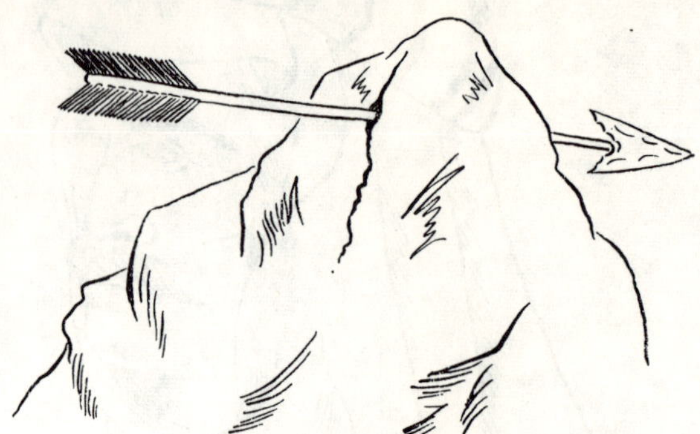

Arrow Rock, Missouri

bank, could hit the white bluff on the opposite shore with an arrow. The winner, who was happily also the maiden's choice, not only hit the bluff with his arrow, but lodged the arrow deeply into it's white side. The bluff was named "Pierre á Flèche," French for Arrow Rock, in the early 1700's when the French explorers mapped this area. The Indian treaty of 1815 made this town an important river crossing on the trail to the West. May 23, 1829, the town of New Philadelphia was platted here, but settlers unhappy with the name voted to change it back to Arrow Rock in 1833. (1)

ARROYOSECO, New Mexico
Located in Taos County, the name is Spanish and means "dry arroyo" (creek or gulch). It takes its name from a small creek that runs through the village, which, in the summer, doesn't run at all. (1)

ASCUTNEY, Vermont
This small Vermont village is located at the base of Mount Ascutney (3,144 feet), from which it gets its name. Tradition tells that it was through this heavily wooded area that slaves were smuggled from the South into Canada. Many times slaves hid out on the mountain, while awaiting transportation. One particular slave slipped on a rocky ledge and cut himself, crying out in pain, "Ah's cut ma knee!" Since it sounded like Ascutney to the hardy mountain folk, they called the unnamed mountain, Mount Ascutney. (1)

ASHEPOO, South Carolina
A tribe of Ashepoo Indians lived along the river bank here. They were visited by Captain Dunlop in 1687, and noted in his diary. The river

was named the Ashepoo and the village took its name from the river. The name Ashepoo is Muskhogean Indian, and means "river seat," or "river dwelling," most likely applying to the location of the Indian village.

During the Civil War this small town suffered much from the depredations that such a conflict spawns. Its homes and churches were looted and burned. According to Bishop Thomas's *History of the Episcopal Church,* General Foster's troops tore some of the weather boarding from the Chapel (The Episcopal Edmundsbury Chapel) to make rafts for crossing the Ashepoo River. There is, today, nothing left of the chapel. (1)

ASOTIN, Washington
Located on the Washington-Idaho border, Asotin has an Indian name that means "Eel Creek." (2)

ASPINWALL, Pennsylvania
Located just across the Allegheny River from Pittsburgh, it was founded in 1796, and named for the Aspinwall family, who were early landowners. (4)

ASSAWOMAN, Virginia
An old Indian name for an old Indian settlement that was once located here, the name is thought to mean "many hills." (1)

ASSININS, Michigan
Father Frederick Baraga founded a mission here in 1843 to educate the Ojibway Indians, and compiled a grammer and dictionary of the Ojibway language. He died in 1868. The name is, of course, Ojibway Indian and means "little rock." (6)

ASSUMPTION, Illinois
First called Tascusha, for Chief Tascusha of a local Indian tribe. In 1856 settlers came here from Louisiana, and when the town was incorporated the name was changed to Assumption, to honor their previous home in Assumption Parish, Louisiana. (2)

ATCO, Georgia
Atco, Georgia, was established by the American Textile Company, and was named after the first letters of the company name. (2)

AU GRÈS, Michigan
For those who yearn for by-gone days, Indian legends tell of Indian boys riding sturgeon on the stony flats of Point Au Grès, and that it is here where the Indians made arrow heads and tomahawks. Later, the Chippewas

conquered the Sanks (for whom the bay is named), when a great Indian battle was fought on Point Au Grès; and to this day the "Monomooses" or spirits of the dead Sanks can sometimes be heard when the wind blows from the east.

Early French explorers, following the Lake Huron shores from the north by canoe, saw alabaster, and called it White Stone Point. The next point was coarse sand, and was named Gravelly Point, and finally they came to a ledge of gritty stone which they called Au Grès.

Wild and wooly in the old lumbering days, it is said that a lumber mill here, worth thousands of dollars, once changed hands in a poker game to the holder of a pair of deuces. (*See* Show Low.) (2)

AU SABLE FORKS, New York

Au Sable Forks, located in Essex County, up-state New York, takes its name from its location near the confluence of the two forks of the Au Sable River. The Au Sable, named by French explorers and trappers, means "river of sand," and is about 50 miles long, and the two branches are nearly equal in volume and meet here. Mail in the pioneer days of the village was addressed to "Forks of the Au Sable."

The reason for the name of the river comes from the mouth, which is about two and one-half miles from the original shore line. The entire area for ten miles is composed entirely of sand brought down by the river through the ages.

The village was settled in the late 1800's by a settler named Rogers, who built a foundry here for making charcoal iron from the nearby mine. (1)

AUSTERLITZ, New York

Settled in 1750 by immigrants from Connecticut and Massachusetts, tradition gives its naming a bit of the unusual. It is said that Martin Van Buren, an admirer of Napoleon Bonaparte, was outraged when another New York town was named Waterloo. It caused him to have the town named Austerlitz in reprisal. Austerlitz, in Czechoslovakia, in Moravia, was where Napoleon defeated the combined forces of the Russian and Austrian armies in 1805. (6)

AVALON, Pennsylvania

Settled in 1802, it was called West Bellevue. It changed to Avalon in 1894, possibly for the Isle of Avalon or "Abode of the Blessed," in the Arthurian tales. (4)

AZLE, Texas

In Tarrant County, was settled in the late 1860's by Joseph Fowler. The community was called Fowler's store until September 5, 1881, when it was changed to O'Bar, for William O'Bar. A quarrel between O'Bar and a Doctor Azle Stewart aroused so much interest and sympathy that the citizens of the town had the name changed to Azle on November 3, 1883. (3)

AZUSA, California

In Los Angeles County, Azusa is known as the "Canyon City," due to its proximity to the San Gabriel Canyon. Azusa, an Indian name, is supposedly derived from Asuaka-gna, a village of Shoshonean Indians, locally known as the Gabrieno, which was located in this area long before the white settlers appeared. As far back as 1769, the area was known as "The Azusa," as evidenced by excerpts taken from the diary of Father Juan Crespi, a member of the famous Portola Expedition.

In 1841, one Luis Arenas was granted a parcel of land by the Mexican Government. This land extended from the San Gabriel River (then known as the Azusa), east along the mountains to the Dalton Canyon, south to the San Bernadino Road, west to the river, then northeast to the point of beginning. This he called "Rancho El Susa." Three years later Senor Arenas sold his holdings to one Henry Dalton for the sum of $7,000 who changed the name of the Rancho to "Azusa Rancho de Dalton." In time it was shortened to Azusa Rancho. The assessed valuation of Azusa in 1965 was $44,394,970.

In the early 1920's, a land boom developed, and for the purpose of promotion, the famous slogan, "Everything From A To Z In the U.S.A.," was coined and has become associated with the name Azusa ever since. (2)

BABY HEAD, Texas

Baby Head, in north central Llano County, was named for Baby Head Creek and Baby Head Mountain. The creek and the mountain were so named about 1850, when early settlers found that the raiding Comanche had killed a captured white baby, and put its head on a pole on the mountain. (3)

BAD AXE, Michigan

Captain Rudolph Papst gave Bad Axe its unique name in the spring of 1861 while surveying the trails between Harbor Beach and Sebewaing. He found an axe in very poor condition. It had been discarded by elk hunters, and as a result he named his surveyor headquarters Bad Axe Camp. Later the intersection of the trails became known as Bad Axe Corners.

For a period of 12 years, after its name had appeared on public records, Bad Axe was just a spot in the dense forest in the center of Huron County.

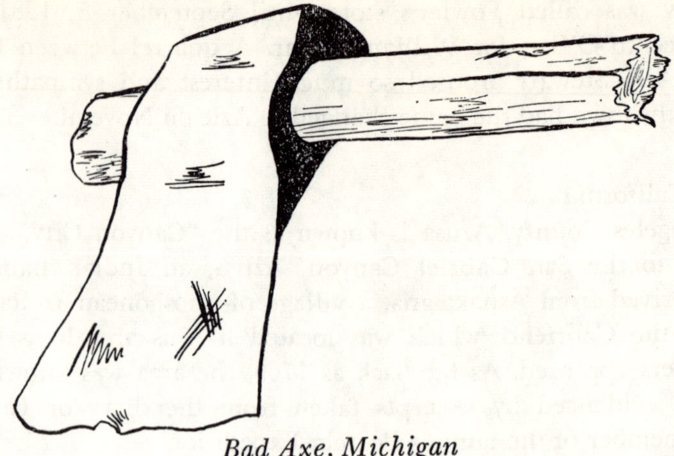

Bad Axe, Michigan

Then, October 15, 1872, the supervisors of Huron County, after much discussion at their fall session held in Port Austin, voted to make the spot, known as Bad Axe Corners, their permanent site for the county seat. The town was platted, settled, and named in 1873. (2)

BALD KNOB, Arkansas
A large flat rock, which covered approximately an acre and stood higher than the rest of the territory, gave the town its name in 1872, when construction of the Missouri Pacific Railroad began. This "Bald Knob" was used by Indians as a camping ground during their hunting trips down into the White Valley. Later it was used as a meeting place for slave traders and, still later, by cattle men for salting, branding, and trading. The rock was destroyed by crushing, by a Commercial organization, before the historical value of it was realized. (2)

BALD RIDGE, Texas
Bald Ridge, in north central Pecos County, on the Kansas City, Mexico, and Orient Railroad, was named by railroad employees for its location on the treeless ridge between Comache Creek and East Mesa.

As early as 1859 a settlement growing up around Fort Stockton spread eastward and adobe huts were scattered over the area around Bald Ridge. (3)

BALL CLUB, Minnesota
This is an Indian Village and was named for a nearby lake, whose shape suggested a lacrosse racket to the Indians. (6)

BALL GROUND, Georgia
Platted in the 1880's, the town received its name from a large field used by the Cherokee Indians to play a ball game, not unlike the game of La-

Crosse. They used a ball made of deer hide, which was stuffed with fur. This ball was batted by a long stick (about 2′ long), which was flat on one end and tapered on the other. Legend has it that all the territory east of the Mississippi was once at stake in one of their contests. (1)

BALLY, Pennsylvania
Laid out in 1742 on ground owned by the Society of Jesus, it was later named for the Reverend Augustin Bally, S. J., who ministered to the Roman Catholics in the surrounding territory between 1837 and 1882. (4)

BALMORHEA, Texas
Balmorhea, on Toyah Creek in southwestern Reeves County, was established in 1906 by a firm of land promoters—Balcolm, Morrow, and Rhea—who used their names to construct the town's name. (3)

BAPTIST, Kentucky
Established in 1917 was named for a primitive Baptist Church located in a lovely Beech grove, a hundred yards from the post office. This church

Baptist, Kentucky

has been here one hundred and thirty years, and was founded by the Reverends Duff and Lykins, who came across the Cumberland Mountains, from Virginia. (1)

BAR CREEK, Kentucky
Local legend has it that explorers came to this virgin land many years ago and camped overnight on a small creek in the area. While they were encamped, a large bear attacked them, and they killed it. Because of this incident they named the creek, Bear Creek. By the time a village had grown up upon its banks and a post office petitioned for, the name had become Bar Creek, due to local pronunciation of "Bar" for "Bear." (1)

BARK RIVER, Michigan
Established in 1871, as a station on the Chicago and Northwestern railroad, it was named for the great quantities of bark found floating on the river. The river was named Bark River. (6)

BASKING RIDGE, New Jersey
Basking Ridge, Township of Bernards, had its name soon after the settlement began. Its earliest known appearance is on the ecclesiastical records of the Basking Ridge Presbyterian Church in the year 1733. As the legend goes the name of the town was derived from the early settlers who had seen wild animals come up from the swampland and bask in the sun, on the side of the ridge. (2)

BATCHTOWN, Illinois
This village, together with the surrounding farms, was first known as Richwoods in the 1850's. Later people called it Sam White's, for a leading merchant of Calhoun County. After this came the name Batchelderville, in honor of William Batchelder, a justice of the peace, merchant, and mill owner. In 1879 a post office was established here and the name shortened to Batchtown. (1)

BATON ROUGE, Louisiana
A tall red cypress tree stripped of its bark once stood on the present site of Louisiana's old state capitol. It marked the boundary between the hunting grounds of the Houma and Bayou Goula Indians. The early French explorers gave the tree a name, "le Baton Rouge," or the Red Stick.

The town of Baton Rouge was incorporated in 1817. Seven governments have held sway over Baton Rouge including France, England, Spain, Louisiana, The Florida Republic, The Confederate States, and the United States. Baton Rouge's military history records three battles, the last in 1862 when the Confederate forces under Breckenridge fought the third battle of Baton Rouge against the Army of Williams and the fleet of Farragut. (2)

BATTLEBORO, North Carolina
Established as a depot for the Wilmington and Raleigh Railroad, it was not named for a famous battle once fought here, but rather for the Battle brothers, James and Joseph, who were large stockholders in the railroad. (6)

BATTLE CREEK, Michigan
The fight that gave the city its name really wasn't much of a battle. Two white members of a surveying party fought with two Indians on the banks of a stream here in 1825. They called the stream Battle Creek. The community was established in 1831, and chartered as a city in 1859. (2)

Battle Ground, Washington

BATTLEGROUND, Indiana
Battleground was established in 1857, adjacent to the mass graves and a monument established by the state of Indiana. The battle of Tippecanoe took place in November, 1811, between a Shawnee chief named Prophet, with his 700 braves, and General William Henry Harrison, and around 1100 soldiers and militiamen. The battle was a resounding military suc-

cess and marked the end of the Northwest Indian Confederacy, although it did not end the Indian "small wars," which continued for sometime.

The founding of Battleground was a planned affair with platted homestead sites a school and a church. Today it is a flourishing city of around 1,000 population. (2)

BATTLE GROUND, Washington

The name of this town is indeed a testament to the lively sense of humor of the early-day settlers. The name is based upon a joke. It was intended to deride a military commander, who with a great deal of hoopla lit out to corral some Indian renegades and then, more or less, *blew the mission.*

On October 26, 1855, Klickitat Indians, numbering about 300, were taken from their homelands along the mouth of the Lewis River and forced to pitch their tepees at Fort Vancouver. Settlers along the river had complained of Indian harassment. An army officer noted that the Indians seemed more frightened than the settlers, and it may have been more for their protection than that of the settlers that the move was made. An Indian named Lukar, a notorious trouble maker among the Indians, passed the rumor that the "Bostons," as the whites were called, had rounded up the Indians for mass slaughter. Being a nervous bunch, about half of them folded their tents and silently stole away.

Panic swept the fort and the surrounding territory, with these "ferocious" Indians on the loose. Captain William Strong, the commander of the fort, gathered together some 30 well-armed troopers, and with a flurry headed out in hot pursuit. A sergeant in the fort recorded at the time: "If they overtake them, Lo, the poor Indian!"

About 16 miles north of Vancouver, Strong and his men came upon their quarry, in fortified positions and apparently ready to fight. Exercising discretion over valor, Strong called for a parley with Umtux, chieftain of the Indians, and they met between the camps on neutral ground. Here they smoked a peace pipe and held a generally happy pow-wow. To placate the nervous settlers, listening from a safe distance of several miles, the pair agreed to discharge all their ammunition, and that the Indians would return peacefully to the fort. Accordingly the Indians let fly some 70 shots in one direction, and the troopers about 50 in the other. With such a volly, news passed quickly back to the fort that Strong had engaged the Indians and was waging a terrible battle.

Unhappily this scene of fun and frolic was marred when the chief, Umtux, was shot and killed by one of his young bucks, who was probably miffed at this "disgusting" turn of events. An investigation was held on the spot by Captain Strong, and this took several days. Meanwhile, back at the fort, the people shuddered and prayed. Finally Captain Strong, concluding that the chief was killed by person or persons unknown, agreed to let the Indians stay on a few days so that they might bury their chief with appropriate honors befitting a tribal chieftain. He would return, and they would follow in a few days.

If the hard-pressed captain had known what was in store for him at the fort, he surely would have made another decision. The settlers undoubtedly were amazed to see Strong ride in with his full complement of 30 troopers, and hardly a soiled uniform among the lot. And even worse, not a single redskin in tow!

The incident was viewed as a scandal, and Strong was mercilessly scorned for what they thought was a botched job. He was presented with a frilly petticoat, for his personal standard. As for the location, well, Captain Strong's "Battleground" lives on for posterity, in the name of the town of Battleground, Washington. (Taken from a story by James Southwell, Staff Writer, *The Oregonian.*) (2)

BATTLE LAKE, Minnesota
Battle Lake, located in Otter Tail County, takes its name from Battle Lake, which was the scene of a battle around 1795, between the Chippewa and the Sioux, over territorial rights. (6)

BAYOU GOULA, Louisiana
French settlers in this area named their little settlement Bayou, for the little river there, and Goula for the name of the local tribe. The Goula Indians (Muskhegean) were of the mound-burying tribes. They buried their dead in huge mounds together with personal belongings, such as arrows, pottery, and other trinkets. When Bayou Goula was settled there was such a mound along the banks of the stream, but it was later dug up and destroyed by the curious and the morbid, looking for curios and souvenirs. (1)

BAZAAR, Kansas
The town was named by Martha J. Leonard, first wife of Doctor M. R. Leonard, in memory of a Shoppe or Bazaar she had owned in Pennsylvania. It was there that she had sold pretty fancy work and infants' clothes. The settlement was started in March 1856, on Rock Creek, about a mile southwest of the present site.

As long as 500 years ago the area where Bazaar now stands was a council grounds for various Indian tribes. (1)

BEANBLOSSOM, Indiana
Located in south-central Indiana, the name of this village came from a

notable Indian who lived here long before the white man arrived.

The village was settled by German pioneers from Georgetown, Ohio, who, happily, chose to give this unique and unusual name to their home. (2)

BEAN STATION, Tennessee
Begun in 1787 when three brothers named Bean erected a fort to protect themselves and other pioneers from Indian attacks. Located near the old Daniel Boone and Great Indian Warpath trails. It was named in honor of the Beans. (1)

BEARDSTOWN, Illinois
Founded in 1819 by Thomas Beard, when he arrived at an Indian village known as Indian Mound, by horseback from Southern Illinois. On his trip northward, over the prairies, he followed streams which fed into the Illinois River, and after a week's travel reached this point. French explorers had previously named the site Beautiful Mound Village, because the Indian camp was located at the base of a large Indian burial mound.

Beard built a log cabin at the river's edge and began trading with the Indians. Soon other settlers arrived and began building around the cabin of Mr. Beard. In 1829, a city was platted here, and named for its first white settler, Mr. Thomas Beard. (2)

BEAR GRASS, Texas
This Texas hamlet was named for the native bear grass that grows in this part of north central Leon County, and was established in the early part of the 1900's. (3)

BEAR RIVER CITY, Utah
Pioneers settled on the banks of the Bear River in dugouts. The Bear River derived its name from Bear Lake, which in turn was named by local Indians, long ago, for the numerous bears in the area. (1)

BEAUTY, Kentucky
This village is situated in the beautiful Kentucky hills, and was once called Himlerville. When the Himlerville Coal Company sold out to J. H. Mandtz, he advertised the coal as "Black Beauty Block," and petitioned the Post Office Department to change the name of the post office from Himlerville to Beauty. Considering the beauty of this spot, and the former name, it was a decided improvement. (1)

BEAVER CITY, Nebraska
Beaver Creek was first named by the Indians for the many busy beavers

who built dams along its winding stretch, and later by white settlers who chased the Indians out and built a town along its banks. They called their town Beaver City, Nebraska. (2)

BEAVER CROSSING, Nebraska
This small town, due to its close proximity to an artesian spring, near the confluence of Beaver Creek and West Blue River, was once a camping ground for westward bound pioneers, and later became a stop for the pony express; a long barn was built here in 1872 to house live stock.

After the Civil War had ended many of its veterans settled here and the Chicago and Northwestern built a line through the town from Linwood to Superior.

The name originated from a Beaver Dam, which bridged Beaver Creek, forming a kind of crossing for animals, Indians, and later for the white settlers to reach the artesian spring. (2)

Bebe, Texas

BEBE, Texas
A rural community in southwestern Gonzales County, it is supposed to have been named for BeBee Baking Powder. (3)

BEE, Virginia

Bee, Virginia, is a very small village, and was named in honor of an equally small girl named Beatrice. (1)

Bee House, Texas

BEE HOUSE, Texas

Bee House, in western Coryell County, was named for the bees and honey found by the pioneers in the cliffs and caves in the vicinity. Settled in the 1850's, its post office was established in 1884, with Joseph L. Rice as the first postmaster. (3)

BEE SPRING, Kentucky

Bee Spring was named for a small spring nearby. This area was "a happy hunting ground" for hunters and they would gather at the spring for water. The area around the spring abounded with bees, and the hunters would drink with one hand and swat bees with the other. It wasn't long before the spring had acquired the name Bee Spring. (1)

BEEVILLE, Texas

First settled around 1830 by immigrants from Ireland, the city took its name from the county in which it is located. Bee County was named for General Bernard E. Bee, who came to Texas from South Carolina in 1836. He was Secretary of War for the Republic of Texas, under President Sam Houston, Secretary of State under President Lamar, and later Minister to the United States.

One of the early settlers, James Hefferman, and his entire family, was massacred by the Indians approximately where the present court house of Beeville now stands. (2)

BEJOU, Minnesota

The extension of the Soo Line Railroad through Northern Minnesota gave birth to a number of new villages on what had been the White Earth Indian Reservation. Passage of the Clapp Amendment in Congress in 1906 gave the Indians title to their land, and the right to sell it. A large part of the White Earth Indian Reservation was sold as a result of this amendment. As the reservation was opened to settlement, the Tribal Council petitioned the railroad to give Indian names to all Reservation towns along the Soo Line. Bejou is Chippewa Indian, and means "hello." (2)

BELL BUCKLE, Tennessee

The town of Bell Buckle, Tennessee, was established in 1850. There are a number of versions as to how Bell Buckle got its unusual name. One says that a large cowbell, with its buckle, was found along the bank of a creek nearby, by early settlers. Another, most often told, is that a bell and buckle were found carved on a beech tree near a spring—the site of an old Indian camping ground—and still another that land dealers sent their agents into these forests in advance of the settlers to classify the land. They blazed the routes traveled through the woods, and the land that they considered arable they marked by carving a plow on a beech tree. Grazing lands were similarly marked by carving a bell and a buckle.

However the name came to be, it has stuck, and Bell Buckle, Tennessee, is well known for its unusual name. (1)

BELLEFONTAINE, Ohio

A Shawnee village once stood here, called "Blue Jacket's Town." Chief Blue Jacket was a white man, captured at age seventeen in Pennsylvania, by the Shawnees, while wearing a blue jacket, and later became chief.

Settled in 1806, high on a watershed, it was given the French name "Bellefontaine," for its natural springs, by French settlers. In 1820 it became the seat of government for Logan County, Ohio. (6)

BELLEFONTE, Pennsylvania

Settled around 1769, the name is French for "beautiful fountain." The name is attributed in story to Talleyrand's exclamation of pleasure upon seeing the big spring here during his exile from France, in 1794–5. (4)

BELLE PLAINE, Minnesota

French for "beautiful plain," Belle Plaine was named for the beauty of the Minnesota Valley, at this spot. (2)

BELLFLOWER, California

Once called Willows and the Wilderness, and briefly, in honor of a would-be subdivider, Firth, was finally christened Somerset. In 1909, when they applied for a post office they were told to search for a new name. To solve the problem the residents turned to an apple orchard. North of town one William Gregory grew beautiful "bellflower apples." They suggested the name Bellflower and it was immediately accepted by the Post Office Department. (2)

BEMIDJI, Minnesota
The town of Bemidji was named for Chief Bemidji, and the chief got his name from Lake Bemidji, which the Indians called Bay-me-ji-ga-maug, meaning a lake with cross waters or a lake lying crosswise, to the general route of travel. The Mississippi River passes through one side of the lake. French fur traders, in the early days of exploration, called the lake "Lake Traverse," because of the sand bar that crossed it. (2)

BEN AVON, Pennsylvania
Incorporated as a borough in 1891, its Scottish name means "hill by the waters." (4)

BEN BOLT, Texas
In east central Jim Wells County, on the Texas and New Orleans Railroad, Ben Bolt is said to have been named, either for an early settler, or for its proximity to Alice, fourteen miles to the north, for as the song goes, "Sweet Alice, Ben Bolt." (3)

BEND, Texas
Bend, on the Colorado River in southeastern San Saba County, was settled in 1854 by three Low brothers from Tennessee. The community was called Schleicher's Bend for Gustav Schleicher in 1856, and in 1858 it was called McAnelly's Bend for the Robert Daugherty McAnelly post office in Lampasas County. Later the names Little Britches, and Bend were submitted with an application for a post office, and on November 24, 1879, Bend Post Office was established. (3)

BENEVOLENCE, Georgia
Thomas Coram drove three yoke of steer, hitched to a big Conestoga wagon into this area and settled here in 1822. He gave five acres of land to the settlement that followed, for a church and a school provided they would guarantee no "red-light" district, no gambling, and no dance halls in the town. They agreed. It was considered a benevolent act, and they called the town Benevolence Homestead. When a post office was established here the name was shortened to Benevolence. (1)

BEN HUR, Virginia
Located in the southwestern tip of Virginia, in Lee County, Ben Hur wasn't named for the famous novel. All the land where the town is now located was owned by one Ben Snead, who constantly referred to his wife as "HER." So when a town was finally established here residents named it in honor of Mr. Ben Snead and his wife "HER," or Ben Hur, as the Post Office Department interpreted it. (1)

BEN HUR, Texas
Ben Hur, an old farm community in Western Limestone County, was named by an early settler impressed by the book *Ben Hur.* (3)

BIG CABIN, Oklahoma
In 1880, when the Missouri, Kansas and Texas Railroad came through here, a name was needed for the switch. A large cabin about 1½ miles northwest of the track was the only visible man-made landmark in sight. First called Big Cabin Switch, and later just Big Cabin, it gradually became a community, and a post office was established. The name Big Cabin was adopted by both the post office and the village. (1)

BIG CHIMNEY, West Virginia
Big Chimney, four miles from Charleston, in Kanawha County, was named for a huge stone foundation of a brick chimney, the remains of an 18th-century Salt Works, that originally spawned the village. (6)

BIG FOOT, Texas
The town was named for William Alexander Anderson Wallace, a native

Big Foot, Texas

of West Virginia, and a noted Indian fighter, who came to Texas to avenge the death of his brother, who had been killed in the battle of the Alamo. He got the nickname, according to tradition, when a large Indian chief was killed during a skirmish, and Wallace tried on the chief's large moccasins. They were a perfect fit, so he wore them and his men began calling him "Bigfoot." He died in Big Foot, Texas on January 8, 1899. He is buried in the State Cemetery in Austin, Texas; however there is a monument and a museum to his memory located in Big Foot, Texas. (Big Foot Museum)

BIG HILL, Texas
In Gonzales County, this town derives its name from its location on the highest of some rolling hills in the section. It had its beginning in 1885 as a railroad stop for the San Antonio and Aransas Pass Railroad. (3)

BIG HORN, Wyoming
Settled around 1878, the village was named for the Big Horn Mountains. This was the first settlement in this part of the Wyoming Territory. The mountains got their name from the Big Horn sheep that used to be found there. (1)

BIG LAKE, Texas
Named for the largest natural lake in the state, the bottom of which covers an area of 1900 acres. It was once a watering hole for buffalo herds, Indians, and later for herds of cattle. Since the turn of the century the lake has held water only during periods of heavy rainfall. When full, which has occurred about once each decade, the lake will hold water for about three years. Rainfall in this area has decreased as the years pass, bringing about long periods when the lake bottom is exposed. The city was formed in 1911, and now has an estimated population of 3,000. (2)

BIG OAK FLAT. California
The town was first called Savage Diggin's, for a prospector who located here with a band of miners in 1848. In 1850 it was renamed Big Oak Flat in honor of a giant oak tree that stood in the center of the town. It was one of the biggest oak trees in the vicinity. Today the remnants of the tree are preserved in a monument built by the Sonora High School boys. (1)

BIG PINE, California
The town is located in a valley at the foot of the steep eastern slope of the Sierras, and was built near a creek running out of the mountains. The prominent vegetation of the untillable parts of the valley is low brush. Large Jeffrey Pines grow along the creek and are conspicuous and striking against the brush. The town was named Big Pine for these big pine trees.

Curiously, many of the trees in the town were removed in favor of buildings, and those out of the town are partially hidden in a canyon. Thus it is that the very trees that gave the town its name are now conspicuous by their absence. (2)

BIG PINEY, Wyoming
Big Piney, Sheridan County, Wyoming, gets its name from the big pine trees that grow along a creek here. (1)

BIG RUN, Pennsylvania
Five miles from Punxsutawney, in Jefferson County, Big Run was founded in 1822 and named for the stream that empties into Stump Creek. (4)

BIG SPRING, Texas
County seat of Howard County, this town is in a rocky gorge between two high foothills of the Cap Rock escarpment in West Texas. The city derives its name from the "big spring" in Sulphur Draw, which was a watering place for herds of buffalo, coyote, lobo, antelope, and wild mustang. The place was also a source of friction between Comanche and Shawnee Indians and a camp site for early expeditions across the western area of Texas. In 1849 Captain Randolph B. Marcy's expedition reached Big Springs on the return trip from Santa Fe, and marked it as a camp site on the Overland Trail to California. It was also a camp site on the Santa Fe Trail from Fort Smith, Arkansas, to El Paso. Organized in 1882, Big Springs was then a settlement of hide huts of buffalo hunters, a few tents, a wagon yard, hotel, and eight saloons, and was made the county seat. Today it is a city of over 31,000 people. (3)

BIG WELLS, Texas
Big Wells, in northeastern Dimmit County, on the San Antonio, Uvalde, and Gulf Railroad, received its name from flowing artesian wells in the area. (3)

BILL, Wyoming
In deciding on a name for a post office, the settlers decided to name it for the first name of most of the citizens. Since the majority had the first name of "Bill," they named the new village and its post office Bill. This information was furnished by O. L. Pellatz, "about the only living original settler of this community left." And his first name obviously isn't Bill.

BILOXI, Mississippi
Pierre LeMoyne d'Iberville, gallant explorer, carried the Fleur-de-Lis flag of France to these shores in the year 1699, and established the first capi-

tal of the vast Louisiana Territory, stretching from the Gulf to Canada. This immense body of land was first governed from Old Biloxi, and gives this coast area the claim of being one of the oldest places in the United States. d'Iberville landed on Biloxi's gulf shore February 13, 1699.

d'Iberville met the Biloxi tribe of Indians upon his arrival on the front of Gulf beach. Even though located on the Gulf of Mexico, the Biloxi Indians were members of the Sioux family, and according to the Smithsonian Institution, "Biloxi," in the Indian language means "The first people." The Biloxians left many beautiful legends, some that correspond to the well-known Aesop fables. Eight flags have flown over Biloxi—French, English, Spanish, West Florida Republic, United States, Mississippi Magnolia, Confederate States, and Mississippi State. (2)

BIMBLE, Kentucky
Will Payne and his wife Rebecca Payne, who established the Bimble post office, located in Knox County, owned a yoke of prize oxen named Bim and Bill. They combined the names of their two oxen to form the name of the new post office, with Mrs. Rebecca Payne as the first postmaster. (1)

Bimble, Kentucky

BIRCH TREE, Missouri
In south-central Shannon County, this town was named for a large birch tree that stood on the bank of a creek, near the site of the new post office. (1)

BIRD CITY, Kansas
Bird City, Kansas, was named for an early bird named Benjamin, who located here in 1885 and took up cattle raising. (1)

BIRD-IN-HAND, Pennsylvania

Bird-In-Hand is located on the old Philadelphia Pike which in pre-Revolutionary and Revolutionary War days was the main highway between Lancaster and Philadelphia. Bird-In-Hand derived its unusual name from a swinging sign which was placed on an old tavern. This sign contained a picture of a hand holding a bird, and the old adage, "A bird in the hand is worth two in the bush." (2)

Bird-in-Hand, Pennsylvania

BIRD ISLAND, Minnesota

Located in Renville County, in southwestern Minnesota, it was once a favorite camping ground for the Indians. They called it "Birds Island" because it was a grove of trees that stood by itself, and was the favorite place of many kinds of birds. (6)

BIRDSEYE, Indiana

Birdseye, located on a crossroads in Dubois County, was settled in 1846. The newly selected postmaster, Thomas A. King, was seeking a good name for his little town, and requested the assistance of a neighboring postmaster, Benjamin T. (Bird) Goodman. Goodman, who was also an eloquent preacher, scanned the map, pointed his finger at the little spot marking the new town, and said, "It suits Bird's Eye, to a T." And with this remark Birdseye, Indiana, got its unique name. (1)

BIRDS LANDING, California

Birds Landing received its name from a Grain Warehouse Landing on the

Montezuma Slough, about 1½ miles southwest of town. They were both named for an early settler named John Bird, who settled here in 1876. The high Montezuma hills and grain country surround the settlement. (1)

BIRTHRIGHT, Texas

Birthright, also known as Lone Star community, began about 1870 as a store in the ranch home of E. C. Birthright in north central Hopkins County. (3)

BISBEE, Arizona

In the summer of 1877 a detachment of the 6th U. S. Cavalry, Commanded by Lieutenant "Tony" Rucker, was returning to Camp Bowie, after its unsuccessful pursuit of a band of renegade Apaches south of the border. Skirting the eastern slopes of Mule Pass Mountains they found a stream of unsavory water flowing into Sulphur Spring Valley. Winding their way upstream they made camp at the base of the famous Iron Rock, and Sergeant Jack Dunn was detailed to continue the search for fresh water. A few hundred yards farther up the canyon he found cool, clean water gushing from Castle Rock, and filled the canteens. While returning he noticed a rock formation across the Canyon that glittered in the sunlight. This was an outcropping of copper ore, rich with silver. Here the first claim was staked on August 2, 1877, and recorded as the Rucker Mine. From this mine and many others located here flowed six and one quarter billion pounds of copper, ninety million ounces of silver, two and a quarter million ounces of gold, two hundred eighty-six thousand pounds of lead and three hundred thirty-five thousand pounds of zinc. All in all, over a billion dollars worth of ore!

Bisbee was a mining town, and takes its name from Judge DeWitt Bisbee, a San Francisco financier, who bought into the mines, and incidentally never set foot in the town that bears his name. (2)

BITTER CREEK, Texas

Bitter Creek, near Sweetwater in Nolan County, was settled by the Bardwell and Montgomery families in 1880–1881. It was named for Bitter Creek, located nearby. There are at least five Texas streams so named, probably for the alkali in the water which makes the taste harsh or bitter. (3)

BITTER CREEK, Wyoming

This small community was named for a muddy stream that runs through the southeastern part of Sweetwater County. What was known as Bitter Creek Canyon was on the route of the overland stage line. This station on the Union Pacific Railroad has been a principal wool and sheep shipping point. (2)

BIVALVE, New Jersey
Was named for the Bivalve, a mollusk having two shells hinged together. There are many shells of this type to be found just below the soil, and many are always turned up when the land is plowed or disturbed in any way. (1)

BIWABIK, Minnesota
In the valley of the historic Embarrass River, traveled by Indians and fur traders, the site evidently was an Indian camping ground. Prospectors visited the location during the 1865–66 Lake Vermilion "gold rush" because the famous Vermilion Trail passed through here.

In 1891, one of the Merritt parties was fine-combing the Biwabik district. With Indians encamped around the location, watching the proceedings with interest, an excitement of discovery mushroomed. A high-grade blue iron ore had been found at what later became the Biwabik Mine. As sleds carried the samples to Duluth, ore was discovered at other nearby locations. A townsite was platted near Merritt (Embarrass) Lake and named Merritt for the pioneering family. Other townsites were platted, including Biwabik, a mile west of Merritt, and north of the Biwabik Mine. Biwabik grew much slower than Merritt, but was incorporated into a village in the fall of 1892. When, in 1893, the railroad ran its line to Biwabik, the village of Merritt was almost destroyed by fire. Merritt's inhabitants moved to Biwabik, and their old town died. From Mesaba Station, about 10 miles away, came the first supplies, and it is told that Biwabik's first beer was floated down the Embarrass River on a raft from Tower.

The name Biwabik is a direct translation of the Chippewa and means "iron," truly a fitting name. (2)

BLACKBERRY CITY, West Virginia
Blackberry City is located in Mingo County, and it is believed to have received its name from Blackberry Creek, which empties into Tug Fork of the Big Sandy River, on the Kentucky side. Tug River is the dividing line between West Virginia and Kentucky. Many years ago a Coal Company was located on this creek and called itself the Blackberry Coal Company. Inasmuch as the company owned the land, which is now known as Blackberry City, the town could have taken its name from both the creek and the company. The Creek was named for the many blackberries growing along its banks.

Blackberry City is in the land of the famous Hatfield and McCoy feud. About three miles up the creek is the scene of the beginning of the feud, which started on the First Monday of August, in 1882. It was also the scene of the bitter mine strike of 1920–1922, resulting in a gun battle between miners and the Baldwin-Felts detectives. It was in one encounter, that lasted two minutes, that ten men were reported to have been killed and five wounded.

From this turbulent past, the peaceful village of Blackberry City, West Virginia lives on. (1)

BLACK BETSEY, West Virginia
Received its name from the coal mine that gave it its birth. Black is for the color of its coal, and Betsey, an affectionate nickname, often used. (6)

BLACK CANYON, Arizona
The town of Black Canyon came from the topographical formation of its location. It is located near the banks of a large fissure in the earth's surface, known also as Black Canyon. The channel of Black Canyon, in places, is quite narrow, with high walls of dark rock, hence the name Black Canyon. (1)

BLACKDUCK, Minnesota
Settled around 1890 in a white pine forest so thick that it was impossible to drive a team of horses through it, this town had its beginning as a Minnesota logging camp. It is thought that it got its name from a Chippewa chief named Blackduck, who had his headquarters on the north side of Blackduck Lake. Chief Blackduck got his name from the thousands of black mallards which covered the lake with their numbers in the fall of the year. They provided a ready source of food for the Indians. Even today this area is a favorite feeding place for the black mallard, and needless to say a sportsman's paradise. (2)

BLACKFOOT, Idaho
Blackfoot is the pioneer city of the Upper Snake River Valley. The town was laid out in 1878 in anticipation of the arrival of the Utah-Northern Railroad. It arrived on Christmas Day, and then the town boomed, and became an industrial center. The railroad accommodated the transfer of supplies and equipment to freight wagons bound for the rich mining country of central Idaho. As freighting decreased and water from the Snake was applied to the fertile soil in the valley, agriculture became, and still is, the most important industry.

The Snake River, west of Blackfoot, was crossed by a ferry established in 1860 and operated until 1880, when the first steel bridge was built. Two stage lines used the stop at the ferry, one crossing the river to Arco, Challis, and Mackay, and the other going on to Montana.

The town was not named for the Blackfoot Indians, as some people believe. That tribe is in Montana. A group of Shoshone Indians came here in 1818, and as they had walked across some freshly burned-over range land, their moccasins were very black. Because of this, the trappers who were here called them Blackfoot, and the name stuck. The river just south of town was called the Blackfoot and eventually the town.

Eagle Rock (now Idaho Falls) and Blackfoot were rivals for the County Seat of Bingham County. Eagle Rock was finally selected, but a delegation from Blackfoot bribed a clerk to change the name on the bill. When the bill was introduced and voted on, nobody noticed the change, and Blackfoot became the county seat, much to the chagrin of Eagle Rock. (2)

BLACK JACK, Texas
Black Jack, in northeastern Cherokee County, was named for the timber found along the bottom of the Angelina River. The first settlement was a sawmill operated in the 1850's. (3)

BLACK LICK, Pennsylvania
The Black Lick Stream that cuts its way through this small town, with clear water and black rocks, was once a favorite "lick" for deer and other wild game of this area due to salt deposits.

Though no longer as clear, and with the black rocks dimly seen, the stream, never-the-less, gave its name to the village of Black Lick, which flourishes upon its banks. (1)

BLACKSHEAR, Georgia
Blackshear, Georgia, located in Pierce County, was incorporated on December 16, 1859, and named for General David Blackshear, noted Georgia Indian fighter. (2)

BLANCO, Texas
Blanco, in southern Blanco County, was first settled in 1853, when pioneer stockmen built cabins along the Blanco River near the present site of the town and prepared to defend themselves and their cattle against the Indians. First named Pittsburgh, for the Pittsburgh Land Company, it was later changed to Blanco, for the Blanco River. Blanco is Spanish and means white. (3)

BLANKET, Texas
Blanket, in eastern Brown County, was supposedly named because early settlers found an Indian blanket on a creek bank near the site. A post office was established here June 10, 1875. (3)

BLESSING, Texas
In northwestern Matogorda County at the junction of the St. Louis Brownsville, and Mexico and the Texas and New Orleans Railroads, this town was established as a post office in 1902 and named by Jonathan E. Pierce, because he considered the arrival of the railroads a blessing. (3)

BLOOMING GROVE, Texas
Settled shortly after the Civil War a few miles north of Dresden, Navarro County, had its origin in a store established by R. J. Grady and Sam Andrews. First called Gradyville, the settlement was named Blooming Grove for a grove of trees nearby, and Blooming Davis, the son of an early settler. The post office commenced in 1869. (3)

Blooming Rose, West Virginia

BLOOMING ROSE, West Virginia
This lovely name was suggested by the profusion of roses that grew there in 1914 and which are still grown there. First a Land Company, about three miles down the hollow, took the name Blooming Rose Land Company, and then the post office, established through the efforts of George W. Midkiff, an old settler, was named Blooming Rose. (1)

BLOWING ROCK, North Carolina
This town was named for *the* Blowing Rock. The winds from down in John's River Gorge, blowing up over the Rock, was the reason for the old settlers naming the rock Blowing Rock. The current of air flowing upward from the rock prompted the Ripley cartoon about "the only place in the world where snow falls upside down." Visible from The Rock, down the gorge to the southwest are Hawksbill Mountain and Table Rock. To the west are Grandfather Mountain and Mount Mitchell. (2)

Blowing Rock, North Carolina

BLUEBALL, Pennsylvania
Blueball, located in Lancaster County, was named for the old Blue Ball Inn, which was established in 1766. (4)

BLUE BELL, Pennsylvania
Formerly called Pigeontown, Blue Bell got its name from the Blue Bell Inn, established around 1743. Blue Bell could never have been called a "one horse town," since it had two. Two colonial inns located here were named The Black Horse, and The White Horse. The Blue Bell Inn is one of the few places in Montgomery County where George Washington never slept. "Mad Anthony" Wayne, however, did stop here the night before his personally requested court-martial.

The town was once called Pigeontown for the large flocks of wild passenger pigeons (now extinct) that once nested here in the early 1800's. (1)

BLUE DIAMOND, Nevada
This town grew up around the Blue Diamond Corporation, named by J. J. Jamison because he felt his quality of lime was comparable to that of the "Blue Diamond," among the most precious of stones. There are

no diamonds here. The company came here from California for its gypsum deposits. When a post office was established the people unanimously selected the name Blue Diamond for their village. (1)

BLUE EARTH, Minnesota

Blue Earth, Minnesota, is located at the junction of the east and west branches of the Blue Earth River, and takes its name from the river. The Indians called it "Mah-ko-Tah," or Blue Earth, due to the blue clay found near its mouth. The Indians used the clay to paint themselves for their ceremonial dances, and for war paint.

When the first white explorer, LeSueur, a French Voyageur, found the blue earth, he thought it was rich in copper ore, and sent tons of it back to France to be assayed. Disappointed when he found the soil valueless as ore, LeSueur never returned to the fort he founded near Blue Earth River's mouth. The joke, however, was really on LeSueur. It was not the small deposit of blue clay, but the abundant, rich black earth that was the Blue Earth Valley's treasure. Its value ranks at the top of Minnesota's farm land. (2)

BLUE EYE, Missouri

Blue Eye is Stone County's southernmost town, lying on the Missouri and Arkansas line. Settled in the 1860's, the post office was established in 1870. The first postmaster was Elbert N. Butler, a blue-eyed Civil War veteran. One of his friends suggested that the post office and the town be named after him, and the people agreed. Why they chose to honor only one eye is not recorded. (1)

BLUE GROVE, Texas

Blue Grove, in central Clay County, was named for its location in a grove of oak trees. Permanent settlement was made in 1882. (3)

BLUE JAY, West Virginia

Blue Jay, West Virginia, was named for Blue Jay Creek, near Sandpatch, Pennsylvania. The Blue Jay Lumber Company had a mill there and when they moved to West Virginia they used the same name. Since the Blue Jay Lumber Company was here when the post office was opened the people elected to call it Blue Jay. (1)

BLUE SPRINGS, Nebraska

First named Blue Springs by the Indians, the town derives its name from a spring which furnishes a never ending flow of pure water, colored blue because of its purity. The town is located on the Big Blue River, two miles south of Wymore. (1)

Blue Eye, Missouri

BLUFF SPRINGS, Texas

Bluff Springs, on Onion Creek in northern Hays County, got its name in 1883, when a school building was erected on a bluff overlooking a spring in the old Speeds and Butler community. (3)

BOARD CAMP, Arkansas

A pioneer and his family stopped here, as there was some sickness, and they decided to camp for a while. Although the custom was to erect log cabins, this pioneer hewed boards out of the logs and built a board cabin. The family stayed for several months and then moved on. The camp they left behind was used by many hunters and travelers and soon became known as Board Camp. Later, silver was discovered nearby, and a town grew up and was named Silver Center. When the mine played out the people decided to change the name back to Board Camp, as it remains to this day. (1)

BOCA GRANDE, Florida

Boca Grande is a Spanish name and means "big mouth." No, it was not

Boca Grande, Florida

named by some early explorer in memory of his wife or his mother-in-law, but for the pass leading to the Charlotte Harbor basin. It is the only deep-water harbor on the West Coast, south of Tampa, which can accommodate freighters.

Local legend has it that the town and pass were named by the pirate Gasparilla, and that he used this locale as his base of operations for raids upon shipping and on the local country side. (2)

BOCA RATON, Florida

It is believed that the giant Abaniki Indians were the very first inhabitants of Boca Raton. They belonged to the Caloosa tribe, and lived along the shores of Lake Boca Raton and Lake Wyman. These eight foot giants were sun worshippers and mound builders. Some of their skeletons, various utensils, arrowheads, and pottery have been found here. Ponce de Leon was the first white man to view this new land, followed by Spanish Conquistadores and swashbuckling pirates because of the easily navigable inlet from the ocean to Boca Raton Lake where they were protected by the high dunes on the beach from raging seas, and prying eyes.

Boca Raton is shown on several sixteenth-century parchment charts of Spanish origin, that have been preserved, as "Boca de Ratones." A very literal translation of this means "mouth of the harbor of hidden rocks," and refers to the Boca Raton Inlet. The town itself was platted in 1897 by T. M. Rickards, and from this beginning the present town of Boca Raton grew. (2)

BOIS D'ARC, Missouri

Settled in the late 1700's, Bois D'Arc, Missouri, is located in Greene County. The name was given to the area in the early pioneer days by French hunters and explorers who learned that the Indians for miles around came here to get wood for their bows. The Osage Orange, as it is known, is a large hedge that once grew in profusion here. The wood of this hedge is very pliable, very strong, and very durable. It made an ideal wood for the Indian bow, thus the name Bois D'Arc, or Wood of the Bows. (1) (*See* Medicine Bow)

BOISE, Idaho

Boise, Idaho's capital city, is the largest metropolitan community in the state. Boise, pronounced Boy-see, derives its name from the early French trapper expression "Les Bois" meaning "The Woods."

The name Boise has been applied to places in a large area. In 1834 British fur traders established a post that soon developed into the Hudson's Bay Company's Fort Boise. This was at the mouth of the Boise River, more than 40 miles from the later city of Boise. Indian trouble along the Oregon Trail in the Boise Valley in 1854 forced the abandonment of the post, which is now usually called Old Fort Boise. The United States Army decided that a new military Fort Boise would have to be built. Before action was taken on the decision, though, energetic prospectors found rich gold deposits in 1862 in Boise Basin less than 40 miles from Boise, and a rush to these Boise mines changed the situation completely. Construction of the new post no longer could be delayed, and within a year Major Pinckney Lugenbeel was on his way to Boise Valley to select a site and build a new fort.

Celebrating July 4, 1863—the day of Gettysburg and Vicksburg—the United States military force sent out to build Fort Boise chose a location, and three days later the townsite was provided for next to the new fort. The new military post was composed of barracks, storehouses, stables, officers' quarters and similar buildings, but was never enclosed by a single defensive wall. The last place that Indians would attack was a United States Army post like Fort Boise.

When in 1864 the territorial legislature met for its second session in Lewiston—the place designated by the governor until a territorial capital could be agreed upon—Boise was chosen to be permanent seat of government, and has remained that ever since.

BOLADA, Arizona
Bolada was wrought of the beginning letters of three families of Yavapai County—Bones, Land and Dandria. (5)

BOLAIR, West Virginia
The name is a corruption of the French "Beau Clair," which was the title of a song popular among the pioneers of that era. (6)

BOLIVAR, Tennessee
Once named Hatchie, Bolivar, located in southwestern Tennessee, in Hardemann County, changed its named to Bolivar in 1825 to honor Simon Bolivar, the "George Washington" of South America. (6)

BOLIVAR, New York
Bolivar, located in Allegany County, near the Pennsylvania line, was named in honor of General Simon Bolivar (1783-1830), a Venezuelan statesman and leader of revolt of South American colonies against Spanish rule. At the time Bolivar was somewhat of a hero to the Americans, who had only recently thrown off the yoke of British rule. (6)

BON AIR, Alabama
The town was founded by a textile firm seeking water from a large spring in 1907. Although the town is composed entirely of Anglo-Saxons of Scotch-Irish descent, they chose a French name for their town, meaning "good air." (1)

BONANZA, Utah
Located in the Uintah Basin of eastern Utah, this is a mining town, where the glitter of gold and silver took second place to a kind of black gold called Gilsonite, asphaltite or Uintaite. It is a natural black hydrocarbon with an appearance similar to coal. The uses are many and varied all the way from asphaltite tile to printers ink. The town is primarily the headquarters of the American Gilsonite Company, and their employees, and has its own post office.

The Uintah Basin was explored by the white man as far back as 1776, with the Spanish taking the lead. Antoine Robidoux, a Frenchman, established the first trading post here in the early 1800's; however, it was destroyed by the Indians in 1844. Kit Carson built a trading post at the junction of the Uinta, White, and Green Rivers. It too was destroyed about the same time as Fort Robidoux. Fort Davy Crockett, known then as Fort Misery, was built by three trappers—Thompson, Craig, and Sinclair in 1837. It suffered the same fate as the other trading posts. Samuel H. Gilson, around 1850, made the discovery of the mineral when he noticed ants carrying bits of shiny black material and traced their path to the "mother lode." Typically, as soon as the value of his discovery was established, the run began and another mining town was born and fittingly named Bonanza for the Bonanza that made it. (2)

BONDUEL, Wisconsin

Started over one hundred years ago as a birch bark chapel, from which Father Floribandt Bonduel, a French Jesuit priest, administered to both the medical and the spiritual needs of the Menominee Indians, long before other white men dared to tread these paths.

The name Bonduel itself has an interesting history, as related by a descendant, Father Andre Bonduel, dominicain, Helsinki, Finland: The name Bonduel (or Bonduelle) is today fairly common in Belgium and in Northern France. The history of Bonduel is uncertain, but there are many theories. Near the town of Lille is a village named Bondues. The meaning of the name of the village would be "The village of the great and good God," or "le village du Bon Dieu". People from this village were referred to as "Bondues," and the name could have started here. (Mrs. Viola Krueger, Bonduel, Wis.)

BONE GAP, Illinois

Long after the red man had been driven west, far beyond the "father of waters," the Mississippi, white hunters were making regular trips up and down the Bompus, Indian, and Buck Creeks. Around 1815 they discovered piles of bones and a number of Indian mounds near a large gap in the timber. The timber, at that time, covered a high ridge extending from north to south, dividing on the east, what was known as Bompus Prairie from Buck Prairie on the west. Because of their grisly find, they named the locale Bone Gap.

While a rustic school, complete with hand-hewn seats, was erected on this spot in 1854, it wasn't until 1867 that the first place of business made its appearance. When the Illinois Central Railroad (then known as the P. D. & E.) built through the area it missed the small settlement of Bone Gap by half-a-mile, so she just lifted up her skirts and moved to the railroad, taking with her her unusual name. In 1892 Bone Gap incorporated as a village. (1)

Bone Gap, Illinois

BONNE TERRE, Missouri

A mining town, it was incorporated in 1864. The community takes its name from the area, which was then known as Bonne Terre by the early day French miners, who were referring to its great mineral wealth. It is located in Saint François County, near the Illinois line. (1)

BON SECOUR, Alabama

In 1699 Pierre Le Moyne, Sieur d'Iberville, planted the banner of France at the mouth of Mobile Bay. He named the spot Massacre Island, but it was later changed to Dauphin, in honor of the Dauphin of France. In 1702, Iberville's brother, Jean Baptiste Le Moyne, Sieur de Bienville, built Fort Louis de la Mobile on the Mobile River at Twenty-Seven Mile Bluff. When this area, around what is now Mobile, was settled in 1702 Iberville and his two brothers, Bienville and Serigny, built a hunting and fishing lodge at Bon Secour.

Bon Secour was named by Jacques Cook, a Frenchman, who came from Montreal, also the birth place of the Le Moyne brothers. Cook used the name Bon Secour from the oldest cathedral, Notre Dame de Bon Secours, in Montreal. The French Canadian name is translated into the English, meaning Safe Harbor. Bon Secour is considered one of the safest harbors along the Gulf Coast, where small pleasure and fishing boats can anchor during squalls and stormy weather. (Meme and Charley Publishing Company, Bon Secour, Alabama)

BOOK, Louisiana

Book post office was established January 10, 1935, and was named in honor of one of its oldest citizens. He had a small family of nine boys and two girls, and was the former postmaster of Argo, Louisiana, long since discontinued. (1)

BOULDER, Utah

Amasa Mason Lyman, first to settle and build in Boulder Valley (1888–1889) states that the country around here was explored for 15 years before he came here. Boulder is located at the foot of Boulder Mountain, which gave it its name.

At one time there was talk of naming the mountain "Thousand Lake Mountain," for the thousand or more lakes located on it, but since the boulders were more prominent and impressive the name Boulder was given instead. Ironically, a mountain some 15 miles across the valley with plenty of boulders of its own, but with only three small lakes, received the name "Thousand Lake Mountain." (1)

BOULDER CITY, Colorado

During the open winter of 1858–59, settlers worked in shirt sleeves, building cabins and laying out a new town. A company for the town was formed on February 10, 1859, and G. W. Gregg and T. W. Fisher were hired to plat a town site. The new town was named Boulder City for the numerous large stones or boulders in the vicinity. (2)

BOUNTIFUL, Utah

According to the Utah Historical Society, Bountiful was the second Mormon settlement in Utah. It was settled in 1847 by Perrigrine Sessions. He found it when he was sent to find new grazing lands. It was called Sessions Settlement in honor of its founder until February 27, 1855. When the Pioneer Fathers first colonized the area they found that the fertility of the soil was such that everything that was planted grew in rich abundance. Because of this and early reference found in the Book of Mormon, the city was renamed Bountiful. (Reference Book of Mormon, First Nephi Chapter 17, verses 5. 6 and 7) (2)

BOWLEGS, Oklahoma

Named for the famous Indian chieftain Billy Bowlegs. Bowlegs' name was

Bowlegs, Oklahoma

a white man's corruption of the Indian name Bolek. The chief was head of the Seminole tribe when the Seminoles and the whites ended their war in 1856 in the territory of Florida. When the infamous "trail of tears" march was made by the Seminole in their removal from Florida to the Indian Territory of what is now part of Oklahoma, the Bowlegs family settled in the area of present-day Bowlegs. Later some of the Seminoles moved back to Florida and settled on reservations in the Everglades. Billy Bowlegs, the son of the famous Seminole chieftain, was living on the Brighton Indian Reservation at the time of his death, February 1965. He left one son. (1)

BOWLING GREEN, Kentucky
Established around 1780, it was so named for the habit of playing "bowls" here on the level, green lawns, particularly on the front lawn of one of its oldest settlers. The expression "Let's go down to the Bowling Green" eventually gave the city its name. (2)

BOX CHURCH, Texas
Box Church, in central Limestone County, four miles south of Groesbeck in the timbered region along McKinzie Creek, was named for a church established in the community before 1860. (3)

BOX ELDER, Texas
Box Elder in southeastern Red River County was named for the trees found along the bottoms of Shawnee and Crooked Branch creeks. Planters settled a scattered community here between 1840 and 1860. (3)

BOYS RANCH, Texas
This community is just what the name implies. It is a ranch that raises boys instead of cattle. Founded in 1939, by Cal Farley, it is a home for homeless boys. (2)

BRAINTREE, Massachusetts
The name Braintree dates from 1632, when the so-called Braintree Company recruited by the Reverend Thomas Hooker, in Braintree, England, sailed here on the ship *Lyon.* On arrival here, they were ordered by the General Court to "sit down" at Mount Wollaston, but finding the area still unsuitable many of them proceeded to move on to Newtowne (now Cambridge) . The name Braintree was probably chosen because many of the followers of Reverend Hooker were from Braintree, a town of Hooker's own parish of Chelmsford, Essex, England. (2)

BRANDYWINE MANOR, Pennsylvania
Was named for Brandywine Creek and the Manor Presbyterian Church, which was built in 1875. (4)

BRATTLEBORO, Vermont
By purchase and inheritance one Mr. William Brattle acquired land on the frontiers of the Colonies. In 1727, he married the daughter of Governor Gordon Saltonstall, and entered the realm of politics. He first intended to enter the ministry, then decided to become a doctor, but finally became a soldier. By 1773 he had become a major general and found himself in hot water over the withdrawal of stores of ammunition he was charged with for the British General Gage. According to the records he "took refuge at Castle William; released his property and let himself be evacuated to Halifax, Nova Scotia." He apparently enjoyed the good food he found there after rationing in Boston. "Brattle died of a surfeit (over indulgence) there on October 1776." All in all William Brattle seems to have been a rather odd and unusual character. While he was living it up in Canada, inflated currency and claims against his estate left it insolvent. In other words he went broke. The province confiscated most of his land, which was to become known later as Halifax, Vernon, Guilford, and Mr. Brattle's Borough, "Brattleboro, Vermont." (2)

BREAKS, Virginia
When the Russel Fork River came this way it looked for a *break* in the Cumberland Mountains. It found one and cut a deep gorge that eventually came to be known as the Grand Canyon of the South. Many cliffs measure 1600 feet to the river bed. Several years ago the states of Kentucky and

Virginia decided to establish a park here and the Breaks Inter-State Park was created. (1)

BRIDAL VEIL, Oregon

Bridal Veil, Multnomah County, Oregon, received its unusual name from a remark made by a passenger going down the river in a boat. The sight of the falls cascading into the river caused her to remark that it looked just like a bride's veil. The locale eventually became known as the Bride's Veil, and later changed to Bridal Veil. When a community grew up here it took the unusual name for its own. (1)

BROKEN ARROW, Oklahoma

The history of Broken Arrow dates back to Indian Territorial days. It was on the site of what is now Broken Arrow that the Indian braves, just returned from the armies of both the North and the South, pledged their friendship, which was symbolized by the breaking of an arrow—thus Broken Arrow was given its name. (2)

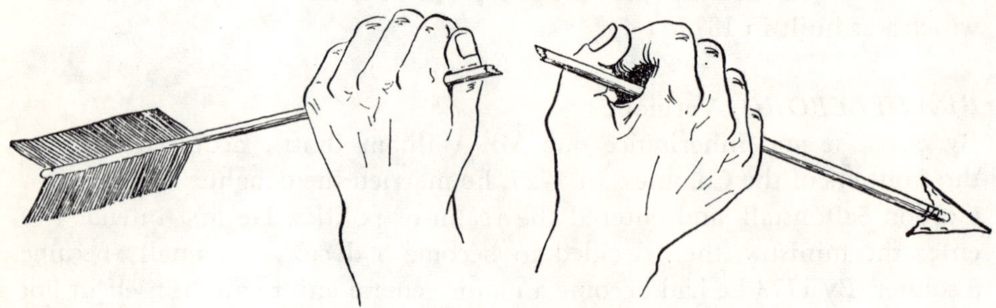

Broken Arrow, Oklahoma

BROKEN BOW, Nebraska

Located in Custer County, where the train conductor on the railroad in 1886 used to chant, "Prepare to meet your maker . . . you are now entering Custer County." The origin of the name is better told in a poem contributed by the Arrow Hotel:

Hewitt, in his dugout, sought a name for his P. O.
He suggested several—but Uncle Sam said, "No,"
His two boys went a hunting; and Indian bow brought back.
'Twas broken, but they hung it upon the dugout shack.
He shouted when he saw it, "This name will surely go!"
And Uncle Sam okayed it, That's why it's Broken Bow. (2)

BROKEN BOW, Oklahoma

Broken Bow got its name from the Dierk's Camp that moved here from Broken Bow, Nebraska, several years ago. When they arrived this town had no name so they adopted the name of their previous camp. (2)

BRONCO, Texas
Bronco, on the western line of Yoakum County, was named for the cowboy sport of riding broncos and was a ranch supply point. (3)

BRYN MAWR, Pennsylvania
Ardmore is the name of a small hamlet in Ireland in County Waterford, 39 miles from the City of Cork. It means the same in Irish as Bryn Mawr does in Welsh—"high ground." Bryn Mawr, however, was the name given by one Rowland Ellis to his Main Line estate after his native town in Wales and it was later applied to the town. (4)

BUCATUNNA, Mississippi
Bucatunna, located in Wayne County, near the Chickasawhay River, was settled around the early 1800's. The name is Indian and means "collected together." (6)

BUCKSKIN JOE, Colorado
Buckskin Joe, Colorado, was a mining town founded in 1859, and first called Laurette. The name was later changed to Buckskin Joe in honor of its founder, whose real name was, of all things, Joseph Higgenbottom! Higgenbottom (or Buckskin Joe) wore buckskin clothes which accounted for his unusual nickname. He hung around the mining town for a while then lit out for the San Juan Mountains where he had heard of a larger gold strike. That was the last anyone ever saw of him. The town of Buckskin Joe has been restored to its original condition by careful planners and is now primarily a show town, giving people a look back through time to the wild and wooly gold mining days of early Colorado. It has a post office, though. (2)

BULLHEAD CITY, Arizona
Over a hundred years ago when the discovery of gold brought the first white settlers, they had the problem of trying to cross the Colorado River. Before the five dams were built, it would flood badly every spring, and there were also treacherous quick sand spots. By watching the Indians, the white men found the safest crossing, which was by a rock cliff shaped like a bull's head. This point became known as Bull's Head, and kept that name until construction of a dam began near this point. A post office was requested for the village, and when it was established the government officials gave it the name Bullhead City, *and the waters rose and covered the bull.* (2)

BULL SHOALS, Arkansas
In 1854, a government survey party traveling up the White River by boat

reached the rapids, where a dam now stands, and it took the "bull strength" of the entire party to get the boats over the shoals. In their field notes they named it Bull Shoals. Later a hill, a dam, and a lake were also named Bull Shoals. The city was platted in 1947, and quite naturally took the same name. (2)

BULLTOWN, West Virginia
The town was named for Captain Bull, a minor chief of a minor tribe of Delaware Indians. (6)

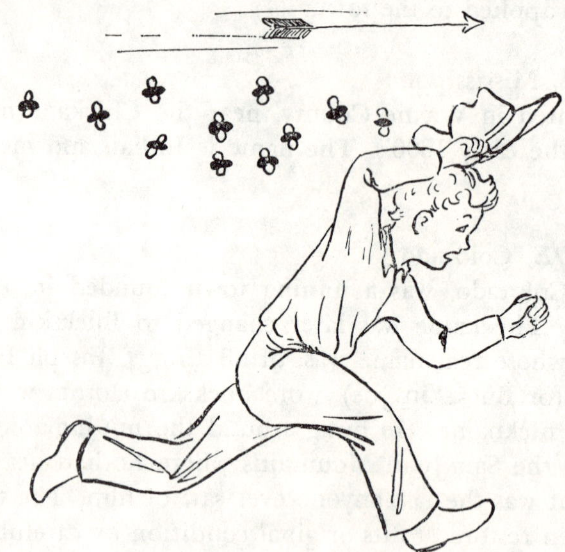

Bumble Bee, Arizona

BUMBLE BEE, Arizona
There are a number of versions about the origin of the name Bumble Bee. One is that the early settlers used to send a boy, each day, to the top of a nearby hill as a lookout for Indians. One day the boy came racing in yelling, "Quick, the Indians are coming and they're as thick as Bumble Bees!" Another credits the name to an Army Scout, sent out from Fort Prescott to look for Indians, and who later reported that "The Indians are thicker than Bumble Bees around the waterholes." (1)

BUMPASS, Virginia
At the time of the building of the Chesapeake and Louisiana Railroad, this village was known as Second Turnout, and the first post office, established in 1847, was known by that name. In 1860 John T. Bumpass became postmaster and had the name changed.

Paradoxically the name Bumpass was French and started out as Bonpass, meaning a good pass, and it was horribly Anglo-Saxonized and Americanized into Bumpass! (1)

BURKBURNETT, Texas
Burkburnett, on Gilbert Creek in northeastern Wichita County, originated about 1867 when D. P. McCracken and H. C. Ackers settled in this area. In the early 1870's the community was known to the cowboys on Samuel Burk Burnett's Four Sixes (6666) Ranch as Nesterville. Once named Gilbert, the town moved about one mile to the railroad townsite, which was then named for Burk Burnett in 1907. The Burk Burnett townsite was named for him, reputedly by personal intercession with the Post Office Department by Theodore Roosevelt, who had been Burnett's guest on a wolf hunt in the area in 1905. (3)

BURNING SPRINGS, Kentucky
The town took its name from a spring of water, with natural gas seeping into it. It would frequently burn when someone touched a match to it. The petroleum floating on the top of the water would burn without any effect from the water under it.

There are several oil companies drilling here for oil. The residents, who drill for water, must first pipe off the natural gas before they can use it. (1)

BURNING SPRINGS, West Virginia
There are several legends as to how Burning Springs was named; however the most authentic is that Indians accidently struck a flint stone too near a water spring which was covered with an oil slick. The spark ignited the oil which burned upon the water causing the Indians to stare in awe at the sight of water burning. They called the strange, and forbidden place, Burning Spring. (1)

BURNT CABINS, Pennsylvania
Was so named because the cabins of the early settlers here were burned down by order of the provincial government in 1750, after the Indians had complained against white encroachment on their lands. (4)

BURNT CORN, Alabama
Burnt Corn, Monroe County, Alabama, is said to have gotten its unique name after Indians stole into the little village one night, killed all the white settlers, burned their homes, and great quantities of corn. (2)

BURNT HOUSE, West Virginia
In the late 1800's an Inn, known as Harris Inn, was located here and was a main stagecoach and travelers' stop. One Sunday night it burned to the ground, and a lot of mystery and intrigue was attached to the incident.

Thereafter the place became known to travelers as the place of the "Burnt House," and the phrase grew into the name of a town that was built on this spot. (1)

BURNT PRAIRIE, Illinois
The town was incorporated as the Village of Liberty; however the post office, in the early 1900's, was named Burnt Prairie because another Liberty was located in Illinois. The name Burnt Prairie had evolved after the area had been burned over, some years ago, and hunters had begun to refer to it as "the burnt prairie." Until February 1965, the post office had one name and the town another. Confusion was so great that a petition was finally drawn up by the townspeople and the name of the town was changed to Burnt Prairie to match the name of the post office. (1)

BUSHKILL, Pennsylvania
Was settled in 1812, at the confluence of Little Bushkill and Big Bushkill Creeks. Bushkill is Dutch, and means "Little River." (4)

Bushyhead, Arizona

BUSHYHEAD, Oklahoma
Named for Dennis W. Bushyhead, at one time (1879–1887) chief of the Cherokee Nation. (6)

BUSTAMANTE, Texas
Bustamante, a town in central Zapata County, was named for Anastasio Bustamante, a former president of Mexico. (3)

BUTTES DES MORTS, Wisconsin

The Winnebago tribe lived here, as there was good hunting and fishing on the Fox River. The Fox Tribe, from Green Bay, with the help of a French fur buyer came up the Fox River in canoes and surprised the Winnebagos. A great battle was fought here on the bank of the Fox River and the Fox drove the Winnebagos out. The evidence of the battle is on the crest of the river bank. Fourteen skeletons were discovered when one basement was dug. Arrow heads, spear heads, and fish hooks made out of stone are often found along the river banks. The name Butte Des Morts is French and means "banks of the dead," referring to the banks of the Fox River. (1)

BUTTERFIELD, Arkansas

This village was named, curiously enough, for a stage line, but not the famous Butterfield Line. It was named, instead, for a man named D. A. Butterfield, who supervised the building of the Diamond Jo Stage Line. (6)

BUTTON PRAIRIE, Texas

Button Prairie, an agricultural community of eastern Milam County, seven miles southeast of Milano, was named for the button-like acorns of the oak trees and for the prairie location. (3)

BUZZARDS BAY, Massachusetts

This village was named by the Indians, who revered a certain type of buzzard. The village is also located on a bay, hence the name Buzzard's Bay. (2)

BYHALIA, Mississippi

Located in northwestern Mississippi, near the Tennessee border, this town was settled in 1830. The name is Chickasaw Indian for Great Oaks, in honor of the giant oaks that once grew here in abundance. (6)

BYLAS, Arizona

The next time someone calls you "Bylas," blush! It is Apache for "One who does all the talking." (5)

CABEZA, Texas

In western DeWitt County near the Karnes County Line, this town was named for its location on the headwaters of Cabeza Creek. In 1888 Robert E. I. Magee taught the first session of the school. The name is a Spanish word meaning "head;" the stream has been called that since 1848, but the reason for the name is unknown. (3)

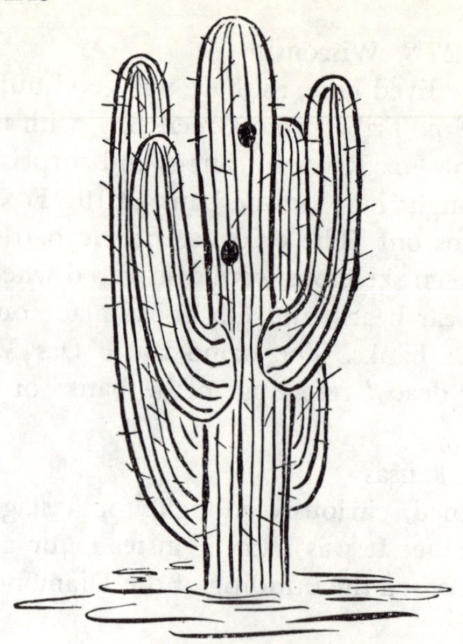

Cactus, Texas

CACTUS, Texas

In northern Webb County, Cactus was established in 1881 as a shipping point on the International-Great Northern Railroad and had a post office before 1900. It was so named for the growth of cacti in the area. Texas contains over one hundred species, representing the widest assortment found in any state. (3)

CADDO, Texas

Located in Milar County, it is a farm community in the northeastern section of the county. Caddo was named for its location on a camp site of the Caddo Indians. N. J. Butler established a store in the late 1870's and became postmaster about 1880. (3)

CADDO GAP, Arkansas

Received its name from the Caddo River, named for the Indians, who once lived in their area, and for the gap of the mountains just below the town. (1)

CADDO MILLS, Texas

On the Missouri, Kansas and Texas Railroad, in Hunt County, was called Caddo for the Caddo Indians, who used the area for a camping ground, until L. T. Johnson erected a sawmill in 1860. It was then changed to Caddo Mills. (3)

CAINS STORE, Kentucky

This post office was established about 1870, by Milford Cain. While a great number of rural post offices are located in the local general store, most of them chose names symbolic to the community, the area, or named it for some prominent citizen. Mr. Cain, being the new postmaster, owning the store where the post office was to be located, probably figured he was just about the most prominent citizen in the village, so he had it named Cains Store. Luckily he didn't operate a mortuary instead of a store! (1)

CALAMINE, Arkansas
Calamine was a little mining town in the 1870's, where zinc was mined and processed. The post office was established in 1871, and named Calamine, which Webster describes as "a mineral, hydrous *zinc* silicate, ZnSiO3 (OH2), an ore of zinc; hemimorphite." (1)

CALAVERITAS, California
Means "small skull." Scene of great mining activity in the early 1850's, it is located near Andreas. Destroyed by fire in 1853, only a few adobe buildings remained. It is located in colorful Calaveral County, California. (2)

CALCIUM, New York
This small hamlet, just five miles north of Watertown, New York, was first called Sanford's Corners. One of the town's most prominent citizens was Mr. Madison Cooper, a pioneer in refrigeration, who used calcium chloride CaC12 in his refrigeration process. In this capacity he received a great deal of mail, and much of it went to Sanfords, New York, which annoyed him a great deal. He finally petitioned the Post Office Department to change the name to Calcium. His request was granted and his mail no longer strayed, as this is the only post office named Calcium in the United States. (1)

CALICO ROCK, Arkansas
There are limestones, flints, sandstones, marbles, granites, but who ever saw a calico rock? Strange as it may seem there are such formations, and it is from the huge bluffs of "calico" striped rock along the White River, that the town of Calico Rock got its name. (City Rexall Drugs, Calico Rock, Ark.)

CALION, Arkansas
The town traces its origin to the Indian village of Utiangue, where DeSoto and his hardy band built a stockade and spent the winter of 1541. It is named for Calhoun and Union Counties, taking the first three letters from Calhoun and the last three from Union.

CALLAO, Missouri
Callao, located in Macon County, was platted in 1858 and when the time came to choose a name, one of the city fathers was blindfolded, while another

spun a globe of the world. By placing his finger on the globe, he stopped it on the town of Callao, Peru, and Callao, Missouri was born. (1)

CALUMET, Minnesota

In 1880 several logging companies were operating near the future site of the village of Calumet. The logging companies, sometimes employing as many as 100 men, brought the first settlers to the Calumet area. The largest number of settlers came from other states, and foreign countries, when iron ore mining gained importance in the area. When the Duluth, Mesabi, and Northern Railway Company moved into the area, the village of Calumet was born. It was officially incorporated June 11, 1909. By July 20, Calumet boasted fourteen saloons!

Named Calumet after the Indian peace pipes, the word comes from the French, and means "reed." (2)

CAMDEN-ON-GAULEY, West Virginia

The town was originally named Camden, for Senator Johnson N. Camden. The remainder of the name was added later to avoid confusion with another West Virginia town named Camden, at the time of the establishment of a post office. It is located on the Gauley River. (1)

CAMP, Arkansas

Originally named Indian Camp, because the presence of mounds nearby suggested to the old settlers that the spot had once been an Indian tribal center. The name was later shortened to Camp. (6)

CANEADEA, New York

Located in northwestern Allegany County, at an altitude of 1200 feet, it rests upon the site of an old Seneca village, from whence it got its name. The name is Seneca Indian and means "where the heavens rest on the earth." The reason for the name is obvious. (6)

CANNON BALL, North Dakota

Cannon Ball, located in Sioux County, derives its name from the many sandstone formations located in the area. These round "cannon ball" formations, caused by ancient glaciers, range from baseball and cannon ball size to one of many tons. They are located on the Sioux Indian Reservation, by the Big Missouri River. (1)

CANNON FALLS, Minnesota

Named for the Cannon River falls. The name originally given the river itself, by early French hunters, was "Rivière de Canot" or Canoe River.

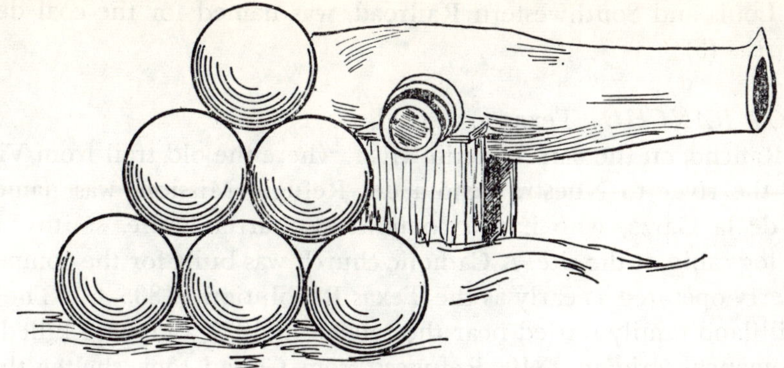

Cannon Ball, North Dakota

Pioneers, who followed later, thought the Indians were calling it the "cannon" river, and marked it that way on their maps, and the Canoe River became the Cannon River. (6)

CANUTILLO, Texas
Canutillo, in El Paso County about fourteen miles northwest of El Paso, was named for a land grant awarded on May 30, 1823, to Juan Maria Ponce de León, and others, under the Mexican Colonization Law of January 3, 1823. (3)

CANYON, Texas
Canyon, near the center of Randall County at a site chosen by Jot Gunter and William B. Munson for headquarters of the T. Anchol Ranch in 1878, was named for the Palo Duro Canyon, and was first called Canyon City. L. G. Conner settled at the site in 1887 and started the village in 1889. His dugout served as a home, general store, and the post office. (*See* Broken Bow) (3)

CARADAN, Texas
Caradan, on north Bennett Creek, in Mills County, was named for Smith Caraway and Dan Bush, early settlers in this area, and was established in 1899. (3)

CARBON, Texas
Carbon in the central part of Eastland County was settled in 1881. The town's name is explained by the mineral deposits in the county. Street names include Lignite, Jet, Coke, Diamond, Anthracite, Cannal, and Coal. (3)

CARBONDALE, Texas
Carbondale, in the coal-mining area of south central Bowie County on

the St. Louis and Southwestern Railroad, was named for the coal deposits in the area. (3)

CARLOS RANCHO, Texas

Carlos Rancho, on the San Antonio River, where the old trail from Victoria crossed the river to Nuestra Senõra del Refugio Mission, was named for Carlos de la Garza, who had a commissary, barrel house, smithy, and a double log cabin at the site. A Catholic church was built for the community, and a ferry operated as early as the Texas Revolution (1835–6). The Johnston Gilliland family settled near the rancho in 1837 and were killed there in a Comanche raid in 1840. Refugees from Goliad took shelter there at the time of the Rafael Vásquez and Andrian Woll invasions of 1842. (3)

CARRIZO SPRINGS, Texas

Carrizo Springs, in northern Dimmit County, was established in 1865 as the first permanent settlement in the county of which it is now the county seat. Early settlers named their community for the reed growing around the springs, using the Spanish name Carrizo. (3)

CARTER NINE, Oklahoma

Carter Nine was founded during the oil boom of the 1920's. It is an oilfield settlement that was started by the Carter Oil Company. They had a large gasoline plant here at the time. The plant was located on lease number 9, so they called it Carter Nine. (1)

CASA PIEDRA, Texas

Casa Piedra, in southeastern Presidio County on Alamito Creek and the Panhandle and Santa Fe Railroad, was established about 1883, and named for a rock house built by Feliciano Mata in 1875. (3)

CASCABEL, Arizona

So lovely to say for the name of a town, but it is Spanish for Rattlesnake! (5)

CASH, Arkansas

Located in Craighead County, 16 miles from Jonesboro, Cash was established in 1894 when the Bonnerville and Southwestern Railroad was built through this area. The new town was first called Soonover, from a remark by a settler that the new town would "soon be over." When the post office was established the name was changed to Cash for the river Cache, which flows nearby. No one knows the reason for the difference in the spelling. Perhaps a postal error.

It is interesting to note that two years after Cash was established as a town, Sedgewick, Phillips and Company created a new town some four miles away, which they called Credit, as a bit of irony against their neighbor Cash. Cash, however, has lasted through the years, while Credit has long since gone out of business. (1)

CASH, Texas
Cash, in south central Hunt County on the Texas and New Orleans Railroad, was named by Edward H. R. Green to honor J. A. *Money,* who worked for the extension of the railroad to the town, and later became its first postmaster. (3)

CASHTOWN, Pennsylvania
The town is said to have been named for an early tavernkeeper's insistence that all patrons pay cash. The Cashtown Tavern is a two-and-a-half-story red brick building dating from 1797. (4)

CASTLE GATE, Utah
Castle Gate obtained its name from the fact that there are two high cliffs about one mile above the town that resemble castles. These cliffs form the doorway to the valley below. Through this gateway flows the water of the Price River, a transcontinental railroad (The Denver and Rio Grande Western), and a coast to coast highway. (1)

CATASAUQUA, Pennsylvania
This small borough, south of Towamensing, was previously called Calisuk and Caladqua, and is Delaware Indian for "Thirsty Earth." (2)

CATAULA, Georgia
Cataula was named for an Indian word, and means "big rock." (1)

CATAWBA, South Carolina
The unincorporated community of Catawba is located three miles from the Catawba River, which gave it the name. On the banks of the river lived the Catawba tribe of Indians. This is the only tribe of Indians now living in South Carolina. At present the Catawba Indian Reservation is so remote and unmarked as to make it almost impossible to find. Many of the Catawbas have intermarried with whites and attend public schools.

The community of Catawba was established about 1870, on the junction of the Seaboard and Southern Railroads, and is also known as Catawba Junction. The story told here is that there was a race between the two railroads to reach this point. The loser was to assume the job of building a trestle to pass over the rails of the winner. The Seaboard won, and the community was established as a junction point and terminus where passengers could change from one railroad to the other. (1)

CATAWBA, Virginia
Located in the beautiful Alleghany Mountains, and still retaining some of its original wilderness appearance, Catawba is a small cluster of houses, gathered around a general store. The name was taken from the Catawba Indians, who were prevalent in this area for hundreds of years. Although they are no longer in evidence, they left behind many relics of their past. The area still abounds in deer, bear, and wild turkey, and must have indeed been a cornucopia of plenty for the Catawba Indians who once lived here. (1)

CAT MASH, Alabama
The small hamlet of Cat Mash, located in the Packer's Bend Area of Alabama, takes its name from Cat Marsh, a swampy area in which wildcats are frequently seen. The name is a derivation of the Cat Marsh. (2)

CAT SPRING, Texas
Cat Spring, southwest of Belleville on the Missouri, Kansas, and Texas Railroad in Austin County, was settled by a group of German immigrants in 1844. Robert Klebert was known as the founder of the village. The name was given when Rudolf von Roeder's son shot and killed a Mexican puma at the spring on their farm. (3)

CAVE CITY, Kentucky
Incorporated in 1866, the city took its name from a large cave located within the city limits. Cave city is also the "gateway" to the famed Kentucky cave area, and is near Mammoth Cave National Park. (1)

CAVE CREEK, Arkansas
Old timers say the town was named for the profusion of small caves and a creek in the area. (1)

CAZENOVIA, Illinois
Located in Cazenovia Township, Woodford County, it, in a round-about way got its name from Lake Cazenovia, New York. It seems there were four brothers-in-law living near Low Point, named Jeter Foster, Eli Rich, Thomas Clark and John Safford. They once had lived near Lake Cazenovia, New York, and talked incessantly of its beauty and its virtues. Finally, the neighbors good-naturedly started calling them "Old Cazenovias," until their real names were almost forgotten.

When Woodford County was laid out and organized into townships in 1852, the problem of a name arose. Someone recommended it be named for the "Old Cazenovias," in jest, but the name was adopted unanimously. The village of Cazenovia took its name from the township. (1)

CEDAR BAYOU, Texas
Cedar Bayou, in southern Harris County, takes its name from its location on a bayou where early settlers found an abundant growth of cedar. It is also known as the home of the farmer-poet John Peter Sjolander. A regiment of the Texas Army camped near the settlement in 1836. (3)

CEDAR LAKE, Texas
Cedar Lake, in southeastern Matogorda County, was named for a cedar brake surrounding a near-by lake. (3)

CEDAR LANE. Texas
Cedar Lane, in Matogorda County, on Caney Creek, was originally a plantation store with an approach through a lane of cedars. (3)

CEE VEE, Texas
Cee Vee, in Cottle County, takes its name from the old CV Ranch. (3)

CENTER POINT, Texas
Located on the banks of the Guadalupe River, the town is ten miles south of Kerrville. Established back in the 1850's, the town was originally called Zenzenburg. In the late 1880's, when Kerrville was established as the county seat, they moved all the county records from Bexar County by ox cart. Halfway from Bexar County to Kerrville, they camped and declared the camp to be "The County Seat for the night." Their camp was at Zenzenburg, which they referred to as the Central Point of their trip. Later the town adopted the name, but modified it to Center Point. (1)

CENTER TUFTONBORO, New Hampshire
Located in the beautiful White Mountains in an area of lakes, such as Lake Winnipesaukee, Mirror Lake and Lake Wentworth, the town takes its name from the township in which it is located and from its position in the township. The name Tufton comes from John Tufton Mason, an Englishman, who was prominent in public affairs.

The village of Center Tuftonboro was once known as Mackeral Corners, for the habit of fishermen of laying their day's catch of mackeral on a large boulder in the town to dry, and later selling it from this very same spot. (1)

CENTURY, Florida
Located in Polk County, Florida, Century was founded in 1900 and received its unique name because it was born at the turn of the century. (2)

CEREDO, West Virginia
Platted in 1857 by Eli Thayer, who named it for the ancient Italian Goddess of Agriculture, Ceres, because of its rich farm land. (6)

CERES, Virginia
Named for the Greek Goddess Ceres, Goddess of Agriculture, this village lies in the western portion of Bland County, Virginia, flanked by the Brushy Mountains on the north and by the Big Walkers on the south.

The Indians called the area Bear Garden, for its many wild bears, and the Cherokees used it as their winter quarters. The post office was established in 1880, by Captain H. C. Graseclose, on the Blue Grass Trail, and named it aptly, for it is still an agriculture community. (1)

CESTOHAWA, Texas
Cestohawa, or Cestochowa, in northern Karnes County, was named for Cestochowa, Poland, and means "saves often." From 1881 to 1891 it was the metropolis of Polish missions in Texas. (3)

CHANCE, Maryland
Originally named Rock Creek, when the first post office was opened, the postmaster chose the name Chance because there was a large farm in the area called the Chance Farms. The Methodists Church in Chance is still named the Rock Creek Methodists Church. (1)

CHAPEL HILL, North Carolina
Chapel Hill was named for the New Hope Chapel of the Church of England, which once stood at the cross of the Petersburg and Salisbury roads. (6)

CHASKA, Minnesota
On the Minnesota River, below Minneapolis-St. Paul, the town was named for a Sioux Indian Chief, whose tribe lived in a nearby village. There are several Indian Mounds in the vicinity. (6)

CHATTANOOGA, Tennessee
The first building in Chattanooga by white men was erected in 1761, and was a trading post called the Old French Store. At that time Chattanooga was inhabited by the Cherokees and until 1835 was the scene of many bitter conflicts with the Indians and was part of the Cherokee Nation until 1837.

The Cherokee alphabet, the only written language developed by any of the American tribes, was invented by Sequoya, a Cherokee whose "hometown" was Chattanooga. The Sequoya Redwoods of California were named in his honor.

Chattanooga owes its origin and name to the Cherokees. It is said to have derived its name from a word in the language meaning "rock coming to a point," describing Lookout Mountain, which stands like a sentinel over the great city. Another interpretation of the word is "hawk's nest." Others claim it came from Tsatanugi, a Cherokee village which was located at the foot of Lookout Mountain.

The extreme valor displayed by Union soldiers in battles around the city during the Civil War brought about the initial awards of the Congressional Medal of Honor, making Chattanooga the birthplace of the nation's highest award. (2)

CHEAPSIDE, Texas

Cheapside is an inland community in Gonzales County located in the rolling hills near the DeWitt County Line. Many of the early settlers were English, and the town was named for a city in England, and for a street in a Virginia town. (3)

CHEBOYGAN, Michigan

Located at the confluence of the Cheboygan River and Lake Huron, Cheboygan takes its name from the river, which was named by the Indians, and means "place of entrance or harbor." A testament to its status as a lumber town was a pile of sawdust, 1,000 feet long, 600 feet wide, and 100 feet high, which represented over 60 years of accumulation. (6)

CHECK, Virginia

When this small village applied for a post office it was necessary to choose a suitable name. Since the post office was to be located in the general store, and since the village loafers were always there playing checkers, the name "Checkers" was chosen.

The Post Office Department turned down the proposed name as there was already another office by that name (since discontinued). The citizens, undaunted, shortened it to Check, and fired it right back again. This time it hit target, and Check, Virginia, was born. (1)

CHEEK, Texas

Cheek, in north central Jefferson County, was laid out in 1907, by a Mr. *Cheek,* as a townsite on the Gulf and Interstate Railroad. A post office, established in 1908, was maintained until 1927. (3)

CHELAN, Washington
Located in the north-central part of Washington, the name is Indian for "deep water," referring to the Chelan Lake. (2)

CHEPACHET, Rhode Island
When the white settlers arrived here they found that the place already had a name, given by the Indians. They called it Chepachet, which means "where the stream begins." The Chepachet River, a major stream that goes on to help form the Blackstone River, starts here. (1)

CHERAW, Colorado
Cheraw is an Indian name and means "sparkling waters." A tribe of Indians once lived along the shores of the river here in mud huts. Arrow heads are still found along the banks by the present residents of Cheraw, giving grim testament to the past residents. (1)

CHERAW, South Carolina
Cheraw, named for an Indian tribe which formerly occupied this area, is the oldest and largest town in Chesterfield County. The first settlement was probably made here about 1752 and was known as Cheraw Hill. It was laid out as a town in 1766 by Eli and Joseph Kershaw, and in 1775 was given the name of Chatham, in honor of the first Earl of Chatham, and whose name it bore until its incorporation in 1820. (2)

CHEROKEE, Alabama
Pioneer settlers migrated from North Carolina and Virginia and built homes in this area around 1820, but it is thought that the town of Cherokee was not actually settled until 1836, when the Memphis to Charleston Railroad (the first in the South) built through. The town was incorporated in 1862.

The name Cherokee was given the town in commemoration of the boundary line between the Chickasaw and the Cherokee Nations. The Chickasaws occupied the land west of Carney Creek in Franklin (now Calbert) County, and the Cherokees occupied the land east of the Creek. (1)

CHERRY FALLS, West Virginia
Located on the Elk River, Cherry Falls was so named for the numerous Cherry trees that grew in the area. (6)

CHERRY LOG, Georgia
Local legend has it that Cherry Log received its name from an old cherry tree that had fallen across a stream near here. The Indians, settlers, and small animals used it in crossing the stream, and it became known as The Cherry Log. (1)

CHERRY TREE, Pennsylvania
A scattered village at the junction of a small creek with the West Branch was founded in 1822, and known to the Indians as Canoe Place. It was renamed for the cherry tree that was used to determine one of the boundaries of the territory conveyed to the Pennsylvania Proprietaries by the Fort Stanwix Treaty of 1768. (4)

CHERRY TREE, Pennsylvania
A farming village, it was so named for the profusion of wild cherry trees in the vicinity. At one time it was named Skidoo. (4)

CHEYENNE, Wyoming
Cheyenne, Laramie County, Wyoming, was named in honor of the Cheyenne Indian tribe. (6)

CHICAGO, Illinois
First incorporated on March 4, 1837, the name is Indian and has many varied meanings. The name was spelled in various ways by the early French explorers, and was used by the Indians to describe anything big

Chicago, Illinois

or strong or powerful, such as wild onions, garlic, and skunks. The Mississippi River appeared on early maps as "Checagou Rivière." A large portage near early Green Bay, Wisconsin, was named the "Checagou Detour," or it could have been the Indians description of Lake Michigan, which is certainly big and powerful. (2)

CHICKAMAUGA, Georgia

The word Chickamauga is derived from a Cherokee Indian word meaning "bloody run" or "river of blood." Prophetic, perhaps, of the fact that it was here that would be fought one of the bloodiest battles of all wars. Over 34,000 fell in the Battle of Chickamauga during the Civil War! (2)

CHICKASAW, Alabama

The town was first established during the early days of World War I, along the Chickasabogue (Chickasaw Creek) by the Tennessee Coal and Iron Company, which selected the name Chickasaw for the town. The early French called the big creek coming in from the northwest by a name something like "Chickasaw Bogue." The name apparently was derived from the fact that the creek came from the direction of the Chickasaw Indian country, in what is now northwest Alabama and northern Mississippi. A group of Indians had lived in the area under the name "Chick-sha," and were apparently a branch of the Choctaw Indians and not really Chickasaws. It appears that the name came down to modern times as a confusion of the words "Chickasaw" and "Chick-sha." (2)

Chicken, Alaska

CHICKEN, Alaska

Chicken was named around 1895, during the gold rush to Alaska. There are several versions of how the name came into being. It was probably named for Chicken Creek, which, legend has it, got its name for the "chicken pay gravel" (that is the small amount of gold found in the gravel of the creek). Another version is that it got its name from the many wild birds found here, such as grouse, and pheasant, or "Chicken of the Flats." (1)

CHICOTA, Texas
Chicota, near Red River and Sanders Creek in Lamar County, was established as a store called Center Springs by Captain Robert Draper, C. S. A. Indians trading at the store spoke of "Checotah" in Indian Territory, and Draper asked for the modified spelling for the name of the post office, which was established here in 1879. (3)

Chili, Wisconsin

CHIEFLAND, Florida
Chiefland got its name in a very unusual way. Dating from old territorial days, it was here that a Creek chieftain and his people laid aside their weapons, took up plowshares, and farmed the land side by side with their white neighbors. This harmonious arrangement continued for many years, until the Indians were forced to move farther southward by what we like to call progress. (6)

CHILI, Wisconsin
In the early 1870's, the railroad crew came through here during the month of January. They were supposed to put up a sign by the depot with the name "Cedarhurst." The report is that it was 47 degrees below zero that morning. One of the men made the remark that this was the "Chilliest"

place he had ever been. Accordingly, rather than make the sign for Cedarhurst, they made it for Chili, and it has been Chili here ever since. (1)

CHILLICOTHE, Ohio
First settled in 1796 by Nathaniel Massie, near the confluence of the Scioto River and Paint Creek, it was incorporated as a city in 1802, and given the name Chillicothe, which is Indian and means "large town." When Ohio became the seventeenth state in 1803, Chillicothe was its first capital. It is the seat of Ross County. (2)

CHINA SPRING, Texas
This community was settled around 1870, as it lay on the old Meridian Highway, laid out in the early 1850's, running from Waco to Meridian. It received its name from a spring, which flowed beside a large Chinaberry tree, located on the side of a hill, north of town. The spring was used as a source of water by Indians, settlers, and cattlemen. (1)

CHINCOTEAGUE, Virginia
Chicoteague (Ching-co-TEEG), meaning "beautiful land across the water," is the largest inhabited island in the state of Virginia. Located on the Eastern Shore, protected from the Atlantic Ocean by Assateague Island, the native home of the famous Chincoteague Wild Ponies. These ponies still roam the salt marshes of Assateague and live wild as they have been doing since the Indians were the only inhabitants. Once a year a pony-penning is held at which time these ponies are rounded-up, made to swim the channel from Assateague to Chincoteague, where they are penned and the smaller ones are sold by auction. This event takes place the last Wednesday and Thursday in July each year. (2)

CHINQUAPIN, Texas
Chinquapin, an old community of eastern San Augustine County, is on the road to Jasper. The name is derived from its location on Chinquapin Creek and from its production of chinquapins. Chinquapin Creek, also known as Egg-Nog Branch, was named for the chinquapin trees growing along its banks. Incidentally the chinquapin is better known as the "dwarf chestnut." (3)

CHISPA, Texas
Chispa, east of Chispa Creek, became a siding on the Galveston, Harrisburg, and San Antonio Railroad (Texas and New Orleans after 1934), in 1882. The site was in Presidio County until Jeff County was created in 1887. The name is Spanish and means "fire" or "spark." (3)

CHOCORUA, New Hampshire
Chocorua is a small village located in the township of Tamworth, New Hampshire, and was named for the famous Indian chief, Chocorua. The chief was so friendly with the first white settlers he left his son in the settler's care. When he returned he found the small boy dead, after having taken poison by mistake. Legend has it that the frantic father massacred the settler family and was, in turn, tracked to the top of the mountains, where he either leaped to his death, or was slain by his pursuers. (2)

CHOICE, Texas
Choice, a Shelby County community about seven miles from Center, on the Santa Fe Railroad was founded about 1904. Unable to choose a name for the post office, the name Choice was given by the Post Office Department. (*See* Mann's Choice) (3)

CHOKIO, Minnesota
Chokia, located in Stevens County, west-central Minnesota, started as an overnight stopping-off station on the Fort Wadsworth Trail from Sauk Centre. The name is Sioux Indian and means "Half-Way." (2)

CHOKOLOSKEE, Florida
Chokoloskee is located on the Island of Chokoloskee—an island believed to have been constructed entirely by Indians. The Calusa Indians once lived in this area in houses constructed on stilts. Each house had a hole in the center of the floor and through these holes the Indians discarded the unwanted shell from their food of shell fish, such as oysters, conchs, etc. Over a period of many, many years these shells built into mounds, the mounds collected silt and eventually an island was unintentionally created.

The settlement is small, the first white settlers coming here in the early 1800's, and the name is Seminole Indian, meaning "old house," presumably for the old stilted houses of the Calusa Indians. (2)

CHRUBUSCO, Indiana
Once called Franklin, the town was required to choose a new name when it was granted a post office. At a meeting held in the log store, a heated argument ensued between an Englishman who wanted to call it Liverpool, a German who thought Brunswick would be a fine name, and a determined Irishman who insisted on Maloney. Peace was restored when a Mrs. Jackson suggested the name Chrubusco, to honor a recent victory by American troops over the Mexicans in the Mexican Border War. The Irishman said he couldn't pronounce it, but if it was for patriotic reasons he would accept it. " 'Cause he was damn if he was going to have a foreign name for his

town!" The motion was carried and the new post office got the distinctive name of Chrubusco. Years later it was discovered that Chrubusco was the War God of the ancient Aztec Indians of Mexico. (2)

CHRISTMAS, Arizona
Was so named because the news of the passage of a bill opening the country for location was received Christmas Day 1902. (5)

CHRISTOVAL, Texas
Christoval, in southern Tom Green County on the Panhandle and Santa Fe Railroad, is said to have derived its name from Christopher Columbus Doty, an early settler. (3)

CHROMO, Colorado
The Navajo Indians thought that a mountain southeast of here was very colorful and they called it Chromo, which was their word for colorful. The word, of course, has other definitions.

The town is sheltered by the Navajo Peak, the Banded Peaks, and the Chromo Peaks, and the Navajo River winds its way through the valley, which is prevalent with deer, elk, and bear. (1)

CHUCKEY, Tennessee
The town was settled sometime between 1850 and 1860, and named Fuller. It was a rail station between Rheatown (a stage coach stop) and the Nolichuckey River. Just prior to 1900 it was changed to Chuckey City, and in 1904 the Post Office Department changed it to Chuckey. The name was taken from the Nolichuckey River, which is Cherokee Indian and means "spruce tree place." An Indian settlement once occupied the site of present Chuckey . (1)

CHUG WATER, Wyoming
Before and during the early days of the white man the Indians hunted buffalo in this area. Local legend has it that they would chase the buffalo over certain cliffs, just above Chugwater Creek, thus killing them, or rendering them easier to be killed. The area was known to the Indians as the place where the buffalo went "Chug," when they hit the "Water." (1)

CHUNKY, Mississippi
Chunky, in Newton County, near the Alabama line, was named for Chunky Creek. The creek was named by the early settlers for their version of the name of an Indian game, once played here by the Choctaw Indians. (6)

CINCINNATI, Ohio
Started as a part of the Miami purchase, between the Miami and the Little Miami Rivers, the town was platted in 1788, opposite the Licking River, and called Losantiville.

In 1790 Hamilton County was organized and Losantiville was renamed Cincinnati, in honor of the Society of the Cincinnati, and made the County Seat. It was incorporated as a town in 1802, and in 1819 as a city.

The Society of the Cincinnati was formed on May 10, 1783, by former officers of the Continental Army as a patriotic and charitable organization. It was named for a Roman General, Lucius Quinctius Cincinnatus, who, after leading his armies to victory, returned to his plow, spurning all accolades before him. (2)

CISTERN, Texas
Cistern, in southwestern Fayette County, was settled in the early 1850's. The community was first named Whiteside Prairie, and then Cockrill, but when each family had to set up a cistern because the well water contained too much iron and sulphur, Cistern became the name of the community. (3)

CLALLAM, Washington
Located on the tip of northwest Washington, on the Strait Juan de Fuca, (named for Apostolos Valerianos), Clallam is an Indian name meaning, "brave people." (2)

CLATSKANIE, Oregon
Clatskanie, in Columbia County, Oregon, was named for the Tlatskani tribe of Indians who lived in the hills south of the river, which now bears their name, and in the Nehalen Valley to the south.

In 1850 white men found Chief Chewan and one hundred of the Tlatskanie, who proved so warlike and formidable that men of the Hudson's Bay Company dared not pass along the river with less than 60 armed men in number. A year later the tribe had been reduced to three men and five women, not by war, but by a more formidable foe, disease! An epidemic (probably smallpox) so decimated the tribe that it later became extinct.

The name Tlatskanie is thought to mean "swift running water," and the beautiful Clatskanie River is truly a swift running stream, and must have given the Indian the idea for the name.

A post office was listed as early as 1871 with E. W. Conyers as the first postmaster. In 1879 Conyers built a small steamboat he dubbed *The Novelty.* which made regular trips out to the Columbia River to rendevous with river boats plying that great stream. Since there were no roads in those days, the boat was the only means of bringing in and taking out people and freight. Finally, in 1898, the railroad built through the area and opened it up for further settlement, and civilization has come to this part of Oregon. (2)

CLAUENE, Texas
Clauene, in south-central Hockley County ten miles from Levelland, is one of the oldest communities in the county. It occupies a site once a part of the Old Savala Ranch. The name Clauene was coined in recognition of the abundance of catclaw bush in the vicinity. (3)

CLE ELUM, Washington
The first white settler arrived in the area of Cle Elum around 1883, but it wasn't until the arrival of the Northern Pacific Railroad that an actual town was established. The name Cle Elum is the English translation of the Indian words "Tle-el-lum," which means "swift water," probably for the Yakma River. (2)

CLIFF, Texas
Cliff, named for cliffs on San Geronimo Creek, is a Medina County community eighteen miles northeast of Castroville. (3)

CLIMAX, Georgia
The word "Climax" was placed on a map being used by the engineers surveying right of ways for what is now the Waycross and Montgomery branch of the Atlantic Coast Line Railroad. It was the highest point between Dothan, Alabama and Waycross, Georgia, and it was at this point that the village of Climax was established. (1)

CLIMBING HILL, Iowa
One of the first settlers in this area was a Mr. Goodrich, who came to Iowa from Canada. He picked a location about a mile east of town and settled on a hilltop. Later, as a village grew up, he petitioned the Post Office Department for a post office. Since he was to be the first postmaster, and the post office was to be located on his hilltop, he named it Climbing Hill. As he later explained, "no matter from what direction you approach the post office, you've just got to climb that hill to get there." (1)

CLOSE CITY, Texas
Close City, in western Graza County, was originally located on the Curry-Comb Ranch and was a part of the area purchased by Charles William Post

for his projected settlement in 1906. It was probably named Close City due to its close proximity to the Curry-Comb Ranch. (3)

CLOSPLINT, Kentucky
Closplint, Kentucky, located in Harlan County, took its name from the Clover-Splint mine—no longer producing. The Clover-Splint mine was so named because it was located on the Clover fork of the river and consisted of a "splint seam". (1)

CLOUDLAND, Georgia
The founder of Cloudland, Georgia, was John W. Ledbetter, who came here from Rome and built a hotel in 1912. He called it the Cloudland Park Club, due to the low scudding clouds that are very prevalent in this area. The post office was already established in the area in 1910 and named Arbutis. It was later moved and the name changed from Arbutis to Cloudland, by its first postmaster, Oscar C. Green. Note: Information furnished by Oscar C. Green.

CLOUDY, Oklahoma
There is a small creek that winds its way around this village, and is always cloudy, never clear. The village takes its name from this creek, which curiously enough is named Cloudy Creek. (1)

COAHOMA, Texas
Coahoma, in east central Howard County on the Texas and Pacific Railroad, takes its name from the Indian word meaning "signal." A small hill nearby is called Signal Mountain. (3)

COAL CREEK, Tennessee
Was originally named "Cole Creek," after an earlier settler named Cole, but later changed to "Coal," when that mineral was discovered in abundance. (6)

COARSEGOLD, California
Once upon a time Dame Nature devised a game, which every living thing on this earth, including mankind, has been trying to win. The Dear Old Lady tucked away in secret places all the needs and the pleasures of all life, and challenged life to find the treasures. In the foothills of the Sierras—just between the valley and the peaks—she found a particularly attractive spot, and there she hid health and happiness. But she knew mankind, so she salted the surrounding hills and streams with nuggets of gold. The ancients and the Red men came in their turn, and sought and found health

and happiness without the need of the yellow metal. Then came the "days of old; the days of gold, and the days of 49." Men, wild in their lust for treasure, rushing to the second great gold strike in California, stopped over night in this little valley on the banks of the Fresno River. Tired, dirty, and hungry they sought rest and refreshments, but found gold—*gold, nuggets of gold.* Little nuggets, big nuggets—not coarser or coarsest, but *coarse gold*—and over night California's third gold strike became a reality and the new town of "Coarsegold" was a thriving city almost between suns. Two Texas brothers found a single nugget worth $15,000 and staked out Texas Flats, which was just a surburb of the town of Coarsegold—a city of 10,000 inhabitants by 1850. By 1866 it was evident to all that the nuggets were dwindling. By 1880 the finds were over but Coarsegold was established. Health and happiness were still here in abundance for those who sought those pleasures of nature. Yosemite, the Big Trees, and the High Sierras were becoming world renowned and Coarsegold became the hostelry of swaying stage coaches, galloping horsemen and wild-eyed wonder seekers. And so it is today—after over a hundred years—the "watering place" of the modern tourist on California's world famous Goldroad Gateway to Yosemite. (1)

COHASSET, Minnesota
This is an Indian name which means "place of pines," due to the heavy timber growth of pines that once grew here. (6)

COKATO, Minnesota
Located in southwestern Wright County, Cokato, as it is with many old Minnesota towns, has an Indian name, which means "stopping place." (6)

COLERAINE, Minnesota
With a population of about 1,300, it is often called the "Model Village" since it was planned and built for its employees by a mining company. In 1905, John Greenway, district superintendent for the company, visited Trout Lake, planned a town, and named it Coleraine, a combination of the names of Thomas F. Cole, president of the company, and a man by the name of Blaine. It was incorporated as a village in 1909. (2)

COLFRED, Arizona
Is named for *Col*onel *Fred* Crocher, Santa Fe treasurer in 1881. (5)

COLLEGE STATION, Texas
The Agricultural and Mechanical College of Texas (Texas A & M) was authorized by the Texas Legislature on April 17, 1871, and was inaugurated

October 4, 1876. There was no post office, and all mail was addressed to Bryan, Texas. February 7, 1877, the Post Office Department authorized the establishment of a post office. The Houston and Texas Central Railroad ran by the campus at that time as a "Flag Stop." The words "College" and "Station" were combined to form the name of the post office, College Station, which it has remained to this day. (Ernest Langford, Archivist, Texas A&M University)

COLONY SETTLEMENT, Texas
In northeastern Bee County, this town was settled between 1884 and 1898 by Norwegians, who developed the section into fine farm land. In 1912 the Colony Lutheran Church was erected; a school was built in 1926. The settlement, most thickly populated of Bee County rural communities, was referred to as the Norwegian Colony, the Menonite Colony, and finally Colony Settlement. (3)

COLT, Arkansas
The village was first named Taylor Creek after Mitchel Taylor. When the Iron Mountain Railroad was built through here the stop was named Colt, after a railroad contractor. Later, the name of the village itself was changed to Colt. (1)

COLTS NECK, New Jersey
How Colts Neck got its name has been lost to the ages; there is no document that positively tells of it. Yet if you follow Yellow Brook and Mine Brook, a neck of land is formed very much like a colt's neck. This, it is believed, is a reasonable explanation as to the name Colts Neck. It was known by that name as early as 1675, long before the Revolution. On June 15, 1676, there is recorded in the minutes of the Board of Proprietors of Eastern Division of New Jersey a Bill of Sale by two Indians for a certain neck of land lying in Monmouth County, called Colts Neck. (2)

COMETA, Texas
Cometa, in southwestern Zavala County, is a rambling community of farms and ranches with a population in 1946 of about one hundred. First settled in the 1860's, the site, about 1900, became the Zavala County headquarters for the T. A. Coleman ranch. The ranch brand was a comet, called "cometa" by the Mexican hands. (3)

COMFORT, Texas
Comfort, second largest town in Kendall County, is about twenty miles from Boerne. On August 27, 1854, Ernst Altgelt led a small body of settlers

to the location. Wearied by their journey from New Braunfels, they were so charmed by the scenery and the sparkling water of the location that they called the place Camp Comfort. (3)

COMMERCE, Texas
Commerce, in eastern Hunt County on the Texas and New Orleans and the St. Louis and Southwestern Railroads, was founded in 1853, and named by Captain William Jernigan, who aspired to make it a commercial center. It is now known as the home of the East Texas State Teachers College. (3)

COMO, Mississippi
In north-central Panola County, and settled in 1856, the town was named for Lake Como in Italy. (6)

COMO, Texas
Como, in southeast Hopkins County on the Louisiana and Arkansas Railroad, was known as Carrol's Prairie when Ferdinand Carrol settled at a teamsters camp site on the road to Jefferson in 1845. A store was opened in 1858, and a post office established in 1870 was first called Bacchus but re-named Carrol's Prairie in 1876. The railroad station was called Carrolton from 1879 until the name Como was accepted in 1894 at the suggestion of settlers from Como, Mississippi. (3)

CONCEPTION, Missouri
The town was established in Nodaway County, in the northwestern tip of Missouri, in 1860 by leaders of the Reading Colony, an organization of Irish Catholics who came here from Reading, Pennsylvania. (1)

CONCRETE, Texas
Concrete, near the east bank of the Guadalupe River in northeastern DeWitt County, was laid out in 1846 on the John McCoy survey. The county's earliest townsite, is named from the vicinity's early-day concrete houses. (3)

CONEJO, Texas
Conejo, in Presidio County on a mail route from Marfa, has a Spanish name meaning rabbit. (3)

CONEJOS, Colorado
Conejos is a Spanish word meaning "rabbits," and the name of this town. It was named due to the abundance of rabbits in the area when pioneers first settled here. It is the site of the oldest church in Colorado, Our Lady of Guadalupe, which was built in 1858. Conejos is the county seat of Conejos

County, and is about seven miles from the northern border of New Mexico. (1)

CONESTOGA, Pennsylvania
Conestoga Township, formed in 1718, took its name from Conestoga Creek, upon whose banks it is located. The creek probably got its name from the Conestogoe Indians, who once lived in this area. The primary village in the township is Conestoga, known prior to World War II as Conestoga Center. The village was platted in 1805 by John Kendig.

While claims have been made that Conestoga was the home of the famous Conestoga Wagons, and a state marker proclaims this, it is most probable that the wagons originated and were built throughout the entire Conestoga Valley, and not just in this specific village.

The Conestoga Wagon was a large, heavy, broad-wheeled covered wagon that the pioneers used in hauling freight and themselves ever westward. (2)

CONNOQUENESSING, Pennsylvania
Is Indian for "a long way straight." Was once named Petersville for Peter McKinney, who settled here in 1792. (4)

CONSHOHOCKEN, Pennsylvania
Incorporated in 1850, the name is Indian and means "beautiful or pleasant valley." The name was given to the valley by the Lenni-Lenape Indians 277 years ago. It is believed that the Colonial Army crossed the Schuylkill River here at least three times, the last being their historic trip to their winter camp at Valley Forge in 1777. (2)

COPPEROPOLIS, California
Founded in 1861, when copper was discovered, it got its fancy name as a result of the copper mines and is located in Calaveras County. Ore was hauled to Stockton by Ox Cart and then shipped to Wales for reduction. Copperopolis was once a city of 10,000 people. The name Copperopolis came, of course, from the ore copper and the Greek word "polis," which means city. (2)

CORAOPOLIS, Pennsylvania
Settled about 1760. According to some the name comes from the Greek Koreopolis, "Maiden City," but others insist it was named for Cora Watson, the daughter of an influential citizen. (4)

CORD, Arkansas
The town got its name from an early settler who opened a blacksmith shop

here around 1890. The settlers took his name, which was McCord, dropped the "Mc," and named their town Cord, Arkansas. (1)

CORDUROY, Alabama
Corduroy, located in Monroe County, Alabama, got such a name due to its location in a low-lying area. To keep the roads passable in inclement weather it was necessary to place logs on the road, about two feet apart, which gave the road a kind of "corduroy cloth" look. From the corduroy road came the name for the hamlet. (2)

CORK, Arizona
Named by a homesick Irishman for County Cork, Ireland. (5)

CORNSTALK, West Virginia
Cornstalk was named for the Shawnee Indian, Chief Cornstalk. West Virginia was a hunting ground for Indians and the early settlers were often attacked by hunting or war parties. In revenge, one day, Chief Cornstalk and his son were ambushed at the battle of Point Pleasant, West Virginia. He was buried there and the state has erected a monument to his memory. (1)

CORNUCOPIA, Wisconsin
Cornucopia, located in northern Wisconsin, was founded in the early 1900's

Cornucopia, Wisconsin

by Thomas J. Stevenson, of Minneapolis. On one of his exploratory trips to this area he was impressed by the abundance of wild fruit and its luxuriant growth of both trees and grasses. When he decided to establish a city here he named it Cornucopia for the fabulous horn of the goat Amalthaea, which suckled Zeus. It is represented as overflowing with flowers, fruit, etc., and commonly known as "the horn of plenty."

To his new village flocked immigrants from Czechoslovakia, and miners from Pennsylvania and Oklahoma. All were of the Greek Catholic faith, and in 1910 they built the Greek-Orthodox Church here. One of the few located in this part of the country. (2)

CORNVILLE, Arizona
Was a post office error. The application for a post office was made for Coanville, in honor of a family, but it was taken for Cornville, in honor of a stalk of corn. (5)

CORPUS CHRISTI, Texas
The City of Corpus Christi began as a frontier trading post, founded in 1838, by Colonel Henry Lawrence Kinney. The small settlement, hard-bitten and lawless, was called Kinney's Trading Post. The Trading Post remained an obscure settlement until July, 1845, when United States troops under General Zachary Taylor arrived on the local scene. Troops, horses, and equipment were lightered ashore. The army remained until March, 1846, when it left to march southward to the Rio Grande, as the beginning of the Mexican War was near. An officer in General Taylor's Army, writing home, said of the post, "It contains a few women and no ladies."

Long before the settlement of Corpus Christi, sea-faring Spanish "Conquistadores" plied the waters of the Gulf of Mexico, and it was one of these, Alvarez Alonzo de Pineda, who discovered the blue waters of Corpus Christi Bay in the year 1519. The event took place on the Festival Day of Corpus Christi, said to have been first proclaimed by Pope Urban IV in 1264. The Bay was named to fit the circumstance. The Spanish, the Portuguese, the English, and the French alternated in making port in Corpus Christi Bay and in visiting the coastal islands, the most famous of which is 110-mile long Padre Island. The galleons of Hernando Cortez appeared here as did the vessels of Jean Lafitte's freebooting band. At one time, the buccaneers held such sway in the area that Padre and Mustang Islands are said to have become mines of buried treasure, and even today a pleasant pastime has become the search for pirate gold in the island sand.

In the year 1847 or 1848 the city took the name of Corpus Christi from the Bay and as one resident put it, ". . . so as to have a more definite postmark for letters." (2)

CORYDON, Indiana

President William Henry Harrison, then governor of Indiana, had the county of Harrison named after him, and was given the honor of naming the county seat. The governor was visiting a friend, Edward Smith, at the time the name was being considered. Smith's daughter had a Missouri Harmony songbook, and she frequently sang "The Pastoral Elegy," the governor's favorite. While listening to it and its plaintive lament for the death of Corydon, a young shepherd, he decided "Corydon" would be a fine name for the county seat of the county that bore his name. In 1840 he was elected the ninth President of the United States, but died one month after his inauguration.

What sorrowful sounds do I hear,
  Move slowly along in the gale;
How solemn they fall on my ear.
  As softly they pass through the vale.
Sweet Corydon's notes are all o'er,
  Now lonely he sleeps in the clay,
His cheeks bloom with roses no more,
  Since death called his spirit away . . .

The town of Corydon was formed around 1812-13, and became the territorial capital of Indiana. The Territory of Indiana became a state December 11, 1816, and Corydon remained the capital until moved in 1825. (2)

COS COB, Connecticut

In the early days of Greenwich (settled in 1640) a gentleman by the name of Coe owned a point of land extending into Long Island Sound. He was English, as many of the early settlers here were, and in England a point of land is known as a "cob." Hence this particular area became known as Coe's Cob. When a village was settled here and a post office established, the name was shortened to Cos Cob. (2)

COST, Texas

Cost, Texas, was originally called OSO. When a post office was requested they found that Texas already had a town by that name, so they put a "C" in front of OSO, and replaced the last "O" with a "T," and came up with Cost. Everybody here lives in a community where they buy their needs at "Cost." (1)

COTOPAXI, Colorado

Cotopaxi is a village of about 100 people located on the Arkansas River, 22 miles above the entrance to the famous Royal Gorge. It is the only town of any size between Canõn City and Salida, Colorado.

Tradition has it that E. H. Salteil, a Russian Jew, was the first settler here. There is an 1871 "water-right" deed to a piece of land he squatted on and built a large house on in the early 1880's. He was a miner, and had been in Equador, where the Cotopaxi Volcano (19,600 feet high) is located. Just south of the town of Cotopaxi, Colorado, is a high peak in the Sangre De Cristo Mountains, that bears a resemblance to the Equadorian Volcano, so Salteil called the location by that name. The name in the language of the Equadorian Indians means "shining pile." (Victor W. Miller, Cotopaxi, Colorado)

COTTON, Texas
Cotton, in northern Grimes County on a mail route from Bedias, was named for the principal crop of the area. The first gin was established in 1890 by R. S. Callender, operator of the general store. (3)

COTTON GIN, Texas
Cotton Gin, in western Freestone County, was named for a cotton gin erected at the site in 1848 by Dr. J. S. Mills. (3)

COTTON PLANT, Arkansas
Cotton Plant lies midway between Little Rock, Arkansas, and Memphis, Tennessee, in north-central Arkansas, and was platted in 1840 by William D. Lynch, who named it for his cotton plantation. (6)

COTTONWOOD, Texas
Cottonwood, Callahan County, was established in 1875 and named for the trees growing at the site. (3)

COUDERSPORT, Pennsylvania
It was named for Jean Samuel Couderc, of the Amsterdam banking firm that managed the interests of some exiled Frenchmen who located in that area. (4)

COUNCIL BLUFFS, Iowa
During their exploration of the Missouri River in 1804 Lewis and Clark were the first white men to stop at the site of what is now Council Bluffs. At this time they held a meeting (or council) with the Otoe and Missouri Indians.

From 1804 until 1853 it was known as Kanesville. It was renamed in 1853, and Brigham Young was the man who succeeded in getting the first post office here. In 1855 Amelia Bloomer, who was already famous for her new type dress for women, arrived to make her home in Council Bluffs.

The Golden Spike Monument is here—a replica of the Golden Spike driven to signify the completion of the Union Pacific Railroad, linking the country coast to coast by rail.

The name Council Bluffs was adopted in 1853, in memory of the council held on the Bluffs by Lewis and Clark and the Indians. (2)

COUNCIL HILL, Oklahoma
According to old timers still residing here, the town received its name because the site was once used by several tribes of Indians to hold their meetings or councils. (1)

COUPON, Pennsylvania
The village of Coupon was first settled in the late 1800's by a family named DeLaney, and called DeLaney. In the year 1893, the Coal Company here began using coupons to pay their employees. These coupons could only be redeemed at the company store, and so infuriated the local postmaster, who also ran the general store, that he retaliated by recommending to the Post Office Department in Washington that the name be changed from DeLaney to Coupon. Thus it was that on June 22, 1894, the town of DeLaney died and the town of Coupon, Pennsylvania, was born! (1)

Cowboy, Texas

COWBOY, Texas
Cowboy, in northeastern McCulloch County in the area occupied by the ranches of W. G. S. Hughes and J. W. Black in 1876, became a townsite in 1880. Hughes was the postmaster for thirteen years. The name Cowboy was chosen for obvious reasons. (3)

COW PEN POND, Florida
Years ago livestock roamed at will over unfenced lands and roads. They were usually given a small amount of supplemental feed in the form of grain and always at the same spot, the most accessible water hole. Consequently they returned to this spot each evening and were penned up for the night as protection against wild beasts. They were released each morning to forage all day. The pens were communal affairs and anyone could pen their animals for the night. The pens encircled the pond and the animals could partake of sufficient water to last them through the following day.

When a settlement formed here it took the unusual name of Cow Pen Pond, Florida. Herman R. Kasper, Marianna, Florida.

COWPENS, South Carolina
Located in Spartanburg County, near the North Carolina border, the town was named for the Cow Pens of Cattleman Hanna, a Tory. (6)

COZAHOME, Arkansas
Approximately 50 years ago, this community was called Pleasant Ridge, but had no post office. When an inspector came to install the post office in the home of the first postmaster, Mrs. George Rhodes, they were discussing a likely name for it. In the course of conversation the inspector commented on what a nice "cozy home" she had. That chance remark gave birth to the nice, new post office of Cozahome, Arkansas. (1)

CRAB ORCHARD, Nebraska
Named for a grove of wild crab apple trees, of which a few still remain near this little village. They have lovely pale-pink blooms. This is a small village in a farming area, with many tree-lined streets of elm and oak. (1)

CRANFILLS GAP, Texas
Located in a gap between two mountains, through which an old Comanche trail meandered, Cranfills Gap was named for George Eaton Cranfill, who came here from Illinois in 1850. (1)

CRIPPLE CREEK, Colorado
Cripple Creek, once known as Pisgah Park, was first settled around 1872 by George and Alonzo Welty. Here, at the foot of the Pisgah Mountain, they built a homestead, which they named the Broken Box Ranch. The remains of this ranch still stand just south of the present town of Cripple Creek. The story goes that while putting a roof on the new ranch house, George fell with a load of shingles still clutched in his arms, and was badly

injured. A couple of days later the hired man, thrown from his horse, broke a leg. This series of accidents caused the ranch wag to suggest that they name a nearby stream Cripple Creek. Cripple Creek, Colorado, took its name from that creek, and became the greatest gold producing-center of the wild, wild west. (Two Mile High Club, Cripple Creek, Colorado.)

CROSS CUT, Texas

Cross Cut, in northwestern Brown County, became a post office with James M. Bloodworth as postmaster on April 9, 1879. The settlement had been called Cross Out because it was across the country and out of the way, but that name was mistakenly read as Cut by the Post Office Department. (3)

CROSS TIMBERS, Missouri

When a post office was established in 1870 it was named Garden City. The name was not approved by the Post Office Department as there was another office by that name only 85 miles away, so a new name had to be selected.

East of the town there were acres of prairie land and in the center of this prairie were two strips of timber, one running north and south, and the other east and west, forming a cross. It was from this unusual growth of timber that the town got its unique name.

Legend has it that there is a lost silver mine here. It was concealed by its owner during the Civil War to prevent the Union Troops from taking it over. It was known as the Old Brooksie Mine, and though people have searched for it over the years, it has never been found. Silver was mined here in the middle 1800's. (1)

CROUCH, Idaho

Crouch, located in Boise County, on the Middle Fork Payette, was settled in the early 1900's by a logger-prospector named William Crouch. He filed homestead rights on 160 acres in Garden Valley, (named by early 1863 pioneers). When the post office was established here in 1933, the postmaster submitted the name Crouch in honor of its first settler, and the name was adopted by the village. The post office was terminated April 22, 1966. (1)

CROW AGENCY, Montana

Crow Agency was so named because it is the Indian Agency for the Crow Indians, and is located in the center of the Crow Reservation. The Bureau of Indian Affairs has an office here where they administer the affairs of the Crow Indians. The Custer Battlefield National Monument is located two miles from here. (1)

CROWHEART, Wyoming
The town was named for Crowheart Butte, 2½ miles southeast of Crowheart. Crowheart Butte was so named because, in 1866, Chief Washakie of the Shoshone Tribe, rather than lose more braves in continuous warfare over territorial rights with the Crow Nation, held a "pow-wow" with the Crow chief, and they both decided to a fight to the death atop the butte. Just the two of them. The winner was to cut the heart out of the loser, and the victor's tribe would have the land forever. The battle was fought and Chief Washakie of the Shoshone won. When white settlers heard of the bloody battle, they named the butte Crowheart. (1)

CRYSTAL CITY, Texas
Crystal City was founded in 1907, from sections of the Cross S Ranch. It was named for the crystal clear water which flowed from the many springs in the area at that time. Since the nearest town was named Carrizo Springs, the town fathers decided to call their town Crystal City rather than Crystal Springs. (2)

CRYSTAL MOUNTAIN, Arkansas
Named for the quartz crystals that abundantly line its sandstone. They are translucent, in hexagon and octagon shapes, and are pointed at one end. With weathering they take on soft tones of rose and yellow. (6)

CUBA, Missouri
The post office of Amanda was established January 2, 1857, and though the town of Cuba was surveyed and laid out in December, 1857, it was not until May 24, 1860 that the name of the post office was changed to Cuba.

Most of the leisure time of the early settlers was spent loitering at the general store, swapping tales, and playing checkers. It was from here that the legend of the naming of Cuba grew.

Among those hardy fellows who frequented this small store was one of nature's less fortunate, insofar as mental ability was concerned. He had taken very seriously, the plight of the peoples of a small island called Cuba, who were, at that time, struggling for their independence from Spain. So greatly had the reports weighed upon him that he repeatedly stated that he was going to Cuba to help them. This young man expressed his intentions so repeatedly that it led to much jesting and when store owner, a Mr. Jaminson, proclaimed that he was going to name his store and post office Amanda, it was immediately suggested that the name Cuba would be better. Initiated as a joke, the insistence continued until it was decided to cast lots to see what the name should be. Cuba won!

From the earliest accounts and indications, Cuba is located at what was once a crossing of the Shawnee Indians in their annual trek from the northeast to the southwest, and return, as they moved with the changes in the seasons of the year. (2)

CUBAGE, Kentucky
The village takes its name from Cubage Branch. The first settlers in this area, according to local legend, found the word "Cub" carved on a beech tree growing along the banks of a stream here, which they later named Cubage Branch. (1)

CUCAMONGA, California
In 1773 the Viceroy of Mexico commissioned Juan Bautista De Anza, a captain, to find a road between Sonora, Mexico, and Monterey. Over thirty men were in Captain De Anza's party. On March 14, 1774 they entered the San Bernadina Valley through the San Gorgonio Pass. March 21, 1774 they camped at Arroyo De Los Osos (Bear Canyon).

The Spaniards found several tribes of Indians that were quite friendly. One of these tribes was the Cucamonga Indians. They had small farms below and among the Red Hills, cultivating the fields, and raising corn and melons. Some of the Cucamonga Indians were here as late as 1873. Tiburcio Tapia, a prominent citizen of Los Angeles and part owner, through inheritance of the Topengo-Malibu grant, petitioned Governor Alvarado for a grant of the property known as Cucamonga. The governor, a friend of Tapia, issued a grant March 3, 1839. From this grant he developed the Cucamonga Rancho, and from the Rancho evolved the present-day city of Cucamonga. The name Cucamonga is Indian, and means "Land of many waters." (2)

CUCKOO, Virginia
The town of Cuckoo was named for a tavern established here in the 1700's. Tradition has it that the tavern had one of the first cuckoo clocks brought to this country. It was from Cuckoo that Captain Jack Jouett started his ride, June 4, 1781, to warn Thomas Jefferson and the Virginia Legislature of the approach of the British, under General Tarleton, thus saving the governor and the legislature from capture by the British at Charlottesville. (Anne Pendleton Forest)

CUT AND SHOOT, Texas
Cut and Shoot, a rural community eight miles from Conroe in Montgomery County, got its unusual name from a community dispute said to have arisen over, of all things, the pattern for a new church steeple! (3)

Cut and Shoot, Texas

CUTHAND, Texas
Cut Hand, settled about 1850, took its name from the Cuthand Creek. The creek is supposed to have been named for a Kickapoo Indian who, working in the bottom of the stream, cut his hand quite badly. (3)

CUT OFF, Louisiana
The Cut Off name apparently originated many years ago when a canal was opened between Bayou Lafourche and Bayou des Amoureux, which gave the lower Lafourche people a "cut-off," or short cut to New Orleans with their produce through Little Lake and Bayou Barataria. (Mrs. Albert Lefturch, Cut-off, La.)

CUTTYHUNK, Massachusetts
The town is really named Gosnold, for Bartholomew Gosnold, who landed on the island of Cuttyhunk and built a fort in 1602. He expected to start a colony, but those of his crew who were supposed to remain here backed out and returned to England. The town of Gosnold is made up of the Elizabeth Islands which run westerly from Woods Hole between Buzzards Bay and Vineyard Sound. The main islands from Woods Hole westerly are Naushon, Pasque, Nashawena, Penikese, and Cuttyhunk. Cuttyhunk is the site of the town hall and the post office and the most populated of all the islands. The name comes from the Indian Poocutohhunkunnoh, which means "point of departnre" or "lands end," since it is the western-

most of the Elizabeth Islands. Gosnold gave the name Elizabeth to the island as a whole in honor of his sister, and his queen, Elizabeth the First, of England.

The Indian name for the entire group of islands was "Nashanow," an Algonquin word meaning "between," probably signifying its location between the Bay and the Sound. The name of each Island is a contraction of an Indian name. Here is a town made up entirely of a collection of islands. Truly a unique town with a group of unique names! (2)

DACONO, Colorado

Dacono was founded by Charles Lockard Baum, organizer and president of the Consolidated Coal and Coke Company. He had to have miners to work the mines, and he had to have houses in which the miners could live, so he established the Dacono Townsite Company.

The town was consolidated in 1908 with the help of the Zang Brewery in Denver. The Brewery put up the necessary money for incorporation and received, in return, an exclusive franchise from the town to sell beer there. In a mining town, that's quite a coup. Rather like being the only one with a lemonade stand in the Sahara.

The town of Dacono was named for three women: the founder's wife, Daisy; a close friend of theirs named Cora; and the minister who married them, Nona Brooks. They took the first two letters of each of their first names and formed the name DA-CO-NO. (1)

DAD'S CORNER, Texas

Dad's Corner, six miles south of Holliday in Archer County, was named for a veteran wild-catter, C. M. "Dad" Joiner, during the old oil boom of the early 1920's. (3)

DAGUSCAHONDA, Pennsylvania

Was founded in 1860, and the name is Indian for "wildcat run." (4)

DAISETTA, Texas

Daisetta, in eastern Liberty County, was established as an oil field town in 1917 in an area settled by planters and lumbering interests as early as 1850. Newt Farris, local store owner, named the place for Daisy Barrett and Etta White. (3)

DALARK, Arkansas

The name of this hamlet is composed of the first three letters of Dallas and the last three letters of Clark, names of the two counties on whose boundary Dalark is situated. (6)

DAMSITE, Texas
Damsite, on Lake Pauline in east central Hardeman County, developed as a work camp for the construction of the lake in the early 1920's and became a tourist and recreation resort. (3)

Daphne, Alabama

DAPHNE, Alabama
Named for the many laurel trees in the vicinity and for Daphne, the nymph in Greek Mythology, who turned into a laurel to escape from Apollo. (2)

DARDANELLE, Arkansas
The town of Dardanelle was named for a small rocky mountain, located at the bend of the Arkansas River. The word Dardonnie is said to be Cherokee or Choctaw, and means to sleep with one eye open. Legend has it that the Indians always kept a lookout on duty on what is known as Dardanelle Rock, located on the bank of the Arkansas River. He was to watch for enemy warriors, and sleep with one eye open. Therefore they were known as Dardonnies.

Another version of the name is that the rock was named for an early French settler, Jean Baptiste Dardenne. Under the Spanish regime, he received a grant of about 600 acres located on the north side of the river, across from the present site of Dardanelle. (2)

DATELAND, Arizona

Like so many small post offices in the Far West, Dateland is a highway stop and a post office that serves the surrounding community. The origin of the name appears to be hazy. There are a number of date trees located around the post office, and although records do not record or indicate it, they probably contributed their name to this oasis in the Arizona desert. (1)

DAWN, Texas

Dawn, in extreme western Deaf Smith County on the Panhandle and Santa Fe Railroad, developed around a store called The Dawn of Civilization, which J. H. Parrish established in 1887. (3)

DEADWOOD, Oregon

Deadwood, located in Lane County, western Oregon, was settled about 1880. When the first settlers arrived here there were little or no forests as there are now, only dead stumps and snags, and a little brush. After surveying the situation they named the stream near their homestead Deadwood Creek, and eventually, when a village grew here and a post office was established, the name became a permanent part of Oregon. (1)

DEADWOOD, South Dakota

Wild Bill Hickok, famous frontiersman of the West; Calamity Jane, whose fame went around the world; Preacher Smith, killed by the Indians in 1876; Jack McCall, the assassin of Wild Bill, who was freed by a miner's court and later hanged by the U. S. Government for the crime—these characters and dozens of others of the tough old days make up Deadwood's colorful past, and contributed, in their own unique way, to the Deadwood of today.

The name describes a gulch or arroyo which was filled with dead and decayed wood, killed by some catastrophe devised by nature. This dead wood was the most outstanding feature of the area at the time of settlement, in the middle 1800's. (2)

DEEPSTEP, Georgia

Local legend has it that as Indians were crossing a small stream near here, one of them stepped into a deep, unseen hole. As he scrambled out he muttered something about that being one hell of a deep step! The legend persisted and when a settlement was established, and a post office requested, the name Deepstep was given to both. (1)

DEER ISLAND, Oregon

The community of Deer Island is not really on an island, nor is there any island in sight. Yet, if one were in a plane there would appear to be a large island in the Columbia River, six miles long and one mile wide. It is diamond shaped, and is formed by two divergent paths taken by the Columbia River at this point. It was named by Lewis and Clark on their exploration in 1805.

An historical marker near the town of Deer Island reads: "Deer Island, in the Columbia was named by Lewis and Clark expedition which was camped here November 5, 1805, on its way down the river. Homeward bound the explorers camped again on March 28, 1806. Captain Clark recorded: 'This morning we set out very early and at 8 A. M. arrived at the old Indian villge on the northeast side of Deer Island, where we found our hunters had halted and left one man with a canoe at their camp. They arrived last evening and six of them turned out very early to hunt. At 10 A. M. they all returned to camp having killed seven deer. The Indians call this large island E-lal-lar, or Deer Island.' " (2)

DEER LODGE, Montana

The Deer Lodge Valley spreads out from five to ten miles wide, between the Rocky and Deer Lodge ranges for a distance of sixty miles.

The origin of the name is credited to the poetic imagination of the Indians. It is derived from a large sugarloaf mound, with a thermal spring on its summit. The mound is over forty feet high, and stands in the midst of a perfectly level valley. From a distance it bears a striking resemblance to an Indian lodge, with smoke rising from it. And so the Indians, true to these facts and weaving with them a happy fancy, named it after that which it most resembled. The Snake hunting parties, approaching the crests of the surrounding mountains, before the pale-face had come to the land, would try the fleetness of their steeds to see who would first catch sight of, and hail, the point of rendezvous—IT SOO-KE EN CAR-NE, "The Lodge of the White-tailed Deer." The early French, appreciating the poetry of the designation, adopted it literally and among them it was known as La Loge du Chevruil. But the laconic, matter-of-fact Yankee pioneer came this way, and without remorse boiled down all its traditions and beauty into the practical appellation "Deer Lodge."

This name was given to the valley, the river, the county, and the town. The town of Deer Lodge was first settled in the middle 1800's. (2)

DeFUNIAK SPRINGS, Florida

In the nineties, any place with a spring was quite apt to become a fine watering spot, or, in short, a resort. Colonel Bonifay, Colonel Chipley, and

Colonel DeFuniak, all officials of the L & N Railroad, were collectively instrumental in projecting the line through this part of Florida. Each of the three wanted the springs named after him. Being gentlemen of the old school, they settled the matter one day at the Pendennis Club in Louisville by dealing a hand of poker, with the obvious result. Of course, both Colonel Chipley and Bonifay eventually had towns named for them. Chipley and Bonifay, Florida, are both down the line a bit from DeFuniak Springs . (2)

DELAWARE WATER GAP, Pennsylvania
Is a small village named for the gap through which the Delaware River flows between Mount Minsi and Mount Tammny of the Kittatinny range of the Blue Mountains. (4)

DELIGHT, Arkansas
Old timers here claim that the first settler made the statement that he hoped this would be a delightful place to live. It proved to be just that, and the town adopted the name of Delight. (1)

DEL RIO, Texas
The first settlement at the site of Del Rio was named San Felipe Del Rio because the place was reached on Saint Phillip's Day. That settlement and a second were unsuccessful, but the third colony was permanent. The post office was called Del Rio (The River), because another settlement in Texas had already secured an office name San Felipe. One section of Del Rio, however, is still called San Felipe. (3)

DEMIJOHN BEND, Texas
Demijohn Bend, a Comal County community in a demijohn shaped bend of the Guadalupe River, was settled in 1850. Farming and ranching are the chief industries of the scenic area. (3)

DENMARK, South Carolina
The name was selected at random by railroad officials establishing "whistle stops" along the route. (6)

DEPUTY, Indiana
Deputy, located in the western part of Jefferson County, was platted in 1871 and named for James Deputy, one of its illustrious and esteemed citizens. The legend of the name Deputy does not end here, however, but goes back to England, the place of its origin. It seems that a foundling was left on the door sill of a Deputy. He reared the child as his own, naming it "Sill Deputy." Generations later, Deputys were still naming their sons "Sill." (2)

DE QUEEN, Arkansas
This town, incorporated in 1879, was originally named Calamity. Later it was changed to DeGeoijen, for a Dutch investor in the Kansas City and Southern Railroad. The name gradually became De Queen, which was much easier to pronounce for the citizens. (6)

DES ALLEMANDS, Louisiana
Located in St. Charles County, near Lac Des Allemands (French for Lake of the Germans) was so named by the French due to the large number of German settlers in the area and the village. (6)

DES MOINES, Iowa
Des Moines had its beginning in 1843 when a fort was built at the fork of the Racoon and Des Moines Rivers to protect the rights of the Indian tribes, the Sacs and the Fox. According to old Indian legends, the river on whose banks this fort was built was known as the "Moingona." The meaning has been lost to history. Later the name was shortened to "Moin," by French explorers who called the stream "La Rivière des Moines." The city got its name from the river.

When the fort was ready (to protect the Sacs and the Fox Indians) the land surrounding it was thrown open for settlement by the whites. In 1853 there were about 500 inhabitants in the settlement and the city of Des Moines was incorporated. It became the capital of the state of Iowa, in 1857. (2)

DEVILS RIVER, Texas
Located on the east bank of Devils River near its confluence with the Rio Grande it takes its name from the River. The River is supposed to be a stream called Laxas (Spanish for slack or feeble), and so named by Gaspar Castano de Sosa in 1590. The stream was also known as San Pedro; at least that name is used in the most typically Texan explanation of its present name. According to legend Captain John Coffee (Jack) Hays of the Texas Rangers, after riding far across barren, rough, and arid country came to a forbidding gorge at the bottom of which was a stream of water. He asked a Mexican the name of the stream and was told that it was "San Pedro's." "Saint Peter's, Hell!" Hayes exclaimed, "It looks like the Devil's river to me." (3)

DEVILS SLIDE, Utah
This town took its name from a natural rock slide formation. The name was probably given by some fanciful pioneer to whom we are all indebted. (1)

DEVILS TOWER, Wyoming

Hardly more than a wide spot in the road, with a general store and a post office, it gets its name from the Devils Tower National Monument, nearby. Colonel Dodge is generally credited with giving the formation its present name. In his book entitled *The Black Hills,* published in 1876, he called it Devils Tower, explaining, "The Indians call this shaft 'The Bad God's Tower,' a name adopted with proper modification by our surveyors." Newton, whose published work on the survey appeared in 1880, explained that the name Bear Lodge (Mateo Tepee) "appears on the earliest map of the region, and more recently it is said to be known among the Indians as 'The Bad God's Tower,' or in better English, 'The Devil's Tower.' " The former name, well applied, is still retained. (Superintendent, U.S. Dept. of Interior, Nat'l Park Svc., Devils Tower Nat'l Monument, Wyoming.)

DEWY ROSE, Georgia

The first postmaster was thinking of a name for the new post office. One Sunday morning, while walking with his young daughter in the yard, she exclaimed, "Oh daddy! Look at the dew on the roses." From this chance remark a village in Georgia became the owner of the lovely name, Dewy Rose. (1)

DIME BOX, Texas

Before there was a post office in Dime Box, early settlers erected a community mail box on the road to San Antonio, and the freighters would pick up mail, for a service charge of a dime, for each round trip. This was from one to four times per month.

When petitions for a post office were sent in, Dr. R. H. Womack requested that it be named Dime Box, so that the old community mail box would not be forgotten. Dime Box was chosen as the starting point for the March of Dimes campaign in 1944. (1)

DINERO, Texas

Dinero, in southeastern Live Oak County, was once called Barlow's Ferry for E. Barlow. The name was changed to Dinero in 1872, perhaps because of the rumor of hidden treasure in the neighborhood. Dinero in Spanish, means "money." (3)

DINGMAN'S FERRY, Pennsylvania

Was founded in 1735 and named for Andred Dingman, the first settler, and operator, of Dingman's Ferry on the Delaware River, going from Pennsylvania to New Jersey. It was later replaced by a bridge. (4)

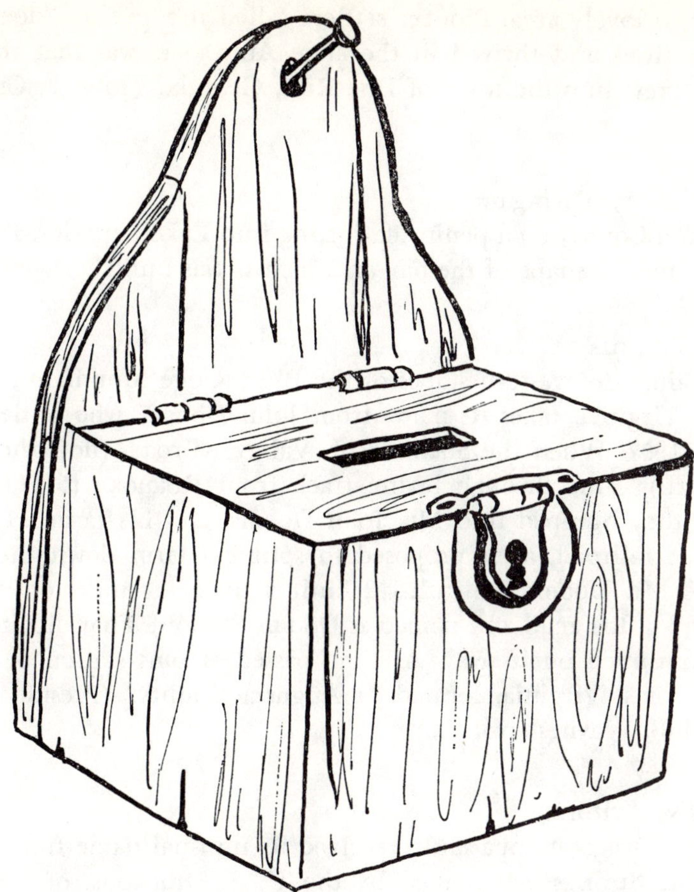

Dime Box, Texas

DIRECT, Texas
Direct, in northwestern Lamar County, got its name from one of two early traditions concerning the settlement—that the Indians across the river were coming there "direct for whiskey," or that a revivalist thought the local people were going "direct to hell." The local church was built with money donated by a converted saloon keeper. (3)

D'LO, Mississippi
In north-central Simpson County, the name is supposed to have come from the name given the Strong River by early French explorers. They referred to the river as "de l'eau," which in their language means "the water."

DOE RUN, Georgia
Small streams ran through the beautiful yellow pines which abounded every-

where in this lovely area. Pioneer settlers called it a perfect "doe run," as many deer lived and thrived in the area. And so it was that their little settlement grew into the town of Doe Run, Georgia. (John F. Craft, Doerun, Ga.)

DOLLAR BAY, Michigan
In Houghton County on a peninsula jutting into Lake Superior, Dollar Bay was named for the shape of the bay on which it was built.

DOOMS, Virginia
Nestled against the western slopes of the Blue Ridge Mountains, the town of Dooms, Virginia, takes its name from John Dooms, who settled in this locality in 1857. When the Shenandoah Valley Rilroad (now the Norfolk and Western) came through laying track from Roanoke to Hagerstown, Maryland, they bumped into Mr. John Dooms, and his farm. He bitterly opposed the railroad, as it proposed to split his farm down the middle. To placate Mr. Dooms the railroad built a depot at the crossing of the railroad and a dirt road and named it Dooms Station. That did it, and the railroad continued on its way. As time passed Dooms station became the town of Dooms, Virginia, located in Augusta County. (President Dooms Ruritan Club, Waynesboro, Va.)

DRAGOON, Arizona
The town of Dragoon apparently received its unusual name from Dragoon Springs. The Springs was named by the U. S. Dragoons, of the United States Army, who discovered the watering place when they were detailed to establish and garrison posts at Fort Buchanan and Tucson in the early part of 1856. Dragoon Springs became a station for the old Butterfield Overland Mail and Stage route, operating between Fort Smith, Arkansas, and Los Angeles, California. It was started in 1858 under the supervision of Silas St. John.

The Dragoon station was the most westerly of the original chain of fortified stone stations erected on the Butterfield route. It was located in the heart of the Apache country, on the war path to Sonora, and was built to withstand Indian assaults. (Amerind Foundation)

DRIP ROCK, Kentucky
This small village, with the post office located in the general store, was named for a nearby rock outcropping, and for the steady dripping of water from the rock. (1)

DRUMS, Pennsylvania
Located in the beautiful Butler and Conyngham Valley it was first known as East Sugarloaf Township, and later was divided and became Butler Township, Luzerne County. It was finally named Drums, for Mr. George Drums. (1)

DRY BRANCH, Georgia
Settled around 1808, the first post office was established here in 1879. The best and most authoritative sources indicate a prohibition influence in the naming of Dry Branch, Georgia.

It is said that many of the local streams, prior to the establishment date of the post office, contained numerous moonshine stills. In 1876 the Georgia Legislature passed the Twiggs Liquor Law governing the production of intoxicating liquors. The law enforcement agencies must have done a commendable job in enforcing the ordinance, because many of the private distilleries, in what is now Dry Branch, began to "dry up." This drying up, is said, by most old timers, to have given rise to the naming of the community. (6)

DRY PRONG, Louisiana
Two streams of water come together near here to form Big Creek. During the 1870's a family moved into this locality and attempted to build a water mill on one of these streams. Having moved here during the winter months, there was plenty of water to operate the mill. However, before construction of the mill was completed, summer arrived and the stream dried up. It was then that the family came to the realization that they had settled on the "dry prong" of the creek. It was from this incident that the name Dry Prong originated.

When a post office was established here in 1906, the name Dry Prong was adopted by both the village and the post office. (1)

DRYTOWN, California
Located in Amador County, Drytown was so named by miners and prospectors, not because there was no water, but rather because on its short main street, at one time, it boasted over thirty saloons.

As a note of interest, near Drytown is Rancheria, the scene of a brutal massacre that occurred August 6, 1855. On that day, well-armed Mexican horsemen had been seen near Drytown and a rider was dispatched to Rancheria to warn them of the suspected bandits. The rider arrived too late. The Mexicans had already sacked the town, leaving nine men and a woman dead, wounding two others and taking $10,000 from the Rancheria strong boxes. The killers were eventually captured and brought to justice. (2)

DUCK HILL, Mississippi
In north-central Montgomery County, Duck Hill is named for a large hill that was once used by a Choctaw Indian chief for his war councils. He was widely known among the Indians and Whites alike, as Duck. (6)

DUCKTOWN, Tennessee
Legend has it that the district took its name from an Indian chief named Duck who once ruled over this portion of the Cherokee Nation. Some of these stories go so far as to designate different sites of Chief Duck's village, where the glum old chief sat while Indian dancers swirled around him. One story places the site of the village near the junction of Tumbling Creek with the Ocoee River. Another story is that the village stood at what is now Staffordtown, about one mile west of Copperhill, and that Duck was buried on one of the adjacent hills.

Turning now to recorded history for light on the origin of the name, it is to be found in the Fifth Annual Report of the Bureau of American Ethnology. In the report a distribution roll of Cherokee annuities paid in the year 1799 shows the number of Cherokee towns in that year to be fifty-one. Included in this list of Cherokee towns are those of Ellijay, Tocoah, and Duck-town. Thus, long before Ducktown was inhabited by white men, it was an established town of the Cherokee Nation. For how long, prior to 1799, it had been such is not known. In all probability the town was one of the oldest of the Cherokee settlements in this part of the tribe's domain.

Authentic scources do not reveal an Indian chief named Duck here. If there was a chief by that name, he probably remained in the seclusion of his mountain lair and did not venture out to make war on white settlers. And if the good chief's social and civic activities among his clan led to the settlement's being named in his honor, then his reign must have dated back into the early 1700's.

The names Cawoneh and Ducktown were at one time used synonymously. Cawoneh was the English version of the Cherokee word Kana'na, meaning "duck." Therefore, what to the Cherokee was "Kana'na" was later to the white man "duck."

From all of this eventually evolved the name of Ducktown, Tennessee, located in Polk County at the junction of Tennessee, North Carolina, and Georgia. (*see* Acknowledgments)

DUE WEST, South Carolina
Due West, South Carolina, as early as 1765 was known to the Indians as

Yellow Water. Where the Keowee Path crossed the Cherokee line was called DeWitts Corner. In 1777 a treaty between South Carolina and the Cherokee Indians was signed there. The present town was first called Due West Corner. Here, in 1839, Ersking College, the state's first four-year church college, was founded by the Associate Reformed Presbyterian Church. With the establishment of a post office here the name was shortened to Due West, South Carolina. (Ersking College, Due West, S. C.)

DUGWAY, Utah

The name Dugway is taken from the Dugway Mountains which lie to the southwest of the installation. The name itself was coined by the early Mormon pioneers and denoted an excavated trench or roadway which they dug to facilitate getting their wagons over the mountains during the westward migrations in the middle 1880's.

The area now covered by Dugway Proving Ground encompasses the Great Salt Lake Desert, remnants of the huge prehistoric Lake Bonneville which existed more than 12,000 years ago. The lake, which is named for Army Engineer Captain Benjamin Bonneville, who charted its history in 1832, once existed as a fresh body of water covering most of western Utah, southern Idaho and eastern Nevada. At its peak, the lake crested at 5,800 feet above sea level.

Although not a town in a true sense of the word, it does have its own post office, and Dugway, Utah (known as Dugway Proving Grounds), is home for an awful lot of good Americans; and the colorful history justified its inclusion in this book.

DUKEDOM, Tennessee

"Duke" A. Beedles was the first merchant here. When the settlement grew to five families he made an application for a post office. He could offer no suggestions as to a name, leaving it up to the Post Office Department. Some wag in the department simply gave the "Duke" his Dukedom. (1)

DURANGO, Colorado

Durango as first laid out was almost entirely a box tent town, except for a few small stores and restaurants, and a number of saloons and dance halls. In December, 1880, the first newspaper gave the population as 2500 to 3000 people. It was a child of the Denver and Rio Grande Railroad, and was named after Durango, Mexico, at the suggestion of Governor Hunt, a stockholder of the railroad, who had recently travelled in that country. (2)

DUSTY, New Mexico

Although the name Dusty would certainly apply to this part of New Mexico, the name was chosen by drawing it from a box. The drawing was held in Santa Fe, to choose a name for the new post office, and for the town. (1)

DUTCH JOHN, Utah

This is the newest town in the book, established in 1959, when the Flaming Gorge Dam was being built. First it was a construction town and now it is a tourist town, as over 100,000 people visit here each year. The entire town is government owned including all the land, houses, and buildings. The town is made up of government or state employees, except the man who runs the service station. The following government agencies are represented: Bureau of Reclamation, Park Service, U. S. Forest Service, U. S. Postal Service, the Utah State Fish and Game Department, and the Utah State Highway Department.

The name Dutch John came from a German horse trader by the name of John Hunslinger, who was called Dutch John due to his German accent. He lived in this area in the 1800's, and herded horses where the town now stands, buying, selling, and trading them with pioneers, mountain men, trappers, and gold seekers. He would winter and fatten up the horses and sell them the following spring. He did this for many years and finally left and was never heard of again. (1)

DUTCH NECK, New Jersey

The year 1737 marks the apparent settlement of the Dutch Neck locality by two Holland Dutch families, the Bergens and the Voorhees, who came here from New Amsterdam (now New York City), or Long Island.

The word "neck" meant a tract of land in the Dutch language, and this is how the village name came into being. It is located in the beautiful Township of West Windsor. (2)

DWARF, Kentucky

The first name of this small town, and the post office established July 24, 1878, was Tunnel Hill. It was named for an extraordinary feat of engineering accomplished by two brothers, Sam and Felix Combs. With the most rudimentary of tools, they dug a tunnel here, over a hundred years ago, to bring water to their mill. The mill has long since fallen into ruin, but the tunnel is still in good condition.

The post office was discontinued in 1881, and when it was re-established July 13, 1883, the name Dwarf was given to honor another Combs, named Jerry, who was an early settler, very small in stature, and known affectionately as "Short Jerry." (1)

Dwarf, Kentucky

EAGLE, Texas

Eagle, a Chambers County village, east of Trinity Bay, is in an area first called Glen. The next name, Eagle Nest, was taken from a nest in a pine on the west prong of Double Bayou. The name was shortened to Eagle when the post office was granted in 1925. (3)

EAGLE GROVE, Iowa

In 1854 Mr. N. B. Paine came to Wright County and built a log cabin near a bluff above the Boone River, upon which stood a large red oak tree that towered many feet above all others in the grove. Perched aloft, in its highest branches, was an eagle's nest, towering some seventy feet above the bluff. The old eagles were at home in the spring and summer of 1855 and 1856. They looked like the old settlers they were, dressed in full plumage, white head and tail—white as the driven snow. Then came other white men with their depredations. It has been said, "where the white man goes, the vulture is not far behind," and so it was that they were shot and killed by a trapper in the spring of 1857.

Eagle Grove was named in honor of the grand old birds of freedom, and for the grove in which they once built their nests. (2)

EAGLE LAKE, Texas

Eagle Lake, in southeastern Colorado County, is the intersection point of several branches of the Gulf, Colorado, and Santa Fe and Cane Belt Railroads. The town and nearby lake were named from a Karankawa Indian legend. (3)

EAGLE MOUNTAIN, California

Eagle Mountain is located in the Josuha National Monument vicinity. It is the special nesting place of the American Bald Eagle (our national bird). Legend has it that iron ore deposits were located here when a prospector's burro, which had metal shoes, stuck to the magnetized rock, indicating the presence of the ore. (1)

EAGLE PASS, Texas

The name Eagle Pass dated way back, long before the town came into existence in 1849. The location was the crossing place on the Rio Grande, on the trade route (wagon trail) from San Fernando, Monclova Viejo, Nava and Allede in the state of Coah, Mexico, to San Antonio, Texas. At that time there were many eagles in this area. One of their favorite roosting and nesting places was in a motte of large pecan trees a few miles southwest of the Rio Grande crossing where the village of Fuentes, Mexico, is now located. The usual flight of the Eagles across the river was where Eagle Pass now stands. Because of this, the Indians, who were prevalent in the southwest at that time, called the crossing "El Paso de Aguila," Spanish for "the pass of the eagles." Early settlers called it Eagle Pass.

During the Civil War Fort Duncan, which was established here, was occupied by Confederate troops, and the port of Eagle Pass was active in cotton trade with Mexico. After the war the last unsurrendered Confederate force, the Shelby Expedition, crossed the Rio Grande at Eagle Pass, and in a silent ceremony buried the last flag to fly over Confederate troops in the river bed. (3)

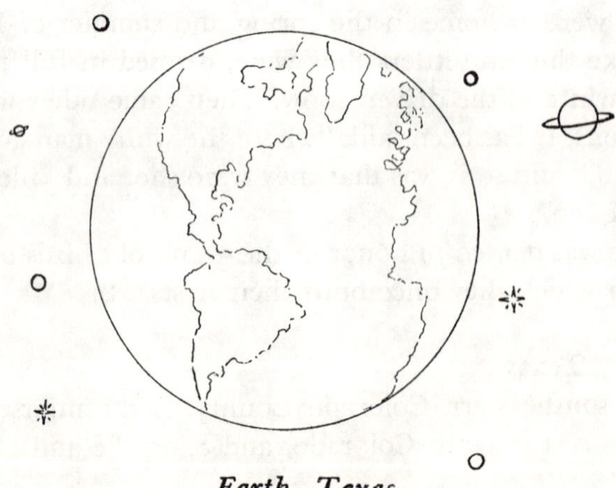

Earth, Texas

EARTH, Texas
Located in northwestern Lamb County, Earth was called Fairleen by W. E. Halsell, who selected the townsite and marked a plot for a hotel. When C. H. Reeves established a store and became postmaster in 1925, the name Fairleen and Tulsa were both rejected. Reeves then named the office Earth, reputedly for a sandstorm then in progress. (3)

EASTANOLLEE, Georgia
Located in Stephens County, the locality was settled by white men around the late 1700's. One of its first settlers was John Stonecypher, who settled here about 1787. This was Indian country, prior to this, and the Indians had a name for the creek. They called it Eastanollee, or "a ledge of rocks across a stream." The Indians had no written language, so the spelling was based upon the way they pronounced the words. The town of Eastanollee took its unusual name from the creek. (Daisy Hayes, Eastanollee, Ga.)

EAU GALLIE, Florida
The Gleason family, from Eau Clair (Clear Water), Wisconsin, settled here in 1884, and recorded the village plat of Eau Gallie. Gleason named it Eau, French for water, and Gallie, a Chippewa Indian word meaning rocky; and it was thus that the town of Eau Gallie had its beginning and its unusual French-Indian name. (2)

EBONY, Texas
Located in northwestern Mills County, Ebony was called Buffalo when it became a community about 1890. With the application for a post office about 1900 the new name was given for Ebony Shaw, a local cowboy. (3)

ECORSE, Michigan
Originally named Grandport, it was established on a Wyandot Indian camping and burial ground around 1812. Later the name was changed to Ecorse, taken from a little stream called Rivière aux Ecorses, by French trappers, which means River of Bark. The banks of the creek were covered with bark, left by the Indians after making enumerable canoes. (6)

EDEN, Arizona
Was so named by its Mormon settlers for obvious sentiments. (5)

EDINBURG, New Jersey
Edinburg was originally the site of an Indian reservation. Formerly known as Assunpink or Sandpink, it was located on the bank of the Assunpink, or what many called Sandpink, Creek.

It received the name of Edinburg by a resolution of its citizens around the mid-1800's, to honor one of its citizens—well liked—who hailed from Edinburg, Scotland. It is located in East Windsor Township. (2)

EFFORT, Pennsylvania
The local citizens of this settlement called a meeting to select a name for the post office. At the first meeting they had no success, as they could not agree upon any of the names proposed. A second meeting was called with the same results, but just prior to their adjournment, one of the settlers jumped to his feet and made a proposition: "Since we have all put forth an effort to select a name for our village, and since we have not agreed to any mentioned, I move we use the name Effort!" The motion was quickly seconded, and carried unanimously, and Effort, Pennsylvania, was named. (1)

EGG HARBOR, Wisconsin
There are two stories as to how Egg Harbor got its unusual name. The first is that there was a sham battle between the crews of two boats stopping at the Harbor in 1825. Each tried to dock first, and in their zeal attacked each other with eggs from their mess baskets. All enjoyed the sport, and news of the battle spread and the area soon became known as Egg Harbor.

The other is that a gentleman with the unlikely name of Increase Claflin, Door County's first settler, named it Egg Harbor when he found a nest full of duck eggs in the harbor. He is also credited with the naming of Horseshoe Bay, Hat Island, The Strawberry Island, and Eagle Island, all near by. (1)

EGG HARBOR CITY, New Jersey
As the Dutch ship *Fortuyn* sailed up the Mullica River in 1614, things looked anything but promising. Sailors from the ship, exploring the lands for wild fruit and berries, found nothing but wild birds' eggs everywhere—it was the nesting season. They called the land they explored "Eyren Haven," or "harbor of eggs," which later was translated into Egg Harbor.

When a village was established here in the Colonial days, taking the name Egg Harbor City, the region was inhabited primarily by Tories, who had fled Philadelphia and the Continental Army. There were also refugees here from the burning of Chestnut Neck, backwoodsmen, and charcoal burners. All in all a motley collection of humanity. The outlaw band of Joseph Mulliner is said to have camped here in the early days. (Joseph Kertz, Elec Svc)

EGYPT, Texas
In northwestern Wharton County on the Gulf, Colorado and Santa Fe

Railroad, Egypt was founded about 1830 by Captain W. J. E. Heard. As the area supplied corn to surrounding settlements during a severe drought, it became known as Egypt. (3)

EIGHTY EIGHT, Kentucky
When the townspeople got together to pick a name for their post office they asked the new postmaster, Mr. Dabnie Nunnally, what his choice was. "Let's call it Eighty Eight," he replied, "I don't write very well and I will just use the figure 88." The name was accepted; however, the post office was not very helpful to Mr. Nunnally, because it insisted that the name be spelled out.

It was in Eighty Eight, during the 1948 elections, that 88 votes were cast for Dewey and 88 votes cast for Truman. (1)

EIGHTY-FOUR, Pennsylvania
In the late 1800's the town was called Smithville, however there was another Smithville in Pennsylvania, and this caused confusion in the handling of mail. In 1884 (the year of the hard-fought campaign, and election of Grover Cleveland) the town fathers decided to change the town's name to Eighty-Four, in honor of the election of Grover Cleveland as President of the United States. (1)

EL DORADO, Arkansas
The original settlers came here from the Carolinas, where the favorite expression had been, "Are you looking for your El Dorado?" and was aimed at any wagon train heading westward. The name El Dorado, of course, means any place of fabulous wealth.

When the settlers reached here, it was the end of their journey—their El Dorado—so they adopted the name for their town. El Dorado is the County Seat of Union County, Arkansas. (Annie L. Spencer, El Dorado Real Estate Co.)

EL CAMPO, Texas
El Campo, in western Wharton County, was called Prairie Switch when it was established in 1881 as a siding and shipping point on the New York, Texas and Mexican Railroad (later the Texas & New Orleans). The siding became the camping place for cattlemen of the area who rounded up their herds at the site and was also a station for construction gangs working on the railroad. In 1890 the name was changed to El Campo (the camp). (3)

ELECTRA, Texas
Located in the western part of Wichita County, the town was twice platted and sub-divided into town lots and three times sold. The town has had

three names—Beaver, Waggoner, and finally Electra. The first settlement followed the building of the Fort Worth and Denver Railroad through this area in 1885. The first post office, in 1889, was named Beaver. It was a trading post for Chief Quannah Parker and his Comanche braves. D. Waggoner, a cattle baron, with his son, moved his headquarters to this vicinity and his holdings almost completely surrounded the town. Supplies were soon to be delivered here addressed Waggoner, thus the depot sported the name Waggoner, while the mail came to Beaver. Becoming a cattle shipping center the herds came from all directions, and trouble erupted between the farmers (nesters), and the cattlemen. To avoid further trouble Mr. Waggoner secured co-operation from the railroad in building a switch track and loading pens at Beaver in 1900. The citizens, in 1902, decided by petition to have the town renamed Electra, in honor of Miss Electra Waggoner, daughter of W. T. Waggoner. (2)

ELECTRIC MILLS, Mississippi
Located in Kemper County, near the Alabama border, it is an industrial town that took its name from a large electric mill. (6)

ELEVEN MILE CORNER, Arizona
It is named for its unique location. It is eleven miles to Casa Grande, eleven miles to College, and eleven miles to Elay, all towns in Arizona. (1)

ELK RIVER, Minnesota
Settled around 1848, and named for the river, which was named for the herds of wild elk that use to roam freely here. The village is on the Mississippi River in Sherburne County, and was platted in 1865 and replatted in 1868. (6)

ELMDALE, Texas
Located in eastern Taylor County, almost within the city limits of Abilene, was established as a stop on the Texas and Pacific Railroad in the early 1880's. Surveyors named it for a mirage which reflected trees and lakes to the prairie travelers. (3)

EL PASO, Texas
El Paso is the extreme western city of Texas. Ciudad Juarez, largest Mexican city on the border, is directly across the Rio Grande. Modern El Paso grew out of four early settlements, the oldest of which was made by Juan Maria Ponce de Léon in 1827. Franklin Coons bought the De Léon ranch area, which covered the present downtown district of the city. In 1849 the California Gold Rush, augmented by cattle drives, began overland travel

through El Paso to the Pacific. Coons was the first postmaster, and named his settlement Franklin in 1852; however he left the area without paying for the land, so the de Léon heirs resold the property to William T. Smith in 1854. From 1858 to 1861 the Butterfield Overland Mail route maintained a station here. The station was erected by Anson Mills, state surveyor for the district, who claimed credit for the changing of the name from Franklin to El Paso when he surveyed the townsite in 1858 and 1859. The name is Spanish and means "the pass," both for its position as the "Pass of the North" through the Rio Grande Valley, and as a gateway into Mexico. A notable episode came in 1877 when one Charles Howard laid claim to the Salt Flats 100 miles east of El Paso. Enraged citizens from both sides of the river, who had long collected the salt free, let their anger overflow in San Elizario, with more than half a dozen deaths resulting, including the fatal shooting of a Texas Ranger. It was the scene of the shooting of John Wesley Hardin, in August 19, 1895. Other notable gunfighters who visited here included Wyatt Earp, Billy the Kid, plus an assortment of hard cases whose names never made it into the history books. (2)

EMBARRASS, Minnesota

The Embarrass River was a means of travel for the early Indians, French fur traders, and missionaries who navigated along the river before the signing of the Declaration of Independence. Records indicate that this area was known as the Embarrass River in the year 1884. The name was possibly first applied to the village by the DM and IR Railway Company, when the depot was established.

A definition for the word Embarrass is found in a letter written by Father du Poisson, a Jesuit Missionary (whose name, incidently, is French and means fish): "What we call an Embarrass is a mass of floating trees which the current drags onward continually. If they snag and form an obstacle, the French call this an Embarrass." (1)

EMBARRASS, Wisconsin

Many of the early lumberjacks in the Shawano and in the neighboring counties were French Canadians. When they attempted to send logs down this particular stream, they found it almost impossible because of the snags in it. They called it Tangle River, which in French is "Rivière Embarrass." The Americans, changing it to English, called it the Embarrass River. The little village took its name from this river. (1)

EMBLEM, Wyoming

Emblem, Big Horn County, Wyoming, was originally named Germania by the first settlers, German immigrants. During and after World War I, because of strong anti-German sentiment, the name was changed to Liberty. Upon learning, through the Post Office Department, that there was already a Liberty in Wyoming, the townspeople adopted the name of Emblem for the town. (*See* Acknowledgements)

EMPIRE, Colorado
Dating from about 1863, the town was settled by early pioneers from New York State. Since their old home state was known as the Empire State, the homesick settlers named the new town Empire. (1)

ENCAMPMENT, Wyoming
Encampment, Carbon County, Wyoming, gets its name from the fact that the area was a noted rendezvous site for trappers and Indians, and was first known as Camp le Grande or Grand Encampment. When the post office was established the name was shortened to Encampment. (*See* Acknowledgments)

ENDEAVOR, Pennsylvania
First named Christian Endeavor by the Christian people that pioneered and settled it, the name was later shortened to Endeavor.

The name was inspired because it took a lot of endurance for young people to remain here, working in a lumber mill, which lacked the modern equipment of today. (1)

ENGLISH TURN, Louisiana
Located in Plaquemines Parish, and formerly called "Détour des Anglais," French meaning "Detour or Turn of the English."

It was here that the French, through trickery, persuaded a British exploration party that the Mississippi River lay farther to the west. They turned and left, leaving this part of the Mississippi Valley exclusively to the French, while they hunted for the evasive Mississippi River. (2)

ENTERPRISE, Arizona
Was so named by its Mormon settlers, who, to say the least, were an enterprising lot. (5)

ENTERPRISE, Utah
An enterprising fellow named Orson W. Huntsman had an idea of building a storage reservoir to catch the spring run-off and carry it in a canal to the valley, some 12 miles below, where there were thousands of acres of fertile land. This in the middle of cow country.

Huntsman took up a homestead at the head of Shoal Creek Wash, in the Escalante Valley, and soon interested some of his neighbors in throwing in with him, locating there and building a town, where there would be room to expand. Building the storage dam, and digging the canal, was a huge enterprise for a few poor people. Huntsman named his town well, for he called it Enterprise. (2)

EOLA, Texas

Eola, in western Concho County, was founded about 1910. In 1940 the town had a population of 250. The origin of the name is not definitely known, but it is probably derived from an Indian word, which means "good luck" or "good returns from the blowing winds." (3)

EPOUFETTE, Michigan

The town was named by early French commercial fishermen for its harbor on Lake Michigan. The name originally meant "peaceful waters," or "quite place to rest." It was used by sailing vessels in the early 1800's as a haven from wind storms and squalls. (1)

ESKOTA, Texas

Eskota, on Sweetwater Creek in southeastern Fisher County, was established as a shipping point on the Texas and Pacific Railroad. The railroad company chose the name, a Spanish word meaning "a basket of fruit," when the Eskota sign was accidentally thrown out instead of a station marker with the name Trent. (3)

ETIWANDA, California

The first house in the valley was built in Etiwanda by Captain Joseph Garcia, a Portuguese sailor, who became weary of life at sea. He bought land and obtained a flock of sheep and settled near the intersection of the old Santa Fe Trail and El Camino Real.

Water rights were established in 1867 by George Day and in 1873 they were extended to cover Day Canyon and East Canyon. Later all rights were consolidated into what was known as the Garcia Ranch.

The Chaffey brothers from Canada came in the early 1880's, and on Thanksgiving Day, 1881, purchased one thousand acres of land and water rights from Captain Garcia. Their uncle who lived in Michigan had written them of an Indian chief there named Etiwanda, so they chose to name their new settlement in California for a Michigan Indian chief! (2)

EUREKA, Missouri

The town was first established as a railroad camp in 1853, by the Missouri Pacific. It is said to have been named by a railroad surveyor who, when finding that the route through this valley would eliminate a lot of work, exclaimed "Eureka!" Eureka, meaning "I have found it," is the reputed exclamation of Archimedes when, after long study, discovered a method of detecting the amount of alloy in the crown of the king of Syracuse.

The town was platted and laid out in 1858 by Messrs. Strody and Shands of St. Louis, Missouri; and they also used the name Eureka. (2)

EUREKA, West Virginia
In Pleasants County, on the Ohio River, Eureka was named when an oil well was finally brought in after many difficulties in 1885.

EXILE, Texas
Exile, in northern Uvalde County, became a post office on the W. C. Lee ranch in 1890. The name supposedly indicated the distance of the ranch from any settled area. (3)

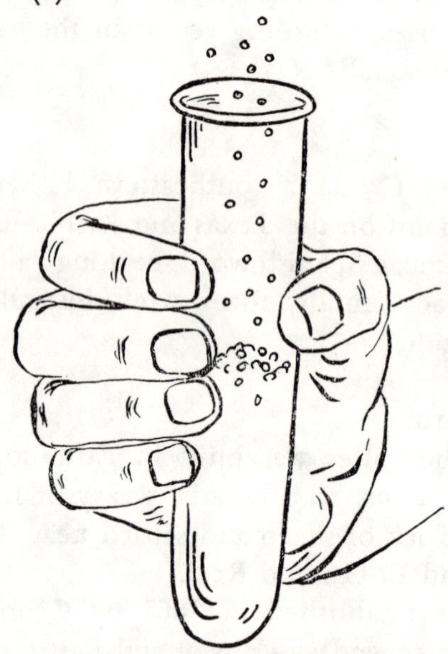

Experiment, Georgia

EXPERIMENT, Georgia
The town was so named because the Georgia Agricultural Experiment Station is located here. Dr. H. P. Stuckey was director of the station and is well-known for his work on scuppernong grapes and pecans. At present work is being done in research on frozen food preservation. (1)

EXPORT, Pennsylvania
Incorporated in 1911, Export was the first town in this area to mine coal for more than local markets, hence the name Export. (4)

EYOTA, Minnesota

The first settlers came here in 1854 from Pennsylvania. The first settler was Benjamin Bear, for whom Bear Creek was named. They first named the village Springfield for the many springs located here. The name was later changed to Eyota, which is an Indian name meaning "superior."

Eyota is located on the highest point of land between the Mississippi and Sioux Falls, South Dakota. They figured it was a superior point and a superior land. (1)

FAIRHOPE, Alabama

The founders of Fairhope were single taxers who came to Baldwin County in November 1894. In February of that year, prior to coming South, they had incorporated in Des Moines, Iowa, as the Fairhope Industrial Association. Ten years later, after favorable legislation had been adopted by Alabama they were reincorporated as the Fairhope Single Tax Corporation. One of the early group is quoted as having said, "There is just a fair hope we might succeed." "That's it!" another exclaimed, "We'll name our town Fairhope." (2)

FAIRHOPE, Pennsylvania

Fairhope is a small village located southwest of the central part of Somerset County. It was laid out after the close of the Civil War, and received its unusual name from the fact that the citizens had a "fairhope" that a railroad would be built through the village. (1)

FAIRPLAY, Colorado

In 1858, the Russel party from Georgia—Whites and Cherokee—discovered gold in feeble streaks in the sands of Cherry Creek near where Denver is now located. This precipitated the mad gold rush of 1859, known as the "Pike's Peak Humbug." Not all of the "fifty-niners" returned home after the swindle of rumor had been realized.

Of the many who continued westward, hundreds drifted into the Tarryall country to make those noted gold finds. These erstwhile, disgruntled, broke, and half-starved gold seekers became encouraged, greedy, and arrogant by their rich findings on the Tarryall. Hence they banded together to run off any late comers. Almost every acre thought to have pay "color" was grabbed up regardless of the recognized rules of possession.

Confronted by this armed attitude the late comers were left with but one alternative—keep going. But in retaliation they renamed the new boom district "Graball." Branded with such a moniker by the weary and hungry prospectors, the Tarryall seemed doomed to leave nothing more to posterity than a frown in history—and acres of clean washed rocks.

But Graball did serve as a stepping stone from which outcast pioneers leaped to the friendly sands of the South Platte where a little band of spurned men were welding a new friendship of their own, led by two pals, Jim Reymonds and Sam Hardesty, that was to grow and blossom into a town "with a touch of gold," destined to become world renown, and sought by every traveler: Fairplay.

"Named by the pioneer miners in expression of their determination for equal opportunity and fair dealing. Site visited by Captain John C. Fremont and Kit Carson in 1844. Fairplay diggings organized and mining laws enacted in April, 1860. Seat of Park County since 1867." Thus reads a marker placed here by the State Historical Society of Colorado, in 1946. (2)

FAIRPLAY, Missouri
The name of this town was originated in the general store, where the townfolk gathered each Saturday for visiting and playing checkers and horse shoes.

Two fellows got into a fight, but it soon became apparent to them both that neither could possibly win, so they just separated and shook hands. A spectator, gripped with the emotion of the moment, jumped up and exclaimed, 'Boys, she sure was Fairplay!" From this incident, the post office and the town was later to be named Fairplay, Missouri. (L. E. Thomason, Alderman)

FAIR PLAY, Texas
Fair Play, in western Panola County, is one of the oldest settlements in the area, occupying part of the Immanuel Antonio Romero grant. The first settler was John Allison, who conducted a general store, boarding house, blacksmith shop, and was county judge when the county was organized in 1846. He was a busy man!

A post office was granted in May, 1851. The site is said to have been named by a traveler who was impressed with the fair rates and treatment he received at Allison's. (3)

FAIRY, Texas
Fairy, in northern Hamilton County, was named for Fairy Fort, daughter of Captain B. Fort, C. S. A., who settled in the area about the year 1873. (3)

FALCON, Texas
Located near the junction of Medio Creek and the Rio Grande in southwestern Zapata County, Falcon is said to have been so named because of its location on the route explored by Miguel de la Garza Falcón in 1755. (3)

Fairy, Texas

FALFURRIAS, Texas
County seat and principal trading center of Brooks County, this town is in the northern part of the county on the Texas and New Orleans Railroad. Established in 1883 by Edward C. Lasater, pioneer Rio Grande Valley developer, the town was given the Spanish name for a desert flower, the "heart's delight."

The original location of the village was near Laguana Salada, a few miles south of the present site, but when the railroad was built through the territory in 1903, Lasater moved his settlement to a more favorable location.

A post office was granted in 1904 with H. R. Rive as post master. The *Falfurrias Facts* began publication in 1906. In 1908 the first creamery in the territory opened and began an industrial change which resulted in the introduction of pure bred Jersey dairy cattle and beef herds to replace the native Texas Longhorn stock. (3)

FALLING WATERS, West Virginia
Located in a bend of the Potomac River, the town was named for a waterfall of a small stream that plunges into the river at this point. The Battle of Falling Waters was fought here in 1863, between the forces of General Robert E. Lee, and General George C. Meade. (6)

FALMOUTH, Florida
Located four miles from the meandering Suwannee River, Falmouth was once called Peacock. Legend has it that a local leading citizen renamed it for a favorite hunting dog, Falmouth, who was killed on a hunting trip. (6)

FANCY GAP, Virginia
Legend tells that during the pioneer days there were only foot trails crossing the Blue Ridge Mountains. One day two pioneers were crossing the mountains on foot, and one of them made the remark that this would be a "fancy place to cross." From then on the pass was known as Fancy Gap.

There are several gaps in the vicinity of this village, with the colorful names of Orchard Gap, Pipers Gap, Low Gap, etc. (1)

FARMERS VALLEY, Texas
Farmers Valley, on the west line of Wilbarger County, was named by E. J. Randal and W. W. Hutchens, who settled there in 1885 and found it a fertile agricultural area. (3)

FATE, Texas
Located in north-central Rockwell County, Fate became a station on the Missouri, Kansas and Texas Railroad in 1886. Many of the residents of Barnes City moved to the new railroad location, and in 1894 a post office, named Fate for Lafayette Peyton, was opened in the community. (3)

FAWNSKIN, California
In the early days this little settlement was known as Grout, for Grout Creek, which empties into Big Bear Lake. Late in the 1800's, travelers coming to the Big Bear Valley by way of the Arrowhead and the Green Valley route had to make their overnight camp in a beautiful little meadow just above Grout Creek Canyon.

On one of these trips, pioneers found many hides of Fawns, which had been slaughtered by a band of hunters, and stretched out against the trees. Thereafter, this spot was often referred to as the "Fawn Skin" Meadows. As the settlement of Grout developed into a more picturesque community, the people searched for a more picturesque name and could find no better than Fawnskin, California. (1)

FEEDING HILLS, Massachusetts
Situated in Hampden County, Massachusetts, the early day settlers of Springfield used this area for the grazing of their cattle and called the locale "feeding hills."

The area is located on high ground, west of the Connecticut River, and is now occupied by the town of Feeding Hills. (1)

FIDDLETOWN, California
Fiddletown, Amador County, California, was settled in 1848 by a group of Missourians, who spent their leisure hours playing the fiddle and dancing. Because of this the town was named Fiddletown.

A snobbish judge from the town had the named changed, in 1878, to Oleta, an Indian name meaning "old home spring," because of the embarrassment it caused him when he would list his home town on the San Francisco hotel registers.

The name of Fiddletown was restored when an interested group of San Franciscans asked the local townspeople to change the name.

In an impressive ceremony in 1936, Fiddletown regained its name, and the noted violinist, Dave Rubinoff, was named honorary mayor.

There was once a large Chinese population in Fiddletown, and today the ruins of their adobe forts, which they built to keep Mexican bandits from robbing them, still stand. Around Fiddletown there were other small communities, with the colorful names of Suckertown, Helltown, Hogtown, and Shirt-Tail. All have disappeared.

Bret Harte added to Fiddletown's fame by writing *An Episode in Fiddletown.* (1) (2)

FIFE, Texas
Fife, in north central McCulloch County just south of the Colorado River, was named by an early settler, Mrs. R. F. Finlay, for her native home, Fifeshire, Scotland. (3)

FIFTY-SIX, Arkansas
When this part of Stone County was settled, there was a "little red school house" located in school district Number 56. A settler named Reva N. Newcomb immigrated here from Springfield, Missouri, and opened a general store. Later it became the post office and he the postmaster. He named his new post office Fifty-six, after the school district. (1)

FIREBAUGH, California
In 1854 Andres J. Firebaugh established a ferry and a trading post on the San Joaquin River for the Butterfield Overland Stages traveling from San Francisco to St. Louis.

Some 60 years after the establishment of Firebaugh's Ferry, the local inhabitants of the settlement that had grown up around it voted to incorporate and name itself the "City of Firebaugh." The vote was 56 to 7, and Firebaugh, California, was established. (2)

FISCHER STORE, Texas

On the Devil's Backbone Drive in the Hill Country of northern Comal County, this town was settled in 1853 by Herman Fischer, who built a one-room log cabin and began raising stock. When neighbors settled nearby, Fischer built a log store which grew from a one-wagon business to a dozen wagon one, drawn by six-mule teams to haul products from the community. The post office, established in 1875, has never failed to have a Fischer for a postmaster. (3)

FISH CAMP, California

Is located about 2¼ miles from the south entrance of the Yosemite National Park, Mariposa County. It started out as a few cabins, providing food and lodging for workers at the Sugar Pine Lumber Mill. Later a fish hatchery was built, and mail began to arrive addressed to Beery's Fish Camp. Mr. Beery finally registered the name with the state, and it made its first appearance on California maps.

When a post office was located here, the Post Office Department, in their desire for short names, reduced the name to Fish Camp. (1)

FISHTRAP, Kentucky

Indians and later white settlers made their livelihood by fishing in this area. Not all fishing was done by poles and nets—the fishermen constructed traps, an unusual method of fishing, and the area soon became known to the settlers and trappers as "Fishtrap." From this unusual method of fishing came the name of the village. (1)

FLAGG, Texas

Flagg, in southwestern Castro County, was originally in the center of a fifty-three section ranch, shaped like a flag, and owned by C. T. Herring. In 1925 the ranch was cut into 160-acre blocks and sold for farms. Flagg is a retail center and post office for a ranching and farming area lying along Runningwater Draw. (3)

FLAG POND, Tennessee

Named for a small pond in the center of the community, completely surrounded by wild iris. The older residents called the iris "flags," and soon referred to the pond as the "Flag Pond." When a post office was established they naturally named it Flag Pond. (1)

FLAGSTAFF, Arizona
The name Flagstaff comes from a pine tree being stripped of its branches to serve as a "flagstaff" for flying the American flag on the 100th anniversary of Independence Day, July 4, 1876. It was on an old wagon train route to

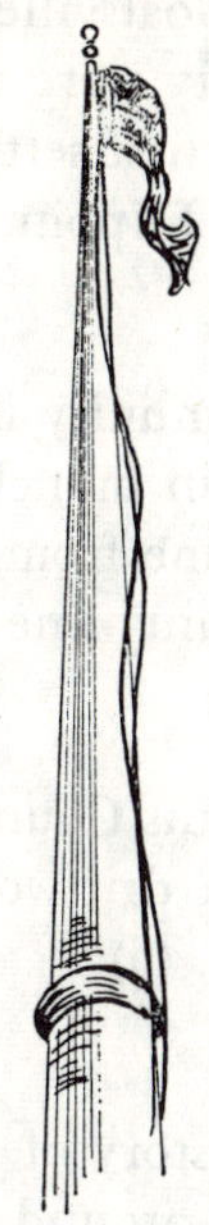

Flagstaff, Arizona

California, and the site of the flagstaff was a popular camping area because of the spring which furnished abundant water. The "Flagstaff' stood for many years to guide other parties along the trail. (2)

FLAT, Texas
In eastern Coryell County twelve miles from Gatesville, Flat was established in 1891 and was first known as Mesquite Flat because of its location upon a flat strip of land covered with Mesquite. (3)

FLIPPIN, Arkansas
The town was named for Thomas J. Flippin, who settled here around 1821. At the time there was a small band of Delaware Indians located nearby, at Big Indian Spring, with a chief called Johnny Cake. A few Shawnee Indians lived at Yellville, but as other white settlers came in the Indians moved out, around 1828.

Flippin was called *Goatsville,* until around 1850. Legend has it that a traveling salesman called upon "Uncle Jim Jackson," who had a general store, flour mill and cotton gin. He had not been very successful in selling the old gent merchandise so he started back to his wagon in a rather vile mood. To add to his woes one of Mr. Jackson's goats took a running tackle at the seat of his pants just as he boarded his hack. After that the enraged salesman referred to the town as Goatsville, and the name stuck.

Settlers of a growing community were unhappy with this moniker and changed their name to honor their first settler, calling it "Flippin Barrens." Later the name was shortened to Flippin. (2)

FLOMOT, Texas
An agricultural and ranching community in the extreme northeastern part of Motley County between the main branch of the North Pease River, and the Quitaque, Flomot takes its name from a combination of the names of Motley and Floyd counties—the county line running north of town. (3)

FLOODWOOD, Minnesota
Floodwood, in southwestern St. Louis County, takes its name from a nearby stream that was always filled with driftwood and logs, which made navigation difficult if not impossible. (6)

FLORISSANT, Missouri
The history of Florissant is the history of America: bloody fights with Indians, which made a log stockade around a spring the only security men knew; dauntless men of God who lived among the savages—men such as the Jesuit Father, Peter DeSmet, whose name has entered American folklore and whose base was Florissant; intrepid men who left their cabins on Coldwater Creek to found cities along the Missouri, in Wyoming and along the Santa Fe Trail.

French farmers and fur trappers looked upon the valley soon after the trading post of St. Louis was established in 1767 and called this spot "Fleurissant" or flowering—flourishing. Some stayed to till the rich, black loam and founded a village.

When the Spanish took over the Louisiana Territory, the havitaciones del establicimiento de Florizan took on the official name of St. Ferdinand until 1939, when the black soil would no longer be denied and the name was officially made Florissant. (2)

FLOURTOWN, Pennsylvania
Founded in 1743, Flourtown was once noted for its flour trade, thus the name. (4)

FLOWERY BRANCH, Georgia
This town, located on an old Cherokee Indian encampment, was not named

for a Flowery Tree Branch, but for a Flowery Creek or Branch. The Indians called the camp ANA-GE-LUS-ky, for the thousands of daisies that grew on both sides of the Branch. The Branch remains, but the daisies have long since passed into memory. (6)

FLOYDADA, Texas
Floydada, on the Pecos and North Texas, and the Quanah, Acme, and Pacific Railroads, in Floyd County, was established in 1890 by M. C. Williams on 640 acres of land donated by J. B. Price of Jefferson City, Missouri.

Originally named Floyd City the site became the county seat in an election on April 14, 1890. When the post office was established in September, 1890, duplication with the name of another post office caused Floydada to be selected. It is a combination of the county name with that of Mrs. Ada Price. (3)

FODICE, Texas
Fodice, a rural Negro community in southern Houston County, was settled in the late 1880's. One explanation of the name is that it is derived from "Four Dice," indicating a favorite occupation of the inhabitants. Another explanation is that the settlers came from Fordyce, Arkansas, and, with a change of spelling, named the new place for their old home. (3)

FOOT, Texas
Was named for a pioneer family of Foots that settled there in the early 1880's. (3)

FOREST HOME, Alabama
Forest Home was named by Miss Hattie Stewart, a school teacher, in Monterey, Alabama, about 1873, because of the number of beautiful trees in the area. Relates an old timer of Forest Home, age ninety-eight. (1)

FORREST CITY, Arkansas
Once a railroad construction camp around 1867, it was named in honor of Nathan Bedford Forrest, a noted Confederate General. (6)

FORT BLISS, Texas
Located on a mesa about three miles from El Paso, Texas, Fort Bliss originated as the Post of El Paso, and was ordered established in February 1848. In September, 1849, Major Jefferson Van Horne arrived with regimental headquarters and six companies to defend against Indians raids and to maintain American authority in the territory recently acquired from Mexico by the treaty of Guadalupe Hidalgo. The post was renamed in 1854 for

Colonel William Wallace S. Bliss, assistant Adjutant General and General Zachary Taylor's Adjutant General during the Mexican War.

With the outbreak of the Civil War, Fort Bliss became headquarters for the Confederate Army in the Southwest. In August, 1862, when the Confederates found increasing adversities too much for them, they burned the fort and moved eastward. The United States flag was soon raised over the ruins, but the fort was not restored until August, 1865. In 1868 the Fort was moved to higher ground, due to flooding by the Rio Grande, rebuilt on a site called Concordia, and called Camp Concordia until 1869, when the former name was resumed.

During the last two years of the Civil War and immediately following, El Paso and Juarez drew a ruffian border population and crime became common. The army here restored order and confidence.

In the middle 1880's Fort Bliss served chiefly as a refitting post for troops who were searching for Geronimo, an Apache chief who was raiding in New Mexico, Arizona, and nothern Mexico. Troops from the fort investigated the Francisco (Pancho) Villa raids in New Mexico in 1912, and a punitive expedition was sent from the fort into Mexico in pursuit of Villa. Troops who served in the two World Wars trained here. (3)

FORT BOGGY, Texas

Fort Boggy, a blockhouse on the north bank of Boggy Creek, about five miles south of Centerville in Leon County, was built about 1840 by a company of minute men under Thomas N. B. Greer. As headquarters for the Boggy and Trinity Rangers in 1840, the fort offered protection for the frontier, and the first settlements of the area on the Leon Prairie grew up around it. The Fort Boggy community retained the name long after the fort itself was abandoned. The name came from the boggy condition of the creek. (3)

FORT DEFIANCE, Arizona

In defiance of the marauding bands of Navajos, Colonel Edwin V. Sumner, in the fall of 1851, selected the site as a military outpost and named it Fort Defiance. Between 1856 and 1863 there was continuous guerrilla warfare between the Navajo and the American military. In April, 1861, Fort Defiance was attacked by some 2,000 Navajos who were finally driven off.

At the beginning of the Civil War, Fort Defiance was abandoned, but was reoccupied in the fall of 1863, and used as Colonel Kit Carson's headquarters during the Navajo campaign. In the fall of that year and the spring of 1864, almost 9,000 Navajos were rounded up and confined at the Fort prior to the "Long Walk" to the Bosque Redondo (Fort Sumner, New Mexico). On their return from Fort Sumner in 1868, the Navajos were placed on a reservation, for which Fort Defiance was the agency. Fort Defiance, which was originally erected to do battle with the Navajo, is today, paradoxically, the administrative center of the Navajo Indian Nation! (Frank H. Carson, Hq. Parks, Recreation & Tourism Development, The Navajo Tribe, Window Rock, Arizona)

FORT DUCHESNE, Utah

The fort was established in 1886 to protect white settlers from the Ute Indians. Said to be the most expensive fort ever erected in America in that day and age, the materials for its construction had to be carried over the mountains from Price, Utah. Wooden walls once surrounded the fort, which was built by two companies of Negro soldiers. The fort was named for the Duchesne River, which in turn was named for a French Trapper. (1)

FORT KLAMATH, Oregon

The original Fort Klamath was established here in March, 1863, and abandoned as a military post June 23, 1890. Though it never moved, the Fort was eventually located in four different counties. The first was Wasco County, then in 1869 it was attached to Jackson County, then into Lake County in 1874, and finally when Klamath County was created and separated from Lake County in 1882, it found itself located there.

Old Fort Klamath was the headquarters for the cavalry during the Modoc Indian Wars, and the present town is on the horse pasture for the cavalry. The wars lasted from November, 1872, to October, 1873, when they ended with the hanging of the four Indian leaders of the "rebellion." Captain Jack, Schonchin John, Black (Shagnasty) Jim, and Boston (Scarface) Charley were hanged at the site of the Fort.

The present town of Fort Klamath lies on the banks of the Wood River one mile west of the site of the old fort. It is high in the Cascade Mountains, still decidedly western in flavor, and surrounded by several large cattle ranches.

The town of Fort Klamath was established about 1885, and was named for the old fort, which itself was named for the Klamath Indians, who still live in this area. (1)

FORT LOUDON, Pennsylvania

Founded in 1795 was named for the Earl of Loudoun, who for a brief period commanded the British forces in the Colonies. (4)

FORT SPUNKY, Texas

Fort Spunky, in the southeastern corner of Hood County, was called Barnardville when it was the site of George Barnard's trading post in 1847.

Its more belligerent name was bestowed after several fights occurred at the time of selecting a name for the new post office. (3)

FORTUNA, California
Is located in the very center of Humboldt County, 260 miles north of San Francisco. Originally called Springville, due to the numerous springs on the hills, and later named Slide, it was finally dubbed Fortuna by a progressive landowner. It is a community of 4,000 located on the north bank of the Eel River. (2)

FORTY FORT, Pennsylvania
The fort was named for the first settlers who came into this valley, and who were forty in number. (4)

FORTY-FOUR, Arkansas
In 1928 a petition for a post office was submitted by this small settlement, located here on Piney Creek. The petition was denied because there was already a town named Piney Creek in North Carolina. The residents, stuck for another name, came up with an inspiration; they simply counted the number of names on the petition. There were forty-four names, so they re-submitted it with the new name Forty-Four, and it was approved. (1)

FOSSIL, Oregon
Fossil, in northwestern Wheeler County, got its unusual name when the post office was established here in February 28, 1876 on the ranch of Thomas B. Hoover, its first postmaster. Mr. Hoover had just discovered and removed the remains of a fossil on his ranch. He recommended the name Fossil for the new post office and the town, and it was adopted.

In the search for stones on which is written the story of ancient life, the folded hills and eroded canyons of Wheeler County, Oregon, have more than yielded their quota. Especially the preserved evidences which depict that critical period known to geologists as the Eocene—when the masters of the earth, giant mammals and seed bearing plants, in their respective fields were striving for dominance.

The Clarno beds alone have yielded some five hundred rare types of fruits and seeds from plants which thrive only in rain forests of tropical climates, and during the past four years more than five hundred bones and fragments from animals which roamed the area some sixty millions of years ago.

Scientists from across the nation hail this as one of the major finds of the century. Among the animals identified were the Amynodon, an elephant-sized rhino and another Rhine-Hyrachus, about the size of a sheep, huge

Titanotheres, Brontotheres (thunder-beasts). Tigers as large as oxen, tapirs, crocodiles, and a fully grown horse which stood only twelve inches in height. None of these animals has been found before west of the Rockies. All these in *tropical* Oregon. (Fossil Community Club, Wheeler County, Oregon)

FOUNTAIN, Minnesota

In central Fillmore County, Fountain is named for its many natural springs or fountains. (6)

FOWLSTOWN, Georgia

November 21, 1817, Fowlstown was a Seminole Indian village. On this date began the first Seminole War. The beginning took place under the command of Major Twigg, who with two hundred and fifty soldiers from Fort Scott tried to capture the Indian braves of Fowlstown for depredations against the whites. The battle ended without a firm decision on either side.

A second battle took place in the village and in the nearby swamp on November 23, 1817, under the command of Lt. Colonel Arbuckle. On January 4, 1818, the village was found deserted and was subsequently destroyed.

Fowlstown, located in the southwestern corner of Georgia, eight miles from the Florida line, was built in the vicinity of the old Seminole village and took the name as its own. (1)

Foxhome, Minnesota

FOXHOME, Minnesota

Foxhome, located on the flats of the rich Red River Valley, was once the largest hay shipping center in the world. When a post office was established here in 1897, it was located in the general store, which was also the home of the first postmaster, a Mr. Fox, who named it for himself. (1)

FREDONIA, Alabama
Fredonia, located in Chambers County, Alabama, got its name in a most unusual way. This part of eastern Alabama was the last to be ceded to the United States by the Creek Indians. This occurred just before the infamous "trail of tears," the great removal of the Indians by United States troops to reservations in the west.

Prior to this unglorious part of our nation's history, two brothers named Hurst (Methodist missionaries to the Indians) came to this area and built a church and a trading post. They were the first white men these Creek Indians had encountered who were honest and who tried to help them. The tribe met and approved a gift of land on which the church and trading post were located. They called the spot Free Donation. Through common usage the name gradually became shortened to Fredonia.

When these Creeks were forced to move to Oklahoma they named their new home Free Donation, to perpetuate the memory of the kind Hurst brothers. (Mrs. Hugh Smith, Station WBMK, West Point, Georgia)

FREEPORT, Pennsylvania
In Armstrong County, Freeport was laid out in 1796 as a free port for river craft, hence its name. (4)

FRENCH CAMP, California
First occupied in the year 1832 by Michael LaFramboise (the Frenchman for whom the camp was named), he established a camp for fur trading with the Indians. The camp soon became known as French Camp, or camp de los Frances, as the Spanish-speaking trappers and hunters called it. It was later abandoned as a hunting and trapping camp, but as it was already established as a spark of civilization in the wilderness, settlers located there and the name French Camp was retained. (2)

FRENCH CREEK, West Virginia
Settled in 1808 by Aaron Gould, the town was named for a local tradition that several Frenchmen panned for gold in the creek here, in 1725. (6)

FRENCH LICK, Indiana
Nearly 200 years ago when a trading post was established, these early settlers discovered that the deer, bear, and fox came to the springs to lick the waters and the wet rock. Pathways from every direction led to the springs, and one of the early white pioneers named it The Lick. Early in the nineteenth century, the French constructed a fort here for protection against the Indians, thus the name was changed to French Lick. (French Lick Sheraton Hotel).

FRIEND, Nebraska

The town was named for C. E. Friend, homesteader of a portion of the land which the city now occupies. He was instrumental in laying out the town site and donated lots for some of the public buildings. The town was originally called Friendville by the railroad construction crew, who reached the site in 1872. The name was later changed to Friend, still honoring the man who gave it such a friendly name. (2)

FRIENDLY, West Virginia

On the Ohio River, and the Ohio border, the village was named for Friend Cochran Williamson, grandson of Thomas Williamson, who settled here in 1785. (6)

FRIO TOWN, Texas

Frio Town, at the Presidio Crossing of the Frio River, witnessed a brief period as a "cowboy capital" and outpost cultural center of southwest Texas during the 1880's. The Presidio crossing at this point, a rendezvous along the approximate route of the Old San Antonio Road, was so named because of numerous cannon balls, swords, and sabers found there. Frio Town was founded in 1871. The last Indian foray occurred during the spring of 1877.

When the International-Great Northern Railroad missed the town, and a new town of Pearsall was established, a general exodus ensued during August, 1883. Most of the residents dismantled their farm buildings and carted them to the railroad. The population of Frio Town in 1945 was twenty. Frio is Spanish and means "cold," and so we have Cold Town, Texas. (3)

FROGMORE, Louisiana

Located between the Little Tensus and the Mississippi Rivers, in Concordia County, tradition has it that a member of a surveying party for the railroad suggested the name because the area had more frogs than he had ever seen, or, at night, ever heard. (6)

FRONT ROYAL, Virginia

In 1778, the town was incorporated as Front Royal, its intriguing name explained by the following tradition: "In Colonial days, a giant oak—the Royal tree of England—stood in the public square, where Chester and Main Streets now join. There on Muster days was drilled the local militia, composed of raw recruits slow to learn military commands and maneuvers. On one occasion, the sorely tried drill sergeant became so exasperated by the clumsy efforts of his troops and their failure to follow his commands that he hit upon a phrase all could understand and shouted: 'Front the Royal Oak!'

"Among the spectators was a Mr. Forsythe who had been a professional soldier, and was so amused by the sergeant's coined order that he and his friends found much sport in telling of the occurrence, repeating the order, 'Front the Royal Oak,' until the area became known as 'Front Royal.' " (2)

FRY, Texas

Fry, in western Brown County, near Coleman county line, was named for a Mr. Fry, who was very active in *oil.* (3)

FYFFE, Alabama

When the town requested a post office, it offered no suggestions as to a name. Some wag in the Post Office Department chose to call it Fyffe, perhaps because he thought it would go well with Drum, Kentucky, and perhaps because he wanted to complete the set. (1)

GAFFORDS CHAPEL, Texas

A Hopkins County church community, this town was named for Mr. Thomas M. Gafford, who deeded land for a church in 1881. (3)

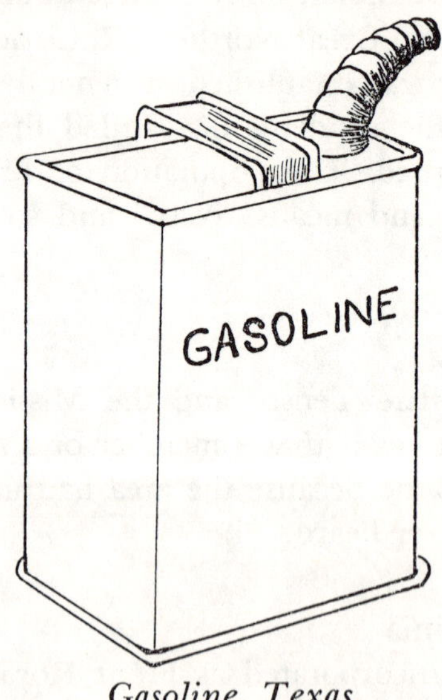

Gasoline, Texas

GASOLINE, Texas

In southeastern Briscoe County, Gasoline originated as a line-camp for cowboys of the early ranches in the area. Farming was introduced in the early 1900's; the early settlers hauling their supplies from Estelline or Plainview. A village developed in 1915, when a gasoline-operated gin was established at the site, and named Gasoline. (3)

GAY, Georgia

The town of Gay came by its name in 1887 when this town applied for a post office. Its name had been Sasserville until that time. It was named for William Sasser who was among the first in the area, in 1829. The Post Office Department refused the application since there was another town in the vicinity named Sasser. The congressman, from this district, was so informed. He knew the Sassers were the Gay's ancestors, and that the town very much wanted a post office so he submitted the name Gay for the town and post office, and it was granted. (1)

GAY HILL, Texas

On the Gulf, Colorado, and Santa Fe Railroad, Gay Hill was settled in the early 1830's and named in 1838 for Thomas Gay and W. C. Hill, both early settlers. (3)

GIBBON, Minnesota

Gibbon, located in Sibley County, Minnesota, was not named for the ape, but for General John Gibbon, who also gave his name to Gibbon, Nebraska. (1)

GIBBON, Nebraska

What is now the town of Gibbon was first named Gibbon Siding by the railroad in 1866; however it was not until 1871 that the first homestead colony settled here. It was named after General John Gibbon, a Westpoint graduate. He was an officer during the Civil War and was sent out here because of the Indian uprisings. He was also the officer in charge of the unit that rescued the survivors of the Seventh Cavalry and buried General Custer and his dead. (1)

GILA BEND, Arizona

Gila Bend is in Maricopa County, located on the Southern Pacific Railroad, about 65 miles southwest of Phoenix. The elevation is 736 feet. It was named for its proximity to the so-called "Great Bend" on the Gila River, which comes in from the north and resumes its westerly flow at this point. The Gila Bend of 1877–1880 was a well-known stage station on the river.

Gila Bend is surrounded by desert and mountains. In some places are fine stands of Saguaro, the giant cactus that takes 150 years to grow up. Other places are full of cholla (Choy-ya) with their silver fuzz of spines and ocotillo (oh co tee yo), like whips. They exist on about six inches of rain a year.

Nobody knows when the first travelers came through Gila Bend, but it was thousands of years ago. Then the Gila River flowed, a green and shady highway through the waterless desert. Archaeologists say Indians came up the peninsula of Baja California, along the Colorado until it joined the Gila, then up the Gila to the northern mountains. East-west trade and travel has also been documented by bits of Pacific Coast and Gulf of Mexico shell ornaments found here.

Father Eusebio Kino, great Spanish missionary, named an Indian settlement on the big bend of the Gila "Uparsoytas," about 1700. The village was still there when Captain de Anza and his colonists went through on the way from Tubac to California, in 1775. (2)

GILL, Texas

Ten miles south of Marshall in Harrison County, Gill was first known as *Terrapin Neck.* About 1894, L. H. Stephens petitioned for a post office and found that a shorter name was required. Because of its brevity he chose the name Gill for a ferry boatman who resided nearby. (3)

GINSITE, Texas

In southwestern Cottle County, Ginsite received its unusual name from the establishment of the Walling Gin in the early 1900's. (3)

GISELA, Arizona

Was taken from the heroine of a book, *The Countess Gisela.* (5)

GLENBAR, Arizona

Glenbar was named by a homesick Scotsman, for his home in Scotland. (5)

GLORY, Texas

Nick Ratliff's glowing description in 1880 of his store's surroundings resulted in the post office being called Glory rather than Richland as he had requested. (3)

GOFORTH, Texas

In eastern Hays County, Goforth was established in 1880, and named for J. T. Goforth, who went forth and became the first merchant here. (3)

GOLD, Texas

The community of Gold, in the eastern part of Gillespie County, was known as "Reingold" or "pure gold" in pioneer days because the earliest settlers, in the late 1840's, were surnamed Gold. Today the community is usually called the Gold Settlement. (3)

Goldenrod, Florida

GOLDENROD, Florida

One evening a discussion was held by the local citizens in the general store. The subject was the name of the town. First named Gabriel, it was later changed to Suburban Heights following a land boom. Now, the people thought it was time for another change because Suburban Heights was just too "high-falutin" a name for a small town so far out in the sticks. Several names were suggested and rejected until one offered the name Goldenrod for that majestic "stink weed," which was in full bloom everywhere at that time. For reasons known only to them, they adopted the name.

All this took place many years ago, when the town was small, and there was much vacant land in and about the town. Today the vacant land is fast disappearing and with it the namesake of the town, its Goldenrod. And Hay Fever reigns no more! (1)

GOLD HILL, North Carolina
In south-central Rowan County, Gold Hill is named for the hill upon which it is located. The hill at one time (1842) contained several gold mines. (6)

GOLD HILL, Oregon
Gold Hill is located in Jackson County, southwest Oregon. It is a pioneer product of those storied frontier days of the nostalgic 1860's when bold men struck for golden riches and the savage Rogue Indians made desperate war to save their land from the white invaders. The "Gold Hill Lode," a fabulous bonanza that yielded untold wealth was located just north of the present townsite and lent its name to this romantic Western town. Gold Hill may well be termed "The Heart of the Rogue River Valley." Snuggled securely and peacefully on the banks of the dashing Rogue, the town is encircled by the superb beauty of hills and tributary valleys, replete with tumbling creeks and evergreen forest bowers.

A short distance from Gold Hill is Table Rock, the curiously formed geologic formation rearing its precipitous walls from the valley floor. This sheer plateau was the reported setting for an all-out battle between the savage Rogue Indians and the white militia, and it is related that many of the Indian braves and their squaws chose death by leaping from the dizzy heights rather than face the dishonor of capture by the hated invaders. The Oregon Vortex, and the House of Mystery are also located here. (2)

GOLD RUN, California
Gold Run was a city carefully laid out in 1861, by an early developer O. W. Hollenbeck, who built a hotel, procured a post office, and christened the neophyte city, first Dixie, and then Gold Run for the small stream that ran nearby.

The town grew quickly and reached its heyday in 1870. The business section included nine saloons, a town hall, a church, the usual stores, a bank, express office, and livery stables. Residents erected what at that time was believed to be the tallest flagpole in the state of California—a claim later disputed by Iowa Hill. (1)

GOLIAD, Texas
Goliad, county seat of Goliad County and one of the three oldest municipalities in Texas, was the site of an Armana Indian village named Santa Dorotea when the mission Nuestra Senõra del Espírito Santo de Zuñiga and the presidio Nuestra Senõra de Loreto were moved there in 1749. The presidio was occupied by Spanish garrisons until the Mexican Revolution of 1810–1812. In 1812 the Gutiérrez-Magee Expedition temporarily occupied the settlement which was then known as La Bahia, the popular name of both the mission and the presidio.

In June, 1817, Henry Perry and his companions attempted to take the presidio, and in the resulting skirmish Perry committed suicide to escape capture. In 1821 James Long's forces made a brief stop at La Bahia. The congress of Coahuila and Texas declared the La Bahia presidio a town in 1829 and changed its name to Goliad, an anagram of (h) idalgo, for Father Francisco Hidalgo.

The post and its supplies were captured on October 12, 1835, by Texans under George M. Collinsworth and Ben Milam. On December 20, 1835, the citizens of Goliad met at the presidio to hear the reading of the Goliad Declaration of Independence. James Walker Fannin, Jr., who occupied the post in the spring of 1836, finally evacuated it on Sam Houston's orders, but Fannin and his men were brought back to the presidio as prisoners following the battle of Coleto and most of them were eventually killed in what is known as the "Goliad Massacre." (3)

GOLLY, Texas

Golly, in southern DeWitt County, was established as a school community in 1884 on land donated by Theresa Hubersberger and was named for Anton Golly, by golly! (3)

GOODNIGHT, Texas

On the edge of the Llano Estacado in northeastern Armstrong County, it was named for Charles Goodnight. He built a home there in 1876, when the total population of the county was thirty, all workers on the Goodnight Ranch.

A private herd of buffalo is maintained on the Goodnight Ranch for the preservation of the species. (3)

GOODYEARS BAR, California

Named for a long bar of land formed by a bend in the north fork of the Yuba River, and for Goodyear, the first settler of the town. He was a mountain man, miner, etc., and is said to have settled Ogden, Utah, before moving here. Goodyears Bar is located in colorful Sierra County. (1)

GORE, Oklahoma

The little town of Gore, situated one-half mile from the famous Arkansas River was once the homeland of many Cherokees, and other Indian tribes, sent here on the infamous "trail of tears." Many relics from old Indian days and Indian wars are to be found along the banks of the Arkansas, near here.

The town was first named Campbell for its founder, but later changed by the Oklahoma State Legislature at the request of the townspeople to honor Senator Thomas P. Gore, who, though totally blind, spent his lifetime fighting for his beloved Oklahoma, and for his Nation. (1)

GOUVERNEUR, New York

In northeastern New York State, in Saint Lawrence County, spread along the banks of the Oswegatchie River, whose name means "black water flowing out," in Indian parlance, the site of Gouverneur was purchased in 1798 by Gouverneur Morris. The village was settled in 1805, and named for the gouverneur. (6)

GOVERNMENT CAMP, Oregon

This area was formerly a camp on the old stagecoach road from The Dalles, over the Cascade Mountains to Oregon City. Traffic flowed over the old Barlow Road, which was a toll road developed by the Barlow brothers.

This village was named in 1849 when U. S. Cavalry troops were forced by deep snows to abandon their wagons and supplies here, and proceed to Oregon City by horse. From that time on the village became known as Government Camp. It is, however, Government Camp in name only, as it is an independent village with its own post office. (1)

GRAND BLANC, Michigan

Grand Blanc, located about eight miles from Flint, Michigan, was first settled by Antoine Campau and a giant of a fellow named Fisher, who established a trading post here for fur trading with the Indians. To the Indians, Fisher was known as "le Grande Blanc," which is French for "the big white." Because of their constant reference to the area as "Le Grand Blanc," the village that grew up here, around the trading post, took the name. (6)

GRAND ECORE, Louisiana

The name is French for "Large Bluff." It was so named for a cliff that overhangs the Red River, and reaches up into the sky for one hundred feet. (6)

GRAND MEADOW, Minnesota

The gently undulating meadow land with its absence of swamps, rocky hills and sand dunes, gave rise to a remark made by a gentleman in the early 1850's that this area was truly a "Grand Meadow."

His remark was destined to name the town that rose on this spot a few years later. (R. T. Hambleton, Grand Meadow, Minn.)

GRAND PORTAGE, Minnesota

The name was given by sixteenth and seventeenth century French explorers and fur traders to a nine-mile portage leading from Lake Superior to the navigable waters of the Pigeon River. "Grande Portage," as it was then called, was a vital link in the water highway of explorers searching for the

"Western Sea," and for the fur traders seeking the riches of the Canadian northwest. With the fall of New France, British fur traders continued to use the "Grande Portage" in their competitive venture with the Hudson's Bay Company. After the passing of the fur trade frontier, the importance of the old portage declined. It retained the name however, and it is after the portage that the Indian village of Grand Portage and Lake Superior's Grand Portage Bay are named. (Superintendent, U.S. Dept. of Interior, Nat'l Park Svc., Grand Portage Nat'l Monument, Grand Marais, Minn.)

GRAND RAPIDS, Minnesota
Grand Rapids, the Itasca County seat, is situated at an altitude of 1,290 feet. No wide spot in the road, Grand Rapids, Minnesota has a population of 8,500 (1965). Between 1870 and 1890 logging grew to major importance in the area near the present site of Grand Rapids. Around 1870 Warren Potter built a log store building on the site of Grand Rapids, thus forming the nucleus for the original settlement which took its name from the rapids on the Mississippi River.

The extension of the Duluth and Winnipeg Railroad to the village in 1890 caused such a stream of settlers that it was incorporated in 1891. When iron ore was discovered on the western Mesabi Range, ore prospectors hurried to the Grand Rapids region. Lumbering, though, continued to be the main industry. (2)

GRAND SALINE, Texas
Grand Saline, in northeastern Van Zandt County, is the site of one of the largest salt plants in the United States. Salt is produced from both mines and wells fed from salt beds extending over an area of some thirty square miles. Early discovery of the salt was made by the Cherokee, Caddo, and other Indian tribes who inhabited the area prior to 1839. The first settler in the vicinity was John Jordan, who in 1845 secured title to an acreage covering the salt deposits, blazed a trail from Nacogdoches and hauled two iron kettles to start a salt works. Later it was purchased by Samuel Q. Richardson, who tried to supply salt for the Confederate Army, but lack of transportation interfered. After the war the salt plant, then called the Grand Saline Company, gave land to the Texas and Pacific Railroad as its main line was extended through Van Zandt County. A new location, just west of Jordan's Saline, was established and named for the Salt Company. (3)

GRAPELAND, Texas
Located in northern Houston County, Grapeland was established in 1872, when the International-Great Northern Railroad built through the county

and was named for the prospective orchards and vineyards planned by its developers.

Located in an oil producing section, Grapeland has oil refineries and recycling plants as well as canning plants, cheese plants, and lumber mills. Not too many grape plants, though, and no winery. (3)

GRAVEL SWITCH, Kentucky
This town was named approximately 150 years ago. The L & N railroad was expanding their lines to the southeastern part of Kentucky for the purpose of hauling coal from the mountains. They needed gravel to make the bed for their road so they built a Switch and a spur line to the North Rolling Fork River to obtain gravel for the fills of their rail beds, and Gravel Switch had its beginning. (1)

GRAVITY, Iowa
Settled in 1881, the railroad came through this little unnamed village in 1882. An old settler named Sara Cox, who ran a boarding house for some of the railroad construction workers persuaded them to name the depot Gravity, because, for the moment, this little settlement had become the center of attraction in the area. The name was finally adopted by the town. (1)

GRAYBACK, Texas
Grayback was originally a line camp at the Grayback Crossing of Beaver Creek on the W. T. Waggoner ranch in southern Wilbarger County. Named for the grayback lice found there, the town was granted a post office in 1920, when an oil field was developed in the area. (3)

GRAYBURG, Texas
Grayburg, in southern Hardin County on the Beaumont, Sour Lake, and Western Railroad, was established in 1905 by the Thompson-Ford Lumber Company, which built a sawmill here. Because all of the buildings were painted gray, Dr. F. L. Thompson, company physician, suggested the name Grayburg. (3)

GREAT BEND, Pennsylvania
Founded in 1787 on the site of a Tuscarora Indian village, and named for its proximity to the deep curve in the Susquehanna's North Branch. (4)

GREAT CROSSINGS, Kentucky
Named because it lay in the old buffalo path that came from the central

part of Kentucky to the confluence of the Ohio River, and Elkhorn Creek. A fort was built here in 1783. (6)

GREENBRIER, Arkansas
When the early settlers came to this part of Arkansas and started clearing the forests for farms and home sites, they found many of the low, fertile pieces of land practically impenetrable, due to the many briars that grew luxuriantly everywhere. Some of the briars would climb trees twenty to thirty feet high. These briars were green all year long, even during the leafless winters. It was from these Greenbriers that the town took its name. (2)

GREENBUSH, Minnesota
On a high sandy ridge a grove of tall spruce trees rose above the surrounding terrain. The evergreens were visible for miles in this low, flat land, and the Indians knew of it as a good camp site. The Chippewa name for this landmark was translated into "Greenbush," by the white settlers. In 1897 a homesteader built his cabin close to the tall trees, and soon others followed. This was the beginning of the village of Greenbush.

When, in 1904, the Great Northern Railroad missed the town by three miles, she simply "lifted up her skirts" and moved to the railroad, carrying with her the name Greenbush. Elm, maple, white oak, Norway pine and spruce were planted, so that today the town is again worthy of the name Greenbush. (1)

GREENCASTLE, Pennsylvania
Established in 1782, by Colonel John Allison and named for his native town, a tiny seaport in County Donegal, Ireland. (4)

GREEN RIVER, Utah
Green River is located in a lush valley, first explored by Lt. Gunnison in the 1850's, and later by Major Powell in 1869 and in 1870. The valley is cut through by the Green River as it leaves Desolation Canyon. Drifting by the Ouray Indian Reservation the river forces its way into the valley. Greenish in appearance, the river is aptly named, as is the town which nestles along its banks.

The town was first named Blake for a pioneer settler who established a ferry here for crossing the river. Then, in 1883, the name was changed to Green River. A young man living here remarks that it was indeed fitting that the town should be named for the river. It was this river that first stopped the pioneers with its deep, rushing waters, and later fed them with its abundant fish. (Mrs. Hazel Ekker.)

GRIT, Texas

Six miles from Mason in Mason County, Grit is said to have derived its name from the gritty soil, and probably the perseverance of its early settlers. The post office was opened here on June 29, 1901. (3)

GROSSE TÊTE, Louisiana

Grosse Tête, in Iberville Parish, near Baton Rouge, means "large or big head" in French. Settled in the early 1830's, it was reputedly named for a rather large skull found here by French explorers. Since only the skull was uncovered, the owner was never identified as to its type. (6)

GROVER'S MILL, New Jersey

Grover's Mill, site of the earliest grist mill in the township, East Windsor, lies about a mile east of Princeton Junction. The territory is drained by Bear Brook, which joins the Millstone River on the north.

There was a small settlement here before the Revolution. The mill was thought to have been built and first operated by Jacob Bergen. Jacob's son, George, operated the mill during the Revolutionary War. At this time the Bergen family was living in the old Hyland house on Cranbury Neck Road on the hill just before crossing the Millstone River into Middlesex County. The Bergens and the Van Nests who settled along the Millstone were two of the oldest families in the area, coming from Holland about the middle of the seventeenth century. It was called Grover's Mill officially about 1859, when Joseph H. Grover became proprietor of the mill.

It was from Grover's Mill that the Martians and Orson Wells invaded the Earth from outer space (via radio) and caused a small nation-wide panic, at 8 P. M., October 30, 1938. NBC is still trying to forget that one! (2)

GRUENAU, Texas

Gruenau, a German farming communitny in northwestern DeWitt County, was opened for settlement in 1890 by Vachel Weldon, Sr. The grass covered prairie suggested the name which is German for "green meadow." Also, many of the early settlers had come from Gruenau, Oldenburg, Germany. The Gruenau Turn and Schuetzen Verein was organized in 1898. Athletic training classes and regular dances were held in the club hall. Each year a shooting contest with neighboring clubs is featured and the winner is proclaimed Schuetzen Koenig, or king of the riflemen. In 1948 the Gruenau Club celebrated its golden jubilee. (3)

GRULLA, Texas

On the Rio Grande in southeastern Starr County, Grulla was formerly a Mexican settlement extending along both sides of the river. The town takes its name from the Spanish word for crane, cranes being common on the lake near the town. (3)

GUASTI, California
First known as South Cucamonga, in 1900 Secondo Guasti came to the area, acquired land and planted grape vines, establishing the largest vineyard in the world. There are over five thousand acres, known as the Italian Vineyard. The name of South Cucamonga was changed to Guasti in honor of Secondo Guasti. (2)

GUIDE ROCK, Nebraska
The first white settlement here along the Republican River was established by Colonel Rankin and four companions. They built a log shelter near the river in May 1870 to store their supplies and assure a good water supply. In the following months more settlers arrived and they erected a stockade for protection against marauding Indians.

South, on the other side of the Republican River, is a high rocky bluff easily seen for miles across the open prairie. This bluff was used as a "guide" by the Indians and trappers, so the new settlers decided to call their stockade-settlement Guide Rock. From this beginning came the present-day town of Guide Rock, Nebraska. (1)

GUNLOCK, Utah
Gunlock was a wide spot in the valley along the Santa Clara River, and a favorite camping spot for travelers along the old "Spanish Trail" to California in the early days of the west.

William Hamblin was a guide for parties traveling along this trail, and being an expert hunter and gunsmith he was called "Gunlock Bill." He liked this little spot and decided to settle here and, with three other families, the town was born, and named Gunlock in honor of Gunlock Bill Hamblin. The year was 1857. (1)

GUNSIGHT, Texas
Gunsight, in southern Stephens County, was named for the nearby Gunsight Mountains and was established as a village about 1879. The Gunsight Mountains have an average elevation of 1,550 feet. The range was named because it runs "as straight as a gun barrel," and has a projecting peak which the early settlers said represented the gunsight. (3)

GUNTOWN, Mississippi
Not as romantic as the name would indicate, it was named for one James Gunn. A Tory, he emigrated from the Carolinas to the Territory of

Gunsight, Texas

Mississippi, which was loyal to the King of England, and was still considered Indian territory. He found the rebellious colonies a little too dangerous for a Tory, and apparently had no stomach for fighting on either side. Here, legend has it, he was taken in by the Indians, and eventually married an Indian Princess, and lived happily ever after. (1)

HACIENDA, Texas
Hacienda, in southwestern Uvalde County, was named for the ranch home of J. T. Hall when it became a post office on the Texas and New Orleans Railroad. (3)

HACIENDITA, Texas
On the Rio Grande in northwestern Presidio County, Haciendita has the Spanish name for "little farm." (3)

HACKBERRY, Texas
Located in Edward County, on the Nueces River, Hackberry was named for nearby Hackberry Canyon and Creek. The area was held by Indians until about 1875 and was then settled by ranchers in the late 1880's. Indian caves in the vicinity have been excavated by scientists since 1920. Both the canyon and creek were named for the abundance of Hackberry trees in the vicinity. (3)

HALFWAY, Kentucky
The town received its name in the early days of our young country, when

it was selected as a "half-way point" for changing horses on the mail route from Bowling Green to Scottsville, Kentucky. (1)

HALFWAY, Texas
Located in Hale County, Halfway became a community center in 1909 when a school was established. It was named because of its location at a point halfway between two county seats, Olton and Plainview. (3)

HAPPY, Kentucky
When a post office was established here the new postmaster was asked to submit a list of desired names. "Happy" was one of the names submitted and was selected by the Post Office Department. The postmaster said he submitted Happy because the people here are always happy. (1)

HAPPY, Texas
Happy, near the northern boundary of Swisher County on the Santa Fe Railroad, derived its name from the fact that it was a "Happy Hunting Ground," because of the water in nearby Happy Draw. (3)

HAPPY JACK, Arizona
Happy Jack was originally known as *Onion Flat,* and later it became known as *Yellow Jacket.* In 1947, Roland Rotty, Timber Management Staffman at the time, and subsequently Forest Supervisor, changed the name to Happy Jack. Happy Jack was a local character who lived on a Ranger District, which Johnson believes was in Wyoming. Rotty worked at this District before he came to the Coconino Forest. Happy Jack is now a logging community and a Ranger Station Headquarters and has been so since approximately 1947. (Forest Supervisor, U.S. Dept. of Agriculture, Coconino Nat'l Forest, Flagstaff, Arizona)

HAPPY JACK, Louisiana
Happy Jack is in Plaquemines Parish, which occupies a neck of land extending out into the Gulf of Mexico, below New Orleans. The land is split down the middle by the Mississippi, on its last leg to the Gulf.

The hamlet takes its name from a small country store that was called "Happy Jack's" and was located in this vicinity. (2)

HARMONY, California
The name Harmony paradoxically grew out of a feud between two families over trespassing. Made up entirely of dairy farmers, one family had to pass over the land of another to reach a country road. A quarrel ensued, and later exploded into a killing feud. To settle the dispute the road was changed to another location.

Years later, when a school was built the road had to be changed again, and it required the cooperation of all the families in the area. When they named the school they called it Harmony, for the harmonious accord finally reached among them. The village eventually grew around the same name, and Harmony has ruled supreme ever since. (1)

HARMONY, Minnesota
Originally located on the old Briggs and Walker Stage Line, it was called Greenfield. About 1870 a narrow gauge railroad came through the area, ½ mile north of the village. The settlers decided to re-locate the village there, and give it a more permanent name. At a village meeting, for the purpose of deciding a new name, the discussion became rather heated. The chairman rapped for order and is reputed to have said, "Gentlemen! Let's have harmony at this meeting." From this chance remark, the people had the name they had been seeking, Harmony. (1)

HARMONY, Pennsylvania
Harmony was the original settlement of the Harmonites, a religious sect that owned all things in common, and believed that the end of the world was at hand. Many of the original homes and historical spots erected by these early settlers may be seen today. And one of the first charcoal blast furnaces to operate in Western Pennsylvania still stands as a monument to the origin of the steel industry in this nation. (2)

HASTY, Colorado
Hasty, Colorado, located in Bent County, was settled around 1910, and named not for its speed or hurried pace but for a settler named Doc. Hasty. In the southeastern part of Colorado, Hasty is only two miles from the large John Martin Reservoir. (1)

HAT CREEK, Wyoming
Is located in central Niobrara County, in eastern Wyoming. The stream Hat Creek is located in the western part of Nebraska, and flows into the Cheyenne River. During the gold rush days the Army sent a detachment to establish a Fort on Hat Creek, but due to unfamiliar terrain they made a slight mistake and set up the Fort on Sage Creek, in eastern Wyoming, and named it Fort Hat Creek. The fort was built, complete with an underground tunnel to a spring. Of the soldiers stationed here, many were remittance men from England, younger sons of English Peers.

Eventually a settlement grew up near the fort, due to its offer of protection against marauding Indians. The first post office was opened March 4,

1884, with John Storrie the first postmaster. The village and the post office took the name Hat Creek, from the fort. For years it was a telegraph and stage station, and one of the first post offices north of Cheyenne, Wyoming.

Although there is a rather large rock southwest of the old fort location named Hat Rock, the village in eastern Wyoming got its name from a creek that flows in western Nebraska. (1)

HAZEL GREEN, Alabama
Hazel Green was named by the wife of its first postmaster, Robert Erwin. They gave her the privilege, and as there were a number of hazel bushes in the vicinity, she called it "Hazel Green." (6)

Hell, Michigan

HELL, Michigan
Back in 1841 whiskey stills were operated here on the banks of a small stream. This notorious place soon became known as Hell and the stream became Hell Creek. Some years later a dam was placed here and the beautiful meandering Hi-Landlake was formed. (2)

HEMATITE, Missouri

Platted in 1861 by Stephen Osburn, the name of the town is the chemical name for iron oxide. Lead and limestone were quarried here, but there is no record that iron was. One possible source of the name could be the railroad that hauled the limestone to St. Louis. The railroad was known as the Iron Mountain Railroad before it was changed to the Missouri Pacific. The depot could have been named Hematite for the "Iron" in the railroad's name. (2)

HEREFORD, Texas

County seat and principal town of Deaf Smith County, Hereford is near the southeast corner of the county on the Panhandle and Santa Fe Railroad. Buffalo Lake, once headquarters of the X I T Ranch, is east of Hereford, and Tierra Blanca Creek runs one mile south. Artesian water in unlimited quantities made Hereford the center of an irrigated farm district. Called "the town without a toothache" because of the fluorine and iodides in the soil, Hereford is the shipping point, educational center, and distribution point for the county.

The first general store (1898) was operated by N. E. Gass; an early postmaster and later judge in the county was Clarence Smith. When the county was organized in 1890, the town had already been named for the herds of Hereford cattle near it. Hereford cattle, a breed which originated in Herefordshire, West England, before 1788, have been instrumental in the disappearance of the Longhorn and the evolution of the high-grade Texas beef herds. (3)

HEREFORD, Pennsylvania

On the Perkiomen River junction, in Berks County, Hereford was settled by German Schwenkfelders in 1732, but named for Herefordshire, in West England. (4)

HESPERIDES, Florida

A small village in Polk County, surrounded by citrus groves, it is said to have been named for the nymph Hesperides. The nymphs, variously given as from three to seven, were said to guard, with the aid of a fierce serpent, a garden at the western extremity of the world. Here grew golden apples, the wedding gift of Gaea to Hera. The garden was sought by Hercules as one of his twelve labors. (6)

HICKORY, Pennsylvania

Is named for Hickory Tavern, a fanciful name given by a party of early road builders to a "hickory tree" at one of their temporary camp sites. (4)

HICO, Texas
In Hamilton County, Hico was named by its founder, Dr. J. R. Alford, for Indians in the area and was originally located on Honey Creek several miles south of the present site. (3)

HIGH ISLAND, Texas
High Island is on Bolivar Peninsula on the extreme eastern tip of Galveston Island. It is on a salt dome, and named for the fact that its elevation of forty-seven feet is the highest point between Point Bolivar and Sabine Pass. During Gulf storms people of the peninsula often seek refuge at the spot. In addition to serving as a supply point for High Island oil field, the village is a collection point for muskrat hides. (3)

HIGHLAND HOME, Alabama
Highland Home was so named because it is the highest point between Birmingham and the Florida coast. People settled here from the surrounding low lands because they felt it had a much healthier climate. (1)

HIGH POINT, North Carolina
Originally settled in 1750 by Quakers, it was named High Point in 1853 because it was the highest point of the railroad between Goldsboro and Charlotte.

HIGHSPIRE, Pennsylvania
Settled in 1775, it is said to have gotten its name from the old church spire there that served as a landmark for Susquehannah River boatmen. (4)

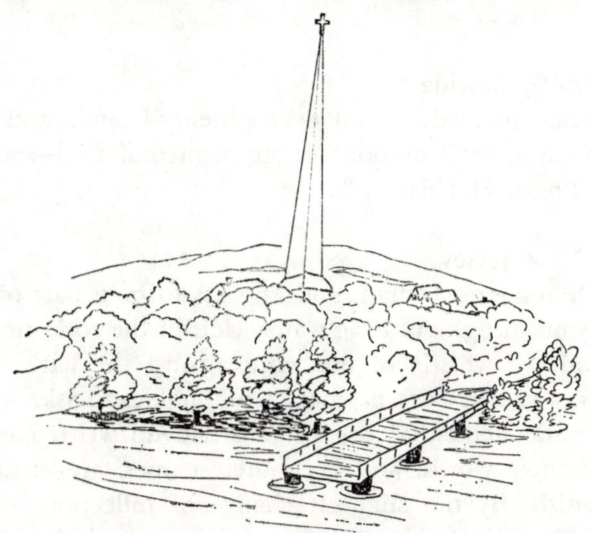

Highspire, Pennsylvania

Hi Hat, Kentucky

HI HAT, Kentucky
Coal mining is the chief industry here. When Hi Hat was named the leading coal company was the Hi Hat Elkhorn Mining Company, producers of high grade or top grade coal. The president of the company petitioned Congress for a post office, later, and asked that it be named Hi Hat. Its name was adopted by the village. (1)

HISSOP, Alabama
This town was founded almost 100 years ago and named for Hyssop, a plant mentioned in the Bible. It is an aromatic labiate herb. Why this town was named for it or why the difference in spelling is anybody's guess. (1)

HOG PEN POND, Florida
Years ago livestock roamed at will over unfenced lands and roads. They were usually given a small amount of supplemental feed—sound familiar? (See Cow Pen Pond, Florida) (2)

HO-HO-KUS, New Jersey
The name is Chihohokies Indian, and appears to be a part of their name. There are many meanings: running water, cleft in the rock, under the rock, hollow rock, and the whistle of the wind against the bark of trees. You can take your pick as there are no more Chihohokies to ask.

It must be understood that the Indians had no written language, and the spellings of their words, and even their names, are entirely English, French, or Spanish. By the slightest change of inflection or by a small gesture an Indian word or phrase could take on an entirely different meaning. Three different people asking an Indian for the definition of an Indian word might receive three different replies. All because they pronounced it slightly different or made some slight gesture that changed its significance. (Ho-Ho-Kus Public Library.)

HOKENDAUQUA, Pennsylvania
The town was named for a small creek which empties into the Lehigh River on the east side, about a half mile above the town. The name is said to be Delaware Indian, a compound of "Hockin," (the first land), and "Dochwe," (searching for). It is said that an Indian village named Hockyondocquay was located on the creek.

The town was established and named by the Thomas Iron Company in 1854. (1)

HOLLIDAY, Texas
In northern Archer County on the Wichita Valley Railroad, Holliday was founded about 1889 and named for nearby Holliday Creek, which was named for John Holliday. Peter Gallagher's diary of the Texas-Santa Fe Expedition records that Holliday carved his name on a tree at the creek.

Fossil remains in the vicinity of Holliday have attracted scientific expeditions which have found vertebrae of ancient amphibians and evidences of reptiles, mastodons, and giant insects.

Near the town is one of the largest Karakul sheep ranches in the United States. (3)

HOLLIDAYBURG, Pennsylvania
Was founded in 1768 by Adam and William Holliday, Irish immigrants, at a time when Indians were still fighting white invasion. (4)

HOLLYTREE, Alabama
Hollytree, in northeastern Alabama, lies almost in the center of Paint Rock Valley, which is split down the middle by a fat little river, the Paint Rock.

The village takes its name from a large grove of Hollytrees, which grew on a nearby hillside. Sad to say, only one tree is left to remind the village of its namesake.

Interesting to note, the post office has been located in the general store for almost a hundred years. The store building was moved once by Ox teams and the post office and the store never stopped operating. (1)

HOMESTEAD, Pennsylvania
Originally was an Amity Homestead and so named. It was renamed and incorporated as a borough in 1880. (4)

HONEYDEW, California
There is a creek flowing into the Mattole River, and the Mattole River flows through here. In the old days the creek was unnamed, and it was during this period that a party of pioneers was traveling through the country. They camped overnight under a grove of Cottonwood trees, beside the creek. In the morning the campers found themselves and their bedding covered with a sweet, sticky substance that had dripped off the blossoms of the trees. It looked, tasted, and smelled like honey, so they called it Honeydew, and the stream was named Honeydew Creek, for the honey that fell in the night like the dew. When a town and post office grew here it was called Honeydew. (1)

HONEY ISLAND, Texas
Honey Island on a high hammock in the fork of Big and Little Cypress Creeks in northwestern Hardin County, was so named because of the number of bee trees found there by the Jayhawkers, who hid in the Big Thicket during the Civil War. (3)

HONEY SPRINGS, Texas
A rural community in central Dallas County, this town is said to have been named for wild bees which early settlers found around some springs in the vicinity. The springs were known to explorers and prospective settlers as early as 1840. (3)

HONOLULU, Hawaii
Statehood bills for Hawaii were introduced into Congress beginning in 1922. For various reasons, Congress was reluctant to make Hawaii a state, one being the fact that it is not contiguous to the continental United States. After the admission of Alaska, the objections seemed to carry less weight. A constitution had been drafted in 1950 and approved that year and again in 1959.

The statehood act was passed by the U. S. Senate on March 11, 1959, passed by the House on the following day, and signed by the President on March 18, 1959 (73 Stat. 4). The President's proclamation admitting Hawaii as the 50th State was signed on August 21, 1959.

The population of Hawaii according to the 1960 census is 632,772. It is interesting to note that of this number, 203,455 are classed as Japanese, 114,405 as Hawaiian, 69,070 as Filipino and 38,197 as Chinese. All these groups have U. S. citizenship.

"Hono" means a valley with a bay in front of it, "lulu" means "sheltered." Thus the name Honolulu is variously translated as "fair haven," "quiet harbor," or "sheltered harbor." Its main beach is named

Honolulu, Hawaii

Waikiki, "Wai," meaning "water," and "kiki," meaning "to spurt," or "spurting water."

Honolulu has been the capital city of the Hawaiian Islands since February, 1845, when King Kamehameha III made it his permanent residence. Prior to this, Kailua in Kona, Hawaii, and Lahiana, Maui, as well as Honolulu had been the residence of the rulers. Present day Honolulu is the capital of our 50th state, Hawaii. (Public Archives, Iolani Palace Grounds, Miss Agnes C. Conrad; State Archivist & Geological Survey Bulletin 1212, U.S. Dept. of Interior.)

HOOLEYAN, Texas
Located in northwestern Hardeman County is also spelled Hooley Ann, and is said to have been named for two members of a pioneer family. It was established in the late 1890's. (3)

HOPATCONG. New Jersey
The name "Hopatcong" or "Huppakong," as it was originally called, is an Indian name given to the lake by the Lenni-Lenape Indians—the first residents here. The name means "honey waters from many streams." The town took its name from the Lake, and is located in Sussex County. (1)

HOP BOTTOM, Pennsylvania
Founded in 1787 and named for the abundance of wild hops that once grew along the banks of Hop Bottom Creek. (4)

HOPE, Arizona

Sprung from the breasts of merchants moving to a new highway alignment. (5)

HOPE, Arkansas

The county seat of Hempstead County, founded in 1852, Hope is 120 miles southwest of Little Rock, 215 miles northeast of Dallas, 300 miles northeast of Houston, 80 miles north of Shreveport and 30 miles from Texarkana. With these directions you might "hope" to locate it with ease.

The name "hope" was given the town in honor of Hope Loughborough, daughter of the Cairo and Fulton Railroad Land Commissioner, who drafted the original plat of the town. (2)

HOPE, Texas

Located in Lavaca County six miles from Yoakum, Hope was named for Hope's Trading Post, established before the Texas Revolution. Germans settled in 1836 and organized a Methodist church in 1837. The first schoolhouse built of logs in 1857 had high steps to keep wild hogs out of the building. Of *one hundred* volunteers from the Hope community serving in the Confederate Army, *ninety-three* were killed!

In 1870 lumber was hauled by ox wagon from old Powder Horn, or Indianola, to construct a new church, which was maliciously burned before it was finished. (3)

HOPE HULL, Alabama

Received its name from Abner McGehee, a prominent citizen and large land owner, who named it for Hope Hull, a Methodist Minister. Hull rode circuit throughout Georgia and parts of Virginia in the late 1700's.

Hope Hull, once an isolated community, is now located only four miles from the city limits of Montgomery, Alabama, and this large city is moving in its direction at a fast pace. Someday Hope Hull, Alabama may be only a memory. (1)

HOPOCA, Mississippi

Settled in 1832 on the site of an old Choctaw Indian Village, the name means "final gathering," and was probably just that to the Choctaws. (6)

HORN HILL, Texas

A farm community in central Limestone County, Horn Hill was named for its location on a hill curved like a ram's horn. The settlement dates from the 1850's. (3)

HORSE CAVE, Kentucky
So named because the Cherokee Indians used a nearby cave as a corral for stolen horses. It is located near Mammouth Onyx Cave, in Hart County. (6)

HORSE CREEK, Wyoming
Horse Creek, the village, took its name from nearby Horse Creek. The Indians and early settlers called it Horse Creek due to the large number of wild horses that watered here.

Horses were not indigenous to America, but were brought here by the Spanish, and many were abandoned when the Spanish Conquistadors departed. They bred and flourished here in the New World. It was from these wild horses that the American Indian got his transportation. (1)

HORSEHEADS, New York
In 1779 General Sullivan with some five thousand soldiers set out to crush the power of the Iroquois Nation, to burn their settlements, and especially to destroy the abundant crops which had helped sustain the British army.

After the battle of August 29, 1779, the Indians and Tories fled northward through this valley with Sullivan at their heels. He had destroyed some forty Indian towns, and most of the agriculture in the area. It was the rainy season and there was a very big swamp in his path.

It was here in this valley that a large number of General Sullivan's horses died from falls, and starvation due to the lack of forage. The number is said to have been close to one hundred. The animals were not buried so their bones lie for many years, bleaching in the sun.

The superstitious Indians arranged the horse heads in a row along the trail, and legend says pioneer children used to step from one horse's skull to another.

Ever afterward the Indians called this "The Valley of the Horse Heads." The white settlers adopted the Indian name and called their little settlement in the valley Horseheads, New York.

When Sullivan's army reached Fort Reed there was a grand celebration at which thirteen toasts were drunk. One of them was of particular interest to the future citizens of Horseheads:

"May the enemies of America be metamorphosed into pack horses and sent on a westward expedition against the Indians." (2)

HORSESHOE, North Carolina
It was named for the horse shoe bend in the French Broad River, west of the village, and is located in Henderson County, in western North Carolina. (1)

HORSE SHOE RUN, West Virginia
The town of Horse Shoe Run was named for the headwaters of a small stream called Horse Shoe Run, and lies in Preston County. (1)

HOSTYN, Texas
A Fayette County Catholic community, which was settled in the early 1840's. Originally part of a section of the county known as the Bluffs, the area was later called Moravan. The present name means "friendly host," in the Czechoslovakian language. The Hostyn community is unique in several respects. It was part of the diocese of Father Michael Muldoon; it was the first Czechoslovakian settlement in Texas (1850), and it organized the K. J. T., a Bohemian Roman Catholic Benevolent Union, which was still functioning. A beautiful grotto in connection with the Catholic church is a favorite shrine for the performance of Czechoslovakian weddings. The Sokol Society meets annually at Hostyn. (3)

HOUMA, Louisiana
Seat of Terrebonne Parish, Houma lies in that part of Louisiana that reaches into the Gulf. It was settled around 1800, and named for the Houma Indians who once made this area their home. (6)

HOWEY-IN-THE-HILLS, Florida
Founded in 1916 by W. J. Howey, whose name it bears, it is located in Lake County, Florida. There is a shortage of hills in Florida yet some of the land can be described as undulating. (6)

HUNDRED, West Virginia
In Wetzel County, near the Pennsylvania line, the town was named for Henry Church, an early settler, who died in 1860 at the age of 109. He was affectionately known as "Old Hundred." (6)

HUNGRY HORSE, Montana
The legend of Hungry Horse: "Two husky freight horses, Tex and Jerry, working in the rugged wilderness of Flathead River's South Fork area, wandered away from their sleigh during the severe winter of 1900-01. After struggling for a month in belly-deep snow, they were found almost starved and so weak considerable care and feeding were required before they were strong enough to be led back to civilization. The name Hungry Horse was given to a mountain, a lake, and a creek in the vicinity of where the incident occurred, and later to the dam and town."

They named a dam, a lake, a city
in memory of, but not for pity—

Hungry Horse, Montana

that hungry horse lost months that winter,
The snow was deep, the cold was bitter.
The rescue came complete with halter
for that horse prone to falter.
He lived to shed six winter coats
and eat ten tons of hay and oats—Len Eriksen, Pres. CofC

HUNLOCKCREEK, Pennsylvania
Is named for the coal-blackened stream that splits it into a number of sections. (4)

HYAMPOM, California
Hyampom, located in Trinity County, California, gets its name from the Indian word *Hiam-pom. "Pom"* means valley, and legend has it that the expression *"Hiam"* means something like "come on in, we have plenty," thus we have "Valley of Plenty," for short.

Located in a valley with fish, deer, good soil, tall timber, and plenty of water, this name would seem to fit quite well. (1)

HYPOLUXO, Florida
Located in Palm Beach County, on the Atlantic Ocean, it was settled in 1873, and has an Indian name meaning "round mound." Part of the village is built on a nearby island. (6)

IAGO, Texas
Located in eastern Whaton County, Iago was established when the Cane Belt Railroad (later the Gulf, Colorado, and Santa Fe) built through the area in 1900. M. D. Taylor, operator of the general store, is said to have named the railroad station and the post office for the Shakespearean character Iago, who was somewhat of a stinker. (3)

IANTHA, Missouri
Local legend has it that in 1875, when the railroad was building its track through this part of the country, there was a pretty Indian girl who hung around the construction camp, associating with the crew. When it became evident that she was going to have a papoose, railroad officials asked her who was responsible. Her only reply was "I and they," as she pointed to the crew.

When they left they named the depot IANTHA, Missouri. (1)

IDALOU, Texas
Idalou, on the South Plains and Santa Fe Railroad in Lubbock County, was laid out in 1911, and named for Ida and Lou Bassett, daughters of Julian M. Bassett. (3)

IDEAL, Georgia
Once called Joetown, for its founder Joe C. Tarrer, it was re-named Ideal by the AB & C Railroad, when they came through here. They thought it an ideal place for a town. (2)

IDLEYLD PARK, Oregon
Idleyld Park, Oregon, was so named by a far-sighted grocer from Roseburg, Earl Vosburgh, who built a small store and a few rough cabins on the bank of the North Umpqua River in the early 1920's. The fishing was good, the scenery beautiful, with a waterfall nearby, and he thought it would be a good place to "idle-a-while," so he named the place Idleyld Park, pronounced "Idle Wild."

The population of the village is around 100. (1)

IGO, California
Mining operations in the late 1850's so undermined the small town of Piety Hill that it was decided to lay out a new town about a half-mile west. Mr. George McPherson, the Mine Superintendent, had a small son, and each day as he started to work on the new town, the little fellow would cry, "Daddy, I Go? I Go?" He finally decided to name the new town IGO, to perpetuate the memory of this. (6)

ILLMO, Missouri
Illmo had its beginning in 1904, and was called Wippervill's Hollow. When a new name was chosen, the settlers used the abbreviations of the states of Illinois and Missouri to form "Illmo." (1)

IMMOKALEE, Florida
In 1869 this town was called Gopher Ridge. Located in Collier County on the edge of the Corkscrew Swamp Sanctuary, the surrounding region is practically uninhabited, and is one of the best hunting grounds in the state. The name is Indian and means "tumbling water." (6)

IMNAHA, Oregon
In 1865 a group of government surveyors came into this lovely valley, deep in canyon country, on the course of a river which flowed into the Snake. It was here that the Nez Perce, under the leadership of Chief Joseph, spent their winters sheltered from the snow and cold. Occasionally they would cross into the territory of Idaho.

During the course of their explorations the surveyors came across a band of Indians led by a chief named Imna. As was the custom in those days, the surveyors adopted his name, adding "ha," and bestowed it upon the canyon country, and the river. The entire name is thought to mean "The land where the Imna dwell," although an accurate translation is not available.

The village of Imnaha is located in Wallowa County, and takes its name from its location at the confluence of the Imnaha and the Snake Rivers. The area where Imnha is located is sparsely settled, and is used primarily as a winter feeding ground for livestock. (1)

INDIAN CREEK, Texas
In southern Brown County, Indian Creek is said to have been named because of frequent fights between Indians and early settlers on a creek near the townsite. A post office was established in Francis Harris' General Store on September 11, 1876. (3)

INDIAN FIELDS, Kentucky
This was once an Indian village named Eskippakithiki, and considered the commercial center and capital of what the Indians called "Kentakee," which is Iroquois for "meadowland." It is believed that from this evolved the name Kentucky.

Indian Fields is located in a valley in the eastern part of Clark County. The valley is drained by the Lubdgee and Upper Howards Creek, and once was covered with forest land.

At one time all Indian trails led to and from Eskippakithiki. One came from the south from Shanoak, a Shawnee town opposite the mouth of the Scioto; another went to Big Bone Lick, forking there to Louisville and Shanoak; another led to Big Sandy, and finally to Ohio. The original village was once burned by hostile Shawnees. Daniel Boone and Stewart, while hunting near Indian Fields in 1769, were captured by the Indians. General Marquis Calmers, a Revolutionary War hero, made a patent at Indian Fields for three thousand acres and while making a survey of his land he met an Indian in the woods. Both were frightened and fled in opposite directions. This was the last Indian seen at Indian Fields—the year was 1774.

Indian Fields got its name because of the agricultural nature of the Indians who live there. They tilled the soil, and grew corn. When the white settlers finally took over the townsite, evidence of the Indians' farming efforts were so apparent that the settlers called their new town Indian Fields. (1)

INDIAN GAP, Texas

Indian Gap is located between the points of two small mountains in the western part of Hamilton County, Texas. This was the ancient home of a group of Comanche Indians, because the hunting here was good. The first white settlers located here around the early 1870's. The first postmaster was Hawley Gerrells. (Isabel Mitchell, great grand daughter of Hawley Gerrells)

Indian Head, Maryland

INDIAN HEAD, Maryland

This legend old, so oft' re-told cannot be proven true.
I do believe it; you may not, but I'll tell the tale to you.

Long years before the white man came to this country's jagged coast;
Algonquin Indians roamed this land; their princess was their boast.
The princess fair, with long black hair, knew of her father's plan
to join together two old tribes, by offering her hand.
To the prince of the great Piscataway, whose father was the king.
Of five great tribes which gathered here, and then, that fateful spring.
An Indian Brave, not prince or king, came from Virginia shore;
he paddled here, devoid of fear, this shoreline to explore.
He saw the Indian princess, and within their youthful hearts,
love sprang to life like a growing thing; that's how love sometime starts.
The proud old chief, her father, demanded love to cease,
and bade the boy depart at once, but growing things increase.
The brave returned to Maryland shore, in the dark of a moonless night;
their plans were set between them to escape before dawn's light.
But the best laid plans of mice or men are apt to go awry,
and fate ordained that, on this night, the Indian boy would die.
When he landed, eager and silent, expecting to find her there,
he found instead her father's guards, and his heart knew stark despair.
They cut his head from his body; mounted it on a spear,
and stuck the spear in the sandy shore to warn those far and near.
They meant it for a message to other Indian braves,
who dared to trespass Maryland land in canoes from 'over the waves.'
The day that followed this dreadful crime, white settlers landed here;
the first raw sight to meet their eyes was the head on the bloody spear.
So Indian Head the town became; It is the same today;
born of love and Indian war; thus legend has its say.
Believe or not, my legend-tale; old times claim it's true.
Algonquin voices from the past would verify it too.—Dorothy Beecher Artes

INGLESIDE, Texas
In San Patricio County, Ingleside was established prior to the Civil War and was named the Gaelic word meaning "fireside." (3)

INK, Arkansas
The name formerly being Quito, in applying for a post office, the people filled out the application in pencil and it was returned with a notation, by the Post Office Department, to "fill it out in ink." Therefore when filling it out again they wrote in "Ink." (1)

INTERCOURSE, Pennsylvania
In Lancaster County, Intercourse was originally called Cross Keys for a log tavern dating from 1754. It was renamed in 1813 because of its location on a prosperous crossroads. (4)

Ink, Arkansas

IONE, California
Ione, Amador County, California, settled in 1848, had many names such as *Dead Dog, Freeze-Out,* and *Bedbug,* and one of the early-day residents wasn't too happy about it. Reading a classic one day entitled *The Last Days of Pompeii* he came across the name of the heroine, Ione. He liked the sound of it. Certainly it was a better name than *Dead Dog, Freeze-Out* and *Bedbug,* so he took it upon himself to change the name to Ione, and Ione it has remained. (2)

IONE, Oregon
E. G. Sperry built a trading post here on the banks of Willow Creek sometime in 1883 to serve settlers raising wheat and cattle in the area. They named the Morrow County community Ione for Ione Arthurs, the first white child to be born here. (1)

IOWA COLONY, Texas
On the Gulf, Colorado and Santa Fe Railroad in northern Brazoria County,

Ione, California

Iowa Colony was founded in 1908 by the Immigration Land Company of Des Moines, Iowa, and named accordingly. (3)

IOWA PARK, Texas
In central Wichita County, Iowa Park was known as Daggett's Switch when it became the temporary terminus of the Fort Worth and Denver Railroad in 1888. The townsite, located in an eighty-acre tract granted in 1885 to G. M. Dodge as surveyor for the railroad, was sold in 1891 to D. C. Kolp of Iowa, who brought settlers from Iowa to the area. The town was incorporated on July 3, 1891 and is named Iowa Park in honor of its Iowa settlers. (3)

IRAAN, Texas
In eastern Pecos County, Iraan became a town in 1928, when oil was discovered on the large ranch owned by Ira G. Yates. The name of the new townsite, chosen in a contest for which a choice lot was the prize, combines the names of the owners, Ira and Ann Yates. (3)

IRON JUNCTION, Minnesota

The village of Iron Junction got its name from the large amount of iron ore which was shipped through here from the great Mesabi Range. It is a child of the Duluth and Mesabi Iron Range Railroad. This is a rail junction for shipment to Duluth and Two Harbors, Minnesota. Although the village is named Iron Junction, it is served by a post office with the singular name of Iron. (1)

IRON MOUNTAIN, Missouri

Iron Mountain was a settlement before the Louisiana purchase, although no record exists as to when the name was given to the village. The name comes from a mountain, which was believed, at one time, to be composed of solid iron. The mines, as a whole, have long since "petered out," and what little mining done here now is expected to end quite soon. (1)

IRONOSA, Texas

A San Augustine County farming community, Ironosa was settled by Lewis Holloway and a man named Ward about 1800. Its name is derived from its location near the mouth of Arnosa Creek. The Spanish name, meaning "Sandy," was corrupted by Anglo-American settlers to Ironosa and Ironore. (3)

IRONTON, Missouri

The town gets its name from the county, of which it is the county seat. Since mining of iron was the main industry of the county, the name is obvious. It is located about 10 miles below Iron Mountain. The town was platted when the county of Iron was organized in 1857. (2)

IRRIGON, Oregon

Irrigon, formerly called Stokes, was founded at a railroad siding seven miles west of the Umatilla River in the later 1800's. In 1905 the name was changed to Irrigon because of the extensive irrigation project that was being constructed. It was incorporated as a city in 1956.

Irrigon is located in the northeast portion of Morrow County. It has very little rain in the summer and in the winter very little snow, so irrigation is a prime factor in the economy. (2)

ISHPEMING, Michigan

The Ojibwa or Chippewa Indians were terribly frightened of the Lake Superior area; therefore, they never settled permanently in this area. They believed the area around Ishpeming and Negaunee to be bewitched. The Indian, in his own tongue, referred to this area as "Ishpeming," meaning "up above" or "higher up." Since Ishpeming is actually higher in elevation than the twin city of Negaunee (meaning low), and is surrounded by hills, the name Ishpeming was adopted. Ishpeming is located in Marquette County. (2)

ISLAMORADA, Florida
Located on Upper Matecumbe Key (a Spanish name "Mata Hombre," meaning "kill man") the name is Spanish and means "purple island."

The area was once the home of the Calusa Indians, who were quite violent, and gave the Spanish and the early American settlers a hard time before they were driven out. (6)

ISLAND POND, Vermont
Island Pond, located in Essex County, derives its name from the lake that borders it. The lake, known as "Island Pond," is two miles long and about one-and-a-half miles wide, with a two-acre island in the center–hence the name.

The name was first adopted by the post office to avoid confusion with the many towns in the United States named Brighton, and is now in every day use by its residents. However, the official name, as used by the state and on legal documents, is still Brighton. (2)

ISLE LA MOTTE, Vermont
This island was granted to Captain LaMotte by the French Government for services rendered. It appeared on all old maps, both French and English as "Isle La Motte."

When the island was finally settled in 1789 by the English, they changed the name to Vingard, but everyone continued to call it "Isle La Motte." After a time, the English gave up, and changed the name back to "Isle La Motte."

Though the island was named for Captain LaMotte, an English translation of the entire name would be "Island of the Lump." (1)

ISRAEL, Texas
Is an unusual religious community in Polk County, founded in 1895 by a sect called Israelites. They settled a trace covering 144 acres and built a church which they named the New House of Israel. They constructed the church in the center of the land, which they deeded to the "Lord God of Israel, Creator of Heaven and Earth." It is duly recorded in this manner in the Polk County courthouse.

Members of the sect wear their hair long; live by agricultural pursuits, and are strict vegetarians. In 1909 there were approximately seventy-five members living in the community. (3)

ITALY, Texas
In southern Ellis County, on the Missouri, Kansas, and Texas Railroad, Italy was originally known as Houston Creek because Sam Houston was supposed to have camped there. That name was rejected by the Post Office Department in 1879, and Gabriel J. Penn submitted the name of "Italy," because the climatic conditions corresponded to "Sunny Italy." This name was accepted on March 24, 1880. (3)

ITTA BENA, Mississippi
Located in Leflore County, the name of this town of about 2,000 is Indian for "home in the woods." (6)

JACKASS FLATS, Nevada
While Jackass Flats is not exactly a town, it has a population of about 1700. The post office here serves only the Nuclear Rocket Development Station.

Jackass Flats was named for the herds of wild jackasses that once roamed the area, and is bordered by Skull and Shoshone Mountains, the

Jack Ass Town, Louisiana

Calico Hills, and 40 Mile Canyon, which pioneers used as a trail crossing the desert to California. (Space Nuclear Propulsion Office, Nevada Extension, Nuclear Rocket Development Sta., Jackass Flats, Nev.)

JACK ASS TOWN, Louisiana
Located in colorful Plaquemines Parish, Louisiana, it derived its *unusual* name from a local politician (apparently a loser) who dubbed the people in this hamlet jackasses. (2)

JACKSON HOLE, Wyoming
"Jackson's Hole" was the name given to this beautiful valley, under the Teton Mountains, in the early 1800's. It was the favorite hunting grounds of David E. Jackson, one of the historic group of venturesome mountainmen who broke the first wilderness trails, trapped beaver in western waters and trekked miles to barter and trade with Indians and fur buyers at their famous yearly rendezvous.

It is guarded on all sides by mountains: the Tetons on the West, the Yellowstone on the north, the Absarkas on the northeast, the Mount Leidy Highlands on the east, the Gros Ventres on the southeast and the Hoback on the south.

The first settlers came in 1883 and it became a cattle center. Jackson Hole has provided rich material for Western stories dealing with those wild and lawless days of horse thieves and rustlers.

Alas, for such a romantic name, it has been shortened and is now known as Jackson, Wyoming. (2)

JALAPA, South Carolina
Named for a Mexican city where several soldiers from this area died fighting in the Mexican Border War. (6)

JANE LEW, West Virginia
In the extreme north central part of Lewis County, it was named for Jane Lewis, mother of Lewis Maxwell, founder of the town, in 1835. (6)

JELLICO, Tennessee
Straddling the Kentucky-Tennessee border in Campbell County, the town was first settled in 1795, and called Smithburg for a number of citizens by that name. History has it that the intended name, when it was incorporated, was Jerrico, but either the name was mis-read, or submitted in bad handwriting, because the name Jellico was the one adopted. (6)

JIGGER, Louisiana
When, in 1933, this small village had grown to sufficient size to petition for

a post office, they were required to submit a list of suggested names for the post office and the town. At a meeting in the general store, many names of historical significance, names of old settlers, etc., were added to the growing list. The son of the owner of the store, and the new postmaster, age five and called Jigger because of his small size, cried out "Daddy, name it for me!" Without much thought given to the matter, and more in jest than in seriousness, they added the name Jigger to the bottom of the list.

That wag in the Post Office Department picked this name, and Jigger, Louisiana was born. (1)

JOB, Kentucky
The post office here was named for the patience of Job. Probably because it took a lot of patience to get a post office for such a small place. (1)

JULIETTE, Georgia
Juliette is located in Monroe County, and the Ocmulgee flows nearby. When the railroad came through this small village in 1882 it received it's Shakespearian name from a railroad official who chose to dub it in honor of his wife, Juliette. (Miss Virginia Williams)

JUSTICEBURG, Texas
Justiceburg, in southeastern Garza County on the south branch of the Double Mountain Fork of the Brazos River and the Pecos and Northern Texas Railroad, became a trading point on the J. D. Justice Ranch about 1907. It was a station on the railroad about 1910, and a post office in 1914. A little poetry gives a clue to its name:

Justiceburg – A good place to live, this one little spot
Just stop and consider the things we've got.
You always find Justice, Duckworths, Cash too.
Forrest and Wood, Bevers, but few
Cobbs, so there's corn, a Miller to stay.
Reed and nice Kropps, Cornetts that won't play.
Find a Cross here, but don't be deceived
We also have a Blacklock, and two sets of Keys,
(And Smithy runs the PO.) (1)

KAHOKA, Missouri
Platted in 1856, the original name of the town was Cahokia, however it was changed to Kahoka with the coming of the post office. This to avoid confusion with Cahokia, Illinois.

The name Cahokia is said to be of Indian derivation, and comes from the Gawkie Indians (Known as the "Lean Ones") who gave us the expression "Gawky." The word Cahokia is translated as "Hill People." (2)

KALAMAZOO, Michigan
Kee-Kalamazoo was the name the Indians gave the river, in which they discovered hundreds of bubbling springs. The names mean "where the water boils in the pot," according to tradition.

The first permanent settler established a trading post here and called it after himself. His name was Titus Bronson, the year was 1829, and he called his establishment and the resulting settlement "Bronson." He was a big, hard-drinking, and outspoken man, whose taste for liquor was not shared by the other townspeople.

In 1836, he was overruled and the name of the settlement was officially changed to "Kalamazoo." They used only part of the river name, but it has remained Kalamazoo ever since. (2)

KAMAY, Texas
In southwestern Wichita County, Kamay was first called Kemp City when it became the site of the Kemp, Munger, and Allen Oil Field in 1919. A post office was requested in 1938, but the Post Office Department refused to accept either the name Kemp City, or K. M. A., so they compromised on Kamay. (3)

KANARANZI, Minnesota
The village of Kanaranzi, the township of Kanaranzi, and a nearby creek all got their names from an early Indian chief, who lived in this area during the 1870's. The Indian name is reputed to mean "crazy woman."

When the white settlers began to flock in, and after a few skirmishes with the Indians, the Indians moved on to the area near Spirit Lake, Iowa. (1)

KANSAS SETTLEMENT, Arizona
This village was colonized by a group of Midwestern settlers. (5)

KARNACK, Texas
In northeastern Harrison County, on the Louisiana and Arkansas Railroad, Karnack is adjacent to The Caddo State Park. The village was named Karnack because it was the same distance from Port Caddo, the northeastern port of entry of the old Republic of Texas, as was Karnack, in Egypt, from Thebes. (3)

KATEMCY, Texas
In northern Mason County, this village is supposedly named for an Indian Chief Katumse, with whom John O. Meuseback is thought to have negotiated a treaty. (You can't get any vaguer than that!)

Settled about 1880, the village had a population of one hundred in 1890 when the post office was established. (3)

KAWKAWLIN, Michigan
A Michigan hamlet, spawned of the days of lumber and lumber kings, the name is Indian for "pickerel," and comes from the Kawkawlin River. (6)

KEEWATIN, Minnesota
It is located in eastern Itasca County, at an altitude of 1,505 feet. Keewatin, which has always been mainly a mining community, was founded when iron ore exploration in the area began. In 1904 large deposits of iron ore were discovered near the present site.

The community took its name from the Objibway word "Giwadin," which means "north" or north wind." (2)

KENOVA, West Virginia
Settled in 1889 its name is the combination of the abbreviations of the states of Kentucky, Ohio, and Virginia, and is located on the border of all three (almost). (6)

KEOKUK, Iowa
The site of Keokuk was known by the early fur traders and other river men as "Foot of the Lower Rapids," while the Indians called it "Puck-e-she-tuck," meaning "Foot of the Rapids."

In 1820 a former Army surgeon, with his Sauk Indian wife, built a log cabin and settled here in the wilderness, at the confluence of the Des Moines and Mississippi Rivers. He was joined later on by others who established a wood yard and lightering service here in 1828 for the steamboats plying the rivers. Next came the American Fur Company, establishing a trading post and a row of houses known as *"Rat Row."*

On July 4, 1829, a group of river men celebrating the glorious Fourth, aboard Captain Culver's steamboat *Missouri,* suggested that the settlement be named Keokuk, in honor of Chief Keokuk, a Sauk Indian, who was friendly with the white settlers.

Years later, his remains were brought back to the city and are interred in Rand Park beneath the stone pedestal and statue erected in his honor.

In the period when the power and influence of the American Indian was rapidly declining, they developed few notable leaders. Most of these were War Chiefs for a lost cause. An outstanding exception was Keokuk, wise courageous leader of the Sauk (Sac) and Fox tribes. Translated into English, Keokuk means "Watchful Fox," an excellent description of the wily rival to the more famous Black Hawk for control of their people.

Keokuk was a rare exception to most of the great chiefs of Indian history because he sought justice for his people through wisdom and oratory . . . and through friendship with the white man, fully recognizing the futility of opposing the United States government, unfair though it may have been in too many instances. (2)

KEOSAUQUA, Iowa

Keosauqua, one of Iowa's older towns, is located on the horseshoe bend of the Des Moines River, in the southeast corner of the state. Located in the center of historic Van Buren County, the town was platted in 1839, by John Carnes, James Hall, James & Edwin Manning, John J. Fairman and Robert Taylor who comprised the "Van Buren Company."

Keosauqua, which was first called Van Buren, and neighboring Des Moines, which is now part of Keosauqua (Not *the* Des Moines), were great rivals in 1838. Both hoped to become the county seat which was to be moved from Farmington. It was finally agreed to unite the towns under the name Keosauqua. At the election on September 10, 1838, Keosauqua was chosen as the new county seat.

The first post office here was established as "Port Oro" (Spanish for "Golden Port") on January 24, 1838. The town was then a part of the Wisconsin Territory. Later, in Iowa territorial days, the post office name was changed to Keosauqua. Keosauqua was incorporated as a city under the general act of the territorial legislature on February 17, 1842.

"Keosauqua!" That's what the Indians called this section after they discovered a number of French Monks dwelling on the bend of the river. *Keosauqua,* "Land of the Monks." (2)

KICKAPOO, Texas

Kickapoo, in western Polk County near the Kickapoo Creek, was named for a remnant of the Kickapoo tribe who settled in the area in the early 1800's. (3)

KILL BUCK, New York

This entire area was once Indian territory, and a large part of it is still occupied by them and known as the Allegheny Reservation.

Kill Buck is located at the confluence of the Allegheny River and Great Valley Creek, which placed it on a well-traveled Indian waterway. The first permanent white settlement in the town of Great Valley (Cattaraugus County), was made by James Green, at Kill Buck in 1812. Kill Buck is a hamlet located in the town of Great Valley. James Green came here in 1812 from New Hampshire and erected a saw-mill, and later an inn.

On the present site of Kill Buck once stood an Indian village of the Seneca nation. The largest tribe of the Iroquois Confederacy of Northern American Indians in western New York, the Senecas were conspicuous for their part in Indian war south and west of Lake Erie.

In the center of this village, on the banks of the Allegheny River, stood the wigwam of Chief Daniel Kill Buck, who was to have his name perpetuated in memory with the naming of Kill Buck, New York. (2)

KILL DEVIL HILLS, North Carolina
In Dare County, this town is located on a narrow strip of land that extends from lower Virginia down, encircling Albermarle and Pamlico Sounds, along the North Carolina coast. It is located halfway between Kitty Hawk and Nags Head.

To the early Dutch settlers a "kill" was a channel, creek, or stream (in this case a channel), and devil was the name for a ridge of land or a small hill (in this case a ridge of land). Thus the strip here developed the name "Kill Devil Hills."

Local legend has it that the name really came from a brand of rum said to be so potent that it could *"kill the Devil."* (6)

KINDERHOOK, New York
Kinderhook is Dutch and means "the children's corner." The name was applied to this locality by Hendrick Hudson, impressed by the many Indian children who had assembled on one of the bluffs along the Hudson River to see his strange vessel, *Half Moon.*

The expression "O.K" was said to have originated with President Martin Van Buren, eighth President of the United States, whose home, Lindenwald, is located here. He is supposed to have used the expression "Everything is Old Kinderhook," which was eventually shortened to O. K. (1)

KING GEORGE, Virginia
King George, Virginia, is the seat of King George County, from whence it takes its name. King George County was named for King George I, and was formed in 1720 from Stafford and Richmond counties. The present boundary lines were surveyed in 1778, and faces on the Potomac and Rapahannock Rivers. (2)

KING OF PRUSSIA, Pennsylvania
Was named for the King of Prussia Inn, which the first proprietor, a native of Prussia, named for the Brandenburg prince, who in 1701 transformed Prussia from a duchy into a kingdom, taking the title of King Frederick I. (4)

KING WILLIAM, Virginia
King William is the county seat of King William County, Virginia. The county was formed from King and Queen County, in 1702, and named for King William, then king of England. (2)

KIOMATIA, Texas
On a bend of Red River in northwestern Red River County, Kiomatia was included in Arkansas Territory when Claiborne Wright settled at Pecan Point on the north side of the river in 1816. After Wright's death his sons crossed the river to settle at Jonesboro and Kiomatia.

A post office granted to Travis George Wright in 1850 was named for the Kiomatia River, called "clear water" by the Indians. (3)

KITTANNING, Pennsylvania
Is Indian for "place of the great river," and stretches along the eastern bank of the clear placid Allegheny. (4)

KITTITAS, Washington
Kittitas, located in Kittitas County, in central Washington, takes its name from the Indian word meaning "grey gravel bank." (2)

KITTY HAWK, North Carolina
Local legend has it that it was named for the swarms of mosquito hawks which once lived here. The name most likely came from the Indian name Chickahauk, which appeared on maps as old as 1729. (*See* Kill Devil Hills). (6)

KLICKITAT, Washington
On the Klickitat River, near the Oregon line, the town gets its name from the Klickitat Tribe of Indians. (2)

KLONDIKE, Arizona
Prospectors returning from the Alaskan gold rush brought back the name Klondike. (5)

KLONDIKE, Texas
On the Texas and New Orleans Railroad in western Delta County, Klondike was settled in the middle 1890's when the Texas Midland Railroad built through the area, and was named for the Alaskan town, then much in the news. (3)

KNIFE RIVER, Minnesota
The name in Chippewa language was "Mokomani-Zibi," which translates

into English as "sharp stones standing on edge in the river bed." That's quite a mouthful for such a short remark. From this long phrase the name was shortened to Knife River.

When the treaty of LaPointe was signed in the fall of 1854, the entire north shore was opened to settlement. The village of Knife River was settled by copper prospectors, but in that era lumber was the real king, and from the late 1880's to the early 1900's Knife River became a prosperous logging center.

Today the busy hustle and bustle has gone, and the prime business at hand is tourists who flock here by the thousands to watch the annual smelt run every spring. (The old timer, KDAL, TV Channel) (1)

KNOB NOSTER, Missouri
Is Latin for "our knobs." Two rather prominent hills lie just to the north of the town. They were used as guides for westward travelers in pioneer days. These hills were believed to be Indian burial mounds. The town moved one mile south of the pioneer trail, with the coming of the railroad about 1860. (1)

KOKOMO, Indiana
County seat of Howard County, Kokomo was founded and named by David Foster, a native of Virginia, who moved his family to a high spot just north of Wildcat Creek in 1842. Ko Ko Mo, which means "black walnut," was a Miami Indian chief of disputed reputation. Some historians record him as a brave, distinguished and honorable war chief, while others claim this as unfounded and untrue; at any rate, soon after the new town was given his name he died, and was buried somewhere within the present limits of his namesake. (2)

KOSHKONONG, Missouri
Koshkonong is an Indian word meaning "wild rice," and was bestowed on this small Missouri settlement by R. R. Hammond, in 1880. He took the name from a lake named Koshkonong, in Wisconsin. (1)

KOSSUTH, Mississippi
In west central Alcorn County, on a mail route from Corinth, it was settled around 1840 and first called New Hope. In 1852 the name was changed to honor Louis Kossuth, an exiled patriot of Hungary, who opposed the unification of Austria and Hungary into the Austro-Hungarian Empire. (6)

KYOTE, Texas
Kyote is a rural community of stockmen and small farmers in Atascosa

County. The name was probably derived from a species of the prairie wolf or coyote which was once numerous in this section. (3)

LA CASA, Texas
In southeast Stephens County, La Casa was established when James C. Bargsley built a log cabin near the site in 1880. The name means "the house," in Spanish. (3)

LACKAWAXEN, Pennsylvania
Is Indian for "swift waters" or "for where the way forks." It was founded in 1770, and lies on the Delaware at the mouth of the Lackawaxen Creek. (4)

LA CRESCENT, Minnesota
Settled around 1851, its name is interesting because it was coined from the Mohammedan Flag Emblem. Rivalry with the town of La Crosse, Wisconsin, was very strong, and the settlers believed, though mistakenly, that La Crosse was named for the emblem of the Crusades, therefore they took their name in reprisal. (6)

LA CRESCENTA, California
In the early 1800's a Dr. Briggs, from Crawfordville, Indiana, came here intending to build a health resort. He purchased a large acreage in the northwestern part of La Canada Rancho from Colonel A. W. William and Dr. J. L. Lanteman.

From the site, Dr. Briggs chose for his home, he had a clear view of the entire valley. From here he saw a series of three crescents. At the foot of the San Rafael hills on the southeast was one; at the Verdugo hills on the southwest was another; and on the north a very large crescent at the foot of the Sierra Madre range. Because of the impressive view he chose the name "La Crescenta" for his home. This name was later adopted by the community that grew and flourished here. La Crescenta is known as "The Balcony of Southern California." (2)

LA CYGNE, Kansas
The town takes its name from the river which flows nearby. The story of the naming of the river was told to W. A. Mitchell, author of *Linn County, Kansas — A History,* by John Roubidoux, head chief of the Miami tribe. It is an Indian legend based in part on a pathetic chapter in American history. The story is authoritatively given as follows:

In 1756 the British carried away bodily the French people in the settlement of Grand Pré (Big Meadow) in Acadia, a colony since peopled by English and called Nova Scotia. It is a tragedy of such great pathos and beauty that it was used by Longfellow as the theme of his poem

La Cygne, Kansas

Evangeline. The heroine being a real character in life who came into the western country in search of her lover, Gabriel Lejeunesse, who with others of the Acadian village had been carried to the shores of Louisiana on the Gulf Coast.

She, bewildered and wondering, set out through the Canadian wilderness, past Quebec, on to Pierre Marquette and down the lakes and the Illinois River, to the Mississippi, up the Missouri to the Osage. It was here that the legend of "Le Marais des Cygnes" begins.

According to the Osage a romance grew and blossomed between a young war chief of the tribe of the prairie, named Coman, and Osa, a princess, and granddaughter of White Hair. He maintained that the hard life of the prairie was not for his granddaughter, who was a child of the forests, and of a land of plenty.

Defying the wishes of the old chief, the two lovers climbed into a canoe on the river and set out. Suddenly some angry thing below seized the boat and drew it downward out of sight. In a flash the two lovers disappeared. As the people watched in horror, two great swans appeared on the place and swam away through the now peaceful waters, under a canopy of vines and wild rice.

From that day forth the place has been referred to as "C'est le Marais de cygnes," French, meaning "It is the marsh of the swans."

From this legend the French explorers named the river "Le Marais des Cygnes," and the town that grew up along its banks became La Cygne. (2)

LA JOYA, Texas
Was named for a nearby lake called "the Jewell" by Mexican ranchers who occupied the area as early as 1774. Located in Hildago County the site became a station and post office on the St. Louis, Brownsville, and Mexico Railroad in 1904. (3)

LAHASKA, Pennsylvania
Is Indian for "great mountain," and was founded in 1725. (4)

LAMESA, Texas
On Sulphur Springs Creek, in central Dawson County, Lamesa was named Chicago when it was established as county seat early in 1905. When the post office was granted on March 20, 1905, the name was changed to Lamesa, from the Spanish description of the flat tableland on which it is situated. (3)

LANGTRY, Texas
The first family to settle in this part of Val Verde County was the Torres, in the early 1870's. The village that finally resulted was named Eagle Nest because of a rather large eagle's nest located in a canyon nearby.

In 1883 the eastern division and the western division of the Southern Pacific Railroad were completed, joined, and the silver spike driven at the end-of-the-track town of Vinegaroon. Vinegaroon was some 15 miles east of the present Langtry where the Pecos River runs into the Rio Grande.

After the completion of the railroad, Eagle Nest began to grow, and

Langtry, Texas

the name was changed to Langtry in honor of a construction engineering foreman on the railroad.

Judge Roy Bean (known as "The only law west of the Pecos"), who was a justice of peace, moved his headquarters from Vinegaroon to Langtry in 1885. He later had a letter written by W. H. Dodd to Mrs. Lillie Langtry, informing her that *he* had named the town for *her*.

Lillie Langtry, known as "The Jersey Lilly," was an English actress who was enjoying great fame at that time. The judge admired her from her pictures in the Police Gazette and thought it would be a complement to her if she thought the town was named for her.

Judge Roy Bean found his place in history in his administration of "justice," from his saloon in Langtry, which he promptly dubbed "The Jersey Lilly." This "hall of justice" still stands and is maintained for its historical significance.

The Judge was short on formal education and long on temper. Some of the judicial decisions he handed down during his tenure in office are classics. Tradition has it that, when a dead cowboy was brought into the Jersey Lilly and searched, twenty dollars was found. The Judge promptly fined him twenty dollars for disturbing the peace, and pocketed the money.

He was succeeded in 1903 by Mr. W. H. Dodd, a friend, who was considerably more learned and less short tempered. (W. H. Dodd, Langtry, Texas)

L'ANSE, Michigan
Located on Keweenaw Bay, in Baraga County, L'Anse is a French name and means "the cove." The town was once a camp site for French explorers, trappers, and missionaries on their way West. (6)

LARIAT, Texas
In southwestern Parmer County on the X I T Ranch, Lariat became a stop on the Pecos and Northern Railroad in 1913. It was named by W. H. Simpson, passenger agent for the road, in honor of the lariat, then in use by the ranch hands. (3)

LAS TIENDAS, Texas
Las Tiendas is a Latin American ranching settlement in western Webb County, and the name is Spanish meaning "the shops." (3)

LAS VEGAS, New Mexico
The first Spanish explorers, who came through this area of New Mexico, during the early 1800's, found a spring, many groves of trees, and grassy meadows in this valley, and named it "The Meadows," or Las Vegas. Las Vegas is located in San Miguel County. (2)

LATEXO, Texas
On the International, Great Northern Railroad in north central Houston County, Latexo was originally called Stark's Switch. Established in 1872 as a shipping point for cotton, lumber, and truck crops, the village was named for the Louisiana and Texas Orchard Company. (3)

LAUREL BLOOMERY, Tennessee
This town was first called Ward, for John Ward who operated a forge or furnace here. The town is located where Laurel and Gentry Creeks come together. Laurel Creek was so named for the profusion of mountain laurel that grows here.

When the post office was established February 13, 1878, it was named Laurel Bloomery, Laurel for both the creek and the mountain laurel, and Bloomery (which means forge or furnace) for the one that was in operation here. (1)

LAWN, Texas
Lawn, on the Pecos and Northern Texas Railroad, originally centered around a school and church known as Oak Lawn from a grove of oak trees. The Post Office Department shortened the name to Lawn, as part of its crusade for short, curt names. (3)

LAZBUDDIE, Texas
On Running Water Creek in Parmer County, Lazbuddie was settled in 1904 and named by combining the nicknames of D. L. "Laz" Green and A. "Buddie" Shirley, ranchers in the area in the early 1900's. (3)

LEADVILLE, Colorado
Leadville is located at the breathtaking altitude of 10,200 feet, and was primarily a mining community and famous as such. The Leadville Lake County Area has produced nearly 400 million dollars in gold, silver, lead, and zinc.

Reminders of Leadville's wild and wooly past are here. The legend of Horace, Augusta and Baby Doe Tabor are still fascinating. A dominant part of the legend is the Tabor Opera House, constructed in 1879, and acclaimed at that time as the finest opera house between Chicago and the West Coast. High on Fryer Hill is the Little Johny gold mine, which J. J. Brown partly owned and was the basis of the Brown fortune. His wife, Margaret Tobin Brown, now is immortalized as the "Unsinkable Molly Brown," by book and movies.

The town was incorporated in February 1878, and by 1879 known as the world's most famous mining camp. The name Leadville was given to the town for its lead producing mines, although Goldville or Silver City would have seemed more appropriate. (2)

LEBANON, Tennessee
Located in Wilson County, this city is abundantly rich in Cedar Trees, and because of them it was named for the Biblical Lebanon, which was also noted for its Cedars. (6)

LEEPER, Pennsylvania
A mining and farming village named for a lumberman who owned most of the land here. (4)

LEE'S SUMMIT, Missouri
Settlers came to what is now known as Lee's Summit during the 20 years prior to the Civil War, migrating from the middle Eastern States, mostly Kentucky. The original settlers liked the high, gently-rolling land with rich soil for their farm houses, and the town of Strother was born October 28, 1865.

November 4, 1868, the town of Strother was incorporated and renamed Lee's Summit, for Doctor Pleasant Lea, the town's physician. He was shot and killed during the Civil War near the present site of the Missouri Pacific Depot. The Summit portion of the name was used since the site 1,050 feet above sea level, is the highest point on the railroad between Omaha and St. Louis. When the railroad established a depot there, it is said to have used a boxcar for want of anything better. On the side they painted the name "Lee's Summit." The name was misspelled and was never corrected. (2)

LIBERTY, South Carolina
One time it was called *Salubrity,* but changed its name in 1776 to Liberty. This in honor of the ringing of the Liberty Bell in Philadelphia, which broke while announcing the winning of freedom from the British. (6)

LIBERTY, Texas
It received its name in the early 1800's. The Villa de la Santisima Trinidad de la Libertad was the original name of this community. Through the years it has been shortened to Liberty. The community was visited in 1690 by Alonso de León, and a mission was established nearby a few years later. The Atascosito Road connected with the Trinity River at this point. Since the Trinity River was navigable and the Atascosito road carried some traffic this community grew as a transportation and trading center for the area. (2)

LIBERTY HILL, Connecticut
First called *Paunch Hill,* it was renamed in 1831, when a liberty pole was raised here. (6)

LIBERTY HILL, Texas
Liberty Hill, Williamson County, on the Texas and New Orleans Railroad, was founded in 1854 by the Reverend W. O. Spence at a site about three miles north of the present town. According to J. Gordon Bryson, in his book *Culture of the Shin Oak Ridge Folk,* the naming of Liberty Hill came about when General Thomas Jefferson Rusk, of the Army of Texas, camped in the Shin Oak Ridge area in 1853, with a company of Rangers going to Fort Grogan (Burnet). The camp was near the home of the Reverend Spence, who invited the General to dinner. After the meal he mentioned to the general that there was no post office between Burnet and Austin, a distance of more than sixty miles. The general just happened to be on the Post Office Committee, and immediately wrote out an order for a post office for the Reverend Spence. "What shall its name be?" he asked. Spence replied that the people living around there were peaceful, liberty-loving folk. "I live on a hill," he continued, "Let's call it Liberty Hill." Thus it was that a post office named Liberty Hill was born in 1853, and the town in 1854. (J. Gordon Bryson.)

LICKING, Missouri
Settled around 1878, Licking took its name from a natural deer lick, which was located within one-quarter mile east of the town, and was alive with deer. Here hunters waited in prey. Therefore, the place became known as The Lick, and later was changed to Licking.

Licking is located in Texas County, named for the state of Texas, while the county seat, Houston, was named to commemorate Sam Houston's victory at San Jacinto. (2)

LIGHT STREET, Pennsylvania
The Reverend Marmaduke Pearce, a Methodist Clergyman, came to the area about 1844 and established a mill. He soon discovered the walk to the nearest settlement post office was a bit too far for his own liking. Being an industrious sort of a man, he applied for his own post office, and when the request was granted, he named it for a street he had lived on in Baltimore, Maryland, named Light.

Shortly thereafter, as both settlements grew, they merged into one long village and took the name Light Street. (1)

LINEVILLE, Iowa
The town of Lineville, Wayne County, is situated on the Iowa-Missouri line, hence its name. It was started as a village sometime in the early 1840's, and was first named Grand River, although the nearest river is some thirteen miles away, and operated a post office under that name in 1851. The coming of the railroad in 1871 boosted the economy, and changed the name to Lineville. (2)

LINN FLAT, Texas
Linn Flat, an agricultural community in northeastern Nacogdoches County, was founded in 1851 and was the scene of the Linn Flat Raid in the carpet bagger days following the Civil War. (3)

LIPAN, Texas
Lipan, in northwest corner of Hood County, was laid out by T. A. Burns in 1873 at the crossing of the Granbury and Palo Pinto roads.

Named for a Texas Indian tribe, the village had strong lodges of Masons and Odd Fellows in the early days. (3)

LITTLE AMERICA, Wyoming
Even though there is a post office located here, Little America is not an incorporated town. Holdings Little America is a travel center, service station, restaurant and motel, located in the desert of southwestern Wyoming, in Sweetwater County. The post office serves the settlers in the area.

The legend of Little America goes thusly: "Away back in the '90's, when I was a youngster and herding sheep in this dreary section of

Little America, Wyoming

Wyoming, I became lost in a raging Northeast blizzard and was forced to 'lay out' all night at the place where Little America now stands. That long January night in that terrible storm, with a fifty mile wind and the temperature about 40 below. . . . "

Thus it was that Holdings Little America had the seed of its beginning. It was named Little America, because it reminded Holdings of pictures he saw of Admiral Byrd's expedition to Antarctica—the two places were equally desolate.

As those who have sought refuge here during some of the bad winter storms will agree, this is an oasis in the bleak wilderness. Just as recently as September 16–17, 1965, when a freak snow storm hit, Little America slept stranded people on the dining room floor because every bed was filled and they couldn't travel any farther. (2)

LITTLE CHICAGO, Texas
Little Chicago, a German farm community in northwestern DeWitt County seven miles north of Yorktown, was started in 1890, when George Langley opened a store named "Little Chicago," to serve the community. (3)

LITTLE ST. LOUIS, Texas
Little St. Louis, a DeWitt County community a mile north of Yorktown, began when Fred Gerrert opened a dance hall by that name. The amusement hall has long since faded into the past, but the little community lives on. (3)

LLANO, Texas
Llano, county seat of Llano County was settled about 1855. During the first year the pioneers had their clothes stolen by Indians, but by 1860 there were stores, a hotel, and plenty of saloons, but no churches. Llano was the center of the mining boom of the 1880's and had a population of seven thousand in 1890. A railroad terminal, it became the distributing point for a large territory. The name comes from the Llano River, and is Spanish meaning "Plain." (3)

LOAFER'S GLORY, North Carolina
Local legend has it that a hard-working woman took one long, hard look at the local male population of this little community, sitting around gabbing and whittling, and remarked, "This place must be Loafer's Glory!" The name stuck. (6)

LOBO, Texas
Lobo, in southwestern Culberson County on the Southern Pacific Rail-

road, was named for the packs of wolves which marauded the flat prairie. The settlement is headquarters for the Texas Mica Co. (3)

LOCO, Texas
Loco, sometimes called New Loco, is a rural community on the Collingsworth-Childress county line. The village grew out of the Buck Creek School District, organized in 1901, and moved to its present site in 1910. Named for the loco weed which crazed but seldom killed the cattle of the early settlers. (3)

LODGE POLE, Nebraska
The town gets its name from a creek that twists and turns its way into one side of the town and out the other. There are several theories as to how the creek came to be called Lodge Pole.

The most accepted theory is that the name was derived from the Dakota Indian words "tushu wakfola," meaning "lodge pole." The tall, straight trees growing along its banks, at one time, did furnish fine lodge poles for the Indians. Another theory has it that poles floated down the creek by lumber jacks constantly lodged in the many twists and turns of the creek, so they called it Lodge Pole Creek. (Margaret Jenike, Teacher, Lodge Pole High School.)

LOGTOWN, Mississippi
Logtown was named for a sawmill located here in 1850. (6)

LOMETA, Texas
Lometa, whose Spanish name means "little mountain," was first called Montavale. Founded in Lampasas County in 1885 as a trading post on the Gulf, Colorado, and Santa Fe Railroad, Lometa is the terminal point for a branch line of the railroad. Lometa has never had a saloon as a result of a pledge made when the town was founded by A. L. Horne, J. W. Stephens, and W. B. Floyd, three early settlers. (3)

LONE GROVE, Texas
The first store in Lone Grove, in 1876, was located in a large grove of Pecan trees, where Little Llano River and Dreary Hollow join. Just a lone store beside the dirt road, in a large field, bare of trees. (2)

LONEJACK, Missouri
The town of Lonejack takes its singular name from a lone tree of the black-jack species, which stood upon the high ridge of prairie dividing the waters of the Missouri and the Osage, in the immediate vicinity of

which was built the little village of Lone Jack. The tree, though dead, was still standing at the time of the battle of Lone Jack, August 16, 1862, and near it were buried the dead of both armies.

A monument or marble shaft has been erected to the memory of the Confederate dead, but the Union soldiers sleep without any. An iron fence encloses both. (*What I saw of Order Number Eleven,* by Fabius Martin Butler)

LONE STAR, Texas

Lone Star, Cherokee County, fourteen miles from Rusk, was established in the late 1850's and was first called *Skin Tight.* A sawmill was in operation before the Civil War. The name was changed when the Lone Star Institute was established and a post office was granted in 1903. As Texas is the Lone Star State, the source of the name is obvious. (3)

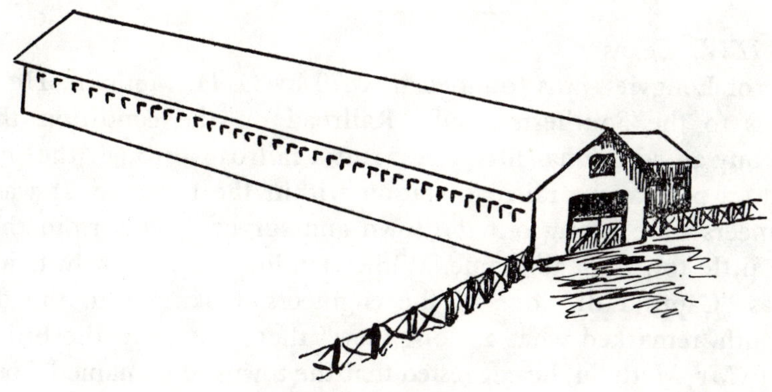

Long Barn, California

LONG BARN, California

Long Barn was named for a long barn, used to house the logging and freighter teams. Long Barn was the last place to rest the horses before continuing over the Sonora Pass into Nevada. The pass is located some 30 miles northeast. The barn housed 70 span of horses (140 in all), and had a feed and tack room in one end, and bunks for stable hands. The expression "Let's meet at the Long Barn," gradually named the location Long Barn, California. (1)

LONG BOTTOM, Ohio

Long Bottom, located in Meigs County, takes its name from its location on the banks of the Ohio River. One side of the river has high cliffs of rock, while the side where the village of Long Bottom lies is flanked by wide, flat bottom lands, hence the name Long Bottom. (1)

LONG MOTT, Texas
Long Mott was settled by German immigrants to Calhoun County in 1853. The first settlements were along the shore of San Antonio Bay in the vicinity of two large clumps or "motts" of trees, one called the Upper Mott and the other the Lower Mott. The Upper Mott was the larger and the longer of the two, and when the post office was established it was called Long Mott. (3)

LONG PRAIRIE, Minnesota
The county seat of Todd County, Long Prairie, is thought to have taken its name from its proximity to a river that flows through flat country, somewhat similar to prairie land.

Located in the heart of Minnesota's dairy country, it is the entrance to the state's lake and resort areas, with lakes Charlotte, Latimer and Osakis quite nearby. (2)

LONGVIEW, Texas
The city of Longview was founded in 1870 by O. H. Methvin. He deeded fifty acres to the Southern Pacific Railroad on the condition that the railroad buy an additional fifty acres; run a railroad through the property, and build a permanent railroad station within the townsite. It was while the engineers were laying out the town and surveying lots from this tract that the little town got its name. While standing on a rock hill, which is known as "Capps Hill," one of the engineers, looking into the distance to the south, remarked what a "long view" there was from the hill. Then, turning to Mr. Methvin, he suggested that the townsite be named Longview. The engineers then incorporated that name into their plat of the town. (2)

LONOKE, Arkansas
The town was named for a landmark of pioneer days, a solitary red oak that stood near the present center of the town. (6)

LOOGOOTEE, Indiana
Loogootee, the only city in the county, was platted on land owned by Thomas Gootee, and recorded on April 4, 1853. The unusual name was derived from a combination of two names, Lowe and Gootee. Lowe was the engineer who surveyed the right of way for the Mississippi and Ohio Railroad through the county and Gootee owned the land. The combination of Lowe-gootee did not look as good as the founders thought it should, so they changed Lowe to Loo, and retained the original pronounciation of Low-go-tee. Loogootee is located in southwestern Indiana, 36 miles east of Vincennes. (2)

LOOKOUT, West Virginia
Near a formation called "Spy Rock," it was used by the Indians, and later by the Union Army, as a lookout point, thus the name. (6)

LOONEYVILLE, West Virginia
Looneyville was named for Robert Looney, a prosperous first settler of British (isle of Man) descent, who came here from eastern Virginia in 1818. (1)

LOOSE CREEK, Missouri
The first settlers in this area were French, who settled along the Osage River at Côte de Sans. They called the creek that flows through here "Louers," because of the many bear found in the area.

About 1840 a large influx of German immigrants came into the area, and the name Louers Creek rolled off their tongue as something like "Loose." Eventually "Louers Creek" became "Loose Creek," and remains to this day. Loose Creek was used by hunters and early settlers as a land mark, and eventually a town grew up along its banks and became the town of Loose Creek, Missouri. It was here that the first court of Osage County was held. (1)

Los Angeles, California

LOS ANGELES, California
Extending from the foothills of the Santa Monica Mountains and the Verdugo Hills, Los Angeles lies on a plain bounded on the south and west by the Pacific Ocean.

In its early days it was a formless community of crude adobe-covered buildings and muddy, crooked streets. An expedition under Gaspar de Portolá reached the present site of the city August 2, 1769. The river here was named "el Rio de Nuestra Señora la Reina de Los Angeles de Porciuncula," or "The River of Our Lady the Queen of the Angels of Porciuncula."

Los Angeles was officially founded by Felipe de Neve, governor of the colonial province of Alta, California, September 4, 1781 and named "El Pueblo de Nuestra Señora la Reina de Los Angeles," "The village of our Lady the Queen of The Angels." Quite a name for a small adobe village to carry!

On March 9, 1842, the first gold discovered in California was made in Placerita Canyon, in the northern part of Los Angeles County, six years before Marshall made his famous strike at Sutter's Mill, and which contributed to the growth of the city of Los Angeles. The driving of the Golden Spike at Southern Pacific's Lang Station in Soledad Canyon, September 5, 1876, connected Los Angeles by rail with the energetic East, and Los Angeles was on its way.

The first complete motion picture to be made in Los Angeles was produced by Colonel Selig in a rented home at Eighth and Olive Streets in 1908. Within the next decade the leading studios of the industry capitalizing on the local climate and topography moved to Los Angeles, and Hollywood (annexed to the city of Los Angeles in 1910) became recognized as the capital of the motion picture industry. (2)

LOS EBANOS, Texas

Los Ebanos, in the southwest corner of Hidalgo County, was supposedly named for the ebony trees in the area. The site was the scene of an engagement between United States customs officers and cattle thieves in November 1875. (3)

LOS FRESNOS, Texas

Los Fresnos, in south-central Cameron, was named for Rancho Los Fresnos, established by Mexican ranchers as early as 1770. Open range grazing, particularly of sheep, continued until after the Mexican War. Railroad construction during the early 1900's brought settlers, and a post office was established in 1915. In 1915 and 1916 the village was raided by Mexican bandits. The Spanish name means "the ash tree." (3)

LOST CABIN, Wyoming

Legend has it that the city was named as a result of this legend: "Three prospectors were mining gold when they were attacked by Indians. Two

Lost Cabin, Wyoming

were killed, and the third was wounded, but managed to try and get help—he was found with a bag of gold in his hand and told of the Indian attack and the killing of his partners, but died before he could tell them where their cabin or gold mine was. People have searched all these years, but no one has ever found a trace of the cabin or the mine." (1)

LOST PRAIRIE, Texas

Lost Prairie, a rural community in southeastern Limestone County, was named for a small prairie area in the timber region. (3)

LOST SPRINGS, Wyoming

Lost Springs, Converse County, Wyoming, was named for a spring at the head of Lost Creek, near the town. The creek was so named because it flows underground in some areas, and is lost to sight. (Wyoming State Archives & Historical Department, Cheyenne, Wyo.)

LOVE, Arizona

Named not for the emotion, but for a World War I casuality. (5)

LOVELY, Kentucky

There are two legends about the name lovely. The first is that the post office was so named because it is situated in the midst of beautiful hills. Just across the river are the equally beautiful West Virginia hills. It was because of such scenic splendor that the name Lovely was chosen.

The other is that it was named for its first business man, S. L. Lovely. The postmaster at Lovely, Mr. Rufus M. Reed, likes the first one, which is indeed more romantic. (1)

LOVING, Texas
Loving, on the route of the Goodnight-Loving Trail in Young County, was named for Oliver Loving, when it was founded in 1903 with the building of the Gulf, Texas, and Western Railroad. (3)

LOWAKE, Texas
Lowake, in northwestern Concho County, was founded about 1910 and named for two of the oldest residents of the region, J. Y. Lowe, and C. G. Schlake. (3)

LOWER PEACH TREE, Alabama
Lower Peach Tree, Wilcox County, got its name from a corruption of "Pitch Tree." There was a tree that the men in the area used for target practice, with knives located on the river bank near here. The tree was known as the "pitch" tree, and the community that grew up here became Pitch Tree, and later through usage of the name, Peach evolved.

The community was obliterated by a tornado back in the teens, and a community, somewhat downstream, replaced it and became known as Lower Peach Tree, Alabama. (Chamber of Commerce, Grove Hill, Ala.)

LOW MOOR, Iowa
The village of Low Moor was surveyed and platted in 1857. When the Chicago, Iowa and Nebraska Railroad came through a few years later it was decided that the town needed a name. Citizens in the town happened to notice the name Low Moor, England, stamped on a pile of rails the railroad was using, and from this chose the name of their young town.

There were two very good reasons for their choice: for one thing most of them were immigrants from Lincolnshire, England, and for another the land was a low marsh land, or a Low Moor, as it would be called in England. The town was incorporated March 1897. (1)

LOYALTON, California
Loyalton, in Sierra County, was originally known as Smith Neck. In the election of 1864, every vote was cast for Abraham Lincoln. The townspeople then and there decided to change the name of their town to Loyalton—to show how loyal they were. (2)

LOYAL VALLEY, Texas
Loyal Valley, near Cold Spring Creek sixteen miles south of Mason, in Mason County, received its name from settlers in the area who remained loyal to the federal government during the Civil War.

The settlement was made earlier than other adjacent communities, but it did not have a post office until 1868. It was a stage stop on the route from Fredicksburg to Mason. (3)

LUCKY FORK, Kentucky
Lucky Fork is located approximately 11 miles from Booneville, Kentucky, where Daniel Boone used to camp. Legend has it that his party often hunted from Booneville, up Indian Creek and through Wolf Gap, to this creek where they always found game plentiful. Boone called it a "lucky fork," and when a village was formed here and a post office established the people chose to call it Lucky Fork. (1)

LUKACHUKAI, Arizona
Is Navajo Indian, and is not a name but a conversation. It means "white patch of reed extends out of the pass." The reason for the name is not known. (5)

LUXOMNI, Georgia
Luxomni started as a flag station for the Seaboard Air Line Railroad in 1891. Railroad employees named the stop Luxomni, which is Latin and means "light for all." Soon a village sprung up around the depot and a post office was established. The town of Luxomni flourishes to this day. (Philip H. Bailey, Boy Scout Troop 99)

MAGALIA, California
This town was a child of the California Gold Rush in 1849, and was first named *Dogtown,* then *Butte Mills,* and finally *Magalia.* As an item in the *Gold Nugget Gazette,* dated December 28, 1861, explains: "Our ancient and lively village of *Dogtown* is as unfortunate as a yearly widow-eternal finding it necessary or convenient to change her name. When the old Dog died, *Butte Mills* slid in through the post office requisition, and now, through the same channel, *Butte Mills* is crowded out of the kennel, and the euphonious *Magalia* usurps the hour. Who discovered the name? Has not the post office department mistaken the word sent on? Was it not *Mahala?* However, the thing is fixed now, and the Dog's dead; the post office of old *Dogtown* in the future to be addressed as *Magalia,* and A. C. Buffum is to be the postmaster." (2)

MAGAZINE, Arkansas
Established in the late 1800's it derives its name from the 2,823 foot mountain that lies just to the east of the town. From the mountain's peculiar form it had received the name "Magazine," meaning barn, from pioneer French hunters. (1)

MAGIC CITY, Texas
Magic City, on North Fork of Red River in west-central Wheeler County, developed when oil was discovered in the area in 1926. It was named for the speed with which a village sprang up on the bare prairie. In 1932 the Fort Worth and Denver Northern Railroad built through the area, and Magic City became a shipping point for cattle and wheat. (3)

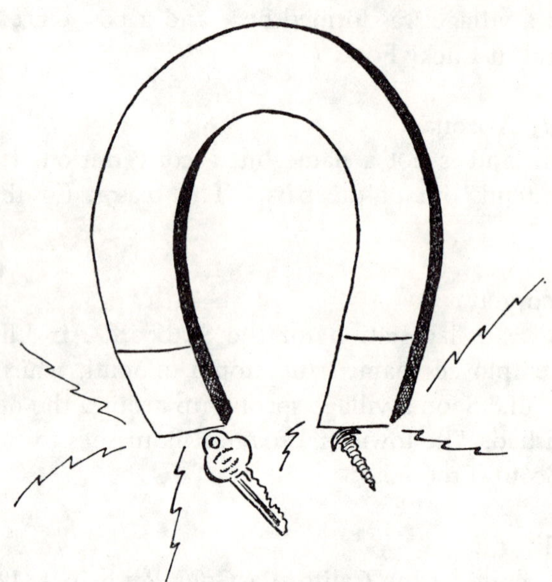

Magnet, Arkansas

MAGNET, Arkansas
Is located in a valley surrounded by low hills. Early Ouachita valley settlers puzzled by the erratic behavior of their compasses discovered quantities of lodestone. The name Magnet was given to the settlement that formed here. In this area have been found over 42 different kinds of minerals, marking this place as one of the most unusual finds of its kind in America. (6)

MAHANOY PLANE, Pennsylvania
A small village which lies between two mountains in the Mahanoy Valley. During the last half of the nineteenth and the early twentieth centuries, this town was a hard coal and railroad center.

A one million dollar plane hoisted coal up and over the mountains to eliminate congestion on the main rail line, thus the name of Mahanoy Plane. (1)

MAHNOMEN, Minnesota
The extension of the Soo Line Railroad through northern Minnesota in 1904 marked the opening of a new area for settlement caused the founding of Manomen County. One of the smaller counties in the state, it was formed from the 16 eastern townships of Norman County, located within the boundaries of the White Earth Indian Reservation. Passage of the Clapp Amendment in Congress in 1906 gave the Indians title to their land and the right to sell it, paving the way for an influx of settlers.

First settled around 1904, Mahnomen is Chippewa Indian and means "Wild Rice." (2)

MAHOMET, Texas
Mahomet, in northeastern Burnet County, near the Williamson county line, was first settled by the Stewart and Williams families during the early 1850's. A post office was established on December 14, 1857, and discontinued July 31, 1916. Mahomet's Mount Horef Lodge is the oldest Masonic lodge in the county, and explains the name of the community. (3)

MAHTOWA, Minnesota
Mahtowa is located in Carlton County, Minnesota, and due to its location was named Mahtowa, which is Indian for "High Point." (1)

MAIDEN CREEK, Pennsylvania
Formerly called Halfway House, for an early Inn, Maiden Creek took its present name from a stream one mile to the north. In this village is a Friend's Meeting House, built in 1759. (4)

MALAKOFF, Texas
Malakoff, in western Henderson County, dated from 1850, when Dr. John Collins applied for a post office and named it for a Russian town that had acquired prominence during the Crimean War. By 1860 the town had two cotton gins from which cotton was floated down the Trinity River or hauled to Navasota or Calvert prior to the building of the railroad in 1880. Silver is supposed to have been mined in the Wild Cat Creek area as early as 1830; in the early 1900's prospectors for silver found lignite deposits and mining began. (3)

MAMMOTH, Utah
In 1870 several roving prospectors filed a claim on a good outcropping of

ore. One of the locations was extremely large, and so impressed one of the prospectors that he exclaimed, "Boys, she a Mammoth—we've got a Mammoth Mine!" As was the case for all rich mines, a town grew up around the find, and took the name of Mammoth, Utah. (1)

MAMARONECK, New York
Located in Westchester County, near Long Island Sound, Mamaroneck was settled by English immigrants in 1650. The name is Indian and is said to mean "He assembles the people." (6)

MAMMOTH SPRINGS, Arkansas
Named for one of the largest springs in the world. A cold torrent of 200 millions of gallons of water pour from the earth each day to form the source of Spring River. (6)

MANILA, Arkansas
Once known as Big Lake Island, the village was settled around 1852 by Ed Smith. When the railroad built through the area it named the little settlement Manila, in honor of Admiral Dewey's victory in Manila Bay, in the Phillipines. (6)

MANILA VILLAGE, Louisiana
Was settled around 1890 by Filipino immigrants, hence the name. (6)

MANISTEE, Michigan
Built around the mouth of the Manistee River, as it enters Lake Michigan, the town occupies what was once a village of 1,000 or more Chippewa Indians, whose name it also took. The name means "spirit of the woods," probably because the area was heavily forested. (6)

MANKATO, Minnesota
The name is Sioux Indian and mean "blue earth," for the blue clay found in the vicinity. The first white men to visit Mankato were a party of Frenchmen during the winter of 1700. They thought they had discovered copper ore in the blue clay along the banks of the Blue Earth River and sent a boatload of it to New Orleans.

The town was founded in 1852 by four sturdy pioneers from St. Anthony (now St. Paul), who selected the site at the bend in the River. By 1873 the village had a population of 4,500. In August, 1862, an Indian uprising took place, and battles were fought at Fort Ridgely, New Ulm, and Birth Cooley. The Indians planned to drive all white settlers from southern Minnesota, but were defeated and surrendered near Montevideo.

Three hundred Indian prisoners were brought to Mankato where they were tried for atrocities and condemned to death. All but 39 were eventually released. One died before execution, and the remaining 38 were hanged. A monument here marks the spot where they were executed on December 24, 1862. (2)

MANN'S CHOICE, Pennsylvania
The name dates from 1890, when a post office was petitioned for by Mr. Job Mann, a congressman. The town, at that time had a tavern, which was also a stage coach stop, and a cluster of houses. The locale was known simply as Foot of the Ridge.

Mr. Mann went to the Post Office Department in Washington and requested a post office. The request was immediately granted, but when asked to furnish a name, Mr. Mann hesitated to suggest one.

The clerk in the Department merely shrugged and entered the name Mann's Choice, and a thriving community was born. (1)

MARBLE FALLS, Arkansas
In the 1830's a village was formed here due to a stream of water, later called Mill Creek, which could furnish water power for mills. The village flourished, and when the Washington Monument was built in Washington, a block of marble was taken from a nearby hill to represent the state of Arkansas. As a result of this the village was called Marble City.

When a post office was established the first postmaster was Armanda Willcockson, and the post office was named after her, although the village kept the name Marble City.

In 1930 an attempt was made to have the name of the post office changed to conform to the name of the village, but this was denied due to a conflict of names with another Arkansas town. One of Arkansas' most beautiful waterfalls is only 1/4 mile from the town so the name Marble Falls was submitted and approved by the Department. (1)

MARBLE FALLS, Texas
Before the lower Colorado River Authority built a series of six dams on the Colorado River of Texas (for flood control and manufacture of electricity) a beautiful little falls could be seen to the south of the Colorado River bridge at Marble Falls. It cascaded over a formation of a series of granite and marble ledges in the river bed. This was a very scenic and beautiful sight. The town of Marble Falls was built on and around the banks of this river, therefore, the name of Marble Falls was given by its founder Adam R. Johnson, in 1887.

When the six dams were built, forming the Colorado River into a series of dams and lakes from Buchanan Dam, Texas to Austin, the lake covered the original falls, so now there is no falls but rather a large lake. Beauty had yielded to progress. (2)

Marblehead, Massachusetts

MARBLEHEAD, Massachusetts

It is said that the first settler, a fisherman, came across the bay from the colony at Salem and lived in a large hogshead on the Marblehead shore, on what is now Peach's Point. Other early settlers came from the Channel Islands of Jersey and Guernsey, in 1629. The settlement was part of Salem until 1649, when the town of Marblehead was incorporated. The original deed of purchase from the Indians may be seen today in Abbot Hall.

A village of fishermen, originally called Marble Harbor because the rocky cliffs looked like marble to the passing fishing boats, usage soon changed the name to Marblehead, suitable because the town is on a rocky headland jutting into the Atlantic Ocean.

From a poor fishing village the town grew and prospered through the clipper-ship days when Marblehead vessels sailed the seven seas, and brought wealth to the "merchant princes." Some of the opulent mansions still stand as fine examples of Colonial architecture.

During the American Revolution the town was a center of blazing patriotism that drove out the few people remaining loyal to the Crown. Marblehead sent an entire regiment under General John Flover, which climaxed its heroic deeds by transporting Washington and his army in the famous crossing of the Delaware. In 1775 General Washington commissioned the *Hannah,* manned and owned by Marblehead men, as the first American warship, thus supporting the town's claim as the "Birthplace of the American Navy." (2)

MARFA, Texas
Marfa, in northeast Presidio County, was established in 1881 as a water stop on the Texas and New Orleans Railroad. It was named by the wife of the president of the railroad for the heroine of a Russian novel. On July 14, 1885, an election transferred the county seat from Presidio to Marfa. Marfa is a ranch trading point which ships cattle, sheep, and mohair. Climate and proximity to the Davis Mountains and Big Bend National Park have made the town a tourist center. (3)

MARINE, Illinois
This Illinois village was so named because it was settled by several sea captains from the east. The name is variously defined as pertaining to the sea, existing in or produced by the sea. (Minnesota Historical Society)

MARINE ON ST. CROIX, Minnesota
The village of Marine Mills, platted in 1853, and incorporated in 1875 received its name from the township in which it is located. It got the additional part of its name when it applied for a post office. The village is located on the St. Croix River, and the addition of "On St. Croix" was made to avoid confusion with another village with the same name, resulting in the lovely name Marine on St. Croix. (Minnesota Historical Society)

MARKED TREE, Arkansas
Many years ago Chief Moonshine and his tribe discovered a good portage from the St. Francis to the Little River, where their favorite hunting grounds lay. To identify this spot, they marked a tree growing along the St. Francis River, where this village is located. In 1881-2, the Kansas City, Fort Scott, and Memphis Railroad built through this area and established a camp at Marked Tree. In 1897 Marked Tree was incorporated as a town. (2)

MASSAPONAX, Virginia
This small village, located in Spotsylvania County, it said to have gotten its name, not from the Indians, but from an exclatation of a Negro slave, who was out looking for his master. After much futile searching, he suddenly spotted his master astride an Ox, and cried out in relief, "Here comes Massa upon an Ox!" (1)

MATADOR, Texas
Matador, seat of Motley County, is one of the most western of Texas towns. It was named for the Matador Ranch, the headquarters of which was established in 1879 at Ballard Springs.

When Motley County was organized in 1891, there was no town in the new county. A townsite, sponsored by H. H. Campbell, was designated. The necessary twenty business houses required by law were supplied by cowboys from the Matador ranch headquarters who set up one-day businesses in order for a patent to be granted by the General Land Office. The town is the principal trading and shipping point for Motley County. (3)

MATAGORDA, Texas
Matagorda, in present Matagorda County, was established in the late 1820's after Stephen F. Austin in 1827 secured permission to build a town at the mouth of the Colorado River. Elias R. Wightman, H. H. League, James E. Austin, and partners Thomas M. Duke and William Selkirk each took one-fourth interest in the townsite. Wightman gathered fifty-two families from New York and New England. On August 1, 1829, the proprietors met and elected the town officers as their constitution provided. They also donated lots to certain individuals for special services.

By 1832 there were 1400 inhabitants within the town and 250 outside, but within its jurisdiction. The town incorporated in 1830, and became the county seat in 1837. The name is taken from the Spanish and means "dense cane," derived from the dense canebrakes that formerly lined the shoreline of Matagorda County. (3)

MATOAKA, West Virginia
Named for the secret or sacred name of Pocahontas, daughter of Chief Powhatan, who is said to have saved Captain John Smith from execution by her father. (6)

MATTAPONI, Virginia
Contrary to the belief of most of those who compose the population of Mattaponi, the name of this village is not Indian. It came about because those who first settled here chose to build their homes along the Mattaponi River, which is made up of the waters from the Matta, Po and Ni Rivers, that flow through northern Virginia. It is possible that one or more of these rivers possesses an Indian name, but the combination has no significent meaning. (Ruth H. Bland)

MAUCH CHUNK, Pennsylvania
Indian for "bear mountain," Mauch Chunk was once called the Switzerland of America, and was settled in 1815. (4)

MAVERICK, Texas
Maverick, in western Runnels County, was named for Samuel A. Maverick who had landholdings in the area. The term "maverick," used after 1845 to designate unbranded cattle, came from the name of Samuel A. Maverick. He is said to have taken some cattle in payment of a debt and put them in the care of a Negro who neglected to brand the calves. Neighbors referred to wandering unbranded calves as "one of Maverick's"; the phrase was shortened to Maverick and gradually came to mean any unbranded stock. (3)

MAXATAWNY, Pennsylvania
Is Indian and means "Bear Path Creek." (4)

MAYODAN, North Carolina
In west-central Rockingham County, the name consists of the combination of the names of the Mayo and the Dan Rivers. (6)

MC KEES ROCKS, Pennsylvania
Settled in 1764, it was named for the massive rock formations along the Ohio River, and for Alexander McKee, an early settler. (4)

MEADOWS OF DAN, Virginia
The Dan River has its headwaters at Meadows of Dan, and the name refers to the meadows along the Dan River, therefore, resulting in the unusual name of the town. (1)

MEANSVILLE, Georgia
Was named for a pioneer settler named John Means. The local school was named John Means Institute. When the railroad was built it missed the town by one mile in order to utilize a gap in the hills.

Since the railroad would not come to the town, the town pulled up its roots and moved one mile to the railroad. So now there is a Meansville and an Old Meansville. (1)

MEDICINE BOW, Wyoming
The area of Medicine Bow, Wyoming, was the buffalo hunting grounds for thousands of Indians for many years. Due to the climate and altitude, no hardwoods are to be found in this area.

Along the banks of the Medicine Bow River the Indians discovered a tough, springy shrub that was suitable for use in making bows. The common name of the shrub is "Buffalo Berry," but it is a variety of sage. Since this was the only suitable wood for hundreds of miles, the Indians made special trips here to secure the Buffalo Berry. This was "good medicine," as the Indians described it. Good medicine for the Bow. The river was named Medicine Bow, and from the river, the Medicine Bow National Forest and the town got their names. (Marvin Cronberg, Medicine Bow, Wyoming)

MEDICINE LODGE, Kansas

The town of Medicine Lodge is an old western Indian village. The Medicine River runs near the south edge of town, and it was the belief of the Indian tribes that the water of this river had some medicinal value. Once a year they would camp near the river to bathe in the waters and absorb its healing qualities.

The last major Indian peace treaty was signed at the river's edge. Every five years this peace treaty of 1867 is relived in Medicine Lodge. The last one was in October, 1967. (Medicine Lodge Indian Peace Treaty Assoc., Medicine Lodge, Kansas)

MEDICINE MOUND, Texas

Medicine Mound, in east central Hardeman County, takes its name from four elevations ranging in height from 200 to 250 feet, called Medicine Mounds. The mounds were camp and ceremonial sites of the Comanche, as medicinal herbs, not available elsewhere, were found here. (3)

MEDICINE PARK, Oklahoma

Between 1910 and 1930 this area was a summer resort, which accounts for the "Park" portion of the name. It is located along a large creek in the foothills of the Wichita Mountains. The creek is named Medicine Creek, which accounts for the "Medicine" portion of the name.

The creek was named by the Indians, probably "Wichitas," long before Oklahoma became a state, though the exact reason for the name is unknown. (1)

MEETEETSE, Wyoming

Meeteetse, Park County, Wyoming, is an Indian word meaning "place of rest," and the area of the town was a general Indian camping ground because of its attractive surroundings. (Wyoming State Archives and Historical Department, Cheyenne, Wyo.)

MELBETA, Nebraska

Melbeta was established as a station for the Union Pacific Railroad and a shipping point for sugar beets, which are raised extensively in this part of Nebraska. It was aptly named Melbeta, which is of German origin and means "sweet beet." There is still a large beet dump here that handles many tons of beets each year. (1)

Melbeta, Nebraska

MELON, Texas
Melon, in south-central Frio County, became a shipping point on the International-Great Northern Railroad about 1910 and was named for the melons which were shipped from the area. (3)

MELONES, California
So named because gold found here was so coarse it resembled melon seeds. Located in colorful Calaveras County it was once called *"Slumgullion."* (2)

MENA, Arkansas
Platted in 1896, the name is a contraction of Wilhemina, and was attributed to the reigning queen of Holland by the Dutch investors in the Kansas City Southern Railroad. (6)

MENAHGA, Minnesota
Menahga is the Chippewa Indian name for the land of blueberries. This is a fitting name because the vicinity abounds with luscious blueberries during the summer months. To add to the blueberry theme, Menahga is located in Blueberry Township, on the banks of the Blueberry River, which flows into Blueberry Lake! (2)

MENDOTA, Minnesota

Settled around 1805, Mendota was first named Saint Peter. The name was changed around 1837 to "Mendota," which is Sioux Indian, and means "Meeting of the Waters." (6)

MENOMINEE, Michigan

Louis Chappee, a fur trader, built a trading post here on the Menominee River in 1796, which became a neucleus for the present town. Bordered on the east by Green Bay, and on the west and south by the Menominee River (its namesake), the name is Indian and means "Wild Rice Country." (6)

MERCURY, Texas

Mercury, on the Fort Worth and Rio Grande Railroad in McCulloch County, was founded by J. A. Austin in 1904 and named for the quantity of mineral found nearby. (3)

MERIDIANVILLE, Alabama

Is on the Huntsville Meridian, from which the surveyors measure—hence its name. (Mrs. Howard C. Jones, Sr., New Market, Ala.)

MESA, Texas

Mesa, in western Grimes County, was named for its location on an elevation above Gibbons Creek. The community was settled by planters in the 1840's and became a flag stop on the Texas and New Orleans Railroad in 1860. (3)

MESHOPPEN, Pennsylvania

Indian for "place of beads," was settled in 1742 as a stagecoach stop. (4)

MEXICAN HAT, Utah

Mexican Hat is a small community separated from the Navajo Indian Reservation by the capricious San Juan River. Monument Valley is just next door to the south, with the canyonlands country virtually on its doorstep.

Mexican Hat is named for a nearby balanced rock which resembles an inverted sombrero. During the San Juan oil boom of 1907-10, the town was located near the rock, and was called Goodridge. (2)

MIAMI, Florida

Because of its climate and natural advantages, the Indians long favored it, the Spanish coveted it, the Seminole Wars caused its evacuation by the Americans; but it has been a place of human habitation long before recorded history. Named for the Miami Indians? Not so! The Miami were a northern tribe who never even heard of Florida.

According to the best authorities the name Miami comes from the Calusa Indian word Mayaimi, meaning "big water." Mayaimi was also the Calusa name for Lake Okeechobee. The Director of the Historical Museum of Southern Florida states that: A west coast Indian tribe, the Calusas, had a word for "great water"—Mayaimi—even before Columbus landed. The word, which described Lake Okeechobee, spread from the Calusas to the Tequesta Indians who lived in this area. By distortion, the word eventually became Miami. Until the city was incorporated in 1896, it was called Fort Dallas. (2)

MIAMI, Missouri
First named Greenville in 1838, the town is located on a bluff ridge, overlooking the Missouri River Valley. The town was named in memory of the short stay of the Miami Indians.

Following their defeat by "Mad" Anthony Wayne in 1791, the Miami Indians began a slow retreat toward the west. In 1815 a band of these Indians settled in the river bottom below here to raise a crop. A band of Sacs and Fox Indians came down from the north and attacked nearby white settlements. After an attack the Miami Indians had the bad judgment to trade the raiders out of some of their loot. The presence of this booty was discovered by the white settlers and an attack was organized. The Miami avoided a fight, however, by moving from their village and after much misunderstanding and hot conversation peace was again established. The following summer the Miami moved farther West, and left only their memory and name behind them. (T. M. Hamilton, Mayor, Miami, Missouri)

MIAMI, Texas
Miami, in southeastern Roberts County, on the Santa Fe Railroad, was named for an Indian word meaning "sweetheart." The town began in 1887 as a construction camp on the railroad. Daily stage trips furnished supplies from Miami to Fort Elliott. Miami was chosen the first county seat, but the election was declared fraudulent, and Parnell, twenty-five miles northwest, was proclaimed legal seat of county government until it was relocated at Miami in 1898. (3)

MIDDLEWATER, Texas
Located in central-western Hartley County on the Rock Island Railroad, Middlewater was first established as a division of the X I T Ranch, and derived its name from nearby Middle Water Creek. (3)

MICO, Texas
In Medina County east of the main dam at Medina Lake and forty miles

west of San Antonio, Mico was named as an abbreviation for the Medina Irrigation Company. (3)

MIDNIGHT, Mississippi

Legend has it that back in the 1800's a number of Southern Gentlemen (plantation owners in this locale) were playing poker. Now these games sometimes got wild and wooly, and the stakes were often very high. One of the gentlemen, running unusually bad luck, put up his plantation as a stake on a particular hand, and lost. It is said that the winner, at this moment, pulled out his watch and remarked, "Well, Gentlement, it's now midnight, and that's just what I'm going to call this piece of land." The legend has persisted through the years and when a town was formed here and a post office established, they, of course, chose the name Midnight. (1)

MILACA, Minnesota

The town is on the shores of the Rum River, which flows from Mille Lacs to the Mississippi. The name Mille Lacs is French and means "thousand lakes." The name of the town is a derivation of Mille Lacs. (6)

MILLER'S TAVERN, Virginia

Miller's Tavern, located in Essex County, Virginia, was named for a tavern and inn established here on a cross roads leading north and south and east and west, by a family named Miller.

The tavern was a favorite stop for the stagecoaches from Tappahannock en route to Richmond. Although the tavern has undergone some changes, it still stands as a monument to the pioneering days. (1)

MILWAUKEE, Wisconsin

The word Milwaukee is Indian and means "beautiful hollow or bay" or "gathering place by the waters." Both were descriptions by the Indians of the seventeenth century and present-day Milwaukee.

The French explorers who were to lend their names to other American towns all stopped here. It was on the confluence of the Milwaukee and the Menominee Rivers, a half-mile from Lake Michigan. As they enter the lake, they are joined by the Kinnekinnic. All the names are Indian, and were the contribution of the Mascoutens, Fox, Winnebago, Potawatomi, and the Menominees.

Known as the founder of Milwaukee was another Frenchman, Solomon Juneau (1793–1856), who came here and founded the most German city in the nation. Milwaukee was incorporated in 1846 and Solomon Juneau became its first mayor. (2)

MINEOLA, Missouri
Daniel Boone came to the Missouri Territory around 1800. He followed the Missouri River (The Big Muddy) to the Loutre River, and went up the Loutre River until he came to Sallee Branch. A few hundred yards from here he discovered a place where the animals were licking the stones for minerals. He called the spot "Loutre Lick."

In the early 1800's Nathan Boone received a grant here from the Spanish Government. In 1815 the grant was purchased by Major Issac Van Bibber, adopted son of Daniel Boone. About 1821 he built a large one-and-a-half story log cabin across Sallee Branch where he lived for 20 years. The house became a tavern, which was a stop for the stage traveling from St. Louis to Howard County, Salt Kilns and on west over Boon's Lick Road.

About 1883 Mr. Harvey Scanland laid out a town around the lick. He called the town Mineola. One of his daughters was named Minnie, and she had a friend named Ola Gregory. The two names made up the name Mineola, but it is also an Indian word meaning "healing waters." The mineral spring water had been found helpful in healing stomach and kidney disorders.

As an interesting sidelight, Issac Van Bibber was unusual in that he believed in the transmigration of souls. He held that there was a complete revolution of nature every six thousand years, and that everything would return to exactly where it had been six thousand years before. He took a great delight in telling of his beliefs, and trying to get converts. Once a party of Kentuckians stopped at his Inn overnight and he launched into his favorite subject. They listened so attentively and seemed so interested that he lay awake almost all night, so convinced was he that he had converted them. The next morning when the men were ready to leave one of them remarked that they were greatly impressed with his theories, and being short of money at the moment, they would return in about 6,000 years and pay their bills. Thinking fast, Major Van Bibber quickly replied, "No. You are the same damn rascals who were here six thousand years ago, and went away without paying your bills, and now you've got to pay before you leave!" They laughed, paid their bill and departed, but the old major had learned his lesson and never again was he to be heard trying to convert others, especially guests in his tavern. (Mrs. Ward F. Darnell, Mineola, Missouri)

MINERAL BLUFF, Minnesota
Named for a bluff, rising more than 400 feet, near the north end of the town. The bluff was found to contain coal, silver, and lead, but not in sufficient quantities to make mining an industry here. (6)

MINERSVILLE, Utah

Not an uncommon name in the pioneer days, the village was named for the mines located around it. The first settlers here worked at Lincoln Head Mine, close to the town. (1)

MINGO, West Virginia

Gets its name from the Mingo Tribe of Indians who once lived and hunted in the surrounding country side, and occupied a village on the present site of Mingo. (6)

MINIDOKA, Idaho

Minidoka, located in Minidoka County, in southeastern Idaho, bears an Indian name, which old-timers say means "water hole." (1)

MINNEAPOLIS, Minnesota

Colonel John H. Stevens filed claim to a large section of present downtown Minneapolis in 1849 and platted it as a town in 1854.

The name Minneapolis was suggested by one Charles Hoag in 1852 as a contraction of Minnehaha, Indian for "falling water," and the Greek word "polis," meaning "city." Thus we have the Indian-Greek name, "Falling Waters, Minnesota." (2)

MINNEISKA, Minnesota

Settled in 1851, Minneiska took an Indian name which means "white water." (6)

MINNETONKA, Minnesota

Minnetonka. The name rolls off the tongue with ease and beauty. It is Indian and means "water, big," as the Indians used the descriptive words separately to describe lake Minnetonka, which is indeed a large and beautiful lake, twelve miles west of Minneapolis.

The lake received its name officially from Governor Alexander Ramsey, of the Minnesota Territory, in 1852, when he visited the area with a party who came up Minnehaha Creek in a large "batteau."

The township was organized May 11, 1858, and called Minnetonka. In 1956, the town of Minnetonka became Minnetonka village. (Dana W. Frear, Local Historian, Minnetonka, Minn.)

MINTER, Texas

Minter, in southeastern Lamar County, was named for Minter Parker, and was originally known as *Parker's Voting Box*. The post office was established in 1882. (3)

MISSION, Texas
Mission, in southwestern Hidalgo County, was named for a mission established in 1824 by priests of the Oblate order on a site three miles south of the present town. An orange grove planted by the priests is said to have been one of the first experiments with citrus culture in the lower Rio Grande Valley. In 1907 John C. Conway and J. W. Holt offered the St. Brownsville, and Mexico Railroad twenty acres of irrigated land to build an extension from Mamie to the present site of Mission, then named Conway. The railroad reached the spot in 1907 and in 1908 the post office was transferred from La Lomita and renamed Mission.

William Jennings Bryan purchased land in the area in 1910, and spent two winters in Mission. Because of Francisco (Pancho) Villa's raids, Texas forces had to be sent to the town in 1911. (3)

MISSOURI CITY, Texas
Missouri City, in eastern Fort Bend County, was promoted in 1890 by the realty firm, Cash and Luckle, which advertised chiefly in Missouri newspapers and brought in a number of settlers. Between 1890 and 1900 the community prospered, and a fair-sized town was built. A storm in 1900 damaged the town severely and it was never completely rebuilt. (3)

Mistletoe, Kentucky

MISTLETOE, Kentucky
Mistletoe is located deep in the Kentucky Mountains, in Owsley County. Years ago, before forest fires and a temperature of 25 below zero, the trees in this area were hung heavily with large bunches of mistletoe. It was from this lush growth of mistletoe that the town and the post office got its unusual name. (1)

MI-WUK VILLAGE, California

The Mi-Wuk Village name comes from the Mi-Wuk or Mi-Wok Indian tribe who lived on an Indian Reservation about ten miles from this town. They used to hunt on what is now a golf course. It was once prevalent with deer, birds, acorns and pine nuts, before the advent of civilization. (1)

MOAB, Utah

The name Moab was chosen by a committee of seven early Mormon settlers. It was suggested by William A. Pierce, a Bible student, who was comparing it to the Biblical, "Far Country of Moab." The naming took place in 1897. (1)

MOBEETIE (Old), Texas

Old Mobeetie, in northwestern Wheeler County, was established in 1875 as a trading post for Fort Elliott and developed from a frontier store on Sweetwater Creek at a buffalo hunter's camp called *Hidetown.* The village was called Sweetwater until a post office was applied for in 1879. Then a duplication in name caused an Indian word meaning sweetwater to be chosen.

Mobeetie became county seat in 1879 and was business center of the Panhandle until the late 1880's. A damaging storm in 1898 and failure to secure a railroad caused the settlement to decline severely; an election moved the county seat to Wheeler in 1907. In 1929 the Panhandle and Santa Fe Railroad built its line two miles north of the site and a new town of Mobeetie sprang up on the railroad. So there are now two towns with the unusual name of Mobeetie, known as "Old" Mobeetie, and "New" Mobeetie. (3)

MOCCASIN, California

A man by the name of Pancoast wrote a book of his adventures in the gold fields of California during 1849. He mentioned Moccasin with the remark that it was so named because of the great number of moccasin snakes found in the creek. In fact he claimed that he found several in his pack after camping on the creek one night. While there are a large number of common water snakes in the creek and numerous rattlesnakes and other varieties in the vicinity, no moccasin snakes inhabit the creek.

It is possible that someone made a mistake and thought the snakes were moccasins. Another version is that a flood occurred in 1849, and after the water subsided, an Indian's moccasin was found hanging from a tree beside the creek, and hence the name Moccasin Creek, from whence the village of Moccasin takes its name. (Carlo M. DeFerrari, Deputy, Board of Supervisors, Sonora, Calif.)

MODESTO, California
The discovery of gold in California brought hordes of men rushing into the nearby Mother Lode. This was the start of early settlements, many of which were along the river. Then, as the area grew, the Central Pacific Railroad made its appearance, and in 1870 surveyors laid out a city.

The name for the city originated when W. C. Ralston, prominent early Californian, declined to have the community named Ralston. His modesty led the people to choose the name Modesto, Spanish for modesty. It was established as the county seat in 1871. (2)

MONUMENT, Kansas
Fort Monument was established during pioneer days to protect settlers of this young land from marauding Indians. The present-day town of Monument, Kansas takes its name from a monument erected on the site of the old fort, by the Government. (1)

Moon, Virginia

MOON, Virginia
Moon is located in Mathews County, on the Chesapeake Bay, and there are two legends as to how it got its name. The first is that the new postmaster, dreaming of the new establishment, and thinking hard for a name, looked out upon a beautiful moon and decided to name it "Moon." The other, less romantic, but probably more factual is that all mail reached this area by boat at noon each day. Because of this the postmaster suggested the name Noon for the new post office, but since he wrote with such a flourishing hand his fancy "N" was mistaken for an "M" and Noon became Moon. (1)

MOOSEHEART, Illinois
Established by the Loyal Order of Moose, Mooseheart is a complete com-

munity in itself. To become a resident of Mooseheart, every child must have lost one or both of its parents, the parents, of course, having been members of the Loyal Order of Moose. The name, as suggested by Congressman John J. Lentz of Ohio, was formally adopted in 1913. (Director, Loyal Order of Moose, Mooseheart, Ill.)

MOOSE PASS, Alaska

Legend has it that about 1901 or 1902 a couple of Eskimo trappers were camped one night in this area. The next morning when they arose, they discovered fresh moose tracks in the snow. One of them said, "Moose pass by in night time." And thus it was that Moose Pass got its name. According to the old-timers. (1)

MOOSEUP, Connecticut

According to local legend some hunters were hot on the trail of a moose, when they suddenly lost it. They asked some of the Indians in a small village here if they had seen the moose, and they replied "Moose-Up," meaning the moose had gone to higher ground. They later referred to the place as Mooseup, and when a post office was established at a new village here years later, the name Mooseup was offered and accepted. (1)

MORA, Minnesota

Settled in 1881, Mora was named for the town of Mora, Sweden. (6)

MOSCOW, Texas

Moscow is on a dividing ridge between the Neches and Trinity Rivers in Polk County. It was founded in 1846 by David Griggs Green, who built a house and a blacksmith shop in the territory on the main road from Burr's Ferry, on the Sabine River, to Patrick's Ferry on the Trinity River. On May 19, 1847, Green's post office was established. A few months later the name was changed to Greenville, and then in 1853, to Moscow. Some people say that the town was given the name of the Russian city because certain residents were admirers of the Russians for their fighting qualities; others suggest that the town was named by David Green for a town of that name in his home state of Tennessee.

The East Texas Pinery, published in Moscow in 1885, boasted of a street car, a vehicle drawn by a mule over a track that led from the railroad to the town's hotel. (3)

MOSSYHEAD, Florida

A river is formed by several creeks coming together and a creek is formed by an abundance of water flowing from a spring. The spring is known as the "head" of a river and/or creek.

Mossyhead received its name from the fact that the spot where the spring rose to the surface was surrounded by trees well loaded with Spanish moss. (Herman P. Kasper, Chamber of Commerce, Marianna, Fla.)

MOUND, Louisiana
Named for the many Indian burial mounds found in the area. (6)

MOUND, Texas
Located in eastern Coryell County on the St. Louis and Southwestern Texas Railroad, it was first called "White Mound," for a nearby white chalk hill. In 1884, when the post office was established here, the name was shortened to Mound. (3)

MOUND CITY, Missouri
First settled in 1840 by Thomas Ferguson, who built a log cabin here, he later sold the cabin to Andrew P. Jackson. The area soon became known as "Jackson's Point," with a tavern and stage stop on the route from St. Joseph to Council Bluffs, Iowa.

The name Mound City was suggested by a mound located in the city limits. This mound is a portion of the range of loess mounds which run north and south of Mound City for several miles. In only two or three places in the world can loess mounds be found and these are reputed to be the finest examples of all of them. (2)

MOUNDVILLE, Alabama
Moundville is situated close to the Black Warrior River in the extreme northern part of Hale County, west central Alabama. The town was incorporated in 1908 when the name was changed from Carthage to Moundville.

The name was selected because of the Indian mounds within the corporate limits. Here is located a prehistoric Indian Village, built by an unknown tribe, as a ceremonial center about 1200 to 1400 A.D. (Town Clerk, Town of Moundville, Ala.)

MOUNDSVILLE, West Virginia
First settled around 1770, it takes its name from a huge Indian Burial Mound located in the heart of the town. Called the Grave Creek Mound, it is almost 80 feet high and fifty feet long. (6)

MOUNTAIN BROOK, Alabama
A relatively young town, incorporated in 1942 from a subdivision south of Birmingham, it was named for two streams that meander through Shade Valley. (City Manager, Dorothy B. Hoyt.)

MOUNTAIN IRON, Minnesota

E. T. Merritt platted the townsite and named it Grant in honor of a railroad contractor. When the first post office was opened the name of the town was changed to Marfield for a post office official.

Both names were later dropped and the corporate name of Mountain Iron was adopted after the great mine which had a "mountain of Iron." On October 17, 1892, thirty-eight inhabitants of the area signed a petition for incorporation and sent it to the County Commissioners of St. Louis County where it was approved a few days later. (Mountain Iron Public Library)

MOUNTAIN RANCH, California

Originally the town of El Dorado but changed when the post office was moved from the original Mountain Ranch. One of the livelier early-day mining camps, it is now famous for its walnuts. The village is located in Calaveras County. (2)

MOUNTAIN TOP, Pennsylvania

So named for its location on the flat summit of Penobscot Mountain, it was founded in 1788. (4)

MOUNT BLANCO, Texas

Mount Blanco started with the building of the first permanent home in northwest Texas, in Blanco Canyon, one mile northeast of Mount Blanco, from which it derives its name.

On the old military trail of Ranald S. Mackenzie, the town is near the place where the United States troops transcended the canyon wall and encountered Quannah Parker and his Comanche bands on October 15, 1871, in the battle of Canyon Blanco. (3)

MOUNT CALM, Texas

The town of Mount Calm, Texas, was named for a French general by the name of Montcalm. General Montcalm showed great bravery, although he did lose his life in the war of 1759 between the English and French at the battle of Quebec. (1)

MOUSIE, Kentucky

Named for a lady named Mousie Martin, who owned several hundred acres of mountain land surrounding the area where the town is located, and "who worked very hard and pulled several strings to get the post office established, and named after her." (Steve Hiche, Postmaster)

MOUTH OF SENECA, West Virginia
Located at the confluence of Seneca Creek and North Fork Rivers, near Seneca Rock. All of the names come from the Seneca tribe that once had a village near here. (6)

MOUTH OF WILSON, Virginia
This little village is located on the mouth of Wilson Creek, hence the name. The creek was named for a pioneer named Wilson, and there are two branches, Big Wilson and Little Wilson.

Mouth of Wilson is located at the confluence of the two. (1)

MUD, West Virginia
Samuel Adkins came here from Kentucky in 1883 by wagon train, and settled with his family. The small village and post office took its unique name from the Mud River, which is small in width, but over a hundred miles long. It eventually empties into the Guyan River at Guyandotte.

The river got its name due to the fact that large amounts of soil and silt, washed down from the hills, keep it in a constant muddy condition. (Lillian Smith, granddaughter of Samuel Adkins)

MUDDY CREEK FORKS, Pennsylvania
There are two large creeks which meet in the center of this small village, forming a fork. The creeks are surrounded by very high and fertile hills which wash rich soil into the creeks keeping them in a muddy condition. This gave the village and the post office its unusual name of Muddy Creek Forks. (1)

MULESHOE, Texas
Muleshoe, county seat of Bailey County, is a trading and shipping center on the Pecos and North Texas Railroad. The town is in Blackwater Valley, part of the shallow water agricultural belt on the South Texas High Plains.

Named for the Muleshoe Ranch, and remaining a typical west Texas cattle town, the national monument to the mule, and his valuable contribution to the settling of this large country, is located here. The Mule Shoe Ranch uses a "mule shoe" as its cattle brand. (2)

MUSCADINE, Alabama
This town got its name from the fruit which grows here in wild abundance. (1)

MUSTANG, Oklahoma

The small town received its name from the many wild horses or mustangs which once freely roamed this area in herds. The mustang, a small wild or half-wild horse of the American plains, descended from horses brought to the American continent by the Spanish during their early day explorations and conquests. (1)

MUSTANG, Texas

In Denton County, Mustang received its name from either the mustang grapes which once lined Mustang Creek on which the village is located or from the large groups of mustang ponies which ranged along the stream as late as 1850. (3)

NACOGDOCHES, Texas

The antiquity of the town is indicated by the presence of four Indian mounds within the city limits. Three of these mounds have been leveled and were found to contain numerous human bones, specimens of pottery, and other artifacts.

The Nacogdoches area was visited by the La Salle Expedition in 1687. The first European settlement was made in June 1716 with the founding by Domingo Ramón of the mission of Nuestra Señora de Guadalupe de los Nacogdoches. Mission life was interrupted between 1718, when the Spanish fled because of threats of invasion by the French, and 1721, when the mission was rebuilt by the Marquis de Aguayo. After France ceded Louisiana to Spain in 1762, Juan María Vincencio de Ripperdá ordered the abandonment of the mission.

In April, 1779, Gil Antonio Ibarvo and his followers resettled Nacogdoches. The importance of the location was recognized by the Spanish authorities because it was the gateway from the east to the Spanish possessions, but under Ibarvo's lax discipline the chief industry seems to have been smuggling contraband between Natchitoches, Louisiana, and the Indians of Texas. It has been stated that he built the Old Stone Fort as a warehouse for his merchandise.

Nacogdoches figured importantly in several of the outstanding events of early Texas history. The town in 1800 was headquarters for Antonio Leal, conspirator with Philip Nolan (the man without a country). It came into prominence again in 1813 with the advent of the Gutiérrez-Magee Expedition and the publication of the first Texas newspapers: The *Gaceta de Tejas,* issued in May, 1813, and *El Mejicano,* which appeared a month later. After the failure of the Gutiérrez-Magee Expedition, Nacogdoches was almost destroyed by forces under Joaquin de Arrendondo. On June 17, 1819, Dr. James Long with three hundred followers entered Texas, occupied the Old Stone Fort, and organized a provisional government for the so-called Republic of Texas. After the defeat of the Long Expedition, the Spanish authorities placed a military force in Nacogdoches and authorized the establishment of a civil government. With the accomplishment of Mexican independence, the municipal government was set up in 1821 with James Dill as first alcalde (mayor). The Fredonian Rebellion in 1826 led to the placing in Nacogdoches of the Twelfth Permanent Battalion, which remained there until the force under José de las Piedras was driven out in the battle of Nacogdoches on August 2, 1832. Nacogdoches continued as a seat of unrest, supplying forces for and largely financing the Texas Revolution. The last uprising centering in the Nacogdoches area, the Condova Rebellion in August, 1838, resulted in the expulsion of the Indians from east Texas.

Nacogdoches, county seat of Nacogdoches County, was named for the Nacogdoches Indians, who originally inhabited the area. (3)

Nags Head, North Carolina

NAGS HEAD, North Carolina
The legend of Nags Head has it that in years gone by, pirates tied a lantern to the neck of a nag and led it across the sand dunes near the ocean on dark and stormy nights. Ships at sea would see the bobbing light and mistake it for another vessel, then move in closer for protection from the storm. As a result they would pile up on the rocks, creating salvage for the pirates.

The less romantic version is that it received its name from one of its early settlers, who, having traveled in England, was reminded of a town called Nags Head when he arrived here.

There are three "Nags Heads" in England. A third guess is that it was named for one of the many British pubs, which frequently featured a sign with a nags head on it. The choice is yours. (2)

NAPOLEON, Ohio
Settled by a group of French in the midst of a preponderately German population they named it for their "greatest" countryman—Napoleon. (6)

NAPFOR, Kentucky
Sitting astride the North Fork of the Kentucky River, at the mouth of Little Meadow Creek, in Perry County, this small town takes its name from an old pioneer expression, and a postmaster's bad handwriting. The pioneers called a man who had less than $100.00 a "Napper," and if he had more than $100.00 he was called a "Napier." Where the expression originated, or what it means exactly is not known.

Local legend has it that the first postmaster submitted the name Napper, and The Post Office Department accepted Napfor. (1)

NAPOLEONVILLE, Louisiana
Settled in the late 1700's and called Courthouse, it was renamed by an early French settler who had once served in Napoleon's Army. (6)

NAPONEE, Nebraska
Originally there was a small settlement located here called Perth. Tradition has it that one day an Indian wandered into town and the only statement the settlers could get out of him was "Na Pony, Na Pony." This incident took place in the late 1800's, and the settlers, apparently tired or dissatisfied with the name Perth, decided to change the name to Naponee, to commemorate the occasion. (1)

NASHWAUK, Minnesota
Nashwauk, location of the first mine in Itasca County, the Nashwauk Townsite Company platted the village on what was once the site of a lumber camp. Its name, from Nashwauk, a river, is of Algonquin origin, and its meaning is thought to be "land between." The village was incorporated in 1903. (2)

NATCHITOCHES, Louisiana
Named for an Indian tribe of the Caddo Group, the Nachitoches (chestnut

or pawpaw eaters). It was first settled by the French in 1714, and is the oldest town in Louisiana. (6)

NATURAL BRIDGE, Alabama
Natural Bridge was formed thousands of years ago by the erosion of a tributary stream. This stream, with the aid of springs, systematically wore away the soft shale of a large deposit of sandstone which had formed more than two hundred million years ago.

The hard sandstone cap was left, leaving two giant arches that compose this beautiful work of nature known as Natural Bridge.

Here, farmers built their homes on ridges so that water falling on one side flows to the north, reaching the Tennessee, Ohio, and Mississippi Rivers, and on the other side, reaching the Sipsey, Warrior, Tombigbee Rivers, and the Gulf of Mexico. What is now officially "The Natural Bridge of Alabama" is near the post office and village of the same name, about ten miles south of Haleyville. (2)

NATURAL DAM, Arkansas
The town takes its name from a natural dam, well known for its scenic beauty. It is a natural formation of stone, on the mountain fork of Lee Creek. The area was settled as early as 1828.

Actually the people of Natural Dam are scattered among the hills here and get their mail at the Natural Dam Post Office. The Dam, itself, is composed of solid rock and is about 7 feet high. (Hubert L. Bass, President R.C.I., Natural Dam, Ark.)

NAYTAHWAUSH, Minnesota
Principal community in the Reservation in Mahnomen County, Naytahwaush is named for an early tribal chief, and is a Chippewa word meaning "smooth sailing." It was mostly the Mille Lac Chippewa Indians who came to the Twin Lakes area of the reservation. (2)

NECESSITY, Texas
Necessity, in southeastern Stephens County, was settled during the Civil War and Reconstruction periods by ranchers who next experienced the drought of 1886, and chose the name when the post office was applied for in the late 1890's. (3)

NEEDLES, California
Needles was founded in 1835 at the western end of construction of the Santa Fe Railroad. The Southern Pacific Railroad built east from Los Angeles and met the Santa Fe at Needles. Later the Santa Fe bought the

Southern Pacific track and right of way from Needles to Los Angeles. Needles has always been the home of the Navajos.

The name of the town comes from the mountain range to the south. Originally it was called "The Needles," taken from the sharp peaks of the mountains, but was later shortened to Needles. (2)

NEEDMORE, Texas
Needmore, Bailey County, was jokingly named by townsite optimists who said that they would "need more" settlers. (3)

NEEDVILLE, Texas
Needville, on the Texas and New Orleans Railroad in lower Fort Bend County, was established in 1891 by August Schendel, who built a home and a store on the high prairie and called it Schendelville. When he made application for a post office, he changed the name to Needmore as a joke, probably meaning he needed more people. Since the name was already in use, the Post Office Department changed the name to Needville. (3)

NEGAUNEE, Michigan
Negaunee, Marquette County, was so named by the Indians prior to the coming of the white man. The Ojibwa or Chippewa Indians were terribly frightened of the Lake Superior area, therefore they never settled permanently in the area. Negaunee is an Indian word meaning "low," referring to the low altitude of the land in the immediate area. Negaunee is the sister city to Ishpeming. (2)

NEOSHO, Missouri
The name, originally spelled Neozho or Neuzhu, is of Indian derivation, and means "abundant" or "clear water." The name comes from nine flowing springs within the city limits, including Big Spring, which played an important role in the town's history.

The town was founded in 1839, and its most famous native son is Thomas Hart Benton, world-famous American artist. (2)

NEOTAU, Oregon
Neotau is located on the 45th parallel, near Lincoln City, at the north end of Devils Lake, northern Lincoln County, a mile and a half from the Pacific Ocean.

When a post office was established here in 1925 the people wanted to call it Devils Lake, but couldn't due to the confusion it would cause with Devils Lake, North Dakota and Delake, Oregon, now a part of Lincoln City. In their search for a unique name they chose Neotau, an Indian name of uncertain origin and almost uncertain meaning. The guesses about the name have ranged from Japanese to Hebrew. The people here insist that the name is Indian and means "devils lake." While there is no evidence to substantiate this there is equally no evidence to the contrary. (1)

NESQUEHONING, Pennsylvania
Was settled in 1824 by Lehigh Navigation and Coal Company and earlier was known as *Hells Kitchen.* The name is Indian for "at the black lick," or "narrow valley." (4)

NEW CASTLE, Texas
New Castle, on the Wichita Falls and Southern Railway in Young County, was founded in 1908. Because of a mine operated there, the village was named for the famous mining town in England. Pioneer Indian fighters held annual reunions at New Castle, which is a few miles north of the site of Fort Belknap. (3)

NEW DEAL, Texas
New Deal was established in 1948, taking its name from a consolidated school located in the community. The school was constructed during the Roosevelt Administration, and took the name for the party motto. (1)

NEW HOPE, Alabama
During the Civil War this town was named Vienna, and it suffered all the hardships visited upon this area during the occupation by the North. Then, after peace was established the people decided to change the name of the town to New Hope, to signify their hope for the future. (Mrs. Howard C. Jones, Sr., New Market, Ala.)

NEW IBERIA, Louisiana
Was named by its Spanish settlers for the ancient name of Spain, which occupies a part of the Iberian Peninsula. The area was first settled around 1785. (6)

NEW MARKET, Alabama
The first settlement in this area was Hillsboro, which had a store. Later another store was built and people began referring to it as the "New Market." Another story that has credence is that there are a number of villages named New Market, and earlier settlers, feeling homesick, might have named the town for their old home. (Kathleen Paul Jones, Genealogist, New Market, Ala.)

NEW PORT, Texas
New Port, in southeastern Clay County, was first settled by L. Hanock, who pre-empted a homestead in 1872. In 1875, a post office was secured with J. H. Hardy as postmaster. The name *Bear Hill* was selected because a bear was killed on the hill at the Hardy home. By 1879 a town had grown up. The name was changed to Newport, the word being formed from the first letter of the names of seven of the leading citizens. (3)

NEW YORK, Texas
New York, on New York Creek in eastern Henderson County, was named in jest when it was located north of the present site about 1860. (3)

NICE, California
Nice, California was named for Nice, France, and is pronounced (Neece). It receives a lot of mail intended for Nice, France, due to the fact that Nice, France, is located in Californie District.

Nice, California, is located on the largest body of natural fresh water in California. (1)

NINE MILE FALLS, Washington
The town was originally called Helen, in 1904, for some pioneer resident. In 1912 the name was officially changed to Nine Mile Falls for one of several power dams on the Spokane River. The spillway or falls is located approximately nine miles below the town, on the Spokane River, which is a tributary of the Columbia that eventually empties into the Pacific Ocean at Portland, Oregon. (1)

NINE POINTS, Pennsylvania
This is a small farming village, made up mostly of Amish farmers who still farm with horses. At one time there were nine roads that converged upon the town, and gave it the name of Nine Points. (Lucy Mendenhall)

NINETY SIX, South Carolina
Ninety Six is first mentioned in 1730 on a map made by George Hunter, which is now in the Congressional Library. He used, as his basis, personal maps of Indian traders. Undoubtedly Ninety Six is older, but how old no one knows for sure.

It is generally believed that Ninety Six was named by Indian traders because it was Ninety-six miles from Keowee, the largest Cherokee Indian town, then located near today's Clemson College.

The first land grant was in 1735, but the early settlers were largely hunters, cow drivers, and squatters, who bothered little with land grants.

They were practical in that a deed or grant automatically became taxable, so few bothered.

About 1751 Robert Gouedy established the first trading post or store in Upper South Carolina at the point called Ninety Six, where the Cherokee Path forked. The first land battle of the Revolutionary War was fought at Ninety Six between the Whigs (Patriots) and the Tories (Loyalists) forces on November 19–21, 1775. The battle was a draw but resulted in the death of the first South Carolinian in the fight for freedom from England. (2)

NIOBRARA, Nebraska

Established in May, 1856, and moved in 1881, because of a destructive flooding of the Missouri River, it is situated along the banks of the Missouri River, just below the mouth of the Niobrara River. It is from the Niobrara River that this town gets its name. Neobrara is an Indian word meaning "running water." (2)

NISSWA, Minnesota

The original town of Nisswa had three lakes on its boundary. The word means *three* in the Chippewa (Ojibwa) language. Nisswa is now a village and has incorporated into an entire township. (1)

NITTA YUMA, Mississippi

Nitta Yuma is Choctaw or Chickasaw Indian meaning "that is a bear," or "those are bears;" also "those are bear tracks," followed by the appropriate gestures.

Tradition has it that Henry Vick, on one occasion, had some Indians spend the night at his lodge. When they went down to the creek to cross in canoes the next morning, one of the Indians pointed down the creek bank and exclaimed "Nitta Yuma."

Henry Vick was so impressed by the beauty of the words that he named his plantation Nitta Yuma. The original plantation is still located here and owned by Vick's descendants. (1)

NOCATEE, Florida

Nocatee, on the Peace River, in DeSoto County, has a real wild name. Nocatee is Indian and means "What is it?" (6)

NOLO. Pennsylvania

Founded in 1858, Nolo was so named because, situated on a mountain pinnacle, it had no low ground. The hamlet was originally called "Stone House, for a stage coach stop tavern of the same name. (4)

NOODLE, Texas

Noodle, in western Jones County, ten miles north of Merkel, was named for Noodle Creek. Anderson Criswell of Fayette County brought 1,500 head of sheep to the area in 1882.

Noodle Creek is an intermittent stream, which twists and turns its way across Nolan, Taylor and Jones Counties, like a noodle. (3)

NOONDAY, Texas

Noonday, Harrison County, was first called "Shortview." In 1876, after a Baptist church was built, a meeting was called to select a new name for the community. It was held at high noon, and "Noonday" was chosen for the name. (3)

NOPEMING, Minnesota

Nopeming consists of a tuberculosis sanitarium established by St. Louis County in 1912. An associated nursing home, added later, and the surrounding rural area use the same post office. The original superintendent, Dr. Arthur T. Laird, had an interest in history and local culture. He felt that an appropriate Indian name might be most suitable for the Sanatorium and post office. On consultation with some local Chippewa Indians, in search of a suitable name, the word "nopeming" was suggested. The meaning they assured him was "out in the woods." This sounded appropriate and was, therefore, adopted.

It has been noted, however, in later years that when other Chippewas are questioned on this point, they seem to respond with hilarity, but refuse to say why. So far no one has been able to explain the source of their merriment. Could it be that the Indian is taking his revenge in some subtle manner? Could it also be that other towns, with romantic-sounding Indian names, variously translated into romantic English, have a different meaning to the wise old Indians? *Could be!* (R. W. Backus, M.D., Nopeming)

NORMANGEE, Texas

Normangee, once known as Roger's Store, is on the Leon-Madison county line near the old San Antonio road. Made a station on the Texas and Brazos Valley Railroad in 1905, the village took the name Normangee from *Norman G.* Kittrell. (3)

NORMANNA, Texas

Normanna, in Bee County, was settled about 1850 and called San Domingo. In 1886, when the San Antonio and Arkansas Pass Railway extended from

Pettus to San Domingo, the name was changed to Walton, honoring D. A. T. Walton, who located there in 1884. A group of Norwegians settled in the community between 1894 and 1898, and the name of the town was changed to Normanna, which means "Home of the Norsemen." (3)

NORWAY, South Carolina
The name was selected at random by railroad employees establishing whistle stops along the right of way. (6)

NOTI, Oregon
One version of the name Noti is that an old trapper by that name once lived in this area and that the village was named for him.

A more colorful and interesting version is that in the pioneer days, when two men were traveling together with only one horse, they would "ride and tie." One would ride on ahead for a given distance, tie the horse and continue on, by foot. When his companion came to the horse he would mount, ride past the first one, who was now on foot, and continue on for a while. When he had ridden the agreed distance, he would then dismount and tie the horse and continue on foot, etc. Noti, Oregon, was said to have gotten its name when a white man and an Indian were sharing a horse. The white man had agreed to tie the horse in the area of Noti. When the Indian came to the spot, he found no horse, as the white man had continued to ride on, whereupon the Indian remarked in disgust, "white man no tie!" (1)

NOTLA, Texas
Notla, in the southeastern corner of Ochiltree County, was named for the reversed spelling of the name of the Alton Grocery Company of Enid, Oklahoma, which owned a store on the site in the early 1890's. (3)

NOVICE, Texas
Novice, in northwestern Coleman County on the Pecos and Northern Texas Railroad, was originally a store and post office on Rough Creek. Later the post office, supposedly named because the store owners were novices in business, was moved to a small store on the Coleman to Abilene stage line. When the railroad was built about 1910, the community was moved one mile north to its present location. (3)

OAK HILL, West Virginia
Named for its location, 2,000 feet high, overlooking rolling wooded hills and green valleys. (6)

OASIS, Utah
Oasis was settled by John Styler between two mountains. The mountains were rich in juniper, oak, pinion pine, maple and quaken aspen. The valley, itself, was covered with salt grass and greasewoods.

John Styler built a house here, dug irrigation ditches, and planted cottonwood trees. The place, thus, became an Oasis—a green spot in the desert. (Elmo Gillen, granddaughter of John Styler.)

OBLONG, Illinois
Before 1854 this town had the hum-drum name of *Henpeck.* No, it wasn't named for some henpecked husband, but for a Mr. Peck, who moved here and opened a store. People would say "Let's go to Henry Peck's store," finally shortening it to "Let's go to Hen' Peck's store."

When a post office was established in 1854, the citizens decided they needed a more sedate name, like Oblong—a name with real class. The name wasn't chosen at random, however, for there was a flat prairie to the north, called that due to its rectangular shape. It had been so dubbed by pioneer hunters and trappers who ventured into the area from Fort Sackville, at Vincennes, Indiana.

Oblong township lies in the southeastern portion of Illinois, in Crawford County. (Charles Michael Price, Senior, Oblong High School)

OBSIDIAN, Idaho
Obsidian nestles in the Sawtooth Valley in Custer County, Idaho, flanked by the scenic Sawtooth Mountains. The entire area is one of breathtaking beauty.

When a post office was requested for the area, the settlers couldn't agree upon a name. Each wanted the honor of naming it for himself. As the time grew short, a Mr. Williams finally suggested the name Obsidian, as the post office was to be located at the bottom of Obsidian Hill. All agreed to the name.

Local legend has it that the name Obsidian is Indian and means "flint rock." The flinty hill, believed to be of volcanic origin, has large outcrops of this flint. The Indians of the area favored it for making tips on their arrows. At this writing there is a bill before the Congress to make the area a National Park.

The dictionary lists the mineral obsidian as a volcanic glass, similar in composition to granite and usually dark in color.

The postmaster relates the story of a pioneer family named Decker, from Colorado, who settled here on the Salmon River. They had a small child of four months who was taken from his makeshift high chair by a cougar, and was never found again. As a result of this bitter and heartbreaking experience, they stayed a short time and then left the area forever. As a result of this incident, a flat here is called Decker Flat, and there is also a Decker Creek, Decker Lake, a Decker Trail and a Decker Peak. Even the postmaster is named Decker (no connection, of course), who is better known as "Trigger Jim," and serves as a guide, packer, and is an excellent gunsmith. (1)

OCALA, Florida
Seat of Marion County, the town's name is a derivation of Ocali, which is Indian for "waters edge." This was the name of a nearby Indian village Hernando DeSoto passed through in 1539 during his explorations in Florida. In 1825 an Indian trading post was established here and in 1827 a fort was erected and named Fort King. This was central Florida headquarters during the Seminole Wars, which continued until August 1842. (2)

OCEANA, West Virginia
In Wyoming County, this village was settled in 1850 and named Cassville, then changed to Sumpterville. In 1855 it was again renamed Oceana, to honor the daughter of an Indian chief named Cornstalk. (6)

OCHLOCKNEE, Georgia
The name of this small town was taken from the Ochlocknee River, which got its name from the Indians. The name is said to mean "crooked waters." There are several different spellings such as Ochlocknee, Ochlochnee, and Ochlockonee. It must be remembered that the Indians had no written language and all spellings are English, French, or Spanish versions of what the Indians said. (1)

OCONOMOWOC, Wisconsin
There are a number of versions of the origin of the name "Oconomowoc," an Indian name credited to both the Winnebago and Pottawatomie tribes. From the time the first Indians paddled their canoes down the "River of Lakes," Oconomowoc has been famed for its waterways. The Winnebago name for the region has been translated as "place where the river falls." On the earliest maps of the lakes in 1837, the Oconomowoc River with its chain of lakes was named Conimauwak Creek. It was the water possibilities in the area that drew the first white settler, Charles B. Sheldon, who built a claim shanty here in April 1837.

In 1844, the town of Oconomowoc came into being, and 1845 Waukesha County and the name Oconomowoc became official.

A legend that grew up about the unusual name Oconomowoc says that a white man came across an Indian who was about to shoot a coon busily eating his corn. When he shot the coon, the Indian threw up his hands and cried "O, Cooney, no mo' walk!" thus the name Oconomowoc, and the nickname of the town "Cooney." Alas for a good tale, that's probably all it was. (Josephine M. Machus, Directory, Oconomowoc Public Library)

OCONTO, Nebraska
Settled in the fall of 1887, local legend has it that the name comes from Oconto, Wisconsin. The name is Menominee Indian and means "place of the pickerel." (1)

OCTAVIA, Nebraska
Octavia is a small village located in the northern part of Butler County, and was named by Mr. Speltz in honor of his daughter with the lovely name of "Octavia Speltz." The village has the distinction of being the only one in the county with no taverns or liquor stores, but boasts a very fine church. (J. J. Papa)

ODD, West Virginia
When it was decided to establish a post office here the old settlers had a meeting to decide on a name. Someone suggested they choose an unusual or odd name. The name Odd was immediately nominated, seconded, carried, and everyone went fishing. (1)

OGALLALA, Nebraska
Gateway of the Northern Plains, that was Ogallala from 1870 to 1885. Hard bitten Wyoming and Montana cattlemen met in Ogallala's hotel and saloons with Texas cattle kings, and bargained over cattle prices. Gold flowed freely across the tables, liquor across the bar, and occasionally blood across the floor—as a bullet brought some unlucky cowhand to his death on the floor boards of "Tuck's Saloon."

Ogallala received its name from the Ogala Sioux Indians. The word mean "scatter," or "scatter one's own." (2)

OHIOWA, Nebraska
This small community was settled and named Ohiowa in 1887, by settlers from Ohio and Iowa, which explains its unusual name.

Ohiowa, suffering the many hardships of the early days and of the dry years of the 30's, hung on, and today some of the first settlers are still here and can recall the town in its beginning.

In the full name of this community you have the name of three states—Ohio, Iowa, and Nebraska. (1)

OIL TROUGH, Arkansas
In south-central Independence County, this town takes its name, according to tradition, from the bear oil shipped out of here in its pioneer days. Being short of barrels, tree trunks were hollowed out with axes, much like dug-out canoes. These trunks (or troughs, as they were called) were packed with bear grease, fastened together to form rafts and floated down as far as New Orleans.

The bear grease was used for cooking, and for hair and leather dressing. (6)

OKABENA, Minnesota
Okabena is a Sioux Indian name meaning "heron's nest" or "nest of the heron," most likely referring to the large blue herons that once frequently nested in this area. A lake near Worington was first named Okabena. When the railroad came through in 1879 a siding was placed at the present town site and named Okabena, by the railroad authorities. (1)

OKAHUMPKA, Florida
The name of this small town is Indian and is variously translated into "lonely waters" or "bitter waters." Since there is no known "bitter waters" here it is believed to mean "lonely waters." It was settled in 1885 by the Reverend Edmund Snyder of Germantown, Pennsylvania, on the site of an old Indian village that stood here until 1835. (1)

OKANOGAN, Washington
In north-central Washington, on the Canadian border, the name is Indian for "meeting place." (2)

OKEECHOBEE, Florida
The name of this town is a shining example of the wide variations in the languages of the American Indian. "Oki" means water, and "chobi" means big, in the language of the Florida Indian, while in Minnesota "Minne" means water, and "Tonka" means big. Thus we have Okeechobee and Minnetonka both meaning "Big Water."

A wild and wooly battle was fought here on Christmas Day, 1837, when Colonel Zachary Taylor, at the head of 1,000 men, attacked about 500 Seminoles under the leadership of Billy Bowlegs (Bolek) and got beaten! (6)

OKLAUNION, Texas
Oklaunion, in northeastern Wilbarger County, received its name from the hope of a junction there between the Fort Worth and Denver Railroad,

and a proposed line into Oklahoma. "Buckskin Joe" Works was the chief promoter of the town, which had a brief boom as a railroad terminus. (3)

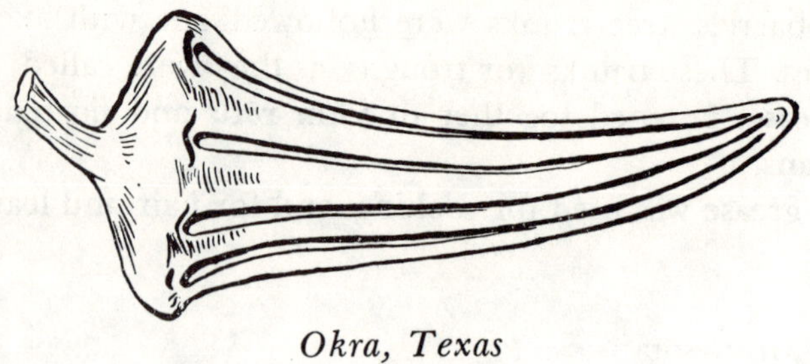

Okra, Texas

OKRA, Texas
Okra, in southwestern Eastland County, is an agricultural community lying along Sabana Creek. It is said to have been named when Live McCulloch, early postmaster, found that the vegetable grew well in the area. (3)

OLD FIELDS, West Virginia
In Hardy County, near the south branch of the Potomac, this town was so called because pioneers discovered an old Indian field there that the Shawnee Indians had plowed, and where they had planted corn. The village was established in the 1750's. (6)

OLD GLORY, Texas
Located in eastern Stonewall County, it was called Brandenberg when it was settled by German families in 1903. In 1917, during the first days of World War I, the residents asked that the name be changed to Old Glory. (*See* Emblem, Wyo.) (3)

OLD HICKORY, Tennessee
Originally named Jacksonville, it was changed to Old Hickory in 1923. Andrew Jackson (known as Old Hickory) had lived in the vicinity for eleven years, and later built the Hermitage, nearby. (6)

OLD HUNDRED, North Carolina
So named because the railroad placed a marker here denoting the spot as being 100 miles to Wilmington. It was later found that the marker was wrong, as it was nearer Wilmington, but the name stuck. (6)

OLD OCEAN, Texas
This community lies about thirty miles from the Gulf of Mexico, which is the nearest thing to an ocean you can find in the vicinity. Just south of

Old Glory, Texas

town, however, there is an oilfield, in what geologists say was the bed of an ancient ocean. At one time the town was known as Chance's Prairie. (1)

OLD TOWN, Florida
In 1818 General Andrew Jackson attacked an Indian village here, and bagged a British officer who had been collaborating with the Creek Chief Hadjo, who himself had previously helped the British in the war of 1812. As a result of his confession he was tried and executed, an act that President John Quincy Adams had a heck of a time explaining to the outraged British.

Old Town, Florida, located in Dixie County, near the Suwannee River, has been the site of human habitation longer than the recorded history of this young nation. It is the site of an old Indian village, and probably the oldest white settlement in this part of Florida. It is thought that the reason for the name is based upon its antiquity. (1)

OLD TRAP, North Carolina
The location was occupied as early as 1681. Located at a busy crossroads it

had several taverns or inns where a number of "painted women" hung out. The commuters who passed through on their way to and from work were often prone to tarry here a while in the evenings. Their wives called it the "Trap." From this inglorious name evolved the eventual name of the town, Old Trap, which now has a population of about 300 people, and no "painted women." (6)

OLD UNION, Texas

Old Union, in southern Limestone County, was named for an early interdenominational church. (3)

OLYMPIA, Washington

Washington's state capital, located at the southern tip of Puget Sound, is one of the oldest communities in the Pacific Northwest. The townsite was started in 1850, and became the territorial capital in 1853.

The name comes from the Olympic Mountains, a part of the Coastal Range in northwest Washington, whose highest peak is Olympus, 8,150 feet. They are believed to have been named for Mount Olympus, legendary home of the greater Grecian Gods. (2)

OMAHA, Arkansas

The town was once known as Sha-wa-nah, and was an important stop on a heavily traveled pioneer trail. Located in northwestern Arkansas, in Boone County, near Bull Shoals Lake, it received the name Omaha, legend has it, to commemorate the Indians by that name. (6)

OMAHA, Nebraska

Manuel de Lisa, a St. Louis fur trader, made his first trip up the Missouri River in 1805, and later established a post near present-day Omaha. The U. S. Army established Fort Atkinson several miles north of Omaha, in 1819. The first permanent white settlement in Nebraska was founded at Bellevue, just south of Omaha, in 1823.

The city of Omaha had its birth in 1854, after the Nebraska territory was organized and the way cleared for settlement of lands west of the Missouri.

The Otoe, Missouri, and Omaha were among the tribes that camped on the bluffs rising on either side of the Missouri River which rolls southward between what are now the states of Nebraska and Iowa. It was from the tribe of Omaha Indians that the city of Omaha took its name. (2)

ONANCOCK, Virginia

Founded in 1680 by a grant from the king of England, the town was incorporated on February 15, 1882 by Act of the General Assembly.

The name comes from the Onancock Indians, and either means "Foggy Place" or "Foggy Bottom." (William H. Chandler, Mayor)

ONAWAY, Michigan
Onaway was founded in 1881 and called Shaw. Largely a resort town the name was changed to Onaway, Indian meaning "Awake." (6)

ONEONTA, Alabama
Variously interpreted as Creek or Cerokee Indian for "The place we seek," it is pronounced OH-nee-AHH-tah, and is located thirty-six miles north of Birmingham. (2)

ONEONTA, New York
Cradled by a ring of hills, Oneonta, Otsego County, and called the "City of Hills," Oneonta has an Indian name meaning "stony place." (6)

ONLY, Tennessee
According to Hickman County history, the place was originally named *Dreamer,* but the citizens being discontent with this name, since it suggested the community must be asleep, decided to rename it.

The most popular version of how Only got its name is that a merchant of the community, each time a prospective customer would ask the price of something, would invariably quote the price as *"only"* so much. Whatever the price might be. (1)

ONO, California
First named Eagle Creek, the town petitioned for a post office, and the request was granted provided they chose a new name. It seemed there was another town named Eagle Creek. It was the minister, a Baptist named William S. Kidder, who suggested the name ONO, taken from the bible. The name was approved and the post office granted in 1882. (6)

ONO, Pennsylvania
According to old timers in this small village it received its unusual name in the identical manner as Onoville, New York. (1)

ONOVILLE, New York
Once named *"Jugville,"* because of the thirsty lumberjacks who made the town, the city fathers decided to change the name to something more sedate when the town began to grow. They held a meeting to entertain suggestions for a new name. Each name suggested would bring the cry "Oh no, not that!" Finally after a number of "Oh no's," someone said, "Why not call it Ono-

Onoville, New York

ville." The name struck their fancy and was accepted and the village of Onoville had its new name. (6)

ONTONAGON, Michigan

Located at the confluence of the Onatonagon River and Lake Superior, at an altitude of 1016 feet, the name comes from the Indian "Nan-ton-a-Gon," which means bowl. It was given as a name to the river because of the bowl-like shape of its mouth. James K. Paul, the first white man to settle here, founded the town of Ontonagon May 3, 1843. He is credited with taking out the famous Ontonagon Copper Boulder, which is on display in the Smithsonian Institution.

When the first white men settled here in 1843, the Indians had no knowledge or legends of this ancient people who apparently came here in the summer months for copper, which they took out of the rock ridges and bluffs using stone hammers, fire and water. Who they were and where they came from is still a mystery—believed by some to have been the Mound Builders and by others the Aztecs. It has been estimated that it took 10,000 men a period of 1,000 years to do the work which was accomplished on the entire copper range, including the Keweenaw peninsula, and that all work ceased at least by 1200 A.D. Many of the grooved hammers are now being found where rock-crushing operations have removed rock piles. Carbon 14 tests have established that this operation took place here three to five thousand years ago. (2)

OOLTEWAH, Tennessee
Is Cherokee Indian for "resting place" or "owl's nest." As is often the case, the Indian language had many meanings, depending upon the pronunciation. The town is the former seat of James County, which in 1919 was combined with Hamilton County. (1)

OPELOUSAS, Louisiana
In central St. Landry County, it was settled in the middle 1700's. It was named for the Opelousa Indian Tribe, a branch of the Attakapas, which were rumored to be cannibalistic. The city has a population of around 18,000. (6)

OPPORTUNITY, Washington
The district known as Opportunity was developed as an area under irrigation in 1905 by a corporation known as Modern Irrigation and Land Company. The real estate agents, Neely and Young, held a contest for suggested names. From the names submitted they selected "Opportunity" as the appropriate one and awarded the winner $10.00. (2)

OQUAWKA, Illinois
Oquawka owes its name to the Indians with whom it was a noted point in their travels and tribal convocations. The word is said to signify the lower end of termination of the Yellow Banks, the point indicated being situated at the termination of a series of high sand bluffs along the river extending at intervals to a point above the town of New Boston, eighteen miles above Oquawka.

Tradition is that the name was that of an Indian chief, but there is no documentary proof of this. (1)

ORACLE, Arizona
Oracle was taken from the ship that brought a young man around the horn. (5)

ORE CITY, Texas
Ore City, a retail market and shipping point in eastern Upshur County, was named for the iron ore mined intermittently since before the Civil War. In 1911, L. P. Featherstone persuaded the Santa Fe Railroad to finance a line for Port Boliver, and by 1914 some thirty miles of road were built, connecting Ore City with Longview. World War I prevented further construction. The line was abandoned in 1927. (3)

ORISKANY, New York

Located halfway between Rome and Utica, in Oneida County, Oriskany sits astride the site of an old Indian village named Oriska, near the confluence of Oriskany Creek and the Mohawk River. It was here that one of the bloodiest battles of the War for Independence started, although it was fought a few miles away. Hand-to-hand fighting between Colonists and Tories and Indians raged all through the night, with the Colonists, battered and bloody, coming out on top. The battle was fought on August 5, 1777. It was called the turning point of the Revolution by many historians. (6)

ORONOGO, Missouri

The name Oronogo has quite an interesting origin. In 1847 ore was discovered along the banks of Center Creek here, in the southern part of this small town. Quickly a settlement grew up here and it had a mining camp name, long since forgotten. When it came time to incorporate, and to get a really permanent name, it was selected in a most unusual way.

When prospectors would come to the settlement to ask for credit they were asked if they had struck ore. If they said no, they were told that it was "ore or no go." When they named the town they chose to call it "Ore or no go," or Oronogo. Many years ago this story was featured in Robert L. Ripley's "Believe it or not" newspaper column. (1)

OSAKIS, Minnesota

Though the name sounds peaceful enough, it is Chippewa or Sioux and means "danger." It probably received this name from the many battles that took place here between the Chippewas and the Sioux. (6)

OSAWATOMIE, Kansas

The territory was first settled by the Massachusetts Aid Society, the town being laid out in 1854 by O. C. Brown, platted in January 1858 by R. J. Roscoe, and recorded in 1860. Osawatomie, named for the surrounding rivers, the Osage and the Pottawatomie, is located in about the center of what was once a government reservation, set apart for the purpose of *domestication* of the Indians! The Indians could not be induced to remain in so small a space and scattered farther west.

Osawatomie has the honor of having the name of "Jayhawker" originate here. Before the sun was up one morning in the fall of 1856, a free-stater by the name of Pat Devlin was seen riding into town on a well-loaded mule. A neighbor remarked, "Pat, you look like you have been on an excursion." Pat answered that he had been "jayhawking." Asked for an explanation he replied that he had been foraging off the enemy; that in Ireland, a bird called the jayhawk worried its prey before devouring it. From this incident came the now familiar name Jayhawker, meaning a person from Kansas. (2)

OSCEOLA, Arkansas
On the Mississippi River, next to the Tennessee line, it was platted in 1830 by William B. Edrington from an Indian village that occupied the site. It was first named Plum Point, but later it was changed to Osceola in honor of the Florida Indian chief of the Seminole Indian nation. Chief Osceola was the chief who defied the U. S. Government when they were moving the Seminoles from Florida to Oklahoma. Osceola is a city of around 7,000 population. (2)

OSPREY, Florida
A fishing village on the Gulf of Mexico, it was named for the osprey, or fish hawk. It is a large hawk which feeds on fish, and often has a wing-spread of four-and-a-half feet. (6)

OSSEO, Minnesota
Platted and settled around 1856, the name for the town was chosen carefully. Located just north of Minneapolis, it was named for the son of the evening star, Osseo, in the *Song of Hiawatha.* (6)

OSSINEKE, Michigan
Located at the mouth of Devil River, on Lake Huron, this small fishing village has an Indian name which is a corruption of Wawsinekie, which means "Image stones." The stones stood on the site of the village prior to 1839. A romantic and fairy-like tale has been woven about these stones by the Indians, who worshipped them. It seems that Chief Shinggabaw told his people that his spirit would return after he died, and would come back to this place. Enemies, finding the idea of the chief returning again too appalling, stole the stones, put them in canoes and started out across Thunder Bay. The angry waters rose up and claimed the culprits, and when the Indians of Chief Shinggabaw's tribe returned to the place of the stones, there they stood in their original place!

The stones have since been lost in the bottom of Lake Huron, and the Indians were driven westward by the white man and his "progress." (1)

OSSINING, New York
In Westchester County, jammed in between New Jersey, Connecticut, and New York City, this city was incorporated in 1813 under the name of *Sing Sing.* Sing Sing prison was built here in 1824, and its fame soon outgrew the town. Finally in 1901, after years of chafing under the weight of tired

jokes about Sing Sing Prison, the city changed the name to Ossining, which is Indian, and symbolically means "stone upon stone." (2)

OSWEGO, New York
The seat of Oswego County, at the confluence of the Oswego River and Lake Ontario, the name is Indian and means "pouring out of waters." (6)

OTOE, Nebraska
The village of Otoe, Nebraska, located in Otoe County, was first named Berlin in 1882. During World War I, feeling was so strong against Germany that the citizens voted to change the name to Otoe, taking the name from the county.

Otoe County was named by the first territorial legislature on March 2, 1855, for the Otoe Indians, a friendly tribe in eastern Nebraska. In 1967, Nebraska celebrated its centennial as a state. (1)

OTTAWA, Ohio
Established in 1833, shortly after the last of the Ottawas had been driven west to reservations. First known as Tawa Town for an Ottawa chief, it was later renamed Ottawa for the Ottawa Indians. (2)

OTTERTAIL, Minnesota
Before there were roads in this wilderness area the best method of transportation was its lakes and rivers. As the Leaf River chain of lakes drain toward the Gulf of Mexico and the Ottertail River flows toward Hudson's Bay, by way of Bois des Sioux, and the Red River of the north, the early explorer could portage from Leaf Lake to Portage Lake to Donald Lake to Pelican Bay and Ottertail Lake then down to the Ottertail River. This journey was an important link in the early transportation chain.

The first explorers on record were through this area in the 1750's. A French explorer named a lake he discovered "Lac Queue Otter," or "Lake of the Ottertail," as there is a sand bar where the river enters the lake that is shaped like an otter's tail.

In 1849 a Hudson's Bay Company trader named Donald McDonald established a trading post here on the east shore of the lake and named it Ottertail. The present village of Ottertail came into being in 1902 when the "Soo" Line Railroad was built through the area and is a mile east of the old village. (G. A. "Jack" Schultz, Postmaster)

OURAY, Colorado
Ouray grew from a miner's pick-and-shovel as did many other gold towns, and the six shooter and rough and tumble brawls were Ouray's teething

ring. From every gulch and hillside someone cried "GOLD!" until Ouray's population reached 3,500. The free gold soon was exhausted and the more substantial mines and miners stayed, while the fortune seekers left for easier pickins elsewhere. A wealth of minerals has been extracted from these hills but geologists claim that the surface has only been scratched.

The town of Ouray is nestled in some of the most spectacular mountain scenery in the Western hemisphere. It was named for the famed Ute chief, Ouray. The valley was a favorite camping place of the Indians who bathed in the curative hot springs bubbling from the floor of the valley. The town was founded in a mining boom in 1876; the most famous discovery was Thomas Walsh's Camp Bird Mine which bought his daughter, Evelyn Walsh McLean, the "Hope Diamond" and launched her in Washington society. Today Camp Bird is still producing. (2)

OVERALL, Virginia

The village and post office was named many years ago for a family of Overalls, who lived here. (1)

OWATONNA, Minnesota

The city was named after the frail, sickly daughter of a mighty Indian chief called Wabena. Legend has it that Wabena brought his ailing daughter here to drink from a bubbling fountain the wondrous healing water called "minnewaucan" (Curing Water). The legend had a happy ending, because when spring time came Owatonna had regained her beauty and health, and joy once again reigned in the teepee of the great chief, Wabena.

Here was the site of the Sioux massacre which began August 18, 1862, and which was incited and conducted by Chief Little Crow. It marks a distinct epoch in the history of the savage butchery of that era. In the short space of thirty-six hours, over eight hundred innocent settlers were butchered, scalped, burned alive, or tortured to death. The Sioux tribes were caused to undergo great privation and suffering by the prolonged delay of the government (then in the throes of the Civil War) to pay their annuities; white traders treated them unfairly, and settlers encroached upon Indian lands. The massacre was prematurely precipitated by two drunken Indians who shot and killed several persons sometime before Little Crow was ready for the wholesale butchery. But it had begun, and fearing the whites would punish the murderers and prepare to resist further attack he ordered the massacre to proceed. Six hundred braves engaged in this terrible work.

A government messenger with $70,000 in gold for the Indians arrived the day after the blow had fallen. This, however, was only a small part of the $555,000 then due the Indians from the government. Yet had this installment arrived earlier, it might possibly have averted the catastrophe. (2)

OWEGO, New York

Owego was built on the site of an old Indian village, Ahwahga, which means, "where the valley widens." The old Indian village was completely destroyed in 1779 by the Sullivan-Clinton soldiers. (6)

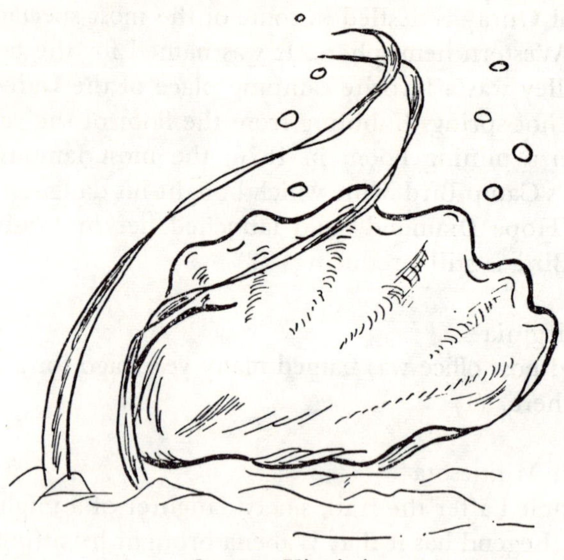

Oyster, Virginia

OYSTER, Virginia

Well, to begin with this is a small fishing village on the edge of mud flats and salt marshes. Why name a town for an oyster? You'd never believe it but here goes anyway: This small village was originally called Cobb's Mill, as a man named Perimeter Cobb had a water-powered grist mill here. Old "Rim" Cobb was interested in sports, but could only scrape up enough athletes for a Shinny team, as this game can be played with as little as two players. It uses a wooden burl, cut from a pine limb, and it is batted back and forth in the manner of ice hockey. As the village continued to grow he finally had enough players for a basketball team, and eventually enough for a baseball team, called Cobb's Mill Mudlarks.

One day the Mudlarks were playing the Cape Charles Sliders. Among the spectators at the game was a postal inspector, along with some friends and relatives, who had come down from Washington to establish some new post offices. The game ended in a fight, with the slinging of fists, bats, and mud. Old Rim Cobb went into the "shucking house" and came out with a gallon of "select" oysters (in those days a "select" oyster was as big as a pork chop) and gave them to his team and hurried back for more. In a matter of minutes the Charles team and supporters had been routed and the Mudlarks were getting into full swing. They let the "select" oysters fly at every individual in sight. The inspector and his friends made a brave stand, but soon left in pain and utter defeat. Folklore has it that no one in the group recovered from the shock—or could say nothing but "Oyster"—for a week or more.

When the post office officials in Washington asked the inspector why he had so many black eyes all he could say was "Oyster." When they asked him why he sat so lightly on his seat, he replied "Oyster." When they asked him if he had established any new post offices, he pointed to a small dot on the map and replied "Oyster!" His refusal to further discuss the details led the Post Office Department to name the little village post office "Oyster," without further questions!

When a northeaster blows and mackerel boats come into this harbor for refuge, the population sometimes grows to almost 200. ("Hardtimes" Hunt, Mayor, Oyster, Virginia)

PAGELAND, South Carolina
Once called Old Store, Pageland was renamed by the Cheraw and Lancaster Railroad for its president S. H. Page, when it established a depot here in 1904. (6)

PAHOKEE, Florida
Located in Palm Beach County, on the banks of Lake Okeechobee, the name is Indian and means "grass water," presumably for its proximity to the lake with its low water, and the reeds and grass that grow in it near the shoreline. (6)

PAINCOURTVILLE, Louisiana
The small town of Paincourtville got its unusual name, according to tradition, when a traveler, angry at his inability to buy a loaf of bread here, dubbed it "Short-of-bread-town," or in French Paincourtville. (1)

PAINTED POST, New York
The Indians who originally occupied the site of the village called it "Tecarnase-tea-ah" or "a hewn sign." According to an account written in 1780 by a prisoner of the Mohawk tribe an Indian chief won a major victory at this spot. Twenty-eight of his enemies were killed and thirty were taken prisoner. The chief is said to have commemorated his victory by erecting a monument at the place of battle. A tree was felled, hewn four square, and painted red.

The twenty-eight dead were symbolically painted in black without heads, while the thirty prisoners were represented in black paint with heads intact. The post, thus erected, gave posterity an account of a battle between whites and Indians. Who they were, however, remains unknown.

The original post endowed this place with a name as unusual as any. By 1803 the first namesake had disintegrated and a fitting substitute was deemed necessary. It was replaced with substitutes for the original also in 1823, and 1893. Finally in 1950 the present monument was erected at which time the citizens held a gala three-day celebration. (2)

PAINT ROCK, Texas
Paint Rock is the county seat of Concho County, and was founded in 1879. The town is located just south of the Concho River, and on the north side, a bluff begins and runs along the river to the west. This bluff is about one hundred feet high and is composed of limestone ledges with considerable overhang. On these stone ledges are some fifteen hundred Indian paintings or pictographs representing many of the Western tribes of Indians. Some go back beyond the white man's knowledge. It is from these paintings that the town of Paint Rock, Texas, takes its name. (1)

PANCAKE, Texas
Pancake, in northwestern Coryell County, had a post office known as Brush, when William W. Balch became postmaster in 1894. By 1901 it was deemed prudent to get a more sedate name for the village and post office, so they had it changed to Pancake, in honor of a Mr. J. R. Pancake. (3)

PANHANDLE, Texas
Panhandle, in south-central Carson County, was named for its location in the Texas Panhandle. Known as Panhandle City, the site was the terminus for the Panhandle and Santa Fe Railroad in 1887, and became county seat when Carson County was organized in 1888. (3)

PANTHER BURN, Mississippi
Legend has it that this small village got its name from a nearby plantation, where panthers (cougar or puma) were so bad that they finally had to burn the woods to get rid of them. Thereafter the plantation was referred to as "The Panther Burn Plantation." (1)

PAOLI, Pennsylvania
Took its name from the General Paoli Tavern, destroyed by fire in 1905. The tavern was named after General Pasquale Paoli, the liberator of Corsica, prior to the American Revolution. Americans, seeking independence from England, felt a close relationship to General Paoli and his cause. (4)

PARADIS, Louisiana
The name is French for Paradise, and it was so called because this area abounded with wild game and was truly a hunter's paradise. (6)

PARADISE, California
The western slope of the Sierra foothills holds a unique settlement appropriately named Paradise. Covering an area of 18 square miles, well above the valley fog, and below the snow, it is high enough to escape the valley heat and is ideal in its seasonal changes for fruits, vegetables, nuts and apples—even people. Altitude 1,300 to 2,300 feet, Paradise was here during the 1849 California Gold Rush.

Surrounding Paradise are such historic mining settlements as *Helltown, Dogtown, Toadtown, Cherokee Diggins, Whiskey Flat, Nimshew, Nelson Bar,* and *Yankee Hill.* Most of these have disappeared into the dim pages of history, but Paradise lives on. (2)

PARADISE, Pennsylvania
Was settled about 1800 by Dunkards and Mennonites. In the year 1812 a settler, Joshua Scott, stood in the middle of the road which connected Philadelphia with Lancaster. As he looked over the beautiful area he was so thrilled with what he saw that he called it Paradise. From this point the community has been named Paradise. (1)

PARADISE, Texas
Located in southwestern Wise County on the Rock Island Railroad, it was called Paradise Prairie in 1873, when Bill Anderson built the first store. Tradition has it that the name was given by pioneers for the beautiful flowers that were in bloom when they first came to this area. (1)

PARAGOULD, Arkansas
Originally a lumber town it was named for two railroad men, J. W. Paramore and Jay Gould. (6)

PARCHMENT, Michigan
Parchment derived its name from the large industry of making parchment paper here. (1)

PARK RAPIDS, Minnesota
Settled in 1880, it received its name from the park-like appearance of a grove of trees, and from the rapids of the Fish Hook River, which has since been tempered by a dam. (2)

Parrott, Virginia

PARROTT, Virginia
This small town was formed in 1900 by a Coal Mining Company, who named the town and the post office in honor of John Parrott. (1)

PARSIPPANY, New Jersey
The name Parsippany is taken from the Indian word "Parsippanong," meaning "the place where the river or brook winds and creeps through the valley!" Darn clever of those Indians to say so much with so little.

In 1644, King Charles II of England granted a vast area of land to Lord John Berkely and Sir George Carteret. Parsippany, Troy Hills Township, was part of that land. In 1928, the township of Parsippany-Troy Hills was incorporated as a separate town. (2)

PASSADUMKEAG, Maine
Located at the confluence of the Passadumkeag and Penobiscor Rivers, the name is Indian and means "quick or running water." The islands in the river still belong to the Indians, and there is an old Indian burial ground located here where arrow heads have been found, and are on display at Bar Harbor, Maine. (1)

PASS CHRISTIAN, Mississippi
In Harrison, on the Gulf of Mexico, the town takes its name from a

channel named "Christian's Pass," which was discovered in 1699 by Christian L'Adnier, a French explorer. (6)

PAUL SMITHS, New York
Apollo A. Smith came into the wild Adirondack country and started a hotel. By 1870 the hotel was attracting guests of wealth and prominence with its excellent food, fine livery stable, telegraph office, barber shop and later mail service. Apollo was a difficult name to pronounce so the guests began to shorten it to Pol and eventually to Paul. Finally a community grew up around the hotel and when the post office was established it was named Paul Smith's.

Eventually an electric railroad was built into the area, and this brought guests from the New York Central Railroad, several miles away. Grover Cleveland, E. H. Harriman, P. T. Barnum, Teddy Roosevelt, Whitelaw Reid, Calvin Coolidge and others were regular guests.

Apollo "Paul" Smith had three children, but they had none. The last surviving son left his estate to found the Paul Smith College, which is named in memory of his father the original Apollo "Paul" Smith. (Historian, Paul Smiths, Town of Brighton, New York)

PAWNEE, Oklahoma
Originally a trading post was made the site of the Pawnee Agency in 1876, when that tribe was moved from its home in Nebraska to Oklahoma. (6)

PAWNEE CITY, Nebraska
Takes its name from the Pawnee Indian Tribe that occupied a small village near the present site of Pawnee City. (2)

PAWTUCKET, Rhode Island
Second largest city in the state, with an Indian name meaning "fall of the water," Pawtucket secured its fame as an industrial center long before its incorporation as a city, in 1885. Its first settler was Joseph Jenks, Jr., a skilled iron worker who established a forge at the falls of the Blackstone River in 1671, initiating the iron industry for which the community was noted in the eighteenth century. (2)

PAW PAW, Illinois
Three miles east of the present site of Pawpaw was a grove of Pawpaw trees. A settlement there was called Pawpaw Grove, then later East Pawpaw. When the Burlington put a branch track through this area, it missed East Pawpaw, so the residents simply moved the town to the railroad and called it Pawpaw, Illinois. (Mrs. Theodore Rosenkrans, Paw Paw, Illinois)

PEACH TREE, Texas
Peach Tree, in northwestern Jasper County, was settled in the 1850's and named for the wild peach trees which grew in the area. (3)

PEA RIDGE. Arkansas
The name Pea Ridge came about naturally. The early community, founded in 1853, was called Pea Vine Ridge, for wild pea vines that were found growing along the neighboring ridge. Later the name was shortened to Pea Ridge.

Just five miles to the east, the greatest conflict of the Civil War west of the Mississippi was fought, March 7–9, 1862. It was a Federal victory that saved Missouri for the Union, and was called the Battle of Pea Ridge. (2)

PECAN GAP, Texas
Pecan Gap, in northwestern Delta County, was established in the early 1880's and named for the pecan trees found by the first settlers. The pecan tree is the state tree of Texas. (3)

PECULIAR, Missouri
In 1887 a petition for a post office was sent to Washington and the name Excelsior was suggested as a possible name for the small Cass County hamlet. Word came back that this name was taken by another new town, and Mr. E. T. Thompson, the new postmaster, sent back word that any name would do, just so it was different or "peculiar." The Post Office Department sent word that the name of the new post office would indeed be "Peculiar," and Peculiar, Missouri, it is. (E. P. Schug, Pres., The Cass County Bank, Peculiar, Missouri.)

PEE DEE, South Carolina
Near the Pee Dee River, in Marion County, this town was named for a tribe of Indians that once occupied this area. (6)

PEEKSKILL, New York
Located in lower southeastern New York State, on the Hudson River, in Westchester County, it was settled in 1665 by Jan Peek, a Dutch trader. He settled along the banks of a creek and named it for himself. The word "Kill" is Dutch and means a channel, creek, stream, or river. (6)

PEEL TREE, West Virginia
Named for a nearby creek of the same name. The town, according to local

tradition, was once named *Scoop Town* because two men working in a mill here had a fight with scoop shovels. (6)

PELAHATCHIE, Mississippi
Located in Rankin County, Pelahatchie is named for Pelahatchie Creek, which is Indian for "hurricane." (6)

PENITAS, Texas
Penitas, in southern Hidalgo County, was the site of a Tejone Indian village called Penitas or "little pebbles," as early as 1625. A Spanish settlement reported to have been made in 1682 was not permanent. In 1904 the present townsite was laid out by the St. Louis, Brownsville, and Mexico Railroad. (3)

PENN'S NECK, New Jersey
Over 250 years ago, along a trail they blazed through virgin forests, the sons of two families related by marriage settled in New Jersey, calling their settlement Penn's Neck. In 1737, Garrett Schenck and John Covenhoven jointly bought a tract of 6,500 acres from three sons of William Penn. They came from Monmouth County and paid 2,175 pounds sterling.

This land had originally been acquired by William Penn in 1693. His holdings formed a neck of land nearly surrounded by water, and it is supposed that this topography gave the tract its name. It extended east to west from the Millstone River to Duck Pond Run and north to south from Stony Brook to Bear Swamp. It is located in West Windsor Township. (2)

PENN YAN, New York
Penn Yan, Yates County, on the upper end of Keuka Lake, got its name as a result of a controversy between settlers from New England and those from Pennsylvania. Unable to agree upon a name, they finally compromised and named it Penn Yan, *Penn* for Pennsylvania, and *Yan* for Yankee! (2)

PEP, New Mexico
A Mr. Bates donated the land for a Mr. Cox to build a store, and a Mr. Hightower furnished the water. When there were enough people living here to justify a post office, with Mr. Cox as the postmaster, he declined to name it for himself, and couldn't name it for Bates without hurting the feelings of Mr. Hightower, and vice versa. Nothing really important had happened here to give it an historical name, so he named it Pep, because he believed the dirt road here would someday become a highway,

and make this a "peppy" town. Pep is located on Highway 18, and is now pretty peppy. (1)

PEP, Texas
Pep, in extreme northwestern Hockley County, developed from the sale of 42,000 acres of land to the Yellowhouse Land Company in 1924 as the site for a Catholic colony. The activity of the people and their spirited manner of getting things done gave it its name. (3)

PERRYOPOLIS, Pennsylvania
Settled in 1814, it was named for the naval hero, Oliver Hazard Perry, 1785–1819, a U. S. Naval officer who defeated the British in the battle of Lake Erie during the War of 1812. (4)

Perth Amboy, New Jersey

PERTH AMBOY, New Jersey
Perth Amboy is situated on a height of land at the junction of the Raritan River and the Arthur Kill Sound. The name apparently evolved through a series of land transactions from the Indian word "Ompoge," meaning "point or elbow of land" to "Emboyle," to "Amboyle" and finally to "Amboy." In the minutes of the board of proprietors of East Jersey, August 14, 1687, the city is referred to as New Perth. The town apparently was first settled around 1651.

The Perth in Perth Amboy was in honor of the Earl of Perth, one of the proprietors of the royal grant of land.

Legend has it that Perth Amboy got its name when the Earl of Perth first came to Amboy. Residents, Indians, and officials went down to the shore to greet him. Being a Scot, Perth wore the kilt. When he came ashore the Indian Chief took one long, hard look at that kilt and those knobby knees and exclaimed, "Perth am girl!" "No," the Earl replied, "Perth am boy!" Alas for a good story, the Earl of Perth never came to America. (2)

PETTY, Texas

In Lamar County, Petty was originally called Lookout because of its elevation. The calling of the station name was said to be so frightening to the passengers that the name had to be changed to Dowlin, in 1881, and to Petty in 1886. The present name honors J. M. Petty, a large landowner. (3)

PEWEE VALLEY, Kentucky

Originally called Smith's Station in 1852, the name was changed to honor the many phoebes or pewees in the area. The pewee or phoebe is a small American flycatcher. (6)

PHOENIX, Arizona

A streak of snobbery in frontier citizenry is revealed in the naming of Phoenix. It was the fancy of "Lord" Darrel Duppa, who foresaw a great civilization rising from the ashes of the old. (5)

PICTURE ROCKS, Pennsylvania

Takes its name from the Indian rock paintings that formerly decorated the precipice overlooking Muncy Creek about a quarter of a mile from the village. The "Murals" have long since been effaced by rock slides and the weathering of the cliff's walls. (4)

PIE TOWN, New Mexico

This little village in New Mexico started out as a gasoline station where Cowboys (the modern ones) bought their gas. Later the proprietor, Clyde Norman, started frying small fruit pies to supplement his meagre income. When Mr. and Mrs. H. L. Craig, who owned a mining claim nearby, bought him out Mrs. Craig kept on cooking and selling the popular pies.

Prosperity brought a garage, a grocery store, a settlement, and finally the need for a post office. While they were scratching for a name, a cowboy suggested Pie Town, because, as he reasoned, "We get our pies here." And Pie Town, New Mexico, it is. (1)

Pie Town, New Mexico

PIGEON FORGE, Tennessee
In Sevier County, near the Great Smoky Mountain Park, this town received its name from an old Iron Foundry located on the Little Pigeon River. (2)

PILLAGER, Minnesota
Just two miles north of the present town of Pillager is a small lake, from which the town got its name. Near this lake, many years ago, lived a band of Chippewa Indians, in their summer camp. The chief of this branch of the Chippewa Tribe was called Pillager, and richly deserved the name. His tribe was known far and wide for their pillaging and stealing. Many of the early settlers lost articles to these sticky fingered Indians, and it was from Chief Pillager, and the Pillager Lake, that the town got its name. (1)

PINECONNING, Michigan
This town near Saginaw Bay, in Bay County, has a name derived from the Indian word Opinniconing, which means "place of the potato." (2)

PINE APPLE, Alabama
First known as Friendship Community in the early 1820's, Pine Apple derived its name from the Baptist Church around which the community was built. This old church, organized in 1825, still bears the name Friendship Baptist Church.

In the 1830's a large apple cider mill was built as the area was rich in apples. Pine trees also abounded here, so when the post office was established the name Pine Apple was coined and given. (Mrs. H. W. Grimes, Greenleaves, Pine Apple, Ala.)

PINE CITY, Minnesota
On the Snake River, near the Wisconsin line, the location was once an Indian village named "Chengwatana," and the name Pine City comes from that name. (6)

PINOPOLIS, South Carolina
In Berkeley County, which borders the Atlantic, it was named for the groves of pines that covered the area in a veritable "sea of trees." (6)

PIONEER, California
When the post office was established here, it took a name common to the area. This is part of the Mother Lode country of California, and there has been a creek by that name for over a hundred years. A school in the area has been here for approximately the same length of time, and was known as the Pioneer Mining District School. (1)

PIPE CREEK, Texas
Pipe Creek, in eastern Bandera County, was established about 1872 and took its name from a nearby creek. The creek, an intermittent stream, rises in eastern Bandera County and flows into the Medina River. The stream takes its name from the fact that a pioneer returned to the creek to get his pipe in spite of the fact that the Comanche were chasing his party. He made the recovery safely and the creek got its name. (3)

PIPESTONE, Minnesota
For at least three centuries a large proportion of the ceremonial pipes used by the American Plains Indians and other tribes was produced from the unusual red stone obtained from the famed quarries near Pipestone, Minnesota, and for which Pipestone was named.

"Amongst the Sioux of the Mississippi, and who lived in the region of Red Pipe Stone Quarry, I found the following and not less strange tradition . . . 'Many ages after the red men were made, when all the different tribes were at war, the Great Spirit sent runners and called them all together at the Red Pipe. He stood on the top of the rocks, and the red people were assembled in infinite numbers on the plains below. He took out of the rock a piece of the red stone, and made a large pipe; he smoked it over them all; told them that it was part of their flesh; that though they were at war, they must meet at this place as friends; that it belonged to them all; that they must make their calumets from it and smoke them to him whenever they wished to appease him or get his good-will. The smoke from his big pipe rolled over them all, and he disappeared in its cloud; at the last whiff of his pipe a blaze of fire rolled over the rocks and melted their surface—at that moment two squaws went in a blaze of fire under the two medicine rocks, where they remain to this day, and must be consulted and propitiated whenever the pipe stone is to be taken away,' " thus wrote George Catlin, the eminent American artist, who traveled among and painted the American Indians from 1829 to 1838. They took him into their confidence and from them came this fascinating story.

Today the stone's use is reserved, by federal law, for the American Indian and is quarried each year under special permits issued by the National Park Service. The Pipestone National Monument is located here. (2)

PIPPA PASSES, Kentucky

Pippa Passes, Kentucky, was named for the poem *Pippa Passes,* by Robert Browning, British poet, 1812–89. Alice Lloyd founded a junior college here for mountain youth. Tuition and board are free.

The college represents "Pippa," the little girl of Browning's poem who, when she passed, had a pronounced effect on the lives of the people she touched. (1)

PISGAH, Alabama

In 1832 Pisgah consisted of three cabins, and the people were just "squatters" until the treaty of New Echota with the Cherokees, about 1835. Located in the Sand Mountain area, a broad flat plateau, it has an average elevation of 1,400 to 1,700 feet. It was during its rowdy era that a visiting circuit rider holding revivals suggested the name as taken from the Bible. Pisgah is a mountain ridge of ancient Palestine, northeast of the Dead Sea, in what is now Jordan. (1)

PLANTATION KEY, Florida

Located on the lower part of the Florida peninsula, Plantation Key is one of a long line of populated keys extending southward to the southernmost tip of Key West.

It received its unusual name from the many pineapple and banana plantations that once thrived here. Unable to compete with lower foreign prices, and occasionally devastated by hurricanes, the plantation owners eventually became discouraged and the plantations disappeared. (6)

PLAQUEMINE, Louisiana

Located in Iberville Parish, just below Baton Rouge, it was named for the Plaquemine Bayou. The Bayou got its name from the Indians who made a bread called "Pikamine" or "Pliakmine" (Indian name for persimmon). Persimmon trees grew wild in this area along the bayou. (6)

PLENTY, Arizona

Once a town named Plenty had a post office and many enthusiastic citizens, but today Plenty doesn't have very much of anything. (5)

PLUSH, Oregon

In southeastern Oregon, on the banks of Lake Hart, is a village with the unusual name of Plush. Across the lake, the verticle escarpments of Hart Mountain rise to more than 4,000 feet above the area they dominate. Plush is located in sage brush country, which gradually rises into the timber-covered mountains. It is here that the tiny streams grow fat with the spring thaw, and cut their way down the mountains, giving life to narrow strips of grassy meadow, where the wild hay grows thick and tall.

It was in this wild and wonderful setting that the village of Plush began in 1904, with the building of a store by Daniel Boone. No, not *the* Daniel Boone, but one with the name and the pioneer spirit of his namesake.

Perhaps the most outstanding segment of the history of Plush was the manner in which it got its elegant name. In the early days a tribe of Piute Indians camped near here for long periods of time. Their chief had been bitten by the gambling bug, and truly loved to play poker. He often played in a local saloon in the town (then unnamed and amply supplied with three saloons). Just what he used for money is not recorded. Probably wives and horses, as this was usually all the Piutes had in the way of trade goods. On one occasion, in a framed game, the chief was dealt a beautiful flush (five cards of the same suit), which is a grand hand, indeed. However the cheats arranged for an accomplice to have one just a wee bit higher. After much heated betting the chief's flush was out-flushed by the higher flush. Apparently smelling a rat, the chief became quite loquacious about that particular game, and he did a lot of talking about the flush he had been dealt. His English was not the best, and each time he tried to handle the word "flush," it came out "plush." He "plushed" the "flush" so often the settlement rocked with the name, and finally adopted it for its own.

Born of a rugged people in a rugged country, where the winters are long and cold, and the summers hot and dry, Plush is anything but Plush. But the people like it here, because there is a fascination about the country that reaches even the most casual visitor. (1)

PLYMOUTH MEETING, Pennsylvania

The town was founded about 1686, by Francis Rawle and family, with nine servants who were passengers of the Ship *Desire,* which sailed from Plymouth, England. The meetinghouse was erected between 1710 and 1712, destroyed by fire and rebuilt in 1867. Originally named Plymouth, confusion arose when another town in the central part of Pennsylvania was also named Plymouth. In 1832, to avoid further confusion, the name was changed to Plymouth Meeting, and has remained so to this day. (Plymouth Meeting Historical Soc.)

POCAHONTAS, Mississippi
In Madison County, this town was named for the daughter of Powhatan, Virginia Indian chief, of the John Smith legend. (6)

POCAHONTAS, Virginia
Named for the daughter of Powhatan and Amonate, Mingo Indians, of the Pocahontas–John Smith legend of American history. (6)

POCATELLO, Idaho
Pocatello, located in southeastern Idaho, near the Fort Hall Indian Reservation, was platted and settled in 1882, and gets its name from Chief Pocatello, of the Bannock Creek Shoshoni or the Kukendeka, meaning "wild wheat eaters." Chief Pocatello, originally called Dono Oso (Buffalo Robe), was a shifty fellow who refused to "follow the road," so his name was later changed to Paughatello or Pocatello, from the Shoshoni words Po (road), Ka (not), and Tello (to follow).

When the old chief died in October, 1878, prior to the birth of his namesake, he had an interesting funeral. He was weighted down with most of his worldly possessions and tossed into a big spring, where the water rolled out of the earth with a roar. The spring was about 20 feet in diameter and flowed hundreds of barrels an hour. (The spring was buried when the American Falls Dam was constructed.) After the chief was so buried, his eighteen head of horses were killed, one by one, and buried after him. It was believed, at that time, by the Indians, that the sacred spring had no bottom. (2)

POINT BLANK, Texas
Among the first settlers in this community was a family by the name of Robinson. They were wealthy planters from Alabama. When their French governess first espied the sea of white cotton in this area, she exclaimed, "Blanc Point!" (French for White Spot.) The community was called Blank Point for years, from this incident, but finally the words were reversed, and the little town is now called Point Blank. (San Jacinto County Historical Assoc., Cold Springs)

POINT CLEAR, Alabama
The point that marks the division between the upper and the lower halves

of Mobile Bay—in earlier times the upper half was markedly cloudier from the silt out of the many rivers than was the lower half—thus the name Point Clear. (2)

POINTE-A-LA-HATCHE, Louisiana
The name Pointe-a-la-Hatche is French and means "Point of the Axe," probably given to this locale because this was a point on the river where ships stopped and took on wood for the boilers, as they plied the Mississippi on its final plunge to the Gulf. It was here, at this point, that axes were needed to chop wood. It is located in Plaquemines Parish. (2)

POINT MARION, Pennsylvania
Settled in 1842 and named for General Francis Marion, the "Swamp Fox," hero of the American Revolution. (4)

POINT OF ROCKS, Wyoming
There are four rocky peaks surrounding the town and some hold that this is the reason for the name. Others say a rock outcropping on the old stage trail which extends from the mountains down to a spring on the trail named Point of Rocks Spring is the source. A mining camp one-half mile east of here was known as Rocky Point. Take your pick, they're all fascinating. (1)

POINT PLEASANT, West Virginia
Has the unique honor of being named by the father of its country, George Washington. In 1770 while he was exploring this territory, located on a headland, shaped something like an arrowhead, he called it a pleasant point. It is located at the confluence of the Ohio and the Great Kanawha Rivers. It was at Point Pleasant that Chief Cornstalk and his son were ambushed at the Battle of Point Pleasant. A monument has been erected here by the state of West Virginia. (6)

POMONA, Tennessee
Received its name from John W. Dodge, a miniature painter, who named it for the Roman Mythological goddess of fruit trees. (6)

POMPEYS PILLAR, Montana
Legend has it that a local Indian chief had a son named Pompey, and he named this large piece of sandstone, setting all by itself, "Pompey's Pillar." When a village was settled near here by white pioneers, they took the name of the most impressive landmark in this part of Montana, Pompeys Pillar. (1)

PONCHATOULA, Louisiana
About twenty-five miles from Lake Ponchartrain, in Tangipahoa Parish, the name is Choctaw Indian for *falling hair.* It was their way of describing Spanish Moss, which is most prolific in Louisiana. (6)

POOLVILLE, Texas
Poolville, in northwestern Parker County, derived its name from a lake called the Big Pool, east of the present town. The lake, once a well-known watering place for trail herds, was filled in after the land was put into cultivation. (3)

POPLAR BLUFF, Missouri
On February 27, 1849, Butler County was created and named in honor of W. A. Butler of Kentucky. John F. Martin and John Stephenson were appointed as commissioners to select a county seat. They selected the present site of Poplar Bluff because it was near the center of the county, on the first high ground on Black River, and was covered with a growth of immense poplar or tulip trees.

This was all uninhabited and virgin territory, but the county secured title from the United States and proceeded to plat the town now known as Poplar Bluff. (2)

PORTAGE, Pennsylvania
Received its unusual name from the old Portage Railroad which was a series of canals and horses and cable cars. Portage is named for the portage over the mountains at this point. (1)

PORTAGE, Utah
Located in Box Elder County, Utah, the town is situated in a small valley, between majestic mountain ranges, at the southern end of Malad Valley. The center is knifed through by the Malad River, coiling from north to south.

The first settlers arrived here in 1867 and built the original settlement on the east side of the valley and called it *Hay Town,* due to the abundance of tall, wild grass. Later settlers, in 1872, moved their log church and homes to the west side about two miles from the old townsite, for the purpose of irrigation as the Malad River was too alkaline for home or irrigation use. They dug a canal 12 miles long from Samaria Lake Springs.

The town received its present name, tradition says, when Lorenzo Snow named it for his birthplace, Portage County, Ohio. The old and new sites, known as East and West Portage, were incorporated on May 26, 1922 under the name Portage. (Portage Town Board President)

Port Wine, California

PORT WINE, California

Port Wine, located in Sierra County, California, was a little mining site of 1850, northwest of Downieville. The site was discovered and named when a group of prospectors found a keg of port wine that had been hidden in the brush by packers. They had themselves a ball forgetting, for the moment, the gold and other matters. When they awoke, later, with throbbing heads and dry mouths, they began to search for water. In their desperate search for water, they uncovered a ravine rich with gold-laden gravel. Needless to say they named the spot and the village that grew there Port Wine. (The Sacramento *Bee*)

POSSUM, Texas

Possum, a rural community in northwestern Palo Pinto County, lies along the eastern edge of Possum Kingdom Lake. Possum Kingdom Lake is the popular name for the reservoir impounded by the Morris Sheppard Dam, so named by an act of Congress.

This area along the Brazos River with its terrain of hills and valleys, post oaks, and cedars was a veritable paradise for opossums. Neither the act of Congress, the $8,500,000 expenditure, nor the inundation of the country has changed it from "Possum Kingdom."

The dam, the first erected by the Brazos River Conservation and Reclamation District, forms a twenty-thousand-acre lake with a shore line of 310 miles which spreads into Palo Pinto, Stephens, Jack and Young Counties.

The lake has a capacity of 724,700 acre-feet and furnishes water for municipal supply, irrigation and power generation. (3)

Possum's Trot, Florida

POSSUM'S TROT, Florida
There are several versions about the origin of the name; however the most accepted version is that a well-defined possum trail existed in the locality, leading to a watering hole or salt lick, and the frequency of passing possums eventually created the name. It is located in Jackson County, Florida. (2)

POST OAK, Texas
Post Oak, a vegetable farming community, was named for its location in the post oak belt in extreme eastern Lamar County. (3)

POTLATCH, Washington
Potlatch is an Indian name which translates variously into "market place," or "gathering place." It was here on the Hood inlet, which empties into Puget Sound, that the Nesbitt Indians would gather for a feast and a bazaar, at which time they would sell anything of value for the right price, even their wives. (1)

POTOSI, Texas
Potosi, in eastern Taylor County nine miles from Abilene, was settled by hide and bone collectors who camped in dugouts along what became the cattle trails to Buffalo Gap. Named for Potosi, Mexico, the village is rail center for an agricultural and ranching community south of Kirby Lake. (3)

POTTER HOLLOW, New York

Potter Hollow, located in the northern foot hills of the Catskill Mountains, was settled in 1806 and named for two of its earliest settlers, Samuel and Timonth Potter. The village is located at the junction of two small creeks, which form a basin or hollow. (6)

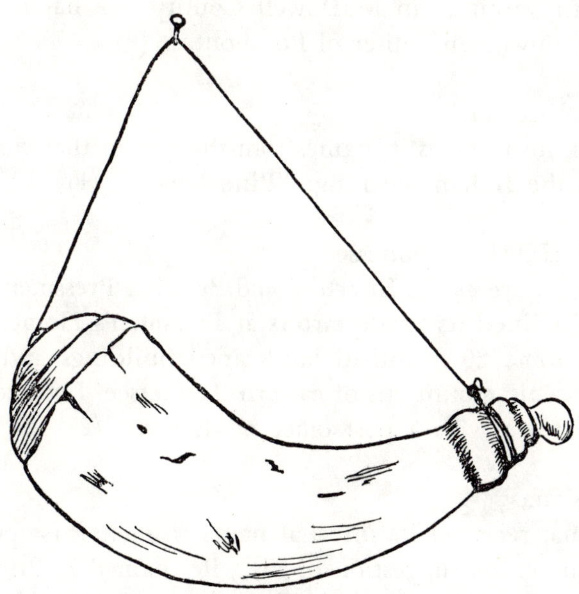

Powderhorn, Colorado

POWDERHORN, Colorado

The village is located in a beautiful valley, about six miles long and two miles wide, nestled in the heart of the western slope of the Rocky Mountains, with an elevation of 8,000 feet.

Originally it was called "White Earth" for the white soda-like mineral found on the ground in many places here. There are numerous soda springs here with naturally carbonated water. Where the water bubbles up and runs over the ground it leaves a white soda deposit.

When a post office was to be established here it was found that there was another "White Earth" in Colorado and that the name would create more postal confusion, so a new name had to be chosen.

The name powderhorn, according to tradition, was chosen from the Powderhorn Creek, a stream that cuts its way down and out of the Rocky Mountains and pours out into the valley in the shape of an Indian Powder Horn. (1)

POWDER RIVER, Wyoming

The village of Powder River, Wyoming, is located near where the south fork of the famous Powder River (Let 'er Buck) springs to life, and takes its name from that river. (1)

POWHATAN, West Virginia

In southwestern Virginia, in McDowell County, Powhatan was named in honor of Chief Powhatan, father of Pocahontas. (6)

POY SIPPI, Wisconsin

Poy Sippi, Wisconsin, takes its name from the stream that runs through the town, and has the Indian meaning: "Pine River." (1)

PRESSMEN'S HOME, Tennessee

For more than fifty years the International Printing Pressmen and Assistants Union has maintained its headquarters at Pressmen's Home, a picturesque community of some 20 beautiful landscaped buildings and 50 residences nestled in the scenic mountains of eastern Tennessee. Located in Hawkings County it is a town with a post office of its own. (2)

PRIDE, Louisiana

Pride, Louisiana, received its unusual name from its first postmaster, Mr. Bill Craig, who, at the suggestion of his wife, named it Pride because she thought they should take pride in having a post office established here. (1)

PRINTER, Kentucky

The small community of Printer, Kentucky, was named for the only Civil War Veteran living in the area at that time. It was named in honor of John Printer Meade. (1)

PROGRESS, Texas

Progress, in extreme northern Bailey County, is a rural trading center and a stop on the Pecos and North Texas Railroad. In 1907 a town site was laid out in anticipation that the area would be favorable for fruit orchards and vegetable farms, but such development did not occur. (3)

PROMISE CITY, Iowa

Located on the Keokuk and Western Railroad, this was one of the early towns of Wayne County. Platted in 1855, a post office was established in 1856. This town, unfortunately, did not live up to the hopes expressed in its fancy name, and the expected growth never came. (History of Wayne County, Corydon Chamber of Commerce)

PROMISED LAND, Louisiana
This small village with a most unusual name is located in Plaquemines Parish, and was originally called "La Terre Promise," by its French settlers. This is probably due to the richness of the soil and the lush growth, which made it seem to them a true promised land. (2)

PROVIDENCE, Rhode Island
In 1636, Roger Williams, exiled from Massachusetts because of his individualistic religious beliefs, came finally to the forests at the head of Narragansett Bay. Here he founded a settlement dedicated to religious and civil liberty, and named "in commemoration of God's Merciful Providence."

In 1644, a royal charter was obtained for the new settlement, which, with Portsmouth and Newport became "Providence Plantation in the Narragansett Bay, in New England." Before the new colony's survival was assured, it faced many hazards, among the most serious of which were sporadic Indian attacks. The struggle with the Indians culminated in 1676 with the bloody King Philip's War.

One of the first blows of the Revolution was struck here in 1772, when a group of patriots led by Samuel Whipple and John Brown captured the British sloop-of-war *Gaspee,* and burned it to the water's edge.

On May 4, 1776, the colony became the first independent republic in the New World, proclaiming her independence two months before the historic Declaration in Philadelphia.

As the city grew the name was eventually shortened to Providence. (2)

PROVIDENT CITY, Texas
Provident City, in the southern "panhandle" of Colorado County, was founded in 1909 and named for the Provident Land Company, which owned much land in the area. (3)

PUMPVILLE, Texas
Pumpville, in Val Verde County, was so named because the Southern Pacific Railroad, about 1887, dug wells there for pumping water for the railroad. (3)

PUNGOTEAGUE, Virginia
The tract on which Pungoteague is situated was patented in 1655 by Nicholas Waddilow, who died in 1660. For about fifteen years, from 1664, the county court held its meetings in this vicinity. Pungoteague has the distinction of being the site of the play, "The Bear and the Cub," the first English Theatrical performance in America. There was criticism of the play resulting in court action, and the court records of Accomack County,

Pumpville, Texas

Virginia, give the date of the play as August 27, 1665. Pungoteague is an Indian word meaning "Sand-fly River." The village is located at the head of Pungoteague Creek in Accomack County. (1)

PUNXSUTAWNEY, Pennsylvania

"In the far west the 'Lenni Lenape' (original people) began life as animals in the mother earth. After ages underground, the Monsi (wolf), Unamis (turtle), and unalachtigos (turkey) came forth to hunt and live as men, forming the three Lenape clans. The Iroquois originated in a like manner seeking fish and game, and they migrated northeast. The Lenape crossed the mountains, settling the Susquehanna and Delaware area, becoming known as Delawares." Thus the legend goes.

Earliest known inhabitants of the Punxsutawney area were the "Alligewi" who first welcomed, then attacked, the east bound Delaware and Iroquois, and finally fled south leaving only their name upon the river and mountains. Their "grandfather," the Groundhog, and other relatives chose to remain in the earth and were never molested by their red brothers.

Punxsutawney was a campsite halfway between the Allegheny and the Susquehanna on the earliest known trail to the east, the Shamokin Path. Because the path at this point separated the two nations, Punxsutawney was sometimes a Seneca (Iroquois), and sometimes a Shawnee (Delaware) camp.

About 1723 seaboard colonization and Iroquois intrigue caused displaced Delawares to build villages at "Chinclamoose" (Clearfield), Punxsutawney, and Kittanning. Between these points the Shamokin Trail became the Chinclacamoose Path.

Withdrawal to Ohio of the main body of coastal Delawares occurred between 1740–1760, many passing by way of Punxsutawney. About 1740 an Indian sorcerer began to appear in various forms and to attack travelers on the path east of Punxsutawney. He was sought out and killed in combat by a young chief. His body was burned to destroy the evil medicine. His ashes, however, turned into ponksad (sandflies) and continued to plague the Indians. From that time the Indians called their town "Ponksaduteney," which means "the town of sandflies."

Punxsutawney, Pennsylvania

The arrival of Punxsutawney's first white settler, Jacob Hoover, in 1814, saw the evacuation of western Pennsylvania by the Indians in accordance with the treaty of Fort Stanwix, New York.

And thus it was that the Delawares left Punxsutawney, leaving behind only their grandfather, the groundhog, to oversee their village, and whose legendary wisdom continues to this day to help shape the destiny of the "Town of the Ponksad." (2)

PUPOSKY, Minnesota

Puposky is the Chippewa Indian name given to this area many years ago, and means "end of the sinking land." By sinking land they were referring to the bog land that is so common north of here. (1)

PUYALLUP, Washington

When the Pacific Northwest was young and Indians came through the mountain passes to barter with the tribes in this green and fertile valley, they found them to be fair in trade. "Puyallups," they called them, "the generous people."

Ezra Meeker, famous pioneer of the Old Oregon Trail days, founded the city in 1877. Incorporation was in 1890. It was he who chose the name and thus prophetically described its bounty. (2)

PYOTE, Texas

Pyote, in Ward County, is said to have been named for the Peyote weed, used in Indian ceremonials. The Peyote is a cactus, containing a narcotic prized by the Indians of certain regions of the southwestern United States and Mexico. The town developed as a shipping point on the Texas and Pacific Railroad in the early 1880's. (3)

QUAKERTOWN, Pennsylvania

Founded in 1715 by the Quakers, it was the center of the "Fries's" or "Hot Water Rebellion." In 1798, when war with France seemed imminent, the federal government endeavored to raise $2,000,000 by levying taxes on land houses and Negro slaves. The house tax was based on the number and size of windows. The sight of assessors carefully measuring windows so irritated the Pennsylvania German housewives that they frequently greeted federal agents with a dash of hot water! (4)

QUAIL, Texas

A post office had been established in 1902 with Sam Wilson as postmaster and the name Quail chosen because of the abundance of the birds in the vicinity. In 1909 a telephone wire was strung on a barbed wire fence to connect Quail with Wellington. *The Quail Feather* was published by Wade Arnold in 1910. (3)

QUANAH, Texas

Quanah, county seat and principal town in Hardeman County, was named for Quanah Parker. Quanah is the site of the annual Texas–Oklahoma wolf hunt, held on the C. T. Watkins ranch.

Quanah Parker, last chief of the Comanche, was born between 1845 and 1852, the son of Chief Peta Nocona and Naduah (Cynthia Ann Parker.) He grew to manhood with the normadic Quahadi, following the buffalo. Refusing to accept the Medicine Lodge Treaty of 1867, he rejoined the Comanche on the Llano Estacado and participated with them in raids which struck past the line of Texas defenses: Forts Richardson, Belknap, Bliss, Stockton, and Griffin. In a battle on Red River, Chief Bear's Ear was killed and Quanah was chosen leader of the tribe. In August, 1871, Ronald S. Mackenzie set out to punish the Quahadi, so Quanah, with a group of braves, stole all the general's horses. Quanah led seven hundred Indians in the battle of Adobe Walls on June 27, 1874. The Quahadi surrendered on June 2, 1875, and were sent to Indian Territory.

Quanah Parker died on February 23, 1911, and was buried in Post Oak Mission Cemetery, four miles from Indiahoma, Oklahoma.

East of the town of Quanah, is a Medicine Mound, which is said to have been the site of religious rites of the Indians. (3)

QUAPAW, Oklahoma
Named after the Quapaw Indians, who were moved to this area around 1833. A large number of Quapaw Indians lived in the town.

The Quapaw Indian Pow Wow, traditionally held July 4, at the Devil's Promenade east of Quapaw on Spring River, is one of Ottawa County's oldest celebrations. (1)

QUECHEE, Vermont
This small Vermont town, located in Windsor County, takes its name from the Ottauquechee River that cuts its way through the town. The name is Indian and means "blackwater." (1)

QUEMADO, Texas
Quemado, on the Rio Grande in northwestern Maverick County, was named for the Quemado Valley, which the Spanish called "burned valley," thinking it had been burned in a volcanic eruption. One of the earliest settlers was Hand Lahrman, as apiarist, and bee culture has been an important industry since the early 1900's. (3)

QUIHI, Texas
Quihi, a Medina County community ten miles west of Castroville, was laid out on Quihi Lake in 1845 by Henri Castro and named for the white-necked Mexican eagle buzzard, the quichie or Keechie. (3)

QUITAQUE, Texas
In Briscoe County, Quitaque was named for the Quitaque Ranch and

Quitaque Creek. The names come from the Quitaca Indians, an unidentified tribe of western Texas or eastern New Mexico. José Pieda Tafoya operated a trading post at the site from 1865 to 1867 to trade dry goods and ammunition to the Indians for rustled cattle.

In 1890 the location became a stage coach stop. (3)

RADIUM, Minnesota

This small town chose to adopt the name "Radium" to commemorate the discovery of radium by Madame Marie Curie, Polish physicist and chemist, in France. (1)

RAGLAND, West Virginia

Located in Mingo County, west-central West Virginia, it was not named because of the people's love of "Ragtime," but rather for an early settler, a Mr. Ragland. (1)

RAGTOWN, Texas

Ragtown, Garza County, was settled about 1906, when Charles W. Post opened the area to immigration. So many of the first inhabitants used tents for homes that the village looked like, and was called, Ragtown. (3)

RAIL ROAD FLAT, California

Located in the heart of the "mother lode" gold country, the forty-niners had almost every foot of ground under claim and gold production or prospecting.

Legend has it that a peddler or drummer came to this gold camp selling novelties and necessities; taking orders for things to be delivered on his next trip. When he asked for the name of the locale he was told there was none.

He looked out across the valley and was struck by the number of tracks leading from each claim. These were rails with small carts so the prospectors could move their ore from the mines to the water, to be washed for gold.

He decided to call it Rail Road Flat because it must have looked like a rail center, and the name stuck. Incidently Rail Road Flat is over twenty-five miles from the nearest Railroad! (1)

RAMARITO, Texas

Originally populated by Mexican ranchers who came here soon after the settlement of Laredo in 1759, no permanent settlement was made until the late 1880's. A. Ramirez established ranch headquarters before the organization of the county in 1913, but since there was another Ramirez it was named Ramarito for the new post office. (3)

RAMPART, Alaska
Rampart was given its name by the early prospectors in 1898. Placer gold was found in the creeks close to this spot on the Yukon River and a village was established. The name Rampart was chosen due to a rock formation slightly above the village. Sheer cliffs or bluffs on the river's shore rise two to three hundred feet high. These bluffs (or ramparts) told the traveler he was nearing the town of Rampart. (1)

RANDADO, Texas
The old ranch settlement of Randado is in Jim Hogg County. The ranch of which it is the center had its inception during 1836, when a sixty-thousand acre grant was awarded to José Policarpo Rodrigues. The name, meaning "fringed with lace," may have been suggested by an itinerant salesman of Spanish lace, or the name may have come from the lace made by the Indians and which they called "randa."

During 1891 Catarino Garza, the Mexican brigand and social equalitarian, encamped a short distance from the community at the head of a revolutionary army. Accompanied by the correspondent Richard Harding Davis, the Eighth Cavalry was dispatched to Laredo, and then marched overland to Randado. Garza, although forced to break camp, was not captured. (3)

Ranger, Texas

RANGER, Texas
This town, in northwestern Eastland County, developed around a Texas Ranger camp. In October, 1880, when the Texas and Pacific Railway built

through the county, the settlers in the tent community called "Ranger Camp Valley" moved two miles west to the railroad and established a town. Oil, discovered in October, 1917, brought a boom which changed Ranger from a village to a city with a population of 16,000 by 1920. A decline in oil production, a series of bank failures in 1920 and 1921, and a disastrous fire in 1924 put an end to the boom, and caused a marked decrease in population. Population in 1950 was 3,951. (3)

RANGERVILLE, Texas

In southern Cameron County on the Missouri-Pacific Railroad, Rangerville was named for the Texas Ranger camps maintained near the Old Military Road. The road was surveyed by the United States Engineers during the Mexican War. Border disturbances kept the Rangers in the vicinity as late as 1917. (3)

RAPID CITY, South Dakota

John Brennan and Samuel Scott, with a small party of men, came to this vicinity in February, 1876. They camped in what is now known as Cleghorn Springs, did some exploring, and decided to lay out the site of the present Rapid City. Rapid City is located on the eastern slope of the central part of the Black Hills region.

Rapid City received its name from Rapid Creek, a fast moving stream of water that originates in the Black Hills and flows through the town. The Black Hills came from the Indian name "Paha Sapa," which is located in the "Badlands," taken from the French name "Mauvais Terres," who got it from the Indians who called it "Mako Sica," or "bad land." All of this is located in South Dakota, which gets its name from the Sioux word "Dacotah," which means "Indian." (2)

RATHDRUM, Idaho

In 1880, when the survey for the transcontinental Northern Pacific Railroad was made across the Idaho Panhandle it touched an area, known then, as "Wood's Ranch." Wide awake businessmen immediately saw the spot as an ideal one for a town. Almost overnight stores and other buildings sprung up, and Mr. Wood, who maintained a stable and horses for his pony express relay station, on his ranch here, was persuaded to plat a portion of his holdings for a townsite to be called Westwood, in his honor. Flattered, Mr. Wood immediately agreed and a village was born.

The railroad reached the village in 1883, and a petition for a post office to be named Westwood was submitted to Washington by Zach Lewis, the new postmaster. The name was denied by the Post Office Department, who decided there were too many Westwoods! Find another name it directed.

Lewis appealed to his friend M. M. Cowley, who maintained a ferry at Spokane Bridge, and he suggested the name Rathdrum, the name of his birthplace in Ireland. He felt sure this name would be unique in the United States, and so it was.

Rathdrum for many years was the county seat of Kootenai County. (Village Clerk, Rathdrum, Idaho.)

RAVEN HILL, Texas
Raven Hill, a rural community on the Walker-San Jacinto county line, was so named because it is at the site of the Sam Houston home called "Raven Hill." (3)

RAVEN ROCK, West Virginia
On the Ohio River, and the Ohio line, it was settled in 1810 by Basil Riggs, and named for the large flocks of ravens that once nested on the rocks near the town. (6)

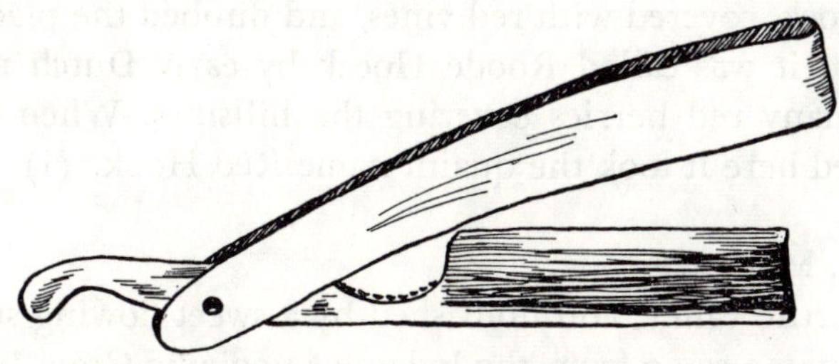

Razor, Texas

RAZOR, Texas
Razor, in northwestern Lamar County, close to Red River, was named by A. K. Haynes for a popular brand of tobacco that he sold. (3)

RED BARN, Texas
Located in Pecos County, Red Barn was named for a large Red Barn that once stood here. The location was originally a winter feeding place for cattle on the western slope of the Pecos. (3)

RED BAY, Alabama
Red Bay is located on the Alabama-Mississippi line, approximately fifty miles southeast of Pickwick Dam, Tennessee. According to legend, Red Bay was named for the red soil and the Bay trees that were so numerous here in the late 1800's. It was named by Edward W. Waldrep, the first postmaster, March 26, 1888. (1)

RED CLOUD, Nebraska

Red Cloud was first settled in 1870 by a group led by Silas Graber, who four years later was elected governor of Nebraska. It was named after Chief Red Cloud, the great Sioux chief. Red Cloud became the county seat of Webster County on May 20, 1871, and the first railroad was built from Hastings to Red Cloud in 1878.

The site of the first stockade and Governor Graber's dugout is located on a natural knoll one mile southeast of the main business section of present-day Red Cloud. (2)

RED HILL, Texas

Red Hill, a post village in central Cass County, was established in the early 1880's. The name comes from the location of the clay bank of south Frazier Creek. (3)

RED HOOK, New York

Local legend has it that some fishermen on the Hudson River saw a hook hanging on a rock, covered with red vines, and dubbed the place Red Hook. Another is that it was called Roode Hoeck by early Dutch navigators because of the many red berries covering the hillsides. When a village was later established here it took the quaint name Red Hook. (1)

RED LODGE, Montana

Located in a fertile valley, and nourished by a sweet flowing stream, legend has it that the name came from the lodges of nomadic Crow Indians, which were colored by the red clay found in the area. Others claim it was because there were so many "red men's" lodges in the area. (2)

RED HOUSE, Virginia

Located in upper Charlotte County, 12 miles from Appomattox, was a hitching post in the 1800's and a tavern located there also served as a stage stop. The name comes from the fact that all houses in this small village were, at one time, painted the same color, red. (1)

RED OAK, Texas

Red Oak, in northern Ellis County, was founded as Navarro County Town before the organization of Ellis County. The post office, established June 14, 1847, was named for the oak trees in the vicinity. The Missouri, Kansas, and Texas Railroad reached the area in 1884. (3)

RED ROCK, Minnesota

A railway village one mile north of Newport, it is near the site of a mission for the Sioux (1837-42). The name came from an oval, rounded boulder of granite, about five feet long, which originally lay on the neighboring bank of the Mississippi, but was eventually removed to the west side of the railroad at the depot.

This rock was held in great veneration by the Sioux, who often visited it until 1862 (less frequently after this), bringing offerings and renewing its vermillion paint. The Indians had painted on it stripes, twelve in number, two inches wide, and from two to six inches long. (Acting Reference Librarian, Minn. Historical Society)

RED ROCK, Texas
In southern Bastrop County, Red Rock is a shipping point on the Missouri, Kansas, and Texas Railroad. The first settler, James Brewer, is said to have used a red rock in the chimney of his house built in the early 1850's and so to have named the settlement.

In 1873 male and female academies were in operation, and an act of the Texas Legislature prohibited the sale of liquors within the two-mile zone around the school. (3)

RED SPRINGS, Texas
Red Springs received its name from the springs flowing from the clay bank of a ravine in the undulating land along the Salt Fork of the Brazos. Red Springs, Baylor County, was a camp site of Indians and a watering place for buffalo as late as 1870. (3)

RED WING, Minnesota
Red Wing derives its name from the leader of friendly Dakota (Sioux) Indians who inhabited this area as their summer hunting and fishing grounds. The chief wore the wing of a wild swan, dyed scarlet and consequently was called "Koo-Poo-Hoo-Sha" or "Red Wing."

Legend persists to this day that old Chief Red Wing is buried on the summit of Barn Bluff (Mt. LaGrange). This landmark of the Mississippi was named by the French Voyageurs in 1680 because to them it looked like a huge barn surrounded by water.

The first white settlement was established in 1849. Soon after, pioneer farmers of Scandinavian descent broke the prairie sod. They farmed so well that by 1873 Red Wing was the primary wheat market of the world. (2)

REFORM, Alabama
Tradition has it that many years ago a preacher rode into town on horse back and for a week conducted a revival meeting, but to no avail—the town contained an appalling number of saloons.

As he rode out of the town, in a very disgusted mood, someone asked him for a name for the new town. He replied, "Reform, brother, Reform!" And Reform it was, and is. (1)

REFUGIO, Texas

On the north bank of Mission River in central Refugio County, Refugio was founded by James Power and James Hewetson in 1834 at the site of Nuestra Señora del Refugio Mission. In accordance with Mexican law the town contained four square leagues of land. The lots were distributed free to the colonists, half of whom were Irish and half Mexican.

In March, 1836, the Mexican Army under José Urrea captured the town, the defending Texas soldiers under William Ward and Amon B. King being captured and executed. The buildings of the town were demolished. During the revolution almost half of the men of Refugio served in the Texas Army, and approximately one-fourth of the male population died in the Goliad Massacre. Refugio County was created in 1836 and organized in 1837 with Refugio as the county seat, but for four years there were not enough men in the county to operate the government. In 1842 Mexican irregulars captured the town and carried all except two of its men to Mexico as prisoners.

The battle of Refugio took place on March 14, 1836. James W. Fannin, Jr., had sent Amon B. King and twenty-eight men to Refugio to help the families besieged there escape to Goliad. King was surrounded by José Urrea's cavalry and took refuge in Nuestra Señora del Refugio Mission and sent a messenger to Fannin for aid. Fannin sent William Ward and one hundred men; they reached Refugio on March 13, but because of jealousy over the command King withdrew from the mission, was lost for two days, and was finally captured and killed by the enemy. Ward held the mission all March 14 against heavy enemy assaults and retreated during the night after receiving Fannin's orders to retreat to Victoria. At Victoria Ward's men were captured and marched to Goliad, where they were killed in the Goliad Massacre. (3)

REGAL, Minnesota

This small village in Kandiyohi County, central Minnesota, was originally called Lintonville. To avoid confusion in mail delivery with nearby towns of Paynesville, and Georgeville, the Post Office Department requested a change of name, if possible. George Weidner, the postmaster, sent a list of suggested names which proved unsuitable to the Department!

A farmer, living on the rural route, suggested the name Ford for the new T Model Ford he had just purchased. Mr. Weidner owned a Regal at the time, so he submitted both names to the Department, and the name

Regal was approved. And so the post office and the town of Regal were named for an automobile. Stanley Steamer would have made a nice name too! (Village Clerk, Regal, Minnesota)

REHOBOTH, Virginia
The name of this small town was taken from the Bible. Rehoboth is the name of Jacobs well, as told in the old testament. (1)

REMLAP, Alabama
When the Louisville and Nashville Railroad was naming its stops along the line, the area known as Palmerdale was named Palmer, after a well-known family living there. When, eight miles north, a stop was needed, Palmer was reversed giving Remlap (an anagram of Palmer) the name it has now. This is confirmed by old timers here. (1)

REMOUNT, Texas
Remount, a station on the Missouri, Kansas and Texas Railroad one mile west of Fort Sam Houston, was named because of the use of the site as a remount station by cavalrymen at the fort. (3)

RENO, Nevada
Reno's history has been one of steady growth from the time of the first discovery of the Comstock lode at Virginia City. The "Biggest Little City" has been a place of importance in northern Nevada since 1859, when it was known as Fuller's Crossing. M. C. Fuller had an inn on the south side of the Truckee then.

In 1863 M. C. Lake purchased Fuller's Inn and a toll bridge at the site of the present Virginia Street Bridge. Virginia City's mines were booming and Lake's Crossing carried a steady stream of wagons ferrying food and other supplies to the Comstock.

Until 1868, Lake had the area that is now Reno all to himself. Then the Central Pacific Railroad pushed its way over the Sierra Nevada Mountains and a land auction was held near the railroad station on May 9, 1868, five days after the railroad had come in. Within a month, 100 homes stood on land where only jackrabbits had lived.

A railroad official named Reno after General Jesse Lee Reno, a Union officer of the Civil War, and the "Biggest Little City" was on its way. (2)

RENOVO, Pennsylvania
Established about 1863 by the Philadelphia and Erie Railroad, it received its name Renovo, which is Latin for "I renew." (4)

REPUBLICAN GROVE, Virginia
There are two local legends as to how Republican Grove got its name. The first is that a church built here was said to have had many sides, and was located in a large grove of trees, attended by all denominations, and called the Republic Church, and from this evolved the name of the town.

Republican Grove, Virginia

The second story is that there was a large grove of trees here, and after an election it was found that one citizen had voted Republican, so he was taken out and hanged in the grove, and from this came the name Republican Grove. This should be a warning to all Republicans! (1)

RETREAT, Louisiana
When the post office was established in this small community in 1940 the name was chosen by the new postmaster, Mrs. Virginia C. Woods, who borrowed it from a nearby plantation named Retreat. The plantation was used as a soldier's retreat or rest camp during the Civil War. (1)

REVLOC, Pennsylvania
The name is an anagram of Colver, a nearby coal town once owned by the same company. (4)

RHODODENDRON, Oregon
This small Oregon village is located in Clackamas County, at the foot of Mount Hood. Both the Barlow Trail and the old Oregon Trail passed

through this area, and four miles east is Laurel Hill where the wagons were lowered down the mountains on ropes and cables. Some of the trees that were used for snubbing are still standing and the rope burns are still visible.

The original name of the village was Rowe, but it was later changed to Rhododendron, in honor of the flowers that grow in great numbers here, and to avoid confusion in mail with the town of Rome. (1)

RHOME, Texas
0riginally called Prairie Point, the community, settled first by Missourians, was extablished on land pre-empted by Samuel Sheets in 1857 and laid out in 1858. A general fight which took place on the day of the survey suggested the name *Scuffletown,* but the present name honored a pioneer rancher, B. C. Rhome. (3)

RICHWOOD, West Virginia
Named Cherry Tree Bottoms until 1900, this lumber camp prospered and grew until a more sedate name was desired. It was named, quite simply, for the product that had spawned it, Wood. (6)

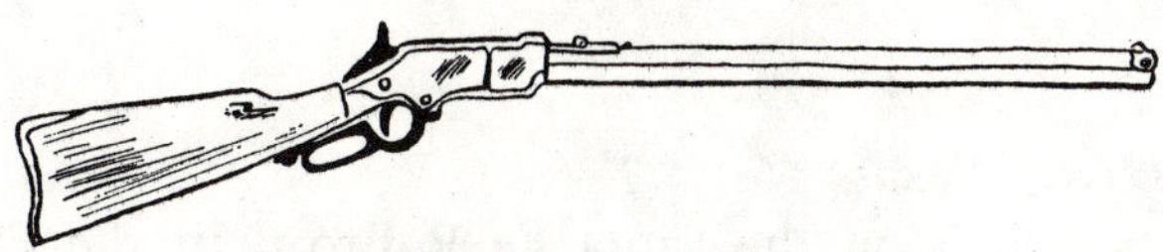

Rifle, Colorado

RIFLE, Colorado
In the mid-1800's a group of adventurous fur trappers traveled through the rich Colorado River Valley, then the home of the Ute Indians, and stopped for a night along a creek near its confluence with the wide Colorado River. After departing, it was found that one of the hunters had left his rifle at the campsite. In a wilderness region where civilized man had yet to penetrate, the incident was indeed a serious one for the loser.

Years later, when the rusted rifle was found on the banks of the creek, it served to name the creek. When hardy settlers finally founded this community, they took the name of the creek and called their village Rifle. (1)

RIO FRIO, Texas
Rio Frio, in Real County, was named for its location on the Frio River, when William Scarbrough secured a post office in his general store in 1890. Frio in Spanish means "cold." (3)

RISING FAWN, Georgia
Settled in 1870, it was originally named Hanna. The Wills Valley Railroad

ran through the town, and later the name was changed to Staunton, and finally to Rising Fawn, for an Old Cherokee Indian village that once was located here. Rising Fawn was a Cherokee Indian Princess. (1)

RISING SUN, Maryland

Originally named Summer Hill, it was settled around 1710-20, when Henry Reynolds built a public house at the crossing of the roads between the markets of Lancaster, Wilmington, and Philadelphia. A large swinging sign was erected depicting the sun at dawn, and the words "The Rising Sun." The old inn soon grew in popularity and the oft heard phrase was "meet you at the Rising Sun." This eventually forced the name Summer Hill into disuse and the swinging sign gave the town a new name. (Town Clerk, Board of Town Commissioners)

ROARING SPRINGS, Texas

Roaring Springs, in southern Motley County, was originally a camp of the Matador Ranch. Named by early cowboys for the natural spring which falls into Dutchman Creek at this point, the town has become a trading center, shipping and recreational point for the surrounding ranching and agricultural territory. (3)

ROCK-CRUSHER, Texas

Rock-Crusher, a switch on the Santa Fe Railroad in the Purcell pasture about eight miles northwest of Coleman, was used to haul crushed rock for construction of the railroad bed. John Saunders of Coleman built a store at the site in 1912, and a small community with a church grew here. (3)

ROCKDALE, Texas

Rockdale, in southeastern Milam County on the International Great Northern and Southern Pacific Railroads, was named by Mrs. B. F. Aekerman in 1873, the name being suggested by a large rock on a prairie nearby. In 1873 the first store was opened in a tent. The town was laid out in 1874 and incorporated in 1878. (3)

ROCK HILL, South Carolina

Located in York County, Rock Hill was established around 1860, and derived its name from a small flinty hill nearby. (6)

ROLL, Arizona

Mr. J. H. Roll opened a small country grocery store in this vicinity shortly after World War I. In 1923 the Southern Pacific Railroad built a line through and constructed a side track and freight house nearby. As was their custom, they named the siding after the nearest landmark, Mr. Roll's store. The name gradually evolved to cover the whole immediate area. (J. H. Roll, Jr., PM)

ROLLA, Missouri
The first settlers came into the area in 1818, and Rolla was officially organized in 1855, its founder being Edmund Ward Bishop.

There are a number of stories as to how Rolla got its name, but the most accepted is that George Coppedge, homesick for his home in Raleigh, North Carolina, asked that it be named Raleigh. As the story goes, he either pronounced it "Rolla," or the early settlers couldn't spell it, or they shortened it because it sounded too highfalutin. Anyway, it is indeed believed that it was named for Raleigh, North Carolina.

The discovery of iron ore in the vicinity in the 1820's and the development of the Meramec Iron Works was one of the reasons the "Frisco Branch" of the Southwest Railroad was built as far as Rolla. During the Civil War this was an important military post, and the existing county courthouse served as an Army hospital. (2)

ROMA-LOS SAENZ, Texas
Roma-Los Saenz in Starr County, directly across the Rio Grande from Mier, was originally a part of José de Escandón's Colony. The name Roma, for Rome, was given to a mission built in 1751; Los Saenz is for a Spanish captain, Miguel Saenz, who received the land in grant in 1767. Roma was an important shipping point on the Rio Grande until the coming of railroads and highways. The river was navigable most of the year, and steamboats carried cotton downstream until after 1886. In the days of the Gold Rush Roma prospered from the trade of the California migrants. Again during the Civil War, Roma was engaged in a lively trade with Mexico. (3)

ROMEO, Michigan
This city was originally settled by immigrants from New England, between 1820 and 1830, and first named for a nearby Indian village.

The people, still New Englanders, chafed under the name for a while, then decided to change it to something short, musical, classical, and uncommon, and Romeo seemed to fit the bill in these areas.

The town has quite a New England look in its architecture, and the population is now approximately 3,500. (Romeo Hist. Soc.)

RONCEVERTE, West Virginia
The Greenbrier River, which threads its way through the narrow valley where Ronceverte is located, was so named for the many greenbriers that

grew along its banks. The town of Ronceverte, located in south-central Greenbrier County, was established around 1800, and is French for Greenbrier, taking its name from the river. (6)

ROODHOUSE, Illinois
The town of Roodhouse, Illinois, was named for its founder John Roodhouse, who left Yorkshire, England, on April 1830, with his parents Benjamin and Jane Roodhouse, at the age of five years for the new land of America. In April 1866 John Roodhouse laid out his town in the virgin land of Illinois and named it Roodhouse, not so much for himself, as for the meaning of the name. The name is Anglo-Saxon and means "house of the holy cross" or simply a church. (John Roodhouse, grandson of John Roodhouse, the founder.)

ROPESVILLE, Texas
Ropesville, in Hockly County, is in the first section of the county to be settled. The W. A. Blankenship family reached there in 1902, followed a year later by twenty-seven families. The first business institution was the South Plains and Santa Fe Railroad, which built through the vicinity in 1917. The depot is named Ropes, and the post office Ropesville, names reminicent of the old cattle range. (3)

ROSEAU, Minnesota
Near the Canadian Border, in Roseau County, on the North Fork of the Rivière aux Roseaux, it takes its name from the river. The name of the river is French and means "river of the rushes." (6)

ROSELAND, Nebraska
Although there are no official records to establish it, there are two local legends regarding the naming of Roseland. The first is that it was named for the tremendous growth of wild roses that abound in this area, and this is probably the true one. The other has it that in 1885 a settler named Rose owned much of the farm land around here, and that the town was named Roseland in his honor. (1)

ROSEVILLE, Texas
Roseville, a school community in Dewitt County, was organized in 1874 and named for the wild roses that bloomed there. (3)

ROSHARON, Texas
Rosharon, near Oyster Creek in northern Brazoria County, was settled before the Civil War by cotton and sugar planters. Called Masterson Switch

when the Columbia Tap Railroad was constructed in 1856, the name was changed by George Colles, plantation manager, in 1910 because of the hedges of wild roses lining the fence rows. (3)

ROUGH AND READY, California

Settled September 9, 1849, by immigrants from Wisconsin, led by a Captain A. A. Townsend, who had served under General Zachary Taylor (Old Rough and Ready) during the Mexican Border War. They called themselves the "Rough and Ready Company."

This all took place during the California Gold Rush of the 49'ers, and the new settlers dug right in. A federal tax on mines so enraged the miners, later, that they organized the "State of Rough and Ready;" wrote a constitution; seceded from the Union, and created an independent country known as "The Great Republic of Rough and Ready!"

Nobody paid particular attention to all these shananigans, especially the federal government who continued to collect its taxes, and the movement finally died for lack of a champion.

The area was later made famous by Bret Harte's story about *The Millionaire of Rough and Ready*. (The Sacramento *Bee*)

ROULETTE, Pennsylvania

Settled in 1816, Roulette was named for Jean Roulette of the Ceres Land Company. (4)

ROUND ROCK, Texas

Round Rock, in south-central Williamson County on the International-Great Northern Railroad, was called *Brushy* by the early settlers who established the town in 1850. T. E. Oatts, the first postmaster and one of the first businessmen, changed the name to Round Rock for an immense round rock, in the bed of Brushy Creek.

The town is best known as the site of the killing of Sam Bass. At Round Rock, where he was planning to rob a bank, he was wounded in a battle with Rangers and other officers on July 19, 1878, and died there two days later. He was buried in Round Rock and soon became celebrated in cowboy songs and legend.

Riding up the trail to Nebraska with a cattle herd in 1876, Bass and several companies went to Deadwood, then in its goldmining boom. They lost their money in gambling and, in the next year, held up seven stage coaches without recouping their fortunes. In search of bigger loot, this band of six, led by Joel Collins, held up a Union Pacific train at Big Springs, Nebraska, in September, 1877. They took $60,000 in gold from the baggage car and several thousand dollars from passengers. Collins and two of the other bandits were killed within a few weeks, but Bass returned safely to Texas, where he formed a new outlaw band with himself as leader. He held up two stagecoaches and, in the spring of 1878, robbed four trains within thirty miles of Dallas without getting much booty. The object of a spirited chase by Texas Rangers and others, he eluded his pursuers until one of his associates informed against him at Round Rock. (3)

ROUNDUP, Montana

Roundup, Montana, located in central Musselshell County, was first settled in 1882 by the arrival of an old trapper and buffalo hunter, named James McMillan, and family. He constructed a log cabin, a small store and a saloon. In less time than it takes to tell about it a settlement began to grow, and McMillan petitioned for a post office, which was granted in 1883 and named Roundup.

It doesn't take too much imagination to guess why the name Roundup was chosen. The cattle industry, as it was conducted in those days, with the vast stretch of open range, was at its height and numerous big cattle outfits were located along the Musselshell River, where the town of Roundup was sitting.

"The Pumpkin Rollers" was the name given the cattlemen of the upper Musselshell, while those in the vicinity of Roundup were nicknamed "Forty Thieves." Creeks in the vicinity go by the name of "Halfbreed," and "Razor," to name a few, as this was a rugged country, peopled by equally rugged men, needed to tame it. (2)

ROUNDUP, Texas

Roundup, on the main line of the Santa Fe Railroad in the northeastern part of Hockley County, was formerly a part of the Spade Ranch. The town had its beginning with the building of the railroad in 1912; the name was suggested by W. H. Simpson, then assistant general passenger agent, for the Texas roundups so common in the area. (3)

RUDYARD, Michigan

The town of Rudyard was originally called Pine River, for the river that flows through it. Log drives started here, in the old days, floating timber southward to St. Martin Bay and Lake Huron.

The famous English poet Rudyard Kipling visited here in the 1880's, as a guest of the "Soo" Line Railroad, and shortly thereafter the depot was named in honor of his visit.

The name change was *suggested* by English capitalists, who had stepped in to help finance the railroad when American money ran out, before the completion of the line. Touched, Kipling wrote a poem about the town of Rudyard, and the town of Kipling, also named in his honor. (2)

RUIDOSA, Texas

Ruidosa on the Rio Grande in Presidio County was established about 1874 when William Russel began farming in the area to supply feed to the cavalry at Fort Davis.

The name, the Spanish word for "noise," is said to be derived from the sound of water falling over a dam in an irrigation canal. (3)

RULE, Texas

Rule, in Haskell County, was named for W. A. Rule, official of the Kansas City, Mexico, and Orient Railroad, when the route was surveyed in 1905. Prior to the coming of the railroad, the territory had been ranch land and was part of a wild horse region where mustangers hunted wild herds and fought Indians for possession of springs near the Double Mountain Fork of the Brazos River.

Rath City, an early buffalo hunting station, was southwest of Rule. (3)

RUSH, Kentucky

At one time this small village was a rich coal mining community. When a rich deposit of coal was discovered here, the town practically grew overnight, with people rushing in from all directions to take part in the prosperity. The miners gave the village the name Rush, because of the rush. (1)

SACRED HEART, Minnesota

A fur trading post was established here about the year 1783, by Charles Patterson. As he always wore a "bearskin hat," the Indians called him the "Sacred Hat Man," for to them the bear was sacred. Usage finally changed the name to Sacred Heart, and eventually became the name of the area, and then the town.

SACUL, Texas

Sacul, in northwestern Nacogdoches County on the Texas and New Orleans Railroad, was named for early settlers, the Lucas family, the name being spelled backwards. (3)

SAHUARITA, Arizona

The plant which enjoys official and popular status as the symbol of the state of Arizona never amounted to much as a place name. The saguaro cactus is dubbed on only one town, Sahuarita, and at that, the place and name are both diminutive forms. (5)

SALLISAW, Oklahoma

Located in Sequoyah County, French trappers named the place Salaison, meaning "salt provision" or "salt meat," because of the large salt deposits nearby. Sequoyah, Cherokee Indian scholar, is buried here, and a monument has been raised to his memory. (6)

SALOL, Minnesota
Legend tells that when a petition was being drawn for a post office no one could think of an appropriate name. A delegation was appointed to go to a neighboring town and ask for suggestions.

The whole affair took on a holiday mood, and rather than getting to the business at hand, the delegation and some of their friendly neighbors got "stoned." The following morning, still without a name, and heavy-headed, the delegation descended on the local drugstore for a hangover cure. While there, one of them saw a drawer entitled "labels," and opening it took out the first one at hand which read "Salol." Happily they returned to their unnamed town, armed with the unusual name they had been sent to find, and were acclaimed heroes.

Salol is a colorless crystalline compound, phenyl salicylate, and is not even good for hangovers. (2)

SALOME, Arizona
The glut of affection may have stimulated Dick Wick Hall to promote his favorite town as Salome, and always with the parenthetical "Where she danced." A phrase duly eliminated by the postal authorities. (5)

SALT CITY, Texas
Salt City, on an early Indian camp site, in Anderson County, was a salt mining center as early as 1840. (3)

SALTILLO, Texas
Saltillo was settled in 1850 by John Arthur, who operated a store, mill, and gin. Its location on the old Jefferson Wagon Road made it a popular camp for teamsters. A new store opened on the opposite side of the road resulted in the temporary name "Twin Groceries." It was renamed Saltillo for a town by that name in Mexico, after a post office was opened February 13, 1860. (3)

SANCO, Texas
Sanco, in central Coke County on Yellow Wolf Creek, lies in a ranching area settled in the early 1870's. The Mexican word, meaning "long step," was chosen as a name for the community in 1883 due to its isolated location. (3)

SAND SPRINGS, Oklahoma
A Creek village was here before 1833, and named Adam Springs, in honor

of a prominent Creek family. It was renamed Sandy Springs for a place of that description, in the nearby Osage Hills. (6)

SANDSTONE, Minnesota
Settled in 1885, Sandstone was named for the pink and red sandstone that was quarried here. (6)

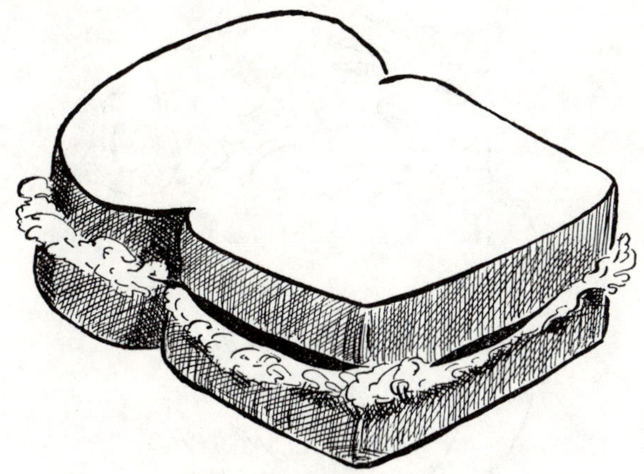

Sandwich, Massachusetts

SANDWICH, Massachusetts
The town of Sandwich was named in honor of the Fourth Earl of Sandwich, John Montague. (Secty., Board of Trade, Sandwich, Mass.)

SANDWICH, New Hampshire
Sandwich was granted in 1763 and first settled in 1767. The name was derived from the Fourth Earl of Sandwich, John Montague, who was the First Lord of the Admiralty, at the time of the American Revolution. His greatest claim to fame is his invention of the sandwich. It was during one of his gaming parties that he asked for a slice of meat between two pieces of bread, as he was too involved in the game to take time out to eat. (1)

SANTA CLAUS, Arizona
Let them belittle the verve of Mrs. Ninon Talbert, when she moved from Los Angeles to the Arizona desert, where she called herself "The biggest real estate operator in the business." At 300 pounds she probably was. She set out to found a town on the windy, waterless, greasewood flats west of Kingman, and she named it Santa Claus! (5)

SANTA CLAUS, Indiana
On Christmas Eve, in 1852, a group of pioneers of German descent were gathered together discussing their big problem—the naming of their little

settlement in northern Spencer County. Just then, the village Santa Claus, laden with gifts, walked in and an idea was born. It was unanimously agreed that their village would be known as "Santa Claus, Indiana."

Santa Claus, Indiana

Today this little community of less than 50 inhabitants commands national attention as the true home of Santa Claus. A fascinating blend of fantasy, pure fun, and history preserves America's most precious folklore heritages in this large and beautiful park of Santa Claus Land. (2)

SANTA FE, New Mexico

Santa Fe (La Villa Real de la Santa Fe de San Francisco de Assisi) was founded in 1610 by Don Pedro de Peralta, governor of New Spain, during the reign of King Charles II of Spain. One or more Indian pueblos stood on the site in prehistoric times. Spanish colonists from Mexico came to the area in 1598, twenty-two years before the Pilgrims landed at Plymouth Rock. Northern Pueblo Indians revolted in the year 1680 and occupied Santa Fe until 1692 when Don Diego de Vargas reached an agreement with the Indians and the city was retaken without bloodshed.

Mexico, which at the time included New Mexico, freed itself from Spain in 1821 and Santa Fe remained the northern capital under the Mexican regime. In 1846, during the Mexican War, the United States took possession of the city. At the outbreak of the War between the States, the Southern Army of the Texas Volunteers invaded the territory and for a brief time both the Texas and Confederate flags were flown over Santa Fe.

Later, Union forces won a decided victory at nearby Glorieta Pass and reoccupied the city. Following the war, the settlement of New Mexico continued, and in 1912, statehood was granted and the "City of the Holy Faith" remained the capital and is the oldest capital city in the United States. Through it all, the distinctive charm and atmosphere of Santa Fe has changed but little.

Santa Fe covers approximately 26.3 miles in the Northern Rio Grande Valley at an altitude of 7,000 feet. It is surrounded by the Sangre de Cristo Range (with peaks rising to 13,330 feet), the Ortiz Mountains on the southeast, the Sandias to the south, and the Jemez range on the west. (2)

SARAGOSSA, Alabama

The town was settled around the year 1890. The first settler, Mr. J. W. Ferguson, gave the location its name. Its tradition here is that he named it after the town of Saragossa (Zaragoza), Spain, although the reason is not known. It is located on the Southern Railroad, ten miles northwest of Jasper, Alabama. (1)

SASCO, Arizona

Came from the abbreviation of the name of the Southern Arizona Smelting Company. S. A. S. Co. (5)

SASPAMCO, Texas

Saspamco, on the north bank of the San Antonio River, near the Wilson-Bexar County line, derived its name from the initials of the San Antonio Sewer Pipe Manufacturing Company, which began using the red clay of the area for the manufacture of tile products about 1910. (3)

SASSAFRAS, Kentucky

In the late 1800's Manton Carnett established a post office near the mouth of a small drain, under the sheltering branches of a huge sassafras tree. The post office served the surrounding rural community, and was named Sassafras.

Later the post office was moved two miles downstream to a small town, which was as yet unnamed. With the post office came the name which the village adopted, to become Sassafras, Kentucky. (1)

SATSUMA, Texas

Satsuma, in western Harris County on the Texas and New Orleans Railroad, was established by C. W. Hahl, who planned to plant satsuma orange groves and named his townsite accordingly. Oil was discovered in 1936, the same year that the townsite was planned. (3)

SAVA, Texas
Sava, in Van Zandt County, is said to have been named by Mexican laborers in R. H. Walker's gin and gristmill when they could not "sabe" his directions. (3)

SCALP LEVEL, Pennsylvania
The area where the town of Scalp Level is now was warranted in the name of Luke Morris, June 25, 1787. Jacob Eash, Jr., erected a grist mill and a saw mill here around 1794, along Paint Creek, which runs through the area. For convenience he decided to have the land around the mills cleared.

All his friends and neighbors were invited to a clearing bee, or frolic, as it was called in those days. In the pioneer days neighbors helped neighbors, and along with the work they managed to make a kind of party of it. While the work was going on Mr. Eash came along with a jug (cost 6½ cents a quart) and yelled to the men clearing the underbrush, "Scalp'em Level, Boys, Scalp'em Level," meaning cut them close to the ground.

They scalped them level, and the local area took on the name "Scalp Level." Interesting to note, Paint Creek, which flows through Scalp Level, got its name because the Indians came here to mix their paint. (S. Newton Yoder, age 80, Windber, Pa.)

SCAPPOOSE, Oregon
There is only one Scappoose! The name is Indian, probably Multnomah, Clackamas, or Kalapooyou, and means "gravelly ground."

Although its most outstanding growth has come in recent years, the history of Scappoose is a long one. Before the arrival of white settlers, the territory, which is surrounded by the streams and forests, became a camping ground for a tribe of Indians known as "Kel-Ass-Sin-O."

The hills west of Scappoose offer an unsurpassed view of four mountain peaks, Mount Hood, in Oregon, and Mount Rainier, Mount St. Helens, and Mount Adams in Washington. On the hills the Indians must have stood in awe at such majestic beauty, and show of force by nature. (2)

SCATTERVILLE, Arizona
A town that rambled in Mohave County became Scatterville! (5)

SCENERY HILL, Pennsylvania
Settled in 1785, it received its name because it affords a splendid view of the valley against a background of ridges. (4)

SCHUYLKILL HAVEN, Pennsylvania
Was settled in 1748 by John Fincher, a Chester Quaker, and took its name from the Schuylkill Canal. Among the earliest settlers were squatters who had trouble with the Indians and with later arrivals bearing evidence of ownership. (4)

SCIENCE HALL, Texas
Science Hall (Hays County) was settled in 1871 by J. L. Andrews and Jimmy Goforth. The communinty took its name from a school named Science Hall. In 1885 the institution became a girl's school called Science Hall Institute, which operated until the district divided between Buds and Dyle. (3)

SCOTLAND NECK, North Carolina
Settled in 1722 on a point of the Roanoke River, there are two schools of thought on the origin of the name. One is that John Nairn, a Scotsman, owned a large farm here, and because its location looked something like a "neck" of land, it was called Scotland Neck.

Another is that it was named by settlers from Virginia where there was another Scotland Neck. (1)

SCRATCH ANKLE, Alabama
Located in Monroe County, Scratch Ankle has two stories behind the name, both similar, and both well worth telling. The first is that there was a rural schoolhouse built on the side of a hill (the entire area is located on a hillside), and in bad weather the goats, cows, mules, sheep, dogs, and other miscellaneous local animals would get under the school, from the lower side, for shelter. Fleas, ticks, and other varmints would come up through the floor and gnaw away at the ankles of the students. As they sat there clawing away at their ankles, they lost no time in dubbing the building, "Scratch Ankle School." The building has been gone for many years, but the community, with its unusual name is still there, located halfway between Franklin and Fountain, Alabama.

The second story is that each time a log train crew came through the village the people would be scratching their ankles. Horses and cows were kept in pens near the railroad, and the yellow flies were thick and bit the people around their ankles. (Chambers of Commerce, Grove Hill and Monroeville, Alabama)

SCURRY, Texas
Scurry, in southwestern Kaufman County, was named for Scurry Dean, who was killed in the Civil War. (3)

SEADRIFT, Texas
Seadrift, a German community in Calhoun County, on San Antonio Bay, secured a post office in 1888. The name Seadrift was chosen because of the debris from the Guadalupe River which collects along the shore of San Antonio Bay. Some of this debris came from the wreckage of the village of Indianola, which was washed away in 1886. (3)

SEATTLE, Washington
Largest city in the Pacific Northwest, this "City of Seven Hills" was named for Chief Sealth, an Indian, who befriended early pioneers. The city is located in King County, on Puget Sound, and has a deep harbor. (Office of Secty of State, Olympia, Washington)

SECLUSION, Texas
Seclusion, on the Navidad River in Lavaca County, was settled by Anglo-American farmers in 1840. A Methodist church and a school were first called *Boxville,* but the name was changed to Seclusion because of the secluded location. (3)

SECURITY, Texas
Security, a lumber shipping point and rural community in Montgomery County, was promoted by the Security Land Company. (3)

SEDALIA, Missouri
The area where the town of Sedalia now stands was once occupied by the Osage Indians. In an attempt to incite the Indians against the Americans in the War of 1812, the British operated in this vicinity. About six miles east of this area, near Flat Creek, a large mound was discovered by Joseph Stephens, Major Stephen Cole, and William Ross. The year was 1818. They found a place where wolves had clawed an opening in the mound; they enlarged it and entered to find a most amazing sight. There sat a British officer, in full uniform, golden epaulettes on his shoulders, cocked military hat, knee breeches, lace stockings, and morocco slippers. He was completely mummified and nothing but the ghastly color and leathery appearance of his skin would hint that he was not alive. What killed him is unknown, but the place was evidently a bunker mound prepared by the Indians for someone they held in awe.

Sedalia, itself, had its beginning in 1857 when George R. Smith, who came from Kentucky, tried in vain to persuade the good people of the village of Georgetown of the merits of financially assisting the railroad which was painfully inching its way west. The Pacific Railroad at that time was experiencing financial difficulty and requiring the counties and towns to assist in the cost of their expansion, provided they wished to have the railroad serve their town. The good citizens of Georgetown weren't the slightest bit interested in subsidizing the railroad, and General Smith, in disgust, predicted that he would live to see the day that bats and owls would make their home in the courthouse of Georgetown, a prediction that came true!

General Smith bought 160 acres of prairie land for $13.00 an acre and filed a plat called Sedville, named for his youngest daughter Sarah F. Smith, whom he called "Sed." Later the name was changed to Sedalia. In a county with an assessed value of $500,000 he raised $170,000 to bring the railroad through the county, and through Sedalia. He persuaded his friends and neighbors to subscribe nearly $2.00 for every $5.00 they owned! (Sedalia Centeniannual)

SEGOVIA, Texas
Segovia, a one-store settlement twelve miles southeast of Junction in Kimble County, was named by the early Spanish settlers of the area who saw a resemblance in the territory to a town in Spain. (3)

SEJITA, Texas
Sejita, in southern Duval County near the Jim Hogg County line, was named for a dam which resembled a "sejita" or "little eyebrow" in shape and which was known as a watering place for early range cattle. (3)

SELLERSVILLE. Pennsylvania
Named for the Old Sellers Tavern, now Washington House, it was founded in 1738. (4)

SENATOBIA, Mississippi
In northwest Mississippi, in Tate County, it takes its name from Senatahoba Creek, and is a derivation of the name. It is Indian and means "white sycamore." (6)

SERGEANT BLUFF, Iowa
The town was started and laid out by J. D. M. Crookwell and a Dr. John Cook, in 1854, and was settled shortly thereafter. It was named for Sergeant Charles Floyd, who was the only man to die on the Lewis and Clark Expedition. Sergeant Floyd actually died on the Nebraska side of the Missouri River, but was buried on a bluff on the Iowa side that overlooks the river.

Interestingly enough, Dr. Cook had a falling out with the townspeople and left to start the city of Sioux City, about eight miles north, at the junction of the Floyd and Big Sioux Rivers, with the Missouri. It prospered at once, and soon outgrew Sergeant Bluff and became the county seat. (1)

SERGEANTSVILLE, New Jersey
Located in Hunterdon County, in the central part of New Jersey, Sergeantsville was originally called *Skunktown,* prior to 1827, because it was frequented by so many skunks (the four-legged kind).

When a post office was established in 1827, the people decided that the village should have a more dignified name than *Skunktown.* Taking a head count, it was found that the Sergeants outnumbered the Thatchers in the area, so the name was changed to Sergeantsville, in honor of the Sergeants. (1)

SEVEN MILE FORD, Virginia
This small village is located seven miles west of Marion, Virginia, the county seat of Smyth County, and the area was used by the Indians as a ford across the river, and later by white settlers. The area became known as Seven Mile Ford and eventually when a village was settled here it adopted the same name. (1)

SEVEN OAKS, Texas
Seven Oaks, in central Polk County on the Texas and New Orleans Railroad, was named by a sawmill operator who had seven oak trees in his front yard. (3)

SEVEN SISTERS, Texas
Seven Sisters, in northern Duval County near the McMullen County line, was named for the Seven Sisters Oil Field, for which it became a supply point in 1932. (3)

SEVEN STARS, Pennsylvania
Gets its name from the Seven Stars Inn, which is still there. The inn was an old stagecoach stop, and tradition has it that an overnight guest asked the inn keeper's daughters if they would play the organ and sing. There were seven of them and their performance so enthralled the guest that he declared that they were indeed "seven stars." The name so pleased the inn keeper that he renamed his inn the "Seven Stars." (1)

SEVEN VALLEYS, Pennsylvania
A sign just before entering the town reads: "Seven Valleys—named for the Siebenthal (Ger) or Seven Valleys within the view of the borough."

Local legend has it that two politicians traveling east from Codorus passed through seven valleys before reaching this town, hence the name. (1)

SHAKOPEE, Minnesota

Named after Chief Shakopee, head of the Little Six Tribe of the Sioux Nation, who lived on the original site of the town, which was founded about 1850. On the eastern edge of the town is the spacious and popular Memorial Park with historic Sioux Indian burial mounds.

It is located in Scott County. (1)

SHANIKO, Oregon

Once a pack train and stagecoach stop, gold was discovered near Shaniko, in 1861. The stop was then known as The Hollow. Located where the old Steens and The Dalles Military Roads crossed one another, a German immigrant named August Schernickau settled here in 1874. He grew in importance and the Indians, unable to handle a name like Schernickau, called him Shaniko. Eventually the village that grew here adopted the name. Shaniko was once the wool center of the world, shipping over 4,000,000 pounds in 1902. (Sue Morelli, *Recorder*)

SHAWMUT, Alabama

Shawmut is reputedly a Creek Indian word for "Living Spring," probably for a large spring that fed the stream that once flowed through the present town of Shawmut.

The town is one of a complex of seven that make up "The Valley," along the Chattahoochee River. They came into being in 1828–29, on the site of very old Creek Indian Villages.

The Spanish census of 1738 and the French census of 1750 list the Indian towns of Ocfuskooche and Ocfuskeenena on the trails of the Creek Indian Nation. These led westward through Georgia and Alabama on the fords of the river, and about six miles from the present city of West Point, Georgia. (News Director, WBMK, Radio, West Point, Ga.)

SHAWNEE ON DELAWARE, Pennsylvania

Originally named Shawnee, for the Shawnee Indians who once lived and hunted here, the name was often confused with another town called Shawneese. Around 1900 the Post Office Department insisted that a less confusing name be chosen. Mr. C. C. Worthington, a large land owner here, who originally came from Irvington-on-Hudson, New York, suggested the name Shawnee on Delaware which was approved and adopted. (1)

SHEBOYGAN, Wisconsin

Sheboygan was incorporated as a village by an act of the territorial legislature approved February 3, 1846. Incorporated as a city in 1853, the corporate name is The City of Sheboygan. The first white settler in Sheboygan was William Farnsworth, who came here in 1814. The early history of Sheboygan is definitely a part of the great American story, including that of the fur trading post, "Indian village," settled by "voyageurs" who penetrated the wilderness with a perseverance and courage matching any in the annals of exploration in this country.

The name Sheboygan is of Indian origin. As of this date there are several theories on its meaning, all legendary. The Potawatomi called it "Shab-wa-wa-goning" meaning "Rumbling Waters" (*see* Wetumpka, Alabama), and also "Waters disappearing Underground." The Menominee Indians, according to the late Chief Reginald Oshkosh, called it "Saw-be-wah-he-con," meaning "Echoes."

The favorite legend among the people—not historians—is that during its pioneer days only boys had been born to the settlers, causing alarm. Each expected birth was awaited by the entire community to see if the "jinx" would be broken, and each time the cry would be "she-boy-again!" Another is that an Indian chief awaiting the birth of his second child proudly went around announcing to everybody, after it came, that "she-boy-again."

Though these legends may have no basis in fact, they are what make the histories of our communities so interesting, and give us an insight into the humor of our forefathers. (2)

SHEEP RANCH, California

So named for the many sheep corrals there in the late 1850's. It is the location of the famous Sheep Ranch Mine once owned by the late George Hearst. It is situated in Calaveras County. (2)

SHELL, Texas

Shell, on the Galveston, Houston, and Henderson Railroad in northern Galveston County, was named by the railroad because of its use as a siding for unloading shell. (3)

SHELL, Wyoming

Shell Creek, Shell Valley and Canyon, and the small town of Shell, Wyoming, in the Big Horn Mountains, are covered with shells of all kinds—large, small, long, pointed, and round. Although located in the Big Horn Mountains, millions of years ago this locality was the bottom of a large ocean. (1)

SHICKSHINNY, Pennsylvania
Is Choctaw Indian for "five mountains," named for a flat above the Susquehanna River, it is ringed by Newport, Lee's, Rocky, Knob and River Mountains. Platted and laid out in 1857, Shickshinny was incorporated November 30, 1861.

Two creeks enter through the mountains and empty into the Susquehanna River within the borough. These streams are paths to Salem, Hunting, Union, Ross and Fairmont Townships. (Borough Secy., Shickshinny, Pa.)

SHINGLETON, Michigan
Shingleton, Alger County, located in northwestern Michigan, was named for a shingle mill that was operated here in the early 1880's. (6)

SHINGLETOWN, California
Years ago there were six shingle mills located in the vicinity of this town, and as a result the town took the name Shingletown. (1)

SHIPSHEWANA, Indiana
Because a little Indian boy once dreamed he saw a lion (cougar), they named him Ship-She-Wana. It was the Potawatomi's way of saying "Vision of a Lion." This boy later became Chief Shipshewana and lived on the shores of the lake with his tribe.

In 1839 the government moved all the Indians from northern Indiana to a reservation in Kansas. Chief Shipshewanna was so heartbroken that they allowed him to come back to his hunting grounds, and eventually named Shipshewana Lake for him. He died in 1841, and a marker to his memory was erected at the entrance to the lake park.

The town of Shipshewana was established in 1888, when the railroad came through the area and was named for the nearby lake. (Lions Club, Shipshewana, Ind.)

SHOSHONE, California
Takes its name from the Shoshone Tribe of Indians that once lived and hunted in this area. The town is located, as they say, "Out where Death Valley begins":

"Oh, it happened in the Valley, to the south of Tonopah
Where there lived a pretty Indian, the young Death Valley Squaw.
Now I wanted so to meet her, at the "Valley" Dance that night,
But I didn't dare to greet her, for she was a little tight.
So to make me more courageous, I just leaned upon the bar;
With a voice a bit bodacious, I just asked for one drink more.
When I turned back to the dancers, a surprise is what I saw,

In my arms there was an Angel, the young Death Valley Squaw.
Her warm cheeks were honey velvet, her wet lips were wild with fire
She could not get me closer, as she quickened my desire.
'Come'n dance with me, my darling, and we'll have ourselves some fun
Come on, handsome, quit your stalling, for you know you're the one.'
Both my hands began to tremble, and my breath was burning hot,
And my heart commenced to tumble, but my head said 'better not.'
'I'm so sorry M'am,' I answered, 'for I've never danced two steps.'
But before I'd said another word, she was kissing my two lips.
Oh, the rapture really thrilled me, so I up and closed my eyes,
But that kiss it nearly killed me, and the stars sparked in my eyes.
The walls were hastily spinning, as I sat down on the floor.
I could hear that Indian grinning, 'Now stand up and have some more.'
The walls, they stopped unreeling, and the dancers all stood still
And my heart was, funny feeling, quite unlike Dan Cupid's quill.
Oh, I never will forget her, the young Death Valley Squaw,
Nor her big old chieftain husband, who just nearly broke my jaw!"
(Charles Brown's, Shoshone, California)

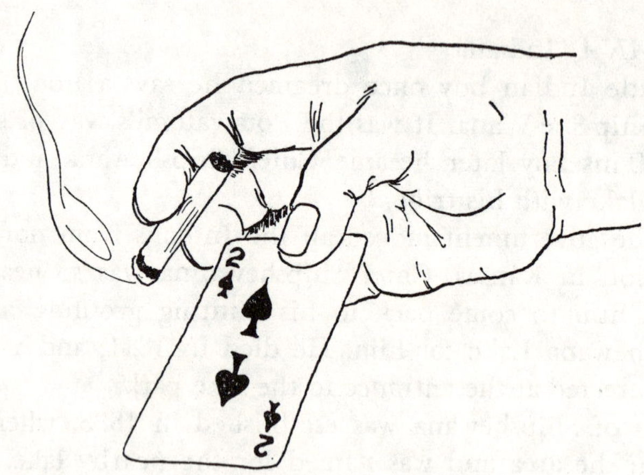

Show Low, Arizona

SHOW LOW, Arizona
Let them contrive a more unusual name than Show Low. Two Arizona pioneers dissolved their partnership in a card game called seven-up. With the townsite as stakes Marion Clark announced, "If you can show low, you win." Corydon Cooley said, "Show low it is," and the turn of his card won-and-named-a-town! Later when the town was laid out Show Low's main street was named "Deuce of Clubs." (5)

SICILY ISLAND, Louisiana
Located in northeastern Catahouia County, tradition has it that an early Italian pioneer thought the vicinity was a lot like his native Sicily, and the

streams and bayous, when flooded, gave the land the appearance of being an island. Because of this he dubbed it Sicily Island, and Sicily Island it is. (6)

SILENT, Arizona

Was not named for the absence of sound but for a judge named Silent. (5)

SILVER CITY, Nevada

The Silver City district has been a continuous producer of silver and gold since 1850. The city was a mining town and took its name from the product that built it, silver. (Nevada Electric Railroad, Silver City, Nevada)

SILVER GATE, Montana

Silver Gate is Montana's northeast entrance to Yellowstone National Park. The park gate is about ½ mile from this little community, which is located on the Beartooth Highway.

The village is located at the foot of Silver Mountain, which is 10,200 feet in altitude. The name Silver Gate is derived from the location of the village, and is very appropriate. The altitude of Silver Gate is 7,500 feet. (1)

SILVER HILL, Alabama

This being a heavily forested area there was not much use for plantations, so the land owners tapped their pine trees for pitch, turpentine, and rosin. They built turpentine stills where the pitch was boiled or distilled into turpentine, with rosin as residue.

An owner in this area built a large turpentine still on a hill to the east, above Silver Creek. All this labor in the forests of tapping, collecting, and hauling by ox, mule or horse, and the distilling, barrelling and hauling to the boats bound for Mobile was done by slaves.

After the War between the States, these laborers had to be paid, and paper money having no value, everyone was paid with silver. Since the still was on a hill and the business office was there too, all the laborers had to "go up the hill" to get their pay or "Silver." Soon the hill was called Silver Hill.

When the Svea Land Company of Chicago bought up the land from Fish River toward the east into what is now known as part of Robertsdale, back in 1896, they were going to call the colony "Svea," as it was to be a Swedish Colony. By then, however, the name Silver Hill was too well established to change. (Clerk, Silver Hill, Alabama.)

SILVER LAKE, Texas

A rural community, Silver Lake was established in 1873 as a stop on the

Texas and Pacific Railroad and was named by railroad men for the silvery appearance of a small lake in the saline creek bottom. (3)

SILVER STAR, Montana

Silver Star, Madison County, Montana, was settled sometime between 1867 and 1869, when the first log cabin was built here. On June 15, 1869, a post office was established, with Mr. John Conner the first postmaster.

This was a pioneer mining town, located near the Jefferson River and Cherry Creek. In 1867 the Iron Rod Mine was discovered, followed by the Broadway, The Hudson, The Owsley, and The Aurora Borealis. Two brothers, George and Bill Boyer, had another mining claim in one of the canyons, east of the Jefferson River, which they called "The Silver Star." It was from this mine that the largest of the two mining camps took its name. The smaller one was called *Rag Town* and later *Iron Rod.*

Silver Star is the third oldest town in Montana, and though the present activities are primarily confined to farming and raising cattle, there is still a little mining done here, and many old timers still hold that "There's Gold in them thar hills!" (1)

SILVER VALLEY, Texas

Silver Valley, in northwestern Coleman County on the Pecos and Northern Texas Railroad, was first settled by B. E. Smith and B. R. Brown about 1886. The community name was attributed both to the fertility of the valley and to possible hopes of early settlers that there was silver in the nearby hills. (3)

SINGER'S GLEN, Virginia

Located in a beautiful valley in Rockingham County, this village, with the lovely and unusual name of Singer's Glen, had its real beginning in 1786 when a family of German immigrants by the name of Funk settled near here.

In 1804 their son Joseph married and left the nest to build a home of his own. He selected a vale, near a spring of cool water. Here he settled, soon to be followed by others, and eventually a village grew to adopt the name of Mountain Valley.

Joseph was a writer and a teacher of music, his most famous work being "Harmoni Sacra." Some twenty or more editions of it have been published. He taught music to the young folk in the valley, and they in turn went out, using his works, and taught.

Because of the musical atmosphere of the village, and the musical talents of its residents, the people of Mountain Valley elected to change the name to Singer's Glen, when a post office was established here in 1860. I doubt they could have chosen a more appropriate or better one. (J. Robert Swank, Singers Glen)

SINKING SPRING, Pennsylvania
The origin of the name Sinking Spring, earlier called the Sunken Spring, was given to the town by the Lenni-Lenape Indians, and was so called because of the periodic appearance and disappearances of a spring located in the eastern end of the borough, founded in 1793. Each February, when the water begins to ooze from the frost-packed ground, the spring flows copiously, but dries up after the spring thaw. (2)

SINNEMAHONING, Pennsylvania
Is Indian for "Stony Lick," and was born of a lumber boom. The wild character of the town in its boom period is reflected in this bit of early nineteenth-century verse:

> There is a place called Sinnemahone,
> Of which but little good is known;
> For sinning, ill must be its fame,
> Since Sin begins its very name.
> So well indeed its fame is known
> That people think they should begin
> To drop the useless word Mahone,
> And call the country simply Sin. (4)

SINSINAWA, Wisconsin
The area around the mound named Sinsinawa was settled by the first white man, General George Wallace Jones, in 1827. In 1844 he sold the property to the Very Reverend Father Samuel Mazzuchelli, O.P., founder of the Dominican Sisters of the Congregation of the Most Holy Rosary. General Jones had acquired the land for lead smelters and used it for that purpose. Father Mazzuchelli bought it for religious and educational purposes and built a college for young men which operated until his death in 1864.

The Dominican Sisters began their institution here, but moved it to Benton in 1852. They returned to Sinsinawa in 1867 and have lived here since. Their Motherhome is located here and they also have an academy for high school girls. The name is Menominee Indian and is believed to mean "home of the young eagle." (Sister M. Lenora, O. P., Postmaster)

SIOUX CITY, Iowa
A French-Canadian fur trapper, Theophile Brughier, was the city's first settler, and his cabin was located near the confluence of the Big Sioux and Missouri Rivers. A friend of the Indians, Brughier married the daughter of the famed Indian chieftain, War Eagle, whose peaceful attitude toward the white man speeded the development of this area.

Dr. John Cook, a government surveyor, platted the town and recorded it May 5, 1855, naming it Sioux City for the River and for the Sioux Nation of Indians. (2)

SISTERS, Oregon

Sisters is located in Deschutes County, Oregon, near Squaw Creek. The name comes from the three peaks of the Cascade Mountain Range, which are now known as North Sister, South Sister, and Middle Sister. They were formerly called Faith, Hope and Charity, and the name, The Sisters, was proposed to the Post Office Department in 1885, but the name Sisters was the one approved. (2)

SISTERSVILLE, West Virginia

Was settled in 1802 by Charles Wells, who had twenty-two children. First called Wells Landing, then Ziggleton, it was finally named Sistersville in honor of Wells' eighteenth and nineteenth daughters. (6)

SIX MILE, Texas

Six Mile, Calhoun County, is a Bohemian community six miles north of Port Levaca, and therein lies the reason for the name. The community was established in 1894. (3)

SKAMANIA, Washington

Skamania, southwestern part of Washington State, has an Indian name that means "swift river." (Office of Secty of State, Olympia)

SKEETERVILLE, Texas

Skeeterville, at the confluence of Wilbarger and Brushy Creeks in northwestern San Saba County, was named in 1920 by Roy Wilson for the prevalence of mosquitoes. (3)

SKINNERS EDDY, Pennsylvania

Named for a tavern erected by Ebenezer Skinner in 1792, and for an eddy in the Susquehanna. (4)

SKULL VALLEY, Arizona

According to *Arizona Place Names* by Willis C. Barnes, the name dates back to 1864 and derives from the fact that soldiers in Captain Hargraves Company, of the First California Volunteers, found piles of bleached Indian skulls here while escorting Cales Bashford to Tucson in March 1864. The skulls were remnants of a battle between Apaches and Maricopas.

In August, 1866, at least 35 more skulls were added to the bleaching bones as a result of a fight between five citizens and four soldiers who battled more than 100 Indians who had stopped the train for the second time that month. A private citizen went for help to Camp McPherson, as

Skull Valley, Arizona

Skull Valley was then called. A bloody conflict followed after which 23 Indians lay dead in the immediate vicinity. The post office of Skull Valley was established April 26, 1869, with John C. Dunn its first postmaster. (1)

SLATE LICK, Pennsylvania
Was named for the fact that deer came here to lick salt from the slate rocks. (4)

SLAUGHTER BEACH, Delaware
Much is left to conjecture as to how the town was named. John Lofland, the Milford Bard, tells a story he says he believes, through much research, to be true. He writes that a vessel from Amsterdam had been stranded on the shore of Delaware Bay. On board was an 18-pound cannon and a vast quantity of powder and shot, intended for colonists farther up the bay. A wanderer came into the settlement suggesting the gun be brought ashore to be used to keep the Indians in subjection. This man, who gave the name of Lander, was recognized by some of the Indians who had seen him on the Brandywine, as one who had killed a fellow tribesman. The Indians vowed vengeance against him. Lander called himself a Swede although he looked more like a half-blooded Indian. The cannon was moved ashore and Lander told the Indians it was the Great Spirit who would speak whenever the

Indians did anything wrong. It was not long before one of the ship's party was murdered. The cannon was fired to tell the Indians they had done wrong. At the thundering sound, the Indians yelled and fell down before the cannon, knowing that it must be The Great Spirit, for nothing human could speak so loud. The cannon was loaded again; the Indians were told to stand before it so that the guilty could be punished. The cannon was fired with a tremendous roar which reverberated throughout the forest and great numbers fell bleeding and writhing in agony. By this means great numbers of Indians were slaughtered; so great was their superstitious terror that they feared to disobey the order to stand before the cannon, having been assured that the firing would kill only the guilty. Those whom Lander and the colonists feared most were placed immediately in front of the cannon that they might certainly be killed. Thus the areas of these slaughterings came to be known as Slaughter Beach and Slaughter Neck. (Slaughter Beach Fire Company)

Sleepy Eye, Minnesota

SLEEPY EYE, Minnesota

The community is an old Indian territory and had few white settlers prior to 1860. During the uprising of 1862 the area was overrun by the Indians and old Fort Ridgey, 11 miles north of Sleepy Eye was the center of the attack.

The village was established in 1872 when the railroad came through, and was named for the beautiful lake which borders it on the north. The lake was named for Chief Sleepy Eye (Ish-Tak-Ba-Ba) in the Indian tongue, friend of the white settlers. His grave and a monument to his memory are located near the depot.

The community's first name was "Village of Sleepy Eye Lake," but some thought that was not sufficiently dignified and induced the legislature to change it to Loreno. People, however, still called it Sleepy Eye, so a second trip was made to the legislature and the name changed back to Sleepy Eye. (2)

SLICK, Oklahoma
Named for the man who platted and laid out the town, T. B. Slick, it was an important oil town and railroad. (6)

SLIDE, Texas
Slide, a rural community in Lubbock County, was first known as *Block Twenty.* The community received its present name because of a "land slide" resulting in a resurvey made by W. R. Standfer in 1903. This caused nearly two hundred sections to be located almost two miles farther west than they were thought to be when first settled. (3)

SLIGO, Pennsylvania
Bisected by Big Licking and Little Licking Creeks, Sligo was named for the Sligo Furnace built in 1845 by four men from Sligo, Ireland. (4)

SLIPPERY ROCK, Pennsylvania
Was called Ginger Hill by early settlers from the local tavern keeper's practice of giving away plenty of ginger with the whiskey he sold.

Slippery Rock Creek is where Captain Samuel Brady is reputed to have crossed in a single 23-foot leap with an Indian right at his heels. The village takes its name from the creek.

Gosh all hemlock, what do I see?
A redskin pointin' his gun at me?
That's right, Pale Face . . . Since I'm discovered
Don't move a step. I've got you covered.
I'm travelin,' Varmint, I'm on my way . . .
My hair won't hang from your belt this day.
You may be fast but I'll have that scalp
If I have to climb the highest Alp.
No Alps for me. I'll chance the creek.
Hurrah! You missed. What a narrow squeak.
There's no use hopping from stone to stone
My tomahawk cleaves the toughest bone.
This Eliza act is durned realistic
Pardon me, Varmint. That's anachronistic.
That two dollar word . . . it may be your last

I've got you, White Man. Your future's just past.
Ha, ha . . . you fell. With all your talk
You didn't see that slippery rock!
The God of Waters is mad at me
Fatherless orphans will fill my tepee.
Oh, no, Redskin. I'm not much fer killin'
You'll yet live to see your wife and your chillen.
But why, White Man? I'd have killed you.
The same fate is right for me, too.
Listen, Varmint, for many a week
I hunted a name for this blamed creek
Something suitable, a name that sticks
And until you fell I was in a fix
But right here and now, without much talk
We've named this creek . . . The Slippery Rock
If a town grows up, that's its name too
If folks think it's funny—what can they do?
We'll be a legend, and we'll be to blame
But they'll have to stick to this funny name.
When I saw you skid for half a block
I knew right then 'twould be—"Slippery Rock." —Jack M. MacDonald

(Slippery Rock Area Chamber of Commerce as furnished by the First National Bank, Slippery Rock, Penn.)

SMACKOVER, Arkansas

Dense sumac thickets in the neighborhood led early French hunters to call the place "Sumac couvert," and the name was eventually "Americanized" to Smackover by the early settlers. (6)

It is located in north central Union County.

SMALL, Texas

Small, in Hudspeth County, was founded prior to 1915 and named for Hank Small, supervisor for the railroad. (3)

SMILE, Kentucky

When this small Kentucky town petitioned for a post office and learned that it had been granted, everyone smiled. No longer would they have to travel six to eight miles to pick up their mail. It was no wonder that they decided to call their new post office Smile. (1)

SMILEY, Texas

Smiley, in southern Gonzales County, was originally called Smiley Lake for the Smiley family. An inland trading point of some importance in the early days, it began to prosper with the building of the San Antonio and Gulf Railroad through the area in 1906. (3)

Smile, Kentucky

SMOKE BEND, Louisiana
Tradition has it that pioneers, rounding a bend in the river, saw smoke rising from Indian campfires, and called the area by that name. (6)

SMYRNA, Texas
Smyrna, a Milam County farming community, church, and cemetery four miles southeast of Milano, was named for the Biblical city of Smyrna. (3)

SNOHOMISH, Washington
Located about thirty miles above Seattle, and ten miles from Puget Sound, Snohomish was named for the Indian tribe of the same name. (Office of the Secty of State, Olympia, Washington)

SNOOK, Texas
Snook, in an agricultural area of Burleson County, had seven stores, a school, and a population of seventy-five in 1940. Snook was named for a postmaster at Caldwell, a Snook, J. S. by name, who was influential in getting a post office for the town. (3)

SNOWFLAKE, Arizona
Snowflake is not named for the cold, white stuff, but rather for its founders, a Mr. Snow, and a Mr. Flake. (5)

Snow Shoe, Pennsylvania

SNOW SHOE, Pennsylvania

Snow Shoe, Pennsylvania, derived its unusual name from a snowshoe found hanging in a tree by first warrant surveyors in 1773. The site was an abandoned Indian campsite near a spring along the Chinclacamoose Indian trail. (1)

SOCIAL CIRCLE, Georgia

Documentary proof is lacking in searching for the origin of the name Social Circle, which this town has always borne; but traditions which have persisted in many families whose ancestors were here in pioneer days are identical and credible. The historical background of the region makes these traditional claims seem plausible.

The east-west and the north-south trails crossed where Social Circle now stands. The ridges around were high and safe from flooding. They were well wooded, and springs were abundant, affording a pleasing place for a night camp.

Tradition has it that on one occasion a stranger arrived and seeing several travelers around a camp fire, and likely passing 'round the familiar jug remarked, "This is indeed a social circle." This incident was followed, when on the morrow as the group began to disperse, by such casual remarks as: "I'll meet you at the Circle in two weeks."

When houses were built here, and a post office established, nobody ever thought of any other name than Social Circle, Georgia. (Frank P. Lane, Georgia Power Company, Social Circle, Georgia.)

SOCIETY HILL, South Carolina
Society Hill was named for Saint David's Society, a society "established purposely for founding a public school in the said parish for educating youths in the Latin and Greek languages, mathematics and other useful branches of learning." The Society was organized in 1777, and was named for Saint David, the patron saint of the Welsh.

The early Welsh pioneers settled along the Pedee River, in South Carolina. The principal settlement was called Long Bluff, and was established along the east side of the river, where the Welsh Neck Baptist Church and cemetery were located. Later they moved out to the surrounding hills, west of the river, where the present town of Society Hill is located.

The Society met on the hill and located their first academy building there, near the present site of Welsh Neck Church. The school was well known in the early days, and is still in existence, although its activities today are limited to the first six grades. (Florence Burn and Postmaster)

SOD, West Virginia
The village was originally called Scioto, but when the post office was organized in 1904 the name was changed to Sod, to honor its first postmaster, Samuel Odell Dunlap. (1)

SODVILLE, Texas
Sodville, in San Patricio County, was established in the early 1900's, when the ranching area was broken up into farm tracts, and appropriately named Sodville. (3)

SOLINO, Texas
Solino, in Hidalgo County, was established in 1927 as a station on the Texas and New Orleans Railroad and was named for the salt lakes found in the region. (3)

SOLO, Missouri
Solo is clustered on a hill around the general store. When a post office was established here in 1897, it was located on low ground, by itself, and so they called it Solo. It is now up on the hill, in the general store, but still named Solo. The village is located high in the beautiful Ozark Mountains in Texas County. (1)

SOPCHOPPY, Florida
Sopchoppy is located thirty-five miles south of Tallahassee, in Wakulla County. The town takes its name from the picturesque Sopchoppy River, with its steep banks overhung with honeysuckle, jasmine and tupelo. The name was given to the river by the Indians, and means "black water." (1)

SOUR LAKE, Texas

Sour Lake, in Hardin County, was originally called Sour Lake Springs because of the mineral springs that fed the lake. The oldest town in Hardin County, it was first settled about 1835, but long before the advent of white settlers, Indians had made use of the mineral waters and of the pitch found around the oil seepages near the lake shores. As early as 1850, Sour Lake was a health resort with good accommodations for health seekers, including Sam Houston in the early 1860's, and so it continued until the discovery of oil in July, 1902.

The Texas Company had its beginning at Sour Lake and still owns the lake and former site of the Sour Lake Springs Hotel. The field had produced about 90,000,000 barrels of oil up to 1948, when it was producing about 3,500 barrels daily and new drilling was being continued. (3)

SOUTHLAND, Texas

Southland, at the edge of the Llano Estacado in Garza County, was named for its location on the South Plains. The Curry-Comb Ranch and several ranches owned by John B. Slaughter were located in the area. (3)

SPANISH CAMP, Texas

Spanish Camp, in Wharton County, was established during the early days of Stephen F. Austin's colony and was named in 1836, when Mexican forces under Antonio López de Santa Anna camped at the springs on Peach Creek. (3)

SPANISH FORK, Utah

Actually, when Spanish Fork was first settled in 1850–51, there were two separate settlements, one located in the river bottoms southeast of the present city and one in the Palmyra area, near Utah Lake, northwest of the town. Fearful of Indian trouble, the two settlements built a fort in 1854, of adobe, with walls 2 feet thick and 20 feet high. The only entrance was through a gate 4 feet thick and 16 feet high. This served to unite the two communities into one, which took its name from Spanish Fork Canyon.

The first white men ever to look upon the present site of Spanish Fork were two Franciscan Friars, Father Sylvestre Velez de Escalante, and Father Francisco Ananasio de Dominguez, who on September 23, 1776, came through Spanish Fork Canyon and camped on the river near the present site of the city. The priests were in quest of a direct route from Santa Fe, New Mexico, to Monterey, California. They also hoped to become better acquainted with the Indians inhabiting this region.

After spending three days visiting the Indian tribes on the east shore of Utah Lake, the Spanish party of nine turned south without visiting Salt

Lake Valley. Fearing a shortage of provisions and the privations of the winter in the mountain region, Escalante and his party turned back toward Santa Fe, after making a short trip farther south in Utah. They arrived at Santa Fe, January 2, 1777, without having reached Monterey, the objective of the expedition. (2)

SPANISH FORT, Alabama
At a junction of the "Old Spanish Trail," stands Spanish Fort, complete with entrenchments and gun placements on one of the best preserved battlefields in North America. It was the scene of many struggles among various European forces in pioneer days, and saw bitter action in the Civil War. Spanish Fort, the town, took its name from the fort. (Eastern Shore Chamber of Commerce)

SPANISH FORT, Texas
Spanish Fort, in a bend of Red River in northern Montague County, was the site of a Taovaya rancheria which was important for Indian inter-tribal trade and as early as 1719 was a French trappers' supply point. In 1759, when Diego Ortiz Parrilla led a punitive expedition to the village, he found it flying the French flag, armed with French guns, and protected behind a crude stockade and moat. He was defeated and forced to retreat. In 1778 Athanase de Mézières visited the village and named it San Teodoro in honor of Teodoro de Croix, commandant general of the Provincias Internas. The pueblo was on the routes of José Mares and Pedro Vial in their explorations of 1786–1788. By 1812 smallpox had decimated the Taovaya, and remnants of the tribe joined the Wichita. Early Anglo-American settlers found traces of the Indians and their Spanish visitors and called the site the Old Spanish Fort.

Permanent Anglo-American occupation was prevented by Indian raids until the early 1870's, when a village called Burlington developed and became headquarters and supply point for early ranchers. A Chisholm Trail crossing of Red River went through the town which came to have a famous cowboy saloon. (3)

SPARKILL, New York
The derivation of the word means "valley of the pine trees," and was so named in 1750 by John DeWindt, a Dutchman who came here from the West Indies. The stone house he built is now a Masonic Shrine and was formerly Washington's headquarters. It was here at the 1776 house that Major Andre was tried and hanged.

Dividing the word into its syllables, Spar-Kill, pine trees were then used as "spars" and masts for ships, and "kill" was the terminology for valley, differing from the Holland Dutch term of kill, meaning a small stream. (Albert W. Munson, D.D.S., Councilman Town of Orangetown.)

SPARROW BUSH, New York
There is no exact record as to the reason for the unusual name, however records indicate that a Mr. H. L. Sparrow owned extensive timber lands near the post office. His timberland might have been called "Sparrow's Bosh," meaning "Sparrow's Slope," or "Sparrow's Bosk," meaning "Sparrow's Thicket of Bushes."

First named Honesville, for the president of the Canal Company, the post office was closed for several years. When it was re-established in 1850 it was given the name Sparrowbush. The former trademark of the Sparrow Bush Tannery consisted of a circle in which sat a sparrow on a twig of a bush. (William J. Darragh, Sparrow Bush, NY)

SPIRIT LAKE, Iowa
Named for Spirit Lake, upon whose shores it was built. Spirit Lake, or "Minnewauken," as it was called in Indian language was regarded in superstitious awe by them. They believed its waters were haunted by spirits. No Dakotah ever dared to cross it in his canoe. In fact no Indian canoe was ever found by the early settlers in the vicinity of this lake. As told by Mrs. A. L. Buckland in 1864:

They saw the beauty of the place,
The lake's walled shore and rippled face,
And asked what name to it belonged.
(For well they knew the Indian tongue.)
"Minnewaukon," the warrior spake;
Translated this means Spirit Lake.
"And why thus called," he asked the brave,
As he looked out upon the wave,
While they the pipe of peace imbibe
He told this legend of his tribe. . . . (2)

SPLENDORA, Texas
Splendora, Montgomery County, was established in 1879 as a stop on the old narrow gauge Houston, East and West Texas Railroad. Splendora was named by M. Z. King, teacher and first postmaster, for the vessel in the song, "The Good Ship That Never Returned." (3)

SPOKANE, Washington
Named for an Indian tribe, the word Spokane means "Chief of the People of the Sun." Located in east-central Washington near the Idaho border, it is in Spokane County. (Off of Sec of State, Olympia)

SPOTSYLVANIA, Virginia
The town got its name from the county, as it is the seat of Spotsylvania County. The county was named for Governor Alexander Spotswood, the first Colonial governor of Virginia. The "Sylvania" portion of the name is old English and means "wood," "woods," or "wooded," and was substituted for the "wood" part of the governor's name. Also the area, at the time, was very heavily wooded with pine trees. (1)

SPRINGTOWN, Texas
Springtown is the second largest town in Parker County. Captain Joseph Ward of New Jersey settled on the site in 1856 and in 1859 laid out the town, which they called Littletonville or Littleton's Springs, for a pioneer family. A petition adopted in the middle 1870's changed the name to Springtown because of the springs which then flowed on the creek bank south of the square. When the town voted dry in 1894, its incorporation was attacked and outlawed so that the saloons might return. (3)

SPRING VALLEY, Minnesota
Located in west-central Filmore County, which borders the Iowa line, it received its name from the many springs or fountains in the area. There are many underground rivers and caves in the vicinity. (6)

SPURGER, Texas
Spurger, Tyler County, is located on a tract conveyed to James Hooks by J. J. Pemberton in 1852. A store and a saloon were at the site as early as 1860. The community is reportedly named from the pronunciation that a local drunk gave the Spurgeon brand of whiskey sold at the local saloon! (3)

STAMPING GROUND, Kentucky
When explorers first came to this section of Kentucky they found a large trail or buffalo road heading in a northeast-southwest direction. The trail led to a large spring of cold, clear water.

The stamping of whole herds of wild buffalo had packed the ground for hundreds of feet around the spring. The explorers called the place "Buffalo Stamping Ground." It was from this that the town of Stamping Ground derived its name, because it was built on this large area and now completely surrounds the spring. (1)

STAR, Texas
Star, on north Simms Creek in eastern Mills County, was first known as Star Mountain for a nearby hill shaped like a five-pointed star. The town was established in the late 1880's by E. A. Street. (3)

STARBUCK, Minnesota
The village of Starbuck, Pope County, was platted in 1882. It was named after Mr. William H. Starbuck of New York, who financed the construction of the Little Falls and Dakota Railroad; a builder of ships and ship owner and a friend of Henry Villard who was president of the Northern Pacific Railway from 1881 to 1884. It is located on the west end of Lake Minnewaska.

Minnewaska, the largest lake in Pope County, was given its name by white settlers, and was made from two Dakota or Sioux words, "minni" or "minne" (water), and "washta" or "waska" (good). The lake was subsequently changed in name to White Bear Lake, and then to Lake Whipple, and finally back to Minnewaska.

The grave of Chief White Bear is an elongated mound at the southern edge of Minnewaska township about 90 feet above the lake. (Who's Who, Starbuck Oil Company)

Steamboat, Nevada

STEAMBOAT, Nevada
Old settlers here claim that Mark Twain (Samuel Clemens) named it while he was a reporter at Virginia City. It is said that he came over the hill and saw all the steam coming from a geyser, and asked, "What is a Steamboat doing out in this desert?" (1)

STEPTOE, Washington
Steptoe, located in Whitman County, Washington, takes its name from beautiful Steptoe Butte, which is nearly 2,700 feet high, and stands all by

itself in the center of wheat, pea, and lentil farms. The nearest mountains are over 18 miles away.

Steptoe Butte was named for Colonel Steptoe. This intrepid Indian fighter, together with 130 dragoons, left Fort Walla Walla and on May 18, 1859, was engaged by 600 Spokane, Coeur d'Alene and Palouse Indians. The soldiers were attacked near Rasalie, Washington, were defeated at Steptoe Butte and retreated by night to the safety of the Snake River Canyon. (1)

STOP OVER, Kentucky

Stop Over, located in Pike County, got its unusual name due to its location at an unmarked junction. People coming and going found it necessary to "stop over" here to ask directions.

The post office is located in the general store and was named by its first postmaster, D. H. Blankenship. The community is located in the heart of a large coal field, and is essentially a mining town. (Anthony Blankenship, Postmaster)

STORY, Wyoming

Story is located well up in the Big Horn Mountains, between North and South Piney Creeks. It is protected by the mountains, and has a generous growth of ponderosa pines, aspen, willow, and wild fruit. Even today it is not unusual to see a moose or elk within the boundary of the community, and deer and bear are a daily sight.

The community was named in honor of Charles Story, representative to Congress in 1902, when the post office was established.

As the present postmaster writes, "We are proud of Story, and echo the words of one of our pioneer citizens—Story is the home of the best people on earth and a few old sore heads!" (1)

STORY CITY, Iowa

In 1855 a small town was platted on the banks of the Skunk River, and named Fairview. In 1856 a post office was established and named "Story City" for the eminent jurist Joseph Story, who was associate justice of the Supreme Court.

Story City was platted in 1878, and joined with Fairview, incorporating as Story City, in 1881. (1)

STRANGE CREEK, West Virginia

Named for Strange Creek which was named for William Strange who strayed from a surveying team near the headwaters of the Elk River in 1795, and became lost. Years later, on the banks of Turkey Run (as Strange Creek was called then), and over forty miles from the spot where he disappeared,

Strange's bones were found beneath a large tree with his rifle and the bones of his dog. Carved in the bark of the tree was this little ditty:

"Strange is my name, and I'm on strange ground.
And strange it is I can't be found." (1)

STRAWBERRY PLAINS, Tennessee

The first settlers came to this vicinity about 1787, and named their settlement Strawberry Plains for the profusions of wild strawberries found in the area. The people liked the name of their town.

When the railroad passed through the town it was said that the flagmen and conductors took to calling it Straw Plains for brevity. Eventually the name on the depot was changed to Straw Plains and even the postmasters changed their postmark to conform, though without official approval. On one occasion the vice-president of the railroad, Mr. Copeman, passed through Strawberry Plains in his private car and stopped for a short visit. The townspeople enjoined him to change the name of their town back to its original one. A short time later the depot name was changed back to Strawberry Plains, and the flagmen and conductors announced the name Strawberry Plains in clear, dulcet tones; the postmaster changed his postmark, and the people of Strawberry Plains breathed a sigh of relief, and settled down to the business at hand. (1)

STRAWBERRY POINT, Iowa

Back in 1841 the Iowa Territorial Legislature appointed a commission to survey and locate a road from Dubuque to Fort Atkinson, Iowa. The road was laid out and the surveyor paid little attention to section lines but surveyed roughly northwest from Dubuque to Fort Atkinson. This road then constituted the main street of several little villages that sprung up along the way, one of them being the town that is now known as Strawberry Point.

Tradition tells that there was a tract of timber about a mile west of the village and that this tract of timber ran to a point along the Mission Road (as it was called). A party of soldiers going from Dubuque to Fort Atkinson camped at this point of timber in the month of June and found an abundance of wild strawberries. The wife of the lieutenant in charge gave the place the name Strawberry Point, and it wasn't long until the name was widely known, not only in Iowa, but in Illinois and states to the east.

The village was platted in 1853 by W. H. and D. M. Sterns and named Franklin in honor of their former home. However, when application was made to the Post Office Department to have this name for the local post office it was found that there was already a Franklin in Iowa, near Keokuk, so the already well-known name of Strawberry Point was chosen.

One would have thought that this would have ended the matter, but not so. When the Davenport and St. Paul Railroad reached Strawberry Point in

1872 and a station was established, officials of the railroad, including a Mr. M. O. Barnes, of Strawberry Point, a vice-president of the railroad, decided the name was not appropriate since it would take too long a sign board for the depot! So they named the station Enfield. Passengers coming from the east often discovered that they were way up the line before realizing that they had passed Strawberry Point, because the conductor had called out "Enfield."

In 1875 the state legislature passed a law requiring a railroad to have the same name for the station as the name of the incorporated town in which the station was located. In 1887 the name "Strawberry Point" was accepted without question. (1)

STRAWBERRY VALLEY, California

Local legend has it that a man by the name of Berry owned the stables during the early days of the settling of this part of California. He always fed the horses straw, more straw, and nothing but straw. He was known throughout the valley as "Straw Berry." When this small town was formed and searching for a name it elected to call itself Strawberry Valley, for old Berry and his incessant straw. Strange were the ways of the wild, wild West! (1)

STRIP, Texas

Strip was established on April 15, 1904. It took its name from its location in what was known as "The Strip," a piece of land one and one-half miles wide and fifteen miles long which lay between two blocks of land patented to railroad companies and settled by homesteaders. (3)

STRONG, Arkansas

Formerly named Victoria, it was decided practical to change the name to avoid confusion with another Arkansas town named Victoria. A meeting was held in Strong's hardware store to decide on a new name. And guess where they got the name? (1)

STUDY BUTTE, Texas

Study Butte, also called Big Bend, in the Chisos Mountains in southern Brewster County in Big Bend National Park. It was named for Will Study, manager of the Big Bend Cinnabar Mining Company, which was established after Frederico Villalva discovered mercury in the area about 1900. (3)

SUBLETTE, Illinois

This small village is located in northern Illinois, in Lee County. It was established in 1854 when the Illinois Central Railroad came through, on the Main Line of Mid-America from south to north. A depot was established here and named Soublette, but later changed to Sublette.

The origin of the name is uncertain, but it is believed by most that the village was named for Thomas Sublette, who fought under Colonel John Dement in Captain Enoch Duncan's company against Black Hawk Indians in the battle of Kellogg's Grove on June 23, 1832. Thomas Sublette, with twenty-two of his comrades, was killed in this battle.

The railroad, beside being a boon to the settlers in the way of freight, mail, etc., was held in considerable reverence by them. Many had never seen steam cars or the roadbed on which they were drawn until the Illinois Central arrived. Because of this, the names the railroad gave to their depots were immediately adopted by the villages. (Farmer's State Bank of Sublette, Ill.)

SUDAN, Texas
Sudan, in western Lamb County, occupies land once a part of the X I T Ranch and owned in 1917 by J. B. Wilson of Dallas, who donated a townsite to the Panhandle and Santa Fe Railroad. The name Jaynes, suggested by the railroad, was rejected, and P. E. Boesen, land agent who surveyed the site, suggested naming the village for the sudan grass just becoming a commercial crop. *The Sudan News* began publication about 1928. (3)

SUGARTOWN, Alabama
The name of this Clarke County community is said to have originated because the people got along so well together. (Chamber of Commerce, Grove Hill, Ala.)

SUNDANCE, Wyoming
Legend has it that the Sioux Indians used the high bald face of the Sundance Mountain for their "Sun Dance." Many historians discount this, but others will verify it with their agreement. Sundance, Wyoming, was named for this mountain. (Sundance Commercial Club)

SUNDOWN, Texas
Sundown, in Hockley County, was laid out in 1928 on part of the old C. C. Slaughter Ranch. The first store was opened in 1929. According to one story the town was named for a motion picture, but another account is that at a meeting held to decide upon a name the villagers debated all afternoon, until almost sundown, then someone suggested that they call the place Sundown and go home. (3)

SUNNY SOUTH, Alabama
Established around 1887, with the coming of the railroad, people from

nearby Airmount (no longer in existence) moved here to be near the depot and the activities that centered about it. The teachers in the local school referred to the new community as "Sunny South" (reason unknown), and when a post office was established later, that name was submitted and approved. (1)

SUNOL, Nebraska

Sunol, Cheyenne County, had its start when the Union Pacific decided to lay a side track here. When two trains approached each other on a single track, one would be sided to allow the passage of the other, thus the necessity for a side track.

Senator Stanfors, of Palo Alto, California, shipped a beautiful young horse named "Sunol" to the Chicago World's Fair, in 1893, over the Union Pacific. The railroad decided to honor the senator by naming this little siding Sunol. When a settlement grew up here, the name Sunol was adopted and later a post office by that name was established here. (1)

SURPRISE, Nebraska

Abraham Towner was the first settler to establish himself in this area, followed in 1881 by George Miller, his wife and two sons. The nearest towns were two day's travel away. Miller established a flour mill along the banks of the Blue River.

As new settlers came over the hills from the north or south, they were always "surprised" to see a mill working this far from established civilization. It soon became known as Surprise Mill, and when enough settlers had arrived to establish a town, it was, of course, named Surprise. (1)

SUNSHINE, Louisiana

Sunshine, Iberville Parish, is in what was known as "The Sugar Bowl," as the growing of sugar cane was the principal industry here for many years. The village first boasted the name of *Forlorn Hope.*

Mail was brought in by the steamboats plying the Mississippi, and picked up at the local general store by the surrounding community. When the railroad came through about three miles away, Oscar Richard, a large sugar plantation owner requested a post office for the area. When it was approved he named it Sunshine, as different as possible from the previous name of Forlorn Hope. (1)

SUNSHINE HILL, Texas

Sunshine Hill, a farming and oil community in Wichita County, was named for a hill which, despite its slight elevation, could be seen for miles around when the sunshine was falling on it. (3)

SWANSEA, South Carolina
A derivation of the German word for twenty (Zwanzig) because the town was located twenty miles from Columbia, South Carolina. (6)

SWEET SPRINGS, Missouri
Settled in 1826 and platted as a township in 1848, it was named for a sweet spring in the town from which flowed several gallons a minute. (6)

SWEETWATER, Texas
Sweetwater, in north-central Noland County, had its beginning in 1877, when Billie Knight, to accomodate buffalo hunters, established a store in a dugout on the banks of Sweetwater Creek. The creek was so named for its pleasant palatable water. On March 31, 1879, with the coming of a few "nesters" and cattlemen, a post office named Sweet Water was established. The village became the temporary county seat in 1881, when the county was organized, and, after moving two miles northeast to the line of the Texas and Pacific Railroad in 1882, remained the seat of local government. Sweetwater has prospered and in 1950 had a population of 13,580. (3)

TABLE ROCK, Nebraska
Settled in 1858 by Charles Woodbury Giddings, who came here from Pennsylvania, Table Rock grew to a city of about 1,000 people at its peak. At one time the city was quite a railroad center, being on the main line of the CB&Q Railroad between St. Joe, Missouri, and Denver by way of Lincoln, Nebraska. The railroad is still here, but just whistles as it goes through now, although the population is about 400 and it is a thriving farm community.

About a mile east of the present site of Table Rock is a bluff and caves where Indians used to live. At this site was a rock that resembled a table, and it was from this rock that the town took its name. The rock does not exist anymore. (1)

TACOMA, Washington
This Puget Sound City has one of the finest harbors in the world and takes its name from the Indian word "Tah-Koma," meaning "the mother of us all," or more simply "the mountain." This city is the gateway to Mount Rainier and White Pass and annually celebrates the Daffodil Festival with nearby valley cities. (Office of the Secty of State, Olympia, Washington.)

TACONITE, Minnesota
Villages were built up all through this area to supply accommodations for the men who worked the mines. Before building a village, the company would "diamond drill" the area to see if there was a chance the proposed

site might someday become a producing mine. If so, they would move the site elsewhere. While test drilling here for the proposed site of a village, they discovered a hard rock, iron bearing, low grade ore. This low grade ore is called Taconite, and is not considered valuable enough for mining.

The village of Taconite was incorporated in 1908, during the great iron ore boom of the Mesabi Range. They named the village for the low grade iron ore upon which it stands.

In the words of its present postmaster, Elwyn Guyer, "Taconite is a village, of low grade ore, and high grade people, 372 strong." (1)

TAHOKA, Texas

Tahoka, in central Lynn County, was named for Lake Tahoka, the name being an Indian word for "deep" or "clear water." The town became the county seat of Lynn County in 1906. (3)

TALLADEGA, Alabama

Founded January 6, 1834, and incorporated January 9, 1835, the town takes its name from the Creek Indian word meaning "border town."

The Battle of Talladega was fought on November 9, 1813, between the Creek Indians and the Tennessee Volunteers led by Major General Andrew Jackson. During this time a small Indian village occupied the site of present-day Talladega. (2)

TALLAHASSEE, Florida

The site of Tallahassee was first occupied by the Apalachee Indians, now extinct. They were dispersed and their villages destroyed by the English and Creek Indians from South Carolina, in the early 1800's. Next to occupy this area were the Seminoles, who were an offshoot of the Creek Nation, the name Seminole meaning "separatist" or "runaway."

In 1821, the United States acquired Florida from Spain, with Andrew Jackson as its first governor. He was succeeded by William P. DuVal of Kentucky, a few months later. The government of the Territory of Florida was in the hands of the governor and a legislative council appointed by the President of the United States. Because Pensacola and St. Augustine were the only two towns of any importance in the territory and each had been the capital of a Spanish providence, the first legislative council met in Pensacola in 1822, while the second was held the next year in St. Augustine. This was such an inconvenient arrangement that the council directed that this quarter section be laid out into a town to be called Tallahassee.

The capital of Florida took its name from the Tallahassee Seminole, who occupied the area, or from one of their villages. The word "Tallahassee" is of Creek derivation meaning literally "old town," but it is frequently translated as "old fields." The legislative council also created Leon County and made Tallahassee its county seat. The county is named for Juan Ponce de León who discovered Florida. (2)

TAMAQUA, Pennsylvania
Is Indian for Beaver. It was started by Berkhard Moser in 1799, when he built a sawmill here, and years later coal was discovered on his land. (4)

TAMARACK, Minnesota
When the Northern Pacific Railroad came through this area shortly after the Civil War, a settler named Sicotts had a trading post here. Eventually a community grew up around the trading post and in 1880 the name Tamarack was adopted due to its location on the edge of a Tamarack swamp. This was a swampy area where Tamarack trees grew very close together. The area has since been burned over several times, and the Tamarack trees are no longer in evidence. (Mrs. Robert H. Harder, School Teacher, Tamarack, Minn.)

TAMINA, Texas
Tamina, in southern Montgomery County, is reputed to have been named by Captain J. H. Berry, who wanted to suggest the name Tammany Hall for the post office. What went wrong? (3)

TAMPICO, Texas
Tampico, in southern Hall County, was the site of a wildcat oil well drilled in 1929. The ambitious operators hopefully named the site for the oil field in Tampico, Mexico. Unfortunately the oil well proved no gusher. (3)

TANGENT, Oregon
No, it was not named for some Indians who went on a tangent. Tangent, in Linn County, northwestern Oregon, got its unusual name when the railroad came through this part of the Willamette Valley in 1871. The stretch of track built through this area was the longest straight piece of track on the line. It ran a long "tangent," thus the name Tangent, Oregon. (1)

TANGIER ISLAND, Virginia
Nowhere in this country is there a purer strain of Anglo-Saxon blood. On this island in the Chesapeake Bay, one can still hear the language spoken in a manner strongly reminiscent of the Elizabethan English of the early seventeenth century.

John Crockett of Cornwall, England, settled the island in 1686 and the majority of the 1100 inhabitants still carry the name of Crockett. Captain John Smith found and named the place Tangier in 1608, for Tangier in Africa, during a sail up the bay for the Virginia Company.

The people here are entirely dependent upon the boat for their livelihood and supplies. There are no roads or automobiles on the island. Eight foot wide asphalt paths serve as a street for the pedestrians and cyclers. Almost everyone makes his living out of the Chesapeake Bay, satisfying the taste of mainland cities for crabs and oysters. (Chamber of Commerce, Eastern Shore of Virginia)

TAOPI, Minnesota
In southeastern Mower County, near the Iowa border, Taopi was named for a famous Sioux chief, who was converted to Christianity and helped the settlers in the territory during the Sioux uprising. The name means "wounded man," though the reason for the name is unknown. (6)

TARENTUM, Pennsylvania
Was laid out in 1829 by Judge Henry Marie Brackenridge, and incorporated as a borough in 1842. A lover of classical lore, the judge named the spot for the ancient city in southern Italy. (4)

TARZAN, Texas
Tarzan, in central Martin County east of Mustang Creek, was located in the area of C. C. Slaughter, John Scarbauer, and Frank Orson ranches before fencing began in 1887. Tant Lindsay opened the first business, a general store, in 1928. A school, church, and gin made up the village in 1929, when a post office was granted and the name Tarzan was chosen from fourteen names sent to the Post Office Department. That Wag was busy again. (3)

TARZANA, California
Once named Runnymede III, this town was originally a part of the historic San Fernando Mission. The change of name to Tarzana was made of necessity on July 20, 1928. The Runnymede Civil Improvement League petitioned for a post office, only to learn that there was another Runnymede in California.

Edgar Rice Burroughs lived on the largest parcel of land in Runnymede. Tarzana Ranch was the oldest in this section of the valley. Through his literary works (creator of Tarzan), he had brought fame and recognition from all parts of the world. On these merits the residents voted unanimously to call their community Tarzana, and asked Mr. Burroughs' permission. He graciously accepted. (2)

TASCOSA, Texas

The valley was settled in the early 1870's by Mexican colonists under Casimero Romero. The sheepman and freighters built adobe huts and irrigation ditches and established plazas along the creeks in the area. Plaza Atascosa, three hundred miles northwest of the line was an easy ford for cattle and freight being accessible at that point, on the Canadian.

After 1875 large ranches occupied the area, and Tascosa became the shipping and supply point for the L. I. T., L. X., L. S., Frying Pan, and the X. I. T. Ranches. In 1876 Henry Kimball set up his blacksmith shop, and a general store and saloon were established. "Dad" Barns carried mail from Tascosa to Dodge City before a post office was established. When the county was organized in 1880, Tascosa became the county seat. Saloons and dance halls sprang up; a stone courthouse was built; Cope Willingham, first sheriff, shot the cowboy who filled the first grave in Boot Hill Cemetery.

Tascosa was called the "Cowboy Capital of the Plains," and as such saw constant conflict between outlaws like Billy the Kid (William Bonney) and Dave Rudabaugh and law enforcement officers like Pat Garrett and Charles A. Siringo.

Tascosa, on the Canadian River, in northeastern Oldham County, was named for Atascosa Creek, which flows into the river at the site of the original settlement. The name is Spanish and means "boggy."

When the railroad missed the town, most of it moved across the Canadian River to the railroad. After the move the town declined steadily, and when the county seat was moved to Vega in 1915, only fifteen persons remained.

The site of Old Tascosa was entirely deserted when Frenchy McCormick was moved in 1939. In June, 1939, Maverick Boy's Ranch was established at the old courthouse and townsite, offering a home and training to underprivileged boys.

Newer Tascosa, on the railroad, is supply point for an agricultural and ranching area. (3)

TATTLERSVILLE, Alabama

These people, years ago, were such notorious tale-bearers, and so disliked throughout the western part of Clarke County that their hamlet soon became known as Tattlersville. The name stuck. (Chamber of Commerce, Grove Hill, Alabama.)

TAYCHEEDAH, Wisconsin

Taycheedah, Fond du Lac County, Wisconsin, has an Indian name which means "my home on the lake." It is named for its location on the Winnebago Lake, which is said to be the largest lake in the United States situated wholly within the boundaries of one state. (Mrs. Harriet R. Dame, Taycheedah, Wis.)

TECOPA, California
The town was named for a Piute Indian chief, Cap Tecopa, who ruled Southern Nevada, and a section of southeastern California which lies in the Amargosa Valley.

You will notice Chief Tecopa's elegant costume in the photograph. Legend has it that Cap Tecopa owned a lead-silver claim in the No-pah mountains, east of Tecopa, which he consistently refused to sell at any price. His vanity, however, was well known as he always dressed in the brightest, glossiest garb he could find.

A smart operator promoted a tall silk hat, and a beautifully embroidered jacket and paraded about where Cap studied him with jealous eyes. He finally took to following the man about caressing the jacket and eyeing the hat. Allowing the chief to try on the hat and the jacket was Caps undoing. The old chief just couldn't bring himself to return them, so he traded his claim for them.

The mine is said to have become one of the richest producers in the area, but Cap never regretted his bargain. After all, wasn't he the best dressed Indian chief in the whole world? (Mrs. Celesta A. Lowe, Southern Nevada Historical Museum Association)

TEHACHAPI, California
The name Tehachapi is of Indian origin and means "Plenty of Acorns and Good Water." The history of Tehachapi dates back to 1854, when the first permanent settler of the area, John Moore Brite, settled in the valley which now bears his name. Brite built an adobe residence where he stocked groceries and miner's supplies for the scattered miners and stockmen who comprised the early population of the mountain district.

Tehachapi was originally located three miles west of the present townsite. With completion of the railroad in 1875, merchants moved to the present site. (Tehachapi Businessmen's Assoc.)

TEHAMA, California
The Indians camped on this site in the early pioneer days to catch Salmon from the Sacramento River. They called the place "Tehama," which, as with many Indian words, has many meanings. It translates into "high water," or "low land." Another version is that it means "shallow water crossing," and the general meaning of all three is about the same. (1)

TEHUACANA, Texas
Tehuacana, in northeastern Limestone County, was named for the Tawakoni Indians, who, with the Waco, occupied the region until the late 1840's. James M. Love set up a blacksmith shop in 1848. In 1852, when Tehuacana Academy was established, the settlement was called Tehuacana Hills for

a nearby escarpment, while the post office was named Tehuacana Springs for the springs at the site of the old Indian village. (3)

TEKAMAH, Nebraska

Tekamah, County Seat of Burt County, was incorporated into a city on March 14, 1855. When this city was just a pioneer camp, the people decided to name it. To choose one each wrote a favorite name on a piece of paper and a drawing was held. The first one drawn was the present name, which is Indian and means "big cottonwoods." It was suggested by a surveyor named William Byers, and the name was well chosen because of the numerous large cottonwood trees that for years graced the banks of Tekamah Creek and were common over the area. (2)

TEKONSHA, Michigan

In central Michigan, this town was built in 1832 on the site of an old Indian village, and was named for the chief of the Potawatomi, Chief Tekonquasha. The chief's body is believed to have been buried somewhere in the village, although the exact site is unknown. (6)

TELEGRAPH, Texas

Telegraph, in Kimble County, sixteen miles from Junction, received its name from the cutting of telegraph and telephone poles from a canyon of the South Llano River, opposite the settlement. (3)

TELL, Texas

Tell, Childress County, was known as Lee when Miss Janie Roberts taught the first school here. According to legend, its later name of Tell Tale Flat came from the propensity of its citizens to reveal much *unsolicited* information to the grand jury. The post office in its zeal for short names whittled this one down to Tell. (3)

TEMPE, Arizona

Was also named by "Lord" Darrel Duppa for a Grecian Vale. (5)

TEMPLE, Pennsylvania

The King Solomon Tavern that stood here, before 1800, gave the town its name. (4)

TENAFLY, New Jersey

The earliest map of this borough shows the name as Tienevly; this was the Erskine map of 1776. If the literal translation of this word of Dutch origin is used, it could be "Ten Swamp." This is not very conducive to settlement, although there is sufficient evidence to indicate there must have been a number of swampy areas here then.

An 1898 map shows the spelling of Tienevlie, but again a Dutch dictionary shows the word "vlie" as meaning a yacht or fly boat, and the Tienekill Brook is not large enough to float a boat of any size. There are several other changes in the spelling before the present name of Tenafly, but the original spelling of 1776, translated into "ten swamp," seems to be the most logical choice.

The borough of Tenafly is located between the Palisades of the Hudson River Valley, in the county of Bergen, New Jersey. (Borough Historian)

TEN MILE, Tennessee

Old timers in this community say the name comes from Ten Mile Creek, which threads its way through this valley. The creek got its name because it is ten miles from the springs (its source) to its confluence with Sewee Creek (its demise). (1)

TENNESSEE COLONY, Texas

Tennessee Colony, in Anderson County, was settled in 1847, when a wagon train of immigrants from Alabama and Tennessee stopped fifteen miles west of Palestine and called the site Tennessee Colony.

All of the first settlers were plantation operators and all brought slaves. The first business was a carpenter shop set up to make household furniture for the settlers—it operated until 1861. In 1860 Tennessee Colony was the center of a Negro uprising instigated by white renegades who were summarily tried, convicted, and hanged. (3)

TEN SLEEP, Wyoming

Ten Sleep, Washakie County, Wyoming, was named by the Indians because it was ten days' travel, or "ten sleeps" from Yellowstone Park and also "ten sleeps" from Fort Laramie. (Wyoming State Archives & Historical Dept.)

TENSTRIKE, Minnesota

When homesteaders came here to settle on claims in the 1890's, the railroad ended at Deer River, and the trip had to be finished by rowboat by way of lakes and streams to this spot.

When one party landed at the lake here, a man observing the beauty of it, with its virgin forests and excellent soil, remarked with satisfaction, "I think we've made a Tenstrike!" (Tenstrike—a term used in tenpins when all pins are knocked down at once.)

Later, when the village was organized, that remark was recalled and

"Tenstrike" was chosen for the name of the new Beltrami County settlement. (A.P.L. Clipping Bureau, Ten Strike, Minn.)

TERLINGUA, Texas

Terlingua, in the Chisos Mountains of southern Brewster County, was named for its location near Terlingua Creek. Terlingua Creek is an intermittent stream, which rises in southwestern Brewster County and flows south fifty miles into the Rio Grande. In the early times the stream was variously called "Tres Lenguas," Spanish for three tongues, Terlingo, Latis Lengua, Latis Lingo, or Tasolingo, which supposedly referred to three tribes of Indians who lived on its three upper branches.

Mexican herders were the first settlers in an area that was known as Apache, Comanche, and Shawnee Indian country. Settlers staked claims as early as 1860 but no permanent community developed until after the discovery of silver in 1890. In the mining boom that followed, over three million dollars worth of quicksilver was mined here.

The townsite and the Chisos Mining Company belonged to Howard E. Perry of Portland, Maine. A post office was established in 1905, and population once reached one thosuand. The Chisos Mine, in operation since 1893, had been flooded, but in 1947 continued to recover quicksilver. (3)

TERRA ALTA, West Virginia

Once called Cranberry Summit because of the many cranberry bogs here, the citizens changed its name to Terra Alta, Latin for "high ground," in 1885. The altitude here is 2500 feet above sea level. (6)

TERREBONNE, Oregon

Terrebonne, Deschutes County, near crooked river, was platted in 1909 and named "Hillman" for a railroad official who helped push the railroad up along the Deschutes River from the Columbia at The Dalles. In 1911, when the post office was established, the name was changed to Terrebonne, French for "good earth," possibly to avoid confusion with Hillsboro, Oregon.

The town's water supply comes from a 385 foot deep well, and the present population is 491. (1)

TERRE HAUTE, Indiana

The city of Terre Haute was founded by a wandering group of French, just after the War of 1812. The city lies on a sixty foot-high embankment, on the east side of the Wabash River, and was called Terre Haute, which is French for "high ground" or "high land." (2)

TESNUS, Texas

Tesnus, in eastern Brewster County, was originally called Tabor, but a conflict with another post office by that name caused its designation to be changed to Sunset, spelled backwards. (3)

TEXARKANA, Texas-Arkansas

Texarkana was named for its location on the state line between Bowie County, Texas, and Miller County, Arkansas, only a short distance above the Louisiana boundary.

The strategic position of Texarkana is the keynote to its history and development. The Great Southwest Trail, for hundreds of years the main line of travel from Indian villages of the Mississippi River country to those of the South and West, passed by the Caddo Indian village which later became the site of Texarkana. Reminders of Caddo occupation and culture are seventy Indian mounds within a radius of thirty miles of Texarkana.

Texarkana has remained a gateway to the southwest. When the builders of the Cairo and Fulton Railroad crossed Arkansas in the late 1850's and by 1874 pushed their rails beyond the Red River to the border line of Texas they met the railhead which the builders of the Texas and Pacific likewise had extended to the state line. The road from the south bank of Red River to the state line was completed on January 15, 1874.

The city of Texarkana had been established on December 8, 1873, at the site where the two roads would join at the state line. Legend has it that Colonel Gus Knobel, who surveyed the route for the Cairo and Fulton Railroad to the Texas Line, wrote Tex-Ark-Ana on a board and nailed it to a tree, saying, "This is the name of the town that is to be built here." There is no doubt that the name combines the syllables taken from the names of the states of Arkansas, Texas, and Louisiana. (3)

TEXOLA, Oklahoma

On the Texas-Oklahoma border, Texola combines syllables from the two state names to form its own. On the west side of town, a historical marker calls attention to the fact that this region was in land claims of fourteen different governments from 1629. (6)

THE DALLES, Oregon

The end of the historical Oregon Trail lies here. The Old Oregon Trail, which began in Missouri and terminated here, was known as "The Longest Road in Human History."

The name "The Dalles" is derived from the French word "dalle," meaning "flagstone." It was applied to the narrows of the Columbia River, above the present city of The Dalles, by French Canadians, employees of the fur companies. Among other things, "dalle" means a stone used to flag gutters, and the peculiar basalt formation along the narrows doubtless suggested gutters. The word is common in America. Well-known dalles are those of

Saint Louis, Saint Croix, Wisconsin, and the Columbia River. The incorporated name of the community is now Dalles City, but the postal name, and the one in general use, is The Dalles.

The neighborhood of Mill Creek, at The Dalles, was called Quenett by the Indians, which meant "salmon trout." Lewis and Clark camped at the mouth of this stream on October 25, 26, and 27, 1805. They recorded the name Que-nett in their journals and on their maps. In April 1806, they named this place "rockfort camp."

The post office was established with the name Dalles on November 5, 1851, with William R. Gibson as the first postmaster. On September 3, 1853, the name was changed to Wascopum, and March 22, 1860, it was changed to The Dalles. In the Dalles they greet strangers by saying: Klichiam Skookum Tillicum, which in Indian means, "How do you do my good friend." (2)

THE GLEN, New York

The Glen, New York, is a small hamlet located on the Hudson River, in the town of Thurman. Settlement of the town of Thurman began about 1785, and The Glen, about 1805. In the early days this hamlet was known as "The Grove" due to its location in a magnificent pine grove on the west bank of the Hudson River.

In the early 1850's, Mr. Robert Gilchrist and Mr. John Thurman established a tannery and a mill here, on Glen Creek. Mr. Gilchrist built a fine home nearby which he christened The Glen. It was from this fine old mansion that The Glen, New York, took its name. (1)

THE KNOBBS, Texas

The Knobbs, named for Yegua Knobs, three small hills in the area, is a farm community of western Lee County. It was a Wendish community, settled in the 1880's. (3)

THE PLAINS, Virginia

The Plains is located in Fauquier County, just west of the Bull Run Mountains. There is an area here of approximately 40 square miles that is very nearly level to gently rolling which is in contrast to the rolling country which surrounds it.

This area was burned and cleared by the Iroquois Indians for buffalo grazing, etc., and was dotted with outcroppings of loose white quartz stone. From this came the first name "White Plains."

When the white settlers came and began to till the soil the white, loose stones were removed and used for houses and fences. Between the years 1829 and 1849 the name gradually changed from White Plains to The

Plains. When a village and post office was established the name The Plains had become firmly established. (Jack L. Middleton, Realtor & Insurance, The Plains, Va.)

THICKET, Texas

Thicket, located deep in the Big Thicket of Hardin County, grew up in 1901 around a flag stop on the Gulf, Colorado, and Santa Fe Railroad. The Big Thicket was the name applied originally to the area between the Old San Antonio Road and the coastal prairie of south Texas from the Sabine River on the east as far west as the Brazos River. Early migrants from Louisiana found their way effectively blocked by impenetrable thickets rooted in the sandy soil of hillsides bordering almost innumerable streams. (3)

THIEF RIVER FALLS, Minnesota

The city takes its name from the river that joins with the Red Lake River at this point. The "Falls" was justified by a dam that converted the Red Lake Rapids into a waterfall.

"Thief River" is the English translation of an Indian name that dates back into unrecorded time. In his book *Pilgrimages in Europe and America,* Beltrami, who passed this way on his journey from the Red River to the headwaters of the Mississippi, reported: "Robber River, called 'Wamans Watpa,' by the Sioux and 'Powisci Sibi' by the Cypowais, so denominated because one of the Sioux, in his flight from vengeance which had been denounced against him for murder, kept himself concealed and robbed on this spot for many years, escaping the observation of his persecutors and enemies by whom he was completely surrounded."

Alexander Henry, an agent of the Hudson's Bay Company, had referred to it in 1880 as "Lac aux Voleurs" and "Rivière aux Voleurs," in French, meaning "lake of thieves," and "river of thieves."

Major S. H. Long of the United States Army, on a map accompanying his report covering his journey up the Red River, referred to it as "thief river," probably the first time the name was set down in its English translation.

In the meantime be assured that the community is no longer infested with thieves, and you may move among the people here, unarmed, in comparative safety. (2)

THORNDALE, Texas

Thorndale, an incorporated town in Milar County, had its beginning when the International–Great Northern Railroad was constructed through the area in 1876. Thorndale was named for the dense thicket of mesquite thorn, prickly pear, and sage brush that covered the site when the town was founded. (3)

THREE RIVERS, California

At an average elevation of 1,000 feet above sea level and embracing an area of approximately 10 square miles, Three Rivers lies in the Kaweah River Canyon at the southern entrance to the Sequoia and Kings Canyon National Parks.

Water flowing from high mountain streams creates the branches of the Kaweah River, three of which join in the community, giving it its name. The community is located in Tulare County, in the beautiful foothills of the Sierra Nevada Mountains. (2)

THREE RIVERS, Texas

Three Rivers, on the San Antonio, Uvalde, and Gulf Railroad, was called Hamiltonburg before it was named for its location near the confluence of the Atascosa, Nueces, and Frio Rivers. (3)

THRIFT, Texas

Thrift, in Wichita County, developed in 1919–1920 at the site of an oil boom settlement called Newton. The name may have been given to the post office because the community was the only one of the boom towns in the northwest extension of the Burkburnett Oil Field that had a bank. (3)

TICKFAW, Louisiana

Tickfaw, located in Tangipahoa County, is a small community of about 300 in population. The name is Indian and means "Pine Rest." (6)

TICONDEROGA, New York

In upstate New York, Essex County, near the Vermont line, and squatting on a neck of land between Lake George and Lake Champlain, is Ticonderoga. Here the French had constructed a fort called "Carillon," which was later changed to Fort Ticonderoga. The name is a derivation of the Indian "Cheonderoga," which quite aptly means "between two waters," or "where the waters meet."

Ticonderoga is located on the site of an old Indian portage. (6)

TIE SIDING, Wyoming

Tie Siding was established in 1867–68 when the Union Pacific Railway, as part of the first transcontinental link, clawed its way westward from Cheyenne through the Laramie Hills. Ties for the railroad were badly needed, and this heavily timbered area furnished many of them. A large stock pile was established at this location, which, at the time was the terminal of the tracks. As the railroad moved on farther west the siding was maintained.

In 1874, J. S. McCoole, a Colorado storekeeper, formally started a townsite here by opening a general store. He was soon to be followed by merchants and saloon keepers. Tie Siding became an important shipping point for railway ties, fence posts, telephone poles, and other timber of various kinds. By the 1880's it had grown to the large size of fifty permanent settlers.

It is almost a ghost town now, and only the name is preserved by the post office, which is still active, and serves the surrounding rural community. (1)

TIFFIN, Texas

Tiffin, a stone and rock loading switch on the Texas and Pacific Railroad in northern Eastland County, is said to have been named in 1880 by an Irish member of the railroad construction gang who designated the spot as the place for tiffin or "lunch." (3)

TILLAMOOK, Oregon

The story of Tillamook begins on August 14, 1788, when Captain Robert Gray, an American sailing the American Sloop *Lady Washington* anchored in Tillamook Bay thinking he had found "the great river of the West." This was the first landing on the Oregon coast and it was not until four years later that Gray found the mouth of the Columbia.

Next came Clark, of the Lewis and Clark expedition, who purchased whale blubber from the Indians at Nehalem to replenish the meat supply at his winter quarters in Clatsop County.

There were three Indian tribes in Tillamook County: the Tillamooks, Nehalems, and the Nestuccas. They lived in the areas which now bear their names. These were a peaceful, friendly people, faithful to their tribal rituals, and like most coastal Indians they were Flatheads, a mark of distinction among the tribes. The "Flathead" was achieved by binding a bag of feathers on the top of the baby's head. They then nursed the baby to sleep and it was removed when he awoke. This was done from birth to about one year of age.

The Northwest Indians were also the only tribe in the northern part of America to build their homes of wood. Because of their skill in building canoes they were also called the "Canoe Indians." Canoes ranged in size from tiny duck hunting canoes to large 40 to 60 man dugouts, which sailed to Astoria and California. The Indian population of Tillamook County was estimated at about 2200 in 1806, and had dwindled to 200 in 1849.

The town of Tillamook, the first community to be settled in the county, is situated on the east shore of Tillamook Bay. It first bore the name "Hoquarten," believed to be an Indian name meaning "the landing;" later the name was changed to Tillamook, meaning "land of many waters."

The first settler in the vicinity was Joseph Champion, who came in 1851 and made his home in a hollow spruce tree which he called his "castle." By 1854 a community had been established here, an election was held, the first census taken, the first school started, and the keel laid for the *Morning Star*.

The *Morning Star* was built out of economic necessity because shipwrecks had destroyed all transportation which had carried the dairy products, fish and potatoes to market. The vessel was built by the combined efforts and the ingenuity of the settlers. Most of the materials came from the forests, but iron work came from a wrecked ship, which was laboriously packed on horseback from Clatsop beaches by way of Neahkahnie Mountain. Sails were purchased from the Indians who had salvaged them from a ship wrecked near Netarts (now part of Tillamook). Pitch was used to caulk the craft, but paint was not available. Nevertheless, this pioneer ship was launched in the Kilchis River on January 5, 1855, and for some years made possible the existence of the pioneers and development of Tillamook City and Tillamook County.

In 1861, Thomas Stillwell, age seventy, arrived with his family from Yamhill and purchased land. The following year he laid out the town of Tillamook and opened the first store. The first public building was the jail, built in 1873; the courthouse and city hall came in the early 1890's. (2)

TINTAH, Minnesota
According to James Denery, an Irish immigrant to Canada, who established a homestead here in 1880, the name is Indian and means "Flower of the Prairie." Mr. Denery still lives on in "Flower of the Prairie," Minnesota, to this date. (Mrs. Laverne Schuster, Postmaster)

TIOGA, Texas
Tioga, Grayson County, was founded about 1881, when the Texas and Pacific Railroad built through the area. The name is an Indian word meaning "fair and beautiful." In a fertile black land farming section, it is said to have particularly fine mineral waters and was at one time a popular health resort. The town was incorporated in 1896. One claim to fame is that it is the home of Gene Autry. (3)

TIONESTA, Pennsylvania
"It penetrates the island," or Indian for "home of the wolves," was first known as Goshgoshing and later as Saqualinquent, Indian for "place of Council." (4)

TISHOMINGO, Mississippi
In northeastern Mississippi, its Indian name means "Warrior Chief." (6)

TISKILWA, Illinois

According to Matson's "Reminiscences of Bureau County," the name Tiskilwa comes from a Pottawatomi Indian chief of that name, who had many wives.

"In a village where the hoot owls hoot,
Fer the want of more to do,
I heer'd a bed time story
An' I'm tellin' it to you.
It's how a hamlet got its name
By the deed of an Injun buck,
Who swung a club on a Mr. Wa
And a Mr. Wa, fergot to duck.
The yarn is told of an Injun brave
Who fell fer a purty squaw.
I don't recall the maiden's name,
But I recollect she called him Wa.
She never told her Lochinvar,
That many moons ago
She got hitched up with a brave named Tis,
Who had a dozen squaws or so.
She couldn't see what dif it made,
To a guy with a dozen squaw
Fer her to play around a bit,
With a handsome Romeo like Wa.
Now course 'twas spring and Mr. Wa
Made a pass at the red skin Miss,
While 'cross the creek the whole darn thing
Was seen by her regular boy friend Tis.
The thing went on fer quite a spell
She kept 'em both at sea,
Until one night it all blew up
And Tis went on a killin' spree.
It seems that one night Mr. Wa
Snuck in with a string of beads,
An' Mr. Tis saw the sneakin' Kuss
As he lay concealed in the brush and weeds,
So he snuck behind the teepee,
Like a tomcat on a hunt.
He slapped the teepee with his club
Then ran around in front.
When Romeo Wa came chargin' out
His liberty in view,
Old Tis wound up and laid him low
'Mid the brush and weeds in the evenin' dew
The glamour gal let out a screech,
At the gruesome thing she saw,
She started howlin' loud and long,
That her lord and master, TIS-KILLED-WA!
And with this gentle yarn, my friend.

The kids their slumbers woo.
Where the hoot owls keep on hooting
Fer the want of others things to do.
(Poem by Perl Smith, as published in the *Tiskilwa Chief*) (2)

TIVYDALE, Texas

Tivydale, a farm community in Gillespie County, was named for Captain Joseph A. Tivy, who, between 1877 and 1885, sold land in the Pedernales River valley to homesteaders. For a consideration of one dollar, Tivy gave forty-three and one-half acres for the school. First known as Bunkesville or Pumpkinville, the community had a group of local musicians known as the "Bunkesville Band," who played old-time German tunes. (3)

TOADVINE, Alabama

Toadvine is a little village below Bessemer on the road to the Warrior River, near Oak Grove, Alabama. At one time it was called Smithville, but a citizen of the town, returning from the Civil War, had the name changed to Toadvine to honor an officer he had served under during the madness of 1861–65. (2)

TOBYHANNA, Pennsylvania

Is Indian for "dark waters" or "alder stream." (4)

TOCCOPOLA, Mississippi

Settled on the site of an old Chickasaw Indian Village, the name is Indian for "crossing of the roads." Several Indian paths converged on this spot at one time. (6)

TODWADDLE, New York

Many years ago there lived here a man of enormous proportions named Tod Nelson. His weight was so great that he waddled like a duck when he walked. Folks in the community used to say, "Guess I'll go up and see Tod waddle." Soon this was shortened to "see Todwaddle," and before anyone realized what was happening they found themselves saddled with the name Todwaddle! (Frank Noble, Town Historian, Bliss, New York.)

TOGO, Minnesota

Togo, Itasca County, was first named in November 1906, by its first postmaster, Miles A. Nelson, who with the help of a friend built its first post office, which also served as their home. Mr. Nelson named his post office for Count Heihachiro Togo, 1847–1934, Japanese Admiral, who met and defeated the Russian Fleet in a war over fishing rights. Admiral Togo sank

Todwaddle, New York

the greatest tonnage ever sunk in a naval battle up to that time, and emerged a hero to all but the Russians. (Miles A. Nelson, age ninety)

TOIVOLA, Minnesota
In 1900 this community was a wilderness of dense forest. First settlers came by boat along the St. Louis River.

In 1905 the church congregation was organized and it was at one of the services that the settlement was named. The Indian names "Era Maa," meaning "wilderness," and "Toivola," meaning "hopeful," were selected and voted upon. The settlers decided to call their new settlement "Toivola."

In 1965 the church congregation voted to call their church "Hope Lutheran Church," thereby carrying on the name Toivola or Hope. (1)

TOKIO, Texas
Tokio, Terry County, is a farming community midway between two oil fields. The name was one of two suggested in 1908 by the first postmaster, a Mrs. Ware, who collected mail for the cowboys in the then sparsely settled area. (3)

TOMAHAWK, Kentucky
Originally settled around the early 1800's the village was once called Wells, for the first postmaster. Later the post office was discontinued, as many of the first settlers moved farther west.

When the village again grew to sufficient size to justify a post office the name Tomahawk, along with others, was submitted for approval by the Post Office Department and was chosen. The name was originally picked by the residents from the name of a newspaper in Inez, Kentucky, called *The Tomahawk News,* and has no other historical significance. (1)

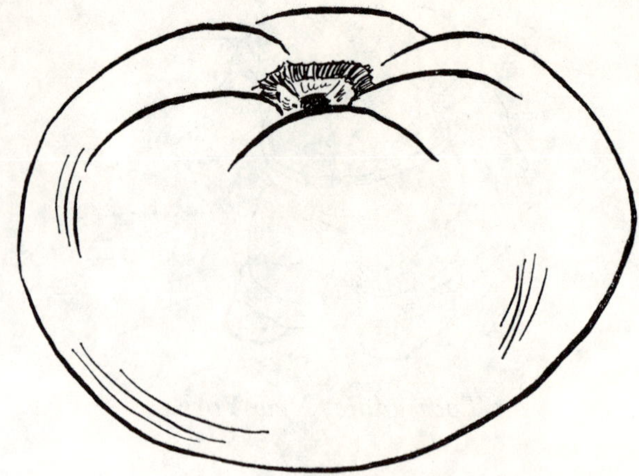

Tomato, Arkansas

TOMATO, Arkansas

The present town of Tomato was a steamboat landing on the Mississippi River. When there were enough settlers to petition Washington for a post office, they gathered in the general store to choose a name. The daughter of one of them came in to pick up some groceries. Overhearing the discussion, she held up a can of tomatoes and said, "Why not name it Tomato, Pops?" Old timers verify this account of the naming. (1)

TOMBSTONE, Arizona

When bearded prospector Ed Schieffelin set out to roam the lonely San Pedro hills in his relentless search for silver, the soldiers at Fort Huachuca warned him of the danger of attack by Apaches saying, "All you'll find is your tombstone." So, in ironic jest, Ed Schieffelin named his first silver claim, discovered in 1877, "The Tombstone."

News of the rich silver strikes brought prospectors, miners, businessmen, fortune hunters, lawmen, and the lawless hurrying to the town which was springing up overnight—the town, which from the outset, bore the name of the mining claim that spawned it.

In January, 1881, it was dedicated as the county seat of the newly formed Cochise County. (2)

TONGANOXIE, Kansas

Located twenty-two miles west of Kansas City, Missouri, Tonganoxie, Kansas, takes its name from Chief Tonganoxie. The chief was widely known on the frontier in the early days of Kansas. He was a large man in stature. Early prints show him attired in frontier garb, flannel shirt and jacket, with a single feather to distinguish him as an Indian.

As the whites immigrated into the territory, his home became a lodge or an inn for early travelers. His hospitality was a legend in days of violence and lawlessness. An incident is told concerning a survivor of a border massacre which occurred a short distance east of Tonganoxie's lodge in the summer of 1856. A survivor was befriended by the chief and hidden in the nearby woods until his assailants had left. (1)

TOOELE CITY, Utah

In 1827, the famed Jedediah S. Smith became the first white man to view the white deserts, junipered hills, and fertile valleys of what is now Tooele County. The name Tooele derives from an Indian word for a water plant which grew near the shores of the Great Salt Lake. Within twenty years, pioneers crisscrossed the land on their way to the West, but studiously avoided any prolonged stay in this barren country.

The Mormon migrations began in the 1840's bringing a desperate people to Utah where they took to the soil to begin building their new home. Tooele City was settled in 1845 by Mormon pioneers who promptly set about to create a small agricultural community. In the 1860's copper and other minerals were discovered and a flourishing mining industry was born. (Dugway Proving Grounds)

Tombstone, Arizona

TOOMSUBA, Mississippi
The town of Toomsuba is named for a small creek with the same "Swahili-sounding" name, that skirts the town on the west.

According to local legend an Indian chief, Choctaw, was attempting to ford this swollen stream, and his favorite horse floundered and drowned in the swift waters. Thereafter the Indians called the creek "Toomsuba," or in the Indian tongue "tomb of the horse."

The Choctaws left this area around 1830, after the treaty of "Dancing Rabbit." Early in this same year white settlers began to move in and in a short time the town of Toomsuba was established. (1)

TOPAWA, Arizona
Is located on the Papago Indian Reservation, in Pima County, and the name is Papago Indian for "it is a bean." (5)

TOPAZ, California
In pioneer days, in Antelope Valley, located in Mono County, T. B. Rickey established a ranch. Years later his headquarters had grown to include a store, saloon, boarding house, houses for his foreman and others, a blacksmith shop and a bunkhouse. In short, it had become a village, and as such had become eligible for a post office.

Mrs. Rickey, his wife, gazing at the beauty of the topaz coloring of the quaking aspens in the mountain canyons, and the cottonwoods and other trees, in a moment of inspiration decided "Topaz" would be a good name for the village. The time was around 1875. (1)

TOPINABEE, Michigan
Located on Mullet Lake the village was founded in 1881. It was named for the Potawatomi chief who signed the peace treaty which gave up the site of Chicago, once called Fort Dearborn. The village, located on a hilly slope, is primarily a resort town. (6)

TORNILLO, Texas
Tornillo, in southern El Paso County on the Texas and New Orleans Railroad, bears the name of a bush-like tree which has screwshaped beans. The site, on the San Elizario Grant, was dedicated by the Tornillo Townsite Company in 1909. (3)

TORONTO, Texas
Toronto, in northwestern Brewster County, is a section house on the Texas and New Orleans Railroad. The community is said to have gotten its name from an old Indian word meaning "rising of the land." (3)

TOUGALOO, Mississippi

Tougaloo, Hines County, has a Swahili-sounding name, but is really Indian, and means "where two creeks meet." (1)

TOUGHKENAMON, Pennsylvania

Toughkenamon, Chester County, was settled sometime in the early 1700's. The name is Indian and means "firebrand," in tribute to a battle fought here between two Indian tribes. Fire brands were used as weapons. A firebrand is a piece of burning wood or other material. This battle was fought between the two Indian tribes long before white man appeared, and its history has been handed down by Indian legend. (1)

TOWAMENSING, Pennsylvania

This village took its name from a Delaware Indian expression, "Towsissinck," which means "the ford," or "fording place at the falls." (Towamensing Mutual Ins. Co., Aquashicola, Pa.)

TOWASH, Texas

Towash, a small town on the left bank of the Brazos River in western Hill County, was established about 1853 on Towash Creek. It is near an old Indian village of Chief Towash, and commonly called the Towash Indian Village. The town was one of the most prominent in the vicinity until the middle 1880's. Towash, a chief of the Hainai Indian tribe which moved from Louisiana to central Texas about 1835, settled with his people on the Brazos River above modern Waco. They remained there until their removal to the Brazos Indian Reservation in 1855. (3)

TOWER, Minnesota

Over inland waterways, as early as 1778, a military trail was operated by British soldiers from Grand Portage to this site, the only such trail in what is now the state of Minnesota. It was visited by adventurous fur traders, who came to nearby Lake Vermilion.

Tower, First City of the Ranges, in the vicinity of Jasper Peak and Lake Vermilion, close to the historic Soudan Mine, to which it primarily owes its existence, is the Minnesota Arrowhead's oldest incorporated municipality north of Duluth.

The town was named for Charlemagne Tower (one of five such towns), a capitalist from the east who became interested in this area in the early days. Although he supplied much of the capital for the development of the area, he never visited his namesakes, and died on July 24, 1889. (2)

TOYAH, Texas

Toyah, on San Martine Draw in Reeves County, bears an Indian name meaning "much water." The townsite was laid out in 1881 as a shipping point on the Texas and Pacific Railroad. (3)

TRAIL, Minnesota

Trail was so named because of the old, well-traveled Indian trail that passed through the present townsite, when the first white settlers moved here about 1900.

This was the route of the Chippewa Tribe as they traveled from the Red Lake Territory to what is now The White Earth Reservation. It also led to the Dakotas and a branch led northwest to Winnipeg, Canada. The first white settlers moved here around 1900 and the railroad (Soo Line) built through the area in 1910. (1)

TRAPPE, Pennsylvania

The origin of the name is uncertain, though many historians declare that an early tavern's high stoop caused it to be called "treppe" (steps) by the German settlers, and that a corrupted form of the word came into popular use. Another explanation is that the tavern's high steps often became a "trap" for its unsteady customers. (4)

TRASKWOOD, Arkansas

The town was platted by the Missouri and Pacific Railroad by two contractors named Trask and Wood. Their names were combined and the new town dubbed Traskwood. (E. A. Still, Mayor.)

TREDYFFRIN, Pennsylvania

The name of this small village, located in the Main Line Area of Pennsylvania, is Welsh and means "valley town." (Chamber of Commerce, Main-Line, Haverform, Pa.)

TRES PIEDRAS, New Mexico

Tres Piedras, Taos County, is a Spanish name and means "three rocks." The rocks that inspired the name are three very outstanding outcrops of granite, which extend about one hundred feet above the ground, and are about five hundred yards apart. (Sam's Chevron Svc)

TRIADELPHIA, West Virginia

Is Greek for "three brothers," and was named for three friends, who settled here together in 1800. (6)

TRIBES HILL, New York
The original name for Tribes Hill was Tripes Hill, as it was named for a Mr. William Tripe, who lived on a hill. The 1829 maps of New York State show the name as Tripes Hill, and the early post office reports, prior to 1842 also record it as Tripes Hill.

The name was changed to Tribes Hill sometime between 1840 and 1842 by the Post Office Department. The reason is obscure, but it could be because they either thought it was a mis-spelled Indian name, or just didn't like the name Tripe. (1)

TRICKHAM, Texas
The oldest town and the first post office in Coleman County, Trickham is on Mukewater Creek, near the Brown County line. It originated in 1856 when Emory Peters, brother-in-law of John Chisum, operated Chisum's combination store and saloon on the *Jinglebob* cattle trail for the convenience of the trail drivers. The original name, *"Trick-em,"* was given because of the many pranks of the cowboys, the change in name being made at the time of the petition for a post office.

Roving bands of Indians disturbed the early settlers, and the cemetery contains graves of at least three persons who were scalped by Indians. (3)

TRONA, California
The post office here in the small town of Trona was established and named in 1914. The name Trona is derived from one of the salts, found in Searles Dry Lake, a vast bottomless lake from which two chemical companies extract a variety of salts and their derivatives. Trona is a mineral, grayish or yellowish, dydrous sodium carbonate and bicarbonate, Na2C03.-NaHC03.2H20, occurring in dried or partly evaporated lake basins.

Searles Valley, in which the town of Trona is located, was named for John Searles, who originally came to the Mojave Desert in search of gold. (Searles Valley Community Services Council)

TRUTH OR CONSEQUENCES, New Mexico
Formerly named Hot Springs, the town voted to take the present name strictly for the commercial advantages offered by a radio program of the same name. (2)

TUJUNGA, California
Rancho Tujunga, later to become the present Tujunga, Los Angeles County, was a separate land grant made in 1840 to the Lopez brothers, Francisco and Pedro. The first owners, Mexicans of high birth, petitioned

the honorable Assembly of the Department of the Californias for a grant of land, known by the name of Rancho de Tujunga, a part of San Fernando Mission, bounded on the south by the Sierra Madre and the Sierre Verdugos, on the east by the oak woodland, on the west by the Pontezuelo (San Fernando Valley), and on the north by the Tujunga Wash.

There have been several stories concerning the meaning of the name Tujunga. According to J. P. Harrington, ethnologist for Smithsonian Institution in Washington, D. C., Tujunga, also spelled Tujugna (pronounced Tujooga) means "old woman's place," the old woman in this case means "our grandmother the earth." Mr. Harrington received this information from an old Indian! (2)

TULARE, California

Early in the 1800's the Spanish noted the abundance of tule (a form of bulrushes) here and referred to the county as "Tulars," which is Spanish for tule. Later the county adopted the name of Tulare, and the town of Tulare was named for the county. (2)

TUMACACORI, Arizona

When the pioneer Jesuit missionary Father Kino visited the Piman Indians of a nearby village in 1691, the native name of the place sounded to him like Tumacacori.

A later missionary, Father Ignacio Pfefferkorn, offered a colorful translation of this Indian word or phrase: "pepper bush; place where the little round pepper is found in abundance." Another translator offered "place of the low fences," while another came up with "light colored rock that bends" or "caliche bend." With such wide variations in the translations of the name of this village, it is too bad we can't ask the Indians, but they left little in the way of records. The Tumacacori National Monument is located here, also. (Superintendent, U. S. Department of Interior.)

TUMTUM, Washington

It is an Indian name taken from the Chinook Indians, and the general meaning is something good or unusual, such as a big tree being a tumtum-tree. There is a large old yellow pine tree standing in the town of Tumtum that was supposedly used as a gallows for both Indians and whites. The locality was also the original camping area of the so-called Chief Tumtum, who always greeted people with, "Hiyu, Tumtum!" or "Good day." (1)

TUNDRA, Texas

Tundra, in south-central Van Zandt County on an undulating strip of western prairie, was named for its appearance. Although explored and surveyed as early as 1845, the area had no permanent settlement until the close of the Civil War. (3)

TUNKHANNOCK, Pennsylvania
Started with a cabin built in 1775, by Jeremiah Osterhout. Its name, of Iroquois Indian origin, is variously translated as "meeting of the waters," "small stream," "wilderness," and "full of timber." It is located at the confluence of Tunkhannock Creek and Susquehanna's North Branch. (Area Resource Development Agent, The Pennsylvania State University) (4)

TUOLUMNE, California
The community was settled shortly after the California Gold Rush of 1849, and first named Summerville. Applying for a post office caused the formation of Carter when Summerville was denied one, and named for Mr. C. H. Carter who had a general store here. Later a lumber company established a post office in their office building for convenience, and named it Tuolumne.

The town now had two post offices. When Carter's post office was discontinued the residents of Summerville, Carters, Long Gulch, Cherokee, and Arastraville all received their mail at "Tuolumne" post office. Gradually through the years the community took the name of Tuolumne. There is no townsite of Tuolumne, and property deeds are recorded as townsite of Carters or townsite of Summerville. Confused? Just write to Tuolumne, and the people of either Carters or Summerville will answer. (1)

TURKEY, Texas
Turkey, just below the Llano Estacado in Hall County, was named for wild turkey roosts discovered on a small creek which took its name from the same source and is called Turkey Creek. The little settlement was first called Turkey Roost, but the name was shortened when a post office was established in 1893. (3)

TUSCALOOSA, Alabama
The history of Tuscaloosa goes back to the dim days in Alabama, when few white men ventured into this Indian country. The area was first visited by Fernando De Soto and his Spanish warriors who waged a bloody battle in 1540 in Mauvila (about 100 miles south of Tuscaloosa). It was there that De Soto's men killed 7,000 Indians, including the great Chief Tuskalusa, a seven-foot giant!

It was from this famous chief that the city and county derived their names, as well as the Black Warrior River, for the word "Tuska" means warrior and "Lusa" means black in the language of the Choctaw and Creek

Indians. The first white explorers to reach the immediate Tuscaloosa vicinity came in 1810 and 1813, but first settlers arrived in 1816 from South Carolina. By 1819 Tuscaloosa was an incorporated town and it grew rapidly becoming the state capital city in 1826. (2)

TUSCUMBIA, Alabama
Tuscumbia was named for an Indian chief by the name of Tascha Kambia, who lived here long before the white invaders. A Cherokee Indian, his name means "warrior who kills." (1)

TUSKEGEE, Alabama
The town took its name from a nearby Indian village called "Taskigi." (1)

TWAIN HARTE, California
Twain Harte was founded back in the '20s, near and around the beautiful meadow which was a favorite spot of the Mi-Wok Indians. It is also near the famous Mark Twain–Bret Harte Trails, which gave the community its name. (2)

TWELVE MILE, Indiana
The exact origin of the name is not known, and there are several conflicting stories regarding it. Old timers here maintain that the village was named for a little creek nearby, which is twelve miles long. Evidence to the contrary lacking, this is the generally accepted explanation. The village is located in Cass County. (1)

TWIG, Minnesota
When a post office was established here in 1904, this small St. Louis County community came up with a brilliant idea. It submitted the name Twig to Washington because they would be just a "small branch" of the Post Office Department. The Department, enchanted with the idea, accepted it immediately! (1)

TWILIGHT, West Virginia
Located in a valley, with high mountains front and back, the town was well named. Twilight is indeed a beautiful time of the day in Twilight, West Virginia.

Originally named Robin Hood, the name was changed to Twilight when a post office was established here. (1)

TWO DOT, Montana
Two Dot was founded in 1908 when the Milwaukee Railroad came through

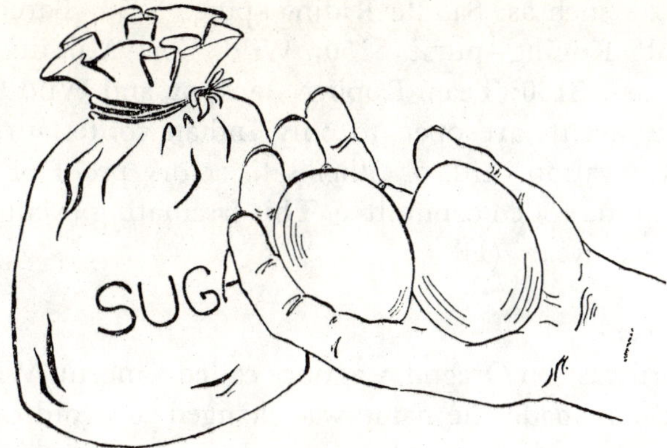

Two Egg, Florida

the area from the East to the West Coast. The townsite was obtained from George Wilson, a rancher here in the late 1860's. His cow brand was two dots (about the size of silver dollars), and he was very pleased when the people voted to name their small village in his honor. (1)

TWO EGG, Florida
Reputedly, Two Egg received its odd name from the custom prevalent in these parts, immediately following the War between the States, of obtaining the necessities of life by means of barter, due to the shortage of actual currency. Residents of the area would go to the local general store to purchase "two eggs" worth of lard, "two eggs" worth of sugar, etc. (Jackson County Chamber of Commerce, Marianna, Florida.)

TWO MILE, Texas
Two Mile, a Milam County farming community, was named for its distance from old Nashville-on-the-Brazos. (3)

TYGH VALLEY, Oregon
Around 1856 the first store was built in Tygh Valley, and it did a flourishing business trading with the Indians and settlers in the area. Tygh Valley, located on the White River, took its name from the Indians prevalent in this part of the country. The name "Tyee" means "the ruler," and "Tyee Valley" means "chief's valley." The name was slightly altered in the spelling, for reasons known only to the original settlers.

Interesting to note, the town of Tygh Valley has five or six Indian families living there today, with ten Indian children going to the local grade school. Indians still fish with nets on the Deschutes River, just eight miles from Tygh Valley, and every year Tygh Valley holds an all Indian

Rodeo with prizes such as: Saddle Riding—purse $250; Bareback Riding—purse $200; Calf Roping—purse $150; Wild Cow Milking—purse $150; Bull Dogging—purse $150; Team Roping—Jackpot, and Wild Horse Racing, $100 a day. The events are open to only Indian contestants, amateur or professional. Reservation card, or other satisfactory proof of Indian status must be shown to the rodeo committee. This fascinating event is held in the middle of May, each year. (1)

UMAPINE, Oregon

Umapine, in northeastern Oregon, was once called Vincent. When a petition for a post office was made the name was changed to avoid confusion with another Vincent. According to old settlers, the name Umapine comes from Chief Umapine of the Cayuse Indians, and was suggested by a settler who had farmed on the Indian Reservation and knew and respected the old chief well. The name Umapine means "friends" in Cayuse language.

An interesting story concerns the father of Chief Umapine. He is said to have saved Pendleton from an Indian attack. During the Piute–Bannock Wars of 1878, Chief Eagen of the Bannocks had been harassing the white people in the Pendleton area for a long time. Finally the settlers offered a $1,000 bounty for Chief Eagen's capture. When Chief Umapine heard of this, he ran Chief Eagen down with a band of his braves and brought in Eagen's head impaled upon a pole! (1)

UMATILLA, Oregon

It was at Umatilla that the Lewis and Clark Expedition entered the Oregon Territory, and the pioneers along the Oregon Trail first sighted the mighty Columbia River. Umatilla is one of the oldest settlements, if not the oldest, in the state of Oregon, and takes its name from the Indian tribe by that name. Umatilla has been translated into "land of the shifting sand," although its exact meaning is unsure.

Located at the confluence of the Umatilla and Columbia Rivers in Umatilla County, the town became an important port for river traffic. The Umatilla Indian Reservation is located some 35 miles southeast of the town, still living in the land of their ancestors. (2)

UNO, Virginia

Uno, Madison County, according to local legend received its unusual name when it consisted of nothing but a bar. Whenever anyone heading for the bar was asked where he was going he would answer, "You know!" When the bar had grown into a village, and the village requested a post office, and the people were asked what they wanted to name it they replied, "Ah, You know!" (1)

Uno, Virginia

UPPER BLACK EDDY, Pennsylvania
The town of Upper Black Eddy is the largest village in Bridgeton township. It takes its name from the eddy in the river, which was well known for tying up rafts in the old lumbering days. The name was probably bestowed by rivermen who manned the Durham boats and rafts on the Delaware River long before the era of canals and railroads. The post office was established here August 2, 1830, with David Worman as the first postmaster. (Bridgeton Township Supervisors, Buck County, Upper Black Eddy, Pennsylvania)

UPPER TRACT, West Virginia
Once the location of an old fort established in 1756, during the French and Indian War, it was known as the "Upper Tract," because of its location at an altitude of approximately 1500 feet. (6)

UTOPIA, Texas
Utopia, in Uvalde County, was settled in 1852 by William Ware, whose tent was the first residence in the area, and named Waresville. Attempts to change the name to Montania in 1883 failed, but by 1886 the name had been changed to Utopia, for the ideal location and climate. (3)

UVALDE, Texas
Uvalde, on the Leona River in Uvalde County, was settled in 1853, when Reading Wood Black and Nathan L. Stratton located a ranch on the main line of travel between San Antonio and Laredo and Fort Duncan and El

Paso. By 1854 Black opened a store, two rock quarries, and a lime kiln; in 1855 he hired William C. A. Thielepope to lay out a town, which he called Encina. Seminole and Lipan–Apache Indian raids and withdrawal of troops from Fort Inge, two miles north, discouraged settlement in the new town, but the village became the temporary county seat of Uvalde County, and in June, 1856, the name was changed to Uvalde honoring Juan de Ugalde. (3)

VALENTINE, Arizona
Was not named for the saint, but for a commissioner of Indian affairs. (5)

VALENTINE, Texas
Valentine is the smaller of the two towns in Jeff Davis County. It lies forty miles west of Fort Davis. The town is a division point on the Texas and New Orleans Railway and was named when the railroad building crew reached the site on St. Valentine's Day, 1882. (3)

Valentines, Virginia

VALENTINES, Virginia
The town was organized in 1887, and the post office located in the general store, operated and owned by Mr. William H. Valentines. Therein lies the reason for the name. (1)

VALLECITO, California
Settled in the spring of 1850, this picturesque little valley was the site of a trading post until discovery of gold in 1852. It is the gateway to historic Moaning Cave, discovered in 1851, by early miners. Located in Calaveras County, the name is Spanish and means "small" or "little valley." (2)

VALLEY COTTAGE, New York
Originally this hamlet was known as "Forest Glen," and geographically it is located in a valley. In the 1870's when the New York Central Railroad was building its west shore line from Weehawken, New Jersey, to Albany, New York, there were very few inhabitants in this area. One of the largest land owners was a Mr. Green, and he lived in a sandstone cottage (which still stands). The railroad wanted to go through his property, and he agreed to let them provided they named the whistle stop, to be located there, after his original "Cottage in the Valley." The railroad agreed and named the depot Valley Cottage, and from this the hamlet of Valley Cottage grew. (1)

VALLEY WELLS, Texas
Valley Wells, in eastern Dimmit County in the irrigated district of the Winter Garden region, was named for artesian wells found in the Nueces (Spanish for Pecan) Valley. (3)

VAL VERDE, Texas
Val Verde, an agricultural community, in northwestern Milam County, was named by its early settlers for its green valleys. (3)

VENUS, Florida
Near the Seminole Indian Reservation in Highlands County, Venus was named for Venus, an ancient Italian goddess of gardens and spring, identified by the Romans with Aphrodite as the goddess of love and beauty. (6)

VERBENA, Alabama
Once named Summerfield, it was later changed to Verbena due to the lush field of wild verbena in the area. It is located in Chilton County and has a 3rd Class Post Office. (6)

VERDIGRE, Nebraska
Named for the Verdigris Creek, which flows through this valley, the name was shortened first to Verdigris prior to 1900, and then changed to Verdigre by the Post Office Department.

The creek was named by French explorers of this area, and means "green," and as applied to the area means "green valley." (Village Clerk, Village of Verdigre, Nebraska.)

VERGENNES, Vermont
Ethan Allen and the Green Mountain Boys decided that the area at the head of Otter Creek would someday be the site of a great city, due to its great natural resources and waterpower. Talking with the French consul

in New York City in the year 1785, Ethan Allen agreed to name the city in honor of the Comte de Vergennes, French Minister of Foreign Affairs (1775–1788). This was in recognition of the assistance of French patriots during the American Revolution.

In 1788 Vergennes was incorporated as a city and received its charter in 1794 on condition that there exist 12 frame buildings. Vergennes comprising 1200 acres (once a part of a French seigniory) was carved out of the towns of New Haven, Ferrisburg, and Panton. (1)

VESUVIUS, Virginia

The history of Vesuvius started with the building of an Iron Furnace in the early part of the 1800's to smelt iron ore mined in the nearby mountains. Later a foundry was built at the same location and both named Vesuvius, for Mount Vesuvius, in Italy.

Vesuvius, Virginia

The cast iron produced here was hauled by wagon to Richmond, and some by the old canal boats that once ran from Lexington to Lynchburg. The furnace ceased its operation December 15, 1854, but the foundry kept the old name alive.

In 1882 the Shenandoah Valley Railroad built through the area and when they established a depot in this little village they hung a sign on it reading "Vesuvius, Virginia," and it's been Vesuvius ever since. (1)

VILLAGE CREEK, Texas

Village Creek, a rural community in Turrant County, takes its name, as does the creek, from the fact that three Indian villages were located there before the white settlement. In 1841 Indians and Texas Rangers under General Tarrant met in The Battle of Village Creek (3)

VILLANOVA, Pennsylvania
The town was named for the Villanova University, which takes its name from a sixteenth-century bishop, Saint Thomas, who was an educator and writer from Villanova, Spain. (Chamber of Commerce, Main Line, Haverford, Pa.)

VIOLET HILL, Arkansas
Violet Hill was named by an old maid school teacher who taught in the little log school house, about 1870, on a hill which was covered with violets. The teacher was named Miss Emma Stevens. (1)

VIPER, Kentucky
According to old timers, Viper, Perry County, received its unusual name when the postmaster, searching for a novel title for his new post office, chanced upon a nest of vipers, and honored them by naming it Viper, Kentucky. (1)

VOLCANO, California
Volcano was named by the first wagon train that came through the area, due to an unusual rock formation. The early settlers thought it surely must be a volcano and named it accordingly.

Located in Amador County, gold was discovered here in 1848, which led to its growth. The town is also the home of "Old Abe," a Civil War cannon that, according to historians, played an important role in the outcome of the Civil War. (2)

WABASHA, Minnesota
Once named "Cratte's Landing" for Oliver Cratte, who built a blacksmith shop here in 1838, it was later re-named in honor of Chief Wabasha of the Sioux Nation.

It was in 1680 that Father Louis Hennepin, then a prisoner of the Dakotas, first laid eyes on the present townsite and named Lake Pepin "The Lake of Tears." The Sioux later established a rich tradition under three generations of a chief named Wabashaw, as their mounds, relics, and arrowheads still attest.

The colorful era of steamboats and rafting further built Wabasha and today the river here is known as the finest open water on the Mississippi. (2)

WABASSO, Florida
Located in Indian River County, on the Atlantic Ocean, the Gaule Indians migrated here from Ossabaw Island, Georgia. The name is Ossabaw, spelled backwards. (6)

WACO, Texas

Waco, near the confluence of the Bosque and Brazos Rivers in McLennan County, was laid out on the site of an ancient village of Waco Indians, at the location of a once famous spring which in 1950 was still flowing with reduced volume. The spring came into recorded history in 1824, when a letter to Stephen F. Austin from a member of one of his scouting parties described the coldness of its waters. About 1830 a group of Cherokee Indians moved into the region and drove the Waco from the village.

The first white settlement on the site of the Waco village was a Texas Ranger outpost, Fort Fisher, established in 1837 far beyond the line of settlement. The post was abandoned after a few weeks, but one of the Rangers, George B. Erath, was later the surveyor of the Waco townsite. The chosen name for the settlement was to be Lamartine, but Erath persuaded them to call it Waco Village. In 1856 it was officially incorporated as the city of Waco. (3)

WAGON MOUND, New Mexico

Wagon Mound, Mora County, was built right across the old Santa Fe Trail. Nearby was a mound that resembled a covered wagon, from a distance, and was used as a landmark by the wagon trains passing this way from Kansas to Santa Fe, New Mexico. From this landmark came the name of the community of Wagon Mound, New Mexico. (1)

WAHOO, Nebraska

Wahoo, Nebraska, was settled around the year 1869, and takes its name from one of the following legends—possibly:

It was derived from an Indian name for "burning bush," which grew along the creek banks west and south of Wahoo, and used by Indian medicine men in the treatment of their patients.

In the spring of 1872, when a blacksmith shop was started by James William, John Lee, John Simpkins, and J. D. Cook, the name was painted on their sign. The shop was a stopoff point for stage-coaches, and this was accepted as the town's name.

Wahoo, settled in 1869 by J. M. and J. R. Lee, has been said to be a corruption of the Indian word "Pahoo," meaning a place without bluffs.

Some people have said Wahoo was named for a Sioux Indian chief named Wahoo, who had a squaw named Wanahoo. They point to a dance pavilion a mile east of Wahoo which for years was named Wanahoo.

Anyway, Wahoo is Wahoo, and the name is unusual, and the people love it that way! (2)

WALHALLA, South Carolina

In 1850 it was settled by General John A. Wagener of the German Colonization Society of Charleston. The settlers thought the land must be as lovely as "Valhalla," the hall of immortality into which the souls of heroes slain in battle are received, according to Norse mythology. (6)

WALHALLA, Texas
Walhalla, a Fayette County community a few miles from Waldeck, was named for the pagan German word for heaven. (3)

WALLA WALLA, Washington
First called Steptoeville, Walla Walla received its present name November 7, 1859. Named after the Indian tribe which inhabited the Walla Walla Valley, the word means literally "many waters," also interpreted as "small, rapid stream."

The city officially became the county seat of Walla Walla County November 17, 1859. The county then included half of what is now Washington, all of Idaho and one-fourth of Montana. The city of Walla Walla was incorporated by an act of the territorial legislature January 11, 1862. (2)

WALLS, Mississippi
Takes its name from the "Walls" group of Indian mounds. It is located near the Tennessee line and Memphis, in DeSota County. (6)

WALLUM LAKE, Rhode Island
According to accepted authorities the name "Wallum Lake" is derived from the Indian word "Allom," which means "fine, handsome, good, etc." Wallum Lake, itself, is a remarkably clear one, and the village was named for the lake. Wallum Lake is a village in the town of Burrillville, Rhode Island.

Interesting to note, Wallum Lake is about five miles from Lake Webster, Webster, Massachusetts, which was once endowed with the Indian name of *Chagogagogchabunagungamaug,* meaning, "You fish your side. I fish my side. No one fish in middle." Probably some sort of treaty among Indian tribes to settle an argument over fishing rights. (Joseph E. Cockayne, Wallum Lake, R. I.)

WANAMINGO, Minnesota
Wanamingo, Minnesota, located in Goodhue County, was first settled in 1855 by James Brown, who platted a town here and named it for the heroine of a novel, very popular in that day. (1)

WAPWALLOPEN, Pennsylvania
The name is Delaware Indian and has had many spellings over the years, such as Whopehawley, Waphallapane, Opolopona, and finally Wapwallopen. The most accepted meaning of the name is "place where the white hemp

grows." It is known that a kind of white hemp grew in this region, which the Indians used to make fish nets, coarse clothing and even bedcoverings.

Wapwallopen is located in the southern part of Luzern County. About two miles from each other, two creeks empty into the Susquehanna River. They are called the Big Wapwallopen and the Little Wapwallopen, and the village is located in between. Some local wag suggested that the name was derived from the fact that the creek water comes "wapping" and "walloping" along. (Rev. Clark Wesley Heller)

WAR, West Virginia
War, West Virginia, is located in McDowell County, and takes its name from War Creek. War Creek was named for a great Indian battle which was fought here between white settlers and Chief Logan. Chief Logan boasted that he would kill ten white men for every Indian killed, and almost made his boast come true.

The city was first called War Creek, and later changed to Miners City, due to the mining done in this locale. When a post office was established the name was changed to War.

Near here is an old Indian trail to Saltville, Virginia, which starts in Logan, West Virginia, where the Minto Indian Tribe was located. (1)

WAR EAGLE, Arkansas
War Eagle, named for Chief War Eagle of the Osage Indians, is one of the oldest settlements in northwest Arkansas and retains the rustic atmosphere of the Ozarks. (Chamber of Commerce, Pea Ridge, Ark.)

WARRIORS MARK, Pennsylvania
The town of Warriors Mark received its unusual name from the large oak trees in the area that were used as targets by Indian warriors. Farmers in the locale have large collections of arrowheads, made of flint stone, which have been extracted from the trees in the area. (1)

WARROAD, Minnesota
Named for the Warroad River, that flows into Muskeg Bay, the town was first settled in the early 1800's. With the town of Warroad sitting astride the river, no other name was probable.

The Warroad River takes its name from the old Indian "War Road" or War Path, that was used by the Chippewa, Cree, Sioux, and Assiniboine Indians. Down the Warroad River came the Sioux Indians from the Dakota Territory on their raids against the Chippewa, and back up the river went the Chippewa in retaliatory raids against the Sioux. (Morris C. Grove, Rainbow's End Farm, McIntosh, Minn.)

WASECA, Minnesota

Waseca, located in one of the richest agricultural counties in the nation, has a population of approximately 6,500 people and is the county seat of Waseca County.

The first settler in Waseca County was Asa Sutlief who brought his family from Wisconsin in 1854. Accompanying him was James Child, who later became the publisher of the county's first newspaper. In the spring of 1855, Sutlief encouraged other settlers to enter the area with the result that the villages of Wilton and Otisco were formed in 1857.

Sutlief and his friends were greatly impressed by the fertility of the soil and asked the Sioux Indians which words best described "rich and fertile." They were given the word "Washecha," which, for purpose of simplicity, they shortened to Waseca. (2)

WASKISH, Minnesota

The name is Chippewa Indian and means "deer." Inasmuch as the area is still famous for deer hunting, the name is easily understandable.

The town is located on the Red Lake near the Red Lake Indian Reservation. (Mabel N. Andersen, Baudette, Minn.)

WATERFLOW, New Mexico

Waterflow, located in San Juan County, was once two separate communities named Jewitt Valley and Kentucky Mesa. When they decided to establish a post office here it was evident that one name would have to be chosen for the two. A meeting was held in the general store, which would also serve as the post office, and a stalemate was soon reached. The people of Jewitt Valley wanted to retain their name and the people of Kentucky Mesa, their name. The storm inside was nothing to the storm that was raging outside at that moment. Water was cascading over the steep, rocky bluff nearby, and someone exclaimed, "Look at that water flow!" From this chance remark the community of Waterflow replaced the communities of Jewitt Valley and Kentucky Mesa, New Mexico. (1)

WATERPROOF, Louisiana

The name of the town of Waterproof had been the brunt of jokes many times. On several occasions water had reached a depth of from two to three feet over the entire town, due to the caving banks of the river, necessitating a relocation of the townsite.

Abner Smalley, one of the earliest citizens of Waterproof, gave a reason for the unusual name of the town in one of his favorite stories. He was standing, one day, high and dry, on a strip of land surrounded, as far as the eye could see, by water, while waiting for a steamboat to land for its usual refueling of cordwood. As the boat landed, the jovial captain called out, "Well Abner, I see you're waterproof." Pleased with this greeting Mr. Smalley gave the name of "Waterproof" to the many acres which he had acquired. This, of course, was before the time of the levee system, and the spot on which Mr. Smalley stood was said to be the highest point of land on the west side of the Mississippi, between Memphis and New Orleans.

Waterproof, Louisiana

Supposition of the early citizens places the first settlement of Waterproof at 1830 or earlier. Pioneers coming down the river on flatboats, or coming from the north and east by covered wagon, stopped on their way to Texas, by the Old Texas Road trail. Tired by their journey, and attracted by the rich fertility of the soil, they made homes here, some engaging in agriculture and others in trading.

Waterproof is rich in early history, and some of its inhabitants were very closely connected with the Confederacy. It is known that General Zachary Taylor resided on a plantation two miles east of Waterproof, and it was here that he was making his home when notified of his election as President of the United States.

Some settlers chose this region as their place of settlement because of the high altitude.

Leading out of Waterproof is an old road that contributed its own bit of historical lore to the pioneer days of the region. It is known as the "Old Texas Road," and was used in the covered wagon days as the highway between Mississippi and the Lone Star State. The crossing of the River was made at Rodney, just opposite Waterproof; as many as fifty wagons in a day were known to pass through Waterproof across Louisiana to Nachitoches and into Texas.

Waterproof has been moved four times because of the caving banks of the river. The original townsite is now in the state of Mississippi. (The Tensas Gazette-St. Joseph, La. & Postmaster)

WATERS MEET, Michigan
Located in northwestern Michigan, near the Wisconsin border, Waters Meet takes its unusual name from its location at the axis of three watersheds. From Waters Meet, the drainage is north to Lake Superior, east to Lake Michigan, and south to the Mississippi. (6)

WATER STREET, Pennsylvania
Cradled by the Canoe, Short and Tussey Mountains, Water Street was so named because the early wagon route, as well as the Pennsylvania Canal, passed along the bed of a shallow stream here on its way through the gap in the Tussey Mountains. (4)

WATERVLIET, Michigan
Watervliet, in southwestern Michigan, was settled in the early 1830's and named for the rapids that once roiled the waters of the Paw Paw River. The name is Dutch and means "flowing water." (6)

WAUBUN, Minnesota
The extension of the Soo Line Railroad through northern Minnesota gave birth to a number of new villages on what had been the White Earth Indian Reservation. Passage of the Clapp Amendment in Congress in 1906 gave the Indians title to their land and the right to sell it. A large part of the White Earth Indian Reservation was sold, as a result of this amendment. As the reservation was opened to settlement, the Tribal Council petitioned the railroad to give Indian names to all reservation towns along the Soo Line. The town of Bement was renamed Waubun, which is Chippewa Indian, and means "rising sun." (Chamber of Commerce, Mahnomen, Minn.)

WAUCHULA, Florida
County seat of Hardee County, Wauchula grew up around Fort Hartsuff, built to protect settlers during the Seminole Wars. Its catchy name is Indian and means "sandhill crane." (6)

WAUKESHA, Wisconsin

This was once the land of the Potawatomi, friendly to the white men, brother of the Menomonee, but distant cousin of the Winnebago who hated the white man. The Potawatomis were natives of Michigan and Indiana, pushed west by the British. The Winnebagos were native of the southland, forced north by the Spaniards; and the Menomonee were natives of Wisconsin and the northland.

The Potawatomis of the 1800's were a part of this virgin forest: eating, living, fighting, and dying here. Their biggest villages were at Me-quan-ie-go-ick (Munwonago), Pee-wauk-ee-win-ick (Pewaukee), Musk-ee-guac (Muskego), and T schee-gas-cou-tak (Waukesha). It was on the former site of "Tschee-gas-cou-tak" that the present city of Waukesha was built and got its name. (2)

WAUTOMA, Wisconsin

Wautoma, county seat of Waushara County, was incorporated as a village in 1901 and became a city in 1940. Its history, however, dates back to the winter of 1848-49 when Philip Green built a log house here, which also served as a tavern or inn.

The name Wautoma was formed from two Indian words, Waugh and Tomah. The words, united, are variously translated into "good earth," or "good life." Tomah was also the name of a Menomonee Indian chief who lived in these parts. (2)

WAUPACA, Wisconsin

The city and county of Waupaca took their names from the river, called "Waupakaw Sepiew" or "Waubuck Sega" by the Menominee Indians and translated as "Clear or pale swift running water."

Legend has it, however, that it was named for a Potawatomi chief, named Wa-puka, who gave the area his name. The chief, with thirty of his people, lived in the area. According to the legend, the chief made a long, tiring speech at Waupaca in which he persuaded his braves not to massacre the white settlers. Then, about to mount his pony, the old chief dropped dead. (2)

WAUWATOSA, Wisconsin

In this once primeval land of gigantic trees, cut through by the Menomonee River, the city of "Fireflies" was born, when in 1842 the town of Wauwatosa was established. The name comes from the Indians who exclaimed, "WAU-WAU-TAE-SIE!" whenever they saw the swarms of fireflies as they flitted through the night. (2)

Wauwatosa, Wisconsin

WAWAWAI, Washington
In the pioneer days the Nez Perce and Palouse Indians camped all along this part of the Snake River, on bars and on the alluvial bottom of the Snake River. The name is Nez Perce, and means "council grounds."

This area was settled by white settlers around the year 1870, and they cultivated fruit orchards on the once old Indian encampment grounds. The town of Wawawai is located on the banks of the Snake River, occupying what was once the Nez Perce council grounds. (June Crithfield, Colton, Washington)

WAWINA, Minnesota
Years ago a tribe of Indians rested here beneath a giant pine tree (still standing), which marked a halfway point between their home and the town where they traded. They called the place "Wawina," which means "place of rest." On one of their trips the wife of the chief gave birth under the tree, and the papoose, too, was named Wawina. When the Indian left, never to return, and the white settlers built their village around the towering pine, they could choose no better name than Wawina, Place of Rest. (1)

WAX, Kentucky
Wax lies along the banks of the Crooked Nolin River, in Grayson County. The name was bestowed upon this community, according to local tradition, by some officials who were traveling around the state to different designated places, and giving them names. They used as their guide anything that impressed them the most, or whatever action might be taking place at the time of their arrival at one of these points. As the officials walked into the

country store here, the storekeeper was weighing bees wax, and "Wax" it was and is! (1)

WAXAHACHIE, Texas

Waxahachie, in central Ellis County on Waxahachie Creek, derives its name from an Indian word meaning "cow" or "buffalo creek." The first settler, Emory W. Rogers, came from Robertson County in 1846. His gift of sixty acres for the townsite aided in the choice of Waxahachie as the county seat in 1850. (3)

WAYSIDE, Texas

Wayside, in the south of Armstrong County, was named by Mr. E. P. Bradford, an early settler, for its location on the "wayside" of the canyon. The territory was in the Indian region of the Panhandle, and the buffalo herds did not disappear until about 1878. The first white settlers were cowhands of the J. A. Ranch who had line camps along the canyon. In 1891 the first road was surveyed to Wayside and was used for crossing cattle and ranch outfits over the canyon. (3)

WAYZATA, Minnesota

Among those who saw the beauty of this area on the banks of Lake Minnetonka was Oscar Garrison, a civil engineer, who hacked a trail to this location from St. Anthony and platted the original townsite. It was first called Garrison's, then Wayzata City, then Freeport, and finally returned to the name Wayzata.

The Dakota, who spent part of their time here, loved Lake Minnetonka—which means "a large piece of water"—and asked that it be reserved to them when they were bilked on their lands in the shameful treaty of 1851. This was denied them.

Wayzata is derived from a Dakota Indian word "Waziah," which can be translated as "one aspect of the beneficent Great Father of all." (2)

WEDDERBURN, Oregon

Wedderburn, Curry County, Oregon, was settled by R. D. Hume, in 1894. A Pacific Coast business man who had fishing interests along the coast and at the mouth of the Rogue River, he established a cannery here. He chose to name the community after his ancestral home in Scotland, Wedderburn. The name Wedderburn, in Gaelic, means "Sheep Creek." Wedder is the old form of "wether," and "burn," means "stream or creek." (1)

WEED, California

The town received its name from the late Abner Weed, a pioneer lumberman and one-time state congressman, who built the first sawmill here in 1900. Weed is located in Siskiyou County, in the northern California mountain country. (2)

WEED, New Mexico
Settled around 1880, the community got its unusual name from a Mr. Weed, who established a general store, which served as a nucleus for the community, and later as the post office.

The community, located in Otero County, high in the Sacramento Mountains, surrounded with ponderosa pines. The main industry is ranching and lumber. (1)

WEEPING WATER, Nebraska
Weeping Water Creek first appears as "L'eau qui pleure" on a French map of 1802, which translated into "the water that cries." Its English name appears on the Lewis and Clark map of 1804. The name is perhaps a mis-translation of the Indian name for the creek, "Nigahoe" or "rustling water," from the sound of water running over low falls. The first settler, Elam Flower, came here in 1855 and here the ghost towns of Caladonia (1857) and Grand Rapids (1858) were platted but never developed. Weeping Water was platted later and was first known as Weeping Waters Falls. Soon there was quite an influx of settlers, many from Tabor and other Iowa communities. The coming of the railroad around 1880 brought an influx of settlers, many of German origin, and the town began to grow fast. At the turn of the century, a large number of Danish arrived and one part of the community is still called "Swede Town." Some feeling of these early days was immortalized in a book by the famous Nebraska author, Bess Streeter Aldrich, *A Lantern in Her Hand.* (2)

WEESATCHE, Texas
Weesatche, in northern Goliad County, was called Middleton in 1891 because it was midway between Goliad and Clinton. The town was renamed for the huisatche shrub that grows profusely in the section. (3)

WELCOME, Minnesota
Welcome is located about halfway between Sioux Falls, South Dakota, and LaCrosse, Wisconsin, in Martin County. The town was named for a man named Welcome, who has several relatives living here. (1)

WESLACO, Texas
Weslaco, on the Missouri Pacific Railroad in Hidalgo County, was named for the initials of the W. E. Stewart Land Company, which promoted the

townsite in the irrigated valley section in 1917. By 1950 the city had grown to 7,487. (3)

WEST POINT, California
Named by Kit Carson in 1845, it being the westernmost point reached by his expedition at that time; it is located in Calavaras County. The county, incidentally has a name derived from "El Rio de las Calaveras," Spanish for "river of skulls," so called by Lt. Gabriel Morago of the Royal Spanish Army stationed at the Presidio of San Francisco. On the river below San Andreas, he and his men found many bones and skulls left there after a sanguinary battle between the valley and hill tribes of Indians. They fought over the fish—principally salmon—with which the river abounded. (Chamber of Commerce, San Andreas, Calif.)

WESTWEGO, Louisiana
West We Go is one of few cities which can claim a complete sentence as its name. And by virtue of its name, it has been the object of much speculation and opinion. West We Go was settled during the 1800's by members of a family named Fredericks. In its early days it was known as Salaville; in fact the two names were used interchangeably until well into the 1900's.

Westwego, Louisiana

Traditionally, residents explain their city's name by saying it was a departure point for adventurers in the rush for gold. Another and more dramatic explanation relates that "West we go!" was the cry of storm refugees from a terrible hurricane of October 1, 1893. The settlement of Cheniere Caminada near Grand Isle was virtually wiped out by the storm—

of the 1,500 inhabitants of the Cheniere, 822 died. The first rescue boat to reach the stricken settlement came from Salaville via the Company Canal, (now defunct) which ran through bayous Barataria and Lafourche. The survivors of the storm, desperate and determined, made up their minds to flee west to higher ground.

Whether "West We Go" came from a cry of jubilation or was one of desperation, and relief, the name is truly unique. (1)

WETUMPKA, Alabama

Wetumpka, the county seat of Elmore County, is located on the Coosa River in the east-central part of Alabama. It is within two physiographic regions in the Piedmont province and the coastal plains. In 1836, two years after its founding, Wetumpka was a growing town of 1200 people. An early eastern newspaper asserted that Wetumpka, Alabama, and Chicago, Illinois, were the two most promising cities of the West. The prosperity flourished until a bank crash in 1837 which caused a long depression.

Elmore County, in which it is located, was once densely populated with Creek Indians. In 1714 the French built Fort Toulouse in Elmore County, and a hundred years later, after the defeat of the Creeks, the name was changed to Fort Jackson. The Fort, originally founded to establish trade with the Indians, was later used to discourage the British (who were very active in Georgia) from moving into the area.

The city of Wetumpka was originally settled on the west side of the Coosa River and named for the nearby Indian village Witumka, which means *Rumbling Waters.* The name is well taken as the Coosa River, on any given day hurls 1,375,300,000 gallons of water through the city, indeed rumbling as it goes. (State Historical Society, and Wetumpka Chamber of Commerce.)

WEWAHITCHKA, Florida

County seat of Gulf County, this town is said to have received its unusual name from its proximity to two twin lakes. The Indians, with their imagination, thought it resembled two eyes. The name Wewahitchka is, of course, Indian and means "water eyes." (6)

WHEELING, West Virginia

Wheeling, located in Ohio County, is halfway up a narrow neck of land which separates Ohio and Pennsylvania, very much like a wedge. It sits on the eastern shore of the mighty Ohio River.

There have been many explanations as to where and how Wheeling got its name. The earliest authentic record is one which antedates the settlement of this site by many years. It is an old map of the interior of America, published in London in 1755. On it appears the name of Weeling Island and Weeling Creek in their locations. The most popular explanation of the name is that given by one John Brittle. He was a Pennsylvania pioneer captured by the Delaware Indians in 1791, near Wheeling. He lived with the tribe for five years. He related that Chief Hainguypooshies (Big Cat) told him: The first white settlers venturing down the Ohio were captured and beheaded by a band of Delawares. Their heads were placed on poles near the mouth of the stream as a warning to other invading whites. The spot became known to the Indians as Weeling, or "place of the skulls." Pioneers, mispronouncing it, called it Wheeling, and as a result the "h" was officially added later, changing it to Wheeling. (2)

WHISKEYTOWN, California
Whiskeytown was named for Whiskey Creek, which got its name based on a terrible chain of events. A mule train was carrying kegs of whiskey on their backs when disaster struck and one of the packs broke loose. The kegs rolled into the creek and floated away (probably into happier hands farther down stream). The government simply would not accept the name Whiskeytown when they applied for a post office, so they were obliged to suffer the indignities of such names as Blair, Stella, and Schilling, before old-timers, fed up, started a long fight for the restoration of their town's rightful name. Finally in 1952, the government bowed to the will of the people and Whiskeytown once again became Whiskeytown. (The Sacramento *Bee,* Questions and Answers)

WHISTLER, Alabama
Whistler has long been the subject of many whimsical legends concerning its name. One of the most persistent is that it was named for a railroad engineer who whistled to his family as he passed through the community. Actually, it was named for Washington Jefferson Whistler, son of the great James A. McNeil Whistler. When the "Great American" series of postage stamps honored Whistler, a number of years ago, thousands of covers were sent to the Whistler post office for cancellation. The community of Whistler grew up around the railroad shops of the Mobile and Ohio Railroad just prior to the Civil War. It was named for Washington Jefferson Whistler because of his prominence as an engineer and planner of railroads in this country and Europe. (Museum Director, City of Mobile, Museum Board)

WHITE BEAR LAKE, Minnesota
Named for the lake with the same name. The lake was named by the superstitious Indians who believed it to be haunted by a large, white bear, slain by one of their braves. It was probably an Albino, as there are no "White" bears indigenous to Minnesota. (6)

WHITE CASTLE, Louisiana
Was named for a large columned plantation or antebellum house that once stood here. (6)

WHITE CLOUD, Kansas
White Cloud, Kansas, located in Doniphan County was settled by white men in the middle 1850's. It became a thriving shipping port on the Missouri River, in the bluffland of extreme northeast Kansas. The town was named for Chief White Cloud, of the Iowa Tribe, who claimed ownership to all of the land in this area. An Indian Reservation was established here giving rights to each Indian family for a farm. The Indians were never intended as farmers, particularly the plains Indians, but they were mighty hunters. After their failures as farmers, the United States Government gave them permission to sell their land and most of it was immediately taken by eager buyers and land speculators. (J. Donald Shreve, White, Kansas)

WHITE CLOUD, Michigan
Tradition has it that Chief White Cloud, a wayward Ottawa warrior turned his face and stepped northward through the western portion of Michigan to avoid white encroachment and to seek a quieter abode, and finally settled here.

In 1868 a lumberman, Colonel L. C. Morgan, established a lumber camp in Chief White Cloud's territory, but managed to secure the chief's blessings and friendship. Colonel Morgan had a beautiful daughter named Minnie, who attracted the unwelcomed affection of a villainous character named Dan Devine, head of an outlaw band, who followed them here. (Sounds a little like an old movie.)

Devine immediately started a war with Chief White Cloud and almost the entire tribe was annihilated. Chief White Cloud escaped to Colonel Morgan's camp, then called Morganville. Devine then kidnapped the lovely daughter and just as an itinerant preacher was about to marry them Chief White Cloud managed, by strategy, to rout the gang and rescue the fair damsel. (Maybe this is where the Perils of Pauline plots came from.) Having learned of the gang's stronghold which was in a dugout cave, five miles west of what is now the village of Brohman, Chief White Cloud led Colonel Morgan and his men in an attack. After wounding several of Devine's men he had the satisfaction of seeing Devine dash away on his horse, never to be seen again.

Because of Chief White Cloud's bravery and friendship, Colonel Morgan changed the name of his settlement to White Cloud, Michigan.

If this all sounds a little like the "Perils of Pauline," it should be remembered that all this took place in March 1877, long before the movies were even dreamed of. (2)

WHITE DEER, Texas
White Deer, Carson County, was named for a legendary white deer, said to have frequented White Deer Creek. The White Deer or Diamond F Ranch occupied the region in the 1880's; its log headquarters building being the first house constructed in the county. Early settlers hauled buffalo bones to the railroad. After the oil boom of the 1920's White Deer was incorporated. A statute of a white deer stands on the main street. (3)

WHITE EARTH, Minnesota
White Earth, Minnesota, located in Becker County, was first named by the Indians for the white clay that predominates here. The name has been perpetuated by the naming of White Earth. (1)

WHITEFACE, Texas
Whiteface, a retail supply point in east-central Cochran County, was established as a stop on the Santa Fe Railroad in 1925, and named for the Hereford cattle grown in the area. (3)

WHITE HORSE BEACH, Massachusetts
This small Massachusetts town was named for a legend which grew out of a shipwreck during the Revolutionary War, and a romance that began in tragedy and ended in tragedy. The two lovers met after the terrible shipwreck which befell the American ship *The General Arnold,* during the American Revolution. Most of the soldiers aboard the craft were badly frozen as the *Arnold* was caught in the ice off Plymouth, and one by one they started to die of the cold. Roland was one of those who survived the terrible night in Plymouth Bay, but was so terribly frozen in his arms and legs that it took three months for Helen to nurse him back to health. Of course, while he was recovering the two fell in love, but neither parent of Helen approved the match, much to the disappointment of both lovers. Finally it was arranged that Helen gallop out on the beach on a white horse, and then into the waves, but it was such a stormy night that she perished in the breakers. At least, that is the way the legend goes. The great rock near where the incident is said to have occurred was called White Horse in honor of the legend. From this came the name of a small town in Massachusetts, called "White Horse Beach." (Picture of a sculpture by Elizabeth MacLean-Smith in Dini's in Boston, Mass. Legend by Edward Rowe Snow.)

WHITE PIGEON, Michigan
In St. Joseph County, White Pigeon was named for an Indian chief. Legend has it that in 1830 many tribes of Indians were gathering near Detroit planning the destruction of any settlements in the area as vengeance for having been driven from their homes.

For reasons known only to Chief White Pigeon, he is said to have run the entire distance to warn the settlers here of their planned fate, and to have died of exhaustion for his efforts. The village was named in his honor. It is located in southwestern St. Joseph County, near the Indiana border. (6)

WHITE PINES, California
Newly developed community in the white pine studded mountains, it takes its name from its surroundings. It is located in Calaveras County. (2)

WHITE ROCK, South Carolina
Located in Richland County, it was named for a nearby outcropping of white flint. (6)

WHITE ROCK, Texas
White Rock, Red River County, was settled as early as 1823, when John Stiles crossed Red River to settle at a spot identified by white rock. (3)

WHON, Texas
Whon, Coleman County, was settled on Camp Creek on a half-section of land bought by S. H. McCain from Mrs. Wagie Cooper in 1902. Mrs. McCain petitioned for a post office and was made postmaster. The name is an Anglicized version of "Juan," the name of a Mexican who lived on the ranch. (3)

WICHITA FALLS, Texas
Wichita Falls, in southeastern Wichita County, was named for the five foot falls on the Wichita River which were later washed away. According to tradition, the area included in the original townsite was covered by script which was won in a poker game by J. A. Scott of Mississippi in 1837. After Scott's death, the land was located in 1854 by his heirs who in 1876 sent M. W. Seeley to map a townsite and project a town. The Tom Buntin family had been living in the area since the late 1860's, hauling buffalo hides to Sherman and clothing their children in tarpaulin bought at Fort Sill. John Wheeler settled within the present city limits in 1875. The townsite as platted by Seeley in July 1876, marked the falls on the river, named the streets and Arabella Lake, and planned the public square north of the river.

By 1909 the town had thirty miles of sidewalks, five miles of sewers, and over one hundred businesses, including twenty-one saloons, which accounted for the nickname of "Whiskeytaw Falls." Wichita Falls earned its title as "The City that Faith Built," when, in the midst of the Depression, it celebrated its fiftieth birthday, in 1932, with a historical pageant and golden jubilee. (3)

WICONISCO, Pennsylvania
Takes its name from Wiconisco Creek, which is Indian for "a wet and muddy camp." The area was used by the Indians as their summer camp and evidently wasn't too good. (1)

WIKIEUP, Arizona
First settled in the late 1800's the town takes its name from Wikieup Canyon which runs from Francis Creek to Pilot Knob, twenty miles east of the Big Sandy. Legend has it that Wikieup Canyon got its name when some early day cattleman found the ruins of an Indian village and its wikieups or tepees. The Hualapai lived in this area for some time. (Irene Cornwall Cofer, Kingman, Ariz.)

WILDCAT, West Virginia
Was named for the many wildcats that once prowled this area. Even today, there are a few of these native American predators to be seen here. (1)

WILD CHERRY, Arkansas
All the postmaster could find to say about the name of his town was: "Wild cherries grow here."

WILD FORK, Alabama
Wild Fork, located in Monroe County, Alabama, got its unusual name for its location on the confluence of two creeks, located in the "wild woods." (2)

WILD ROSE, Wisconsin
Settlers of this village in Waushara County came from Rose, New York. The settling and the naming of Wild Rose is told beautifully in the following legend: "The band of weary, footsore travelers halted, their sweat-grimed faces pink in the sunset. Pleasure was stamped on these faces, for the land about them was rich with an abundance of natural blessings. 'Here?' someone asked. 'Here!' the rest chorused. 'Let us call this spot Rose, after our old home,' one of the group suggested. A woman sitting on the ground plucked a small spray of wild roses. It was not the season for wild roses. Was this an omen? 'Wild Rose,' she amended, 'let's call it Wild Rose.' Wild Rose seemed fitting, and has been the name of this little Wisconsin community ever since." (Wild Rose Craft Shop)

WILLOW STREET, Pennsylvania
The post office was established on February 1, 1840. There are no records available to tell if the village was here before that time. The town is situated along the main road, south from Lancaster, and is strung out along both

sides of the road, and both sides were also lined with Weeping Willow Trees, therefore the town became known as Willow Street, and has remained so to this date. (1)

WIND GAP, Pennsylvania
Incorporated as a borough in 1893, it was named for Wind Gap, which is a deep cleft in the Blue Mountains southwest of the Delaware Water Gap, and extends from the top of the ridge almost to the floor of the valley. The early Germans called it "Dei Wind Kaft" because of the strong winds blowing through it. (4)

WINDOW ROCK, Arizona
Window Rock is one of two locations of various agencies of the Navajo Indian Nation. In 1936 the Commissioner of Indian Affairs, John Collier, selected the site for the proposed Navajo Central Agency. Buildings of russet-colored sandstone, quarried in the vicinity, were constructed for use by the Bureau of Indian Affairs, the Navajo Tribe, and Public Health Service. Today, the community of Window Rock is bustling with activity as the various departments of the Bureau and tribe help to govern the sprawling Navajo Reservation.

The name comes from a large sandstone formation which was deposited during the Jurassic Period of the Mesozoic Era and dated back about 165,000,000 years. The window has subsequently been formed by erosion from wind, water, and blowing sand. (Frank H. Carson, Head Parks, Recreation & Tourism Development, the Navajo Tribe, Window Rock, Arizona)

WING, Arkansas
This community was known as Fair Hill when the post office was established in 1882. For some reason the Post Office Department instructed the postmaster to find a shorter name for the locale. Checking the directory of post offices, he selected Wing for its brevity and because there was no other office by that name. At that time mail came in by saddlebag from Danville. (1)

WINNEBAGO, Illinois
Founded July 3, 1854, the town was named in honor of the Winnebago Indians which once occupied all of this area. (1)

WINNEBAGO, Minnesota
Once the site of the Indian Agency for the Winnebago Indians in this area, they were later moved to a reservation near the Missouri River, in Ne-

braska. The reservation is not too far from Sioux City, Iowa, named for the Sioux Nation. The Winnebago were a branch of the Sioux. (1)

WINNECONNE, Wisconsin

The Winnebago tribe, having been driven from the banks of the Fox River (Butte des Morts), went west up the river three and one-half miles and settled in Winneconne. The name Winneconne is, of course, Winnebago Indian, and means "The last stand." The Indians numbered about one thousand when they settled Winneconne. The Fox tribe did not follow them from Buttes des Morts. (Postmaster, Butte des Morts)

WINNEMUCCA, Nevada

This town came into existence because of its location along the route taken by gold-seeking 49'ers. The locale was the only place for miles where the Humboldt River could be forded with wagons. The first name given the settlement was French's Ford, although no one can remember who "French" was. Around the middle 1800's an Army survey party came into northern Nevada, mapping the principal mountains, valleys, and other land marks. The lieutenant in charge was apparently hard pressed for names, and when he reached this area no one could give him a logical explanation for the name French's Ford. He decided the settlement should have a better name so he renamed it for the local Indian Chief, Winnemucca. Now this chief, head of the Piute tribe, was quite old at the time, and completely won over by the white men with their whiskey and gambling. On formal affairs he wore a U. S. Army general's uniform, and the only known picture of him shows him so attired.

While he is revered as a great chief today, a close study of the picture brings one to the conclusion that the people of his era probably look upon him as just another "begging ole Injun!" The story goes that, as a small boy, the chief had a hard time keeping both feet shod at the same time, hence he was given the name of Winnemucca, or "one moccasin."

Wild little Injin,' Only had one shoe.
Must have lost the other, In the Humboldt River's goo.
He grew to be a mighty chief, his warriors brought him fame.
A town, a lake and a mountain, were honored with his name.
So the Piute named "One Moccasin," given by his kin.
Is now said "Winnemucca," with the accent on the "Win." (Lee Berk)

WINONA, Minnesota

It was in October, 1851, when Captain Orrin Smith, owner of the steamer *Nominee,* landed Erwin H. Johnson and Caleb Nash on the river banks here. They staked out a townsite, and others arrived the following month. Captain Smith decided to name the settlement Montezuma, and ordered that maps and records show it as the name. Other settlers said the name was not appropriate, and proposed "Wenona," name of the beautiful Indian princess, daughter of Wa-pah-sha, chief of the Sioux. Irate citizens held a secret meeting and the map maker was bribed to change it to Wenonah, but he misspelled the name. Since 1852 it has been named Winona.

Winona, Minnesota, received its name from an Indian legend. Wenonah was the daughter of Wa-pah-sha, chief of the Sioux Indian Tribe, which had a village named Keona, standing between the great river Kitchee See-bee and the blue water now called Lake Winona. Wenonah, whose first name means "first born daughter," was so beautiful that she was often called "Wild Rose of the Prairie." A young hunter played his reed flute to her and won her heart, but her father and brothers favored another suitor, a terrible warrior named Tamadoks, who was wealthy. Time went on and the tribe paddled canoes up Lake Pepin many miles to a place where they could find clay for making pottery. Here Tamadoks again pressed his suit so, that the father set the wedding day and prepared a great feast. Wenonah, in despair, climbed to the top of a high rock where she was heard singing her death dirge. Her people below, realizing her purpose, hastened to stop her, the swift Tamadoks leading them all. Before they reached the cliff, however, Wenonah had disappeared in the dark water below. Ever since, the place has been known as Maiden Rock or Lover's Leap. (2)

WINSTON–SALEM, North Carolina

Salem was founded in 1766 and Winston in 1849. The two towns united in 1913, each agreeing to keep its own identity, thus the hyphenated name. (6)

WISACKY, South Carolina

Wisackey, Lee County, was once a council ground and meeting place for many South Carolina tribes. Its first name was Warsaw, named for one of the tribes of Indians. Later Warsaw was changed to Warsacky, then to Warsocky, and finally to Wisacky, its present name. (1)

WITHEE. Wisconsin

The village was named for a school teacher, Hiram H. Withee, who came to the county from Maine in 1870. He was a familiar figure in the logging camps of Clark County, and did much to shape the policy of the county. He became its treasurer in 1875 and served until 1882. He owned much land and built several large farms in the county, known as Withee Farms. (1)

WIZARD WELLS, Texas

Wizard Wells, in eastern Jack County, was named by early explorers of the territory who found flowing mineral wells, believed by the Kiowa (who occupied the area) to have medicinal value. (3)

WOLF, Wyoming

Wolf is located entirely on a large dude and livestock concern known as "Eaton's Ranch." The post office serves a sizeable rural community, but all the buildings in Wolf belong to Eaton's Ranch. Wolf took its name from Wolf Creek, which was named by Indians long ago, probably due to a great abundance of wolves in the vicinity. The post office was established in the late 1800's. (1)

WOLF CREEK, Montana

Wolf Creek is a small community located where the Prickly Pear and Wolf Creeks meet and flow into the Missouri River. In 1843, Captain John Mullan hitched four teams of mules to a wagon to show the possibility of a route for a new road from Fort Benton to his main camp in the Bitter Root Valley. "The Mullan Road," as it was named, cost $400 a mile and was 630 miles long. It started at Fort Benton, the head of navigation on the Missouri, and ended at Walla Walla, Washington. With the coming of the road, the build-up of the Montana Territory commenced. Soon Wolf Creek came into being.

In 1862 Congress passed the Homestead Act, and with these rights Martin Lemline came in 1877 and laid claim to a quarter section, which included the site of Wolf Creek. In 1864 Congress, to encourage the building of a railroad and telegraph line between Lake Michigan and Puget Sound, passed an act granting to the Northern Pacific Railroad Company a piece of every odd section through the states as it crossed the country. With the coming of the railroads (including the Montana Central) Wolf Creek became the main business center of the area. In later years Wolf Creek declined in importance.

In the early 1900's a few Indians of the Cree Tribe came to the Wolf Creek area from Canada, and settled. They were friendly and caused no trouble. Many of their descendants live on the Rocky Boy Indian Reservation today.

The community of Wolf Creek took its name from the stream Wolf Creek. The Creek was so named by the Indians to commemorate a hunting incident. They used a nearby cliff as a buffalo jump. In this hunting maneuver, the Indians would chase a number of buffalo over a cliff, killing them, thus securing a great number of buffalo with a minimum of effort. During one of their drives not only the buffalo went over the cliff, but somehow a wolf got caught in the stampede and went over too. From that time on, the creek below was known as Wolf Creek to the Indians. (L. Walker, Postmaster)

WOLF LAKE, Indiana
The town was settled in 1829 and platted in 1832. It was primarily a stopping point for travelers between Fort Wayne and Goshen, Indiana. One of the first buildings of the community was the Tamarack Inn, which not only was a stage coach stop, but served also as a rendezvous point for local horse thieves, who plagued the countryside. They would meet here and do their horse trading.

Named for nearby Wolf Lake, the name came from the Miami Indians, who once camped upon its southern shores. Since the area of the lake was heavily infested with wolves, the name Wolf Lake was well chosen. (1)

WOLF PEN, West Virginia
Early trappers built wolf traps (or pens) at the head of Wolf Pen Branch to catch wolves for their hides. Wolf Pen Branch got its name from this practice of trapping wolves, and when a post office was established it was named for the branch. (1)

WOLF POINT, Montana
The name Wolf Point is said to have originated during the winters of the 1870's when trappers stacked great piles of frozen wolf carcasses on a sand bar point in the Missouri River just south of the present site of this town. In the spring, these were skinned out and the furs shipped by boat to St. Louis. The "Wolf Point" became a familiar sight to the river travelers at that period. The "Wolf Point" was considered the halfway point between Bismarck, North Dakota, and Fort Benton, Montana, at that time. (2)

WOLVERINE, Michigan
In the winter of 1881, George Richards, on snow shoes, was carrying the mail over the trail between Gaylord and a small settlement twenty miles to the north. Along the West Branch of the Stugeon River he was attacked by a pack of vicious wolverines. Woodsman that he was, he killed several of the beasts until his ammunition was exhausted and he then used his axe to drive them off. As a result of this experience and upon his request to Washington, D. C., Wolverine was fittingly named and Mr. Richards became its first postmaster. This event had nothing to do with the state's nickname, the Wolverine State. This nickname for Michigan apparently came from a spirit of derision as was common to many other states. The wolverine is noted for its savage disposition and disgusting habits. Records

show mention of Michigan as the Wolverine State, as far back as 1834. (Edna Dodge, Clerk, Village of Wolverine)

WONEWOC, Wisconsin
Wonewoc, Juneau County, has a Chippewa Indian name which has been translated in many different ways. According to the State Historical Society of Wisconsin and Father Chrysostom Verwyst of Bayfield, Wisconsin, who was a missionary among the Chippewa Indians, the name is a derivation of the Chippewa Indian word "Wo-No-wag," pronounced "Wo-nowaug," and meaning "they howl." They were probably referring to the howling of wild animals (wolves) prevalent in the area then. (William T. Brady, Attorney-at-law, Wonewoc, Wis.)

WOODLAND, Pennsylvania
Founded in 1820, Woodland was named for the surrounding forests. (4)

WOODS CROSS, Utah
Daniel Wood and his family arrived in this valley July 24, 1847. On a choice portion of land near a clear mountain stream he built his farm. Around him grew a community of his fellow men.

As early as 1852 the Utah Territorial Legislature petitioned the Congress of the United States to extend the railroad service from the Mississippi River on to the Western Territories, but it took an additional thirteen years before the project got going. On May 10, 1869, the Union Pacific and Central Pacific roads were joined at Promontory Point at the north end of the Great Salt Lake and the famed Golden Spike ceremony took place, thus joining the eastern and western portions of the United States together by rail.

President Brigham Young, of the Mormon Church, was greatly disturbed to learn that the railroad would not come into Salt Lake City, the capital of the Territory. He immediately set plans into motion to extend a branch line from Ogden, Utah, to Salt Lake City, which brought Mr. Daniel Wood into the picture. The railroad would go through the valley, and through a section of Mr. Wood's farm community. When the original survey was presented it had Mr. Wood's consent, but when the surveyor, a Mr. Jesse N. Fox, examined the location he decided it was quite unsuitable and proposed another site. Mr. Wood insisted that the road be laid where it was originally intended, and suggested that Mr. Fox could use a little more education in his chosen profession as a surveyor.

The matter of the right-of-way, and the depot, were laid before President Brigham Young for decision. When President Young asked Fox about Mr. Wood's feelings in the matter, Mr. Fox replied that Mr. Wood was considerably upset and quite *cross.* President Young decided that the railroad survey would remain as designated and Mr. Wood be compensated from the railroad company, and that the depot would be named Wood's Cross.

Placated, Mr. Wood accepted the decision, but when he questioned Mr. Fox about the addition of the word "Cross" in the agreed name of the depot, Mr. Fox muttered something about a crossroads, and left. Later he admitted to him that a crossroads had nothing whatsoever to do with the name Cross, but that it was indicative of his (Wood's) former mood. They both laughed and Wood's Cross, Utah, was born. (Nina F. Moss, Historian Camp Eutaw, Daughters of Utah Pioneers)

WOODY, California

Named for Sparrell W. Woody's Ranch, established in March 1862, at the foot of Blue Mountain. His descendants still live at the original home site and continue to run cattle. (Woody Centennial, 1862–1962)

WOONSOCKET, Rhode Island

Woonsocket was founded in 1666, chartered as a village in 1837, and incorporated as a city in 1888. The great waterfall which gave Woonsocket its name—the Indians called the place Woone (thunder) Suckete (mist), or Thundermist—has been replaced by a huge dam, and the falls are no more, but the Blackstone River that furnished the falls still snakes its way through the city. (2)

WOOSUNG, Illinois

Woosung, Illinois, was founded June, 1855, by three sea captains— Samuel A. Brimblecom, Harvey Roundy, and John H. Anderson. They were said to have made their fortunes in the China trade and came to this spot to retire. Because the rolling prairies reminded them of the country surrounding Woosung, China, on the Yangtse River, they named their new home Woosung, which means "Haven of Rest" in Chinese. (1)

WOUNDED KNEE, South Dakota

Two braves were in love with the same Indian maiden and while practicing with their bows and arrows near the headwaters of a creek, one of the Indians saw what he beieved was an opportunity to disqualify his companion in the eyes of the maiden. Therefore he "accidentally" shot an arrow through the knee of his companion. This made him a cripple, and thus a poor hunter, and poor prospect for a husband. The area became known as Wounded Knee, the creek taking the same name. When a small village grew up here with the Indians all around, it took the name Wounded Knee.

Wovoka, Nevada Paiute Indian, "False Prophet of Ghost Dance

Miracles," Big Foot, Sioux Band Chief, and Colonel Forsyth, in charge of 7th Cavalry at Wounded Knee: these three men are the leading characters in one of the darkest pages of our "American Heritage," The Wounded Knee Massacre!

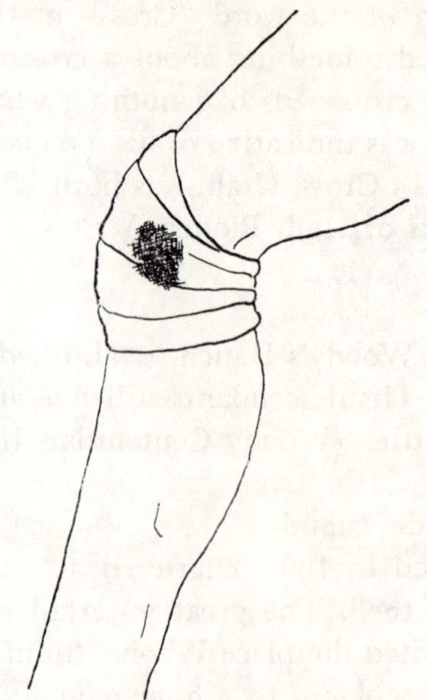

Wounded Knee, South Dakota

December 29, 1890—"Wakan Tanka, the Great Spirit," no doubt very saddened, looked down on Wounded Knee where troops of the 7th Cavalry were deployed, waiting for Chief Big Foot and his band of Sioux men, women and children. The Indians were on their way to the "Cuny Table Flats" where Chief Red Cloud and about 2,000 faithful followers were gathered to celebrate the Ghost Dance Ritual. Knowing the 7th Cavalry was based at Pine Ridge, South Dakota, and well armed, Red Cloud prepared an earthen breast-works as a protection in case of an aggressive action to break up the gathering.

Sitting Bull, Chief Medicine Man of the Sioux people, interested in knowing more about the Ghost Dance, sent a delegation from his camp on the Grand River, about 15 miles south of Standing Rock Agency. Crossing the Cheyenne River Reservation, they picked up Kicking Bear and his followers around Cherry Creek, crossed the Cheyenne River again, traveled south through the Bad Lands on the east, through Interior, Potato Creek, Kyle, camped on American Horse Creek, passed through Porcupine and traveled south toward Wounded Knee.

About five miles from Wounded Knee, near Porcupine Butte, they were apprehended by a contingent of the 7th Cavalry and brought into Wounded

Knee. Tired, hungry, cold, some sick, including Big Foot, they offered no resistance but willingly came into Wounded Knee and immediately set up their camps. Sustenance came mostly from hunting along the way. Together with the Indians waiting at Wounded Knee they numbered about 300 men, women, and children.

There was tension and restlessness throughout both camps. The appearance of armed troops could very well mean encounter, and such was far from the minds and plans of the Indians who had been subdued and ignominously humbled on reservations, poorly fed, clothed and sheltered, and surrounded by the military.

It is said and written that John Barley Corn was in evidence in the Cavalry camp, which alone is an assurance of restlessness, enough to electrify the air and set up over-anxious trigger fingers; also, that Big Foot lay helpless and a prisoner in a trooper tent, leaving the Indians without their leader.

December 29, 1890: By accident or not, it is written also, that without order or command a deadly rifle fire broke out beyond the control of commanding officers. It is also recorded that a shout rang out, "Remember Custer." From there on, between rifle and heavy Hotchkiss one-pound fire, no mercy was shown the Indians. Fire ceased only when their targets were either down or flight had carried them beyond range.

A ghostly hush slowly crept over a field of the dead and dying. Only the mournful whine of a freezing north-wester, the chilling heart-cry of a baby still clinging to the breasts of its mother who was beyond hearing, for she too was numbered among the dead, were the only sounds to break the numbness of the spell.

Several hundred lay in the slumber of death or were dying. Twenty-nine cavalrymen fell in their own crossfire. The Indians, the dead now frozen stiff, were picked up like cordwood, thrown into wagons and hauled away for burial. One hundred and twenty or more were stacked into a long mass grave, dug on the hillside-spot where the Hotchkiss guns were set for action.

Big Foot lay in frozen death along with his faithful followers and so was buried in the long grave. The ghost shirt shield of armor worn by the Indians was now punctured with bullets of death. Wovoka, the Paiute Indian prophet, now had the most costly material proof that Wakan Tanka, The Great Spirit doesn't act as the will of man directs or wishes, but as we all well know, will act in judgment of right over wrong.

One can only try to picture Colonel Fortsyth standing with head bowed, and a prayer of deep grief in his heart as the true picture of death and suffering unfolds before him. Perhaps as great a grief was the failure of the command to orderly carry out the mission of peace without bloodshed. It could very well have been done.

This is a part of the picture Wakan Tanka, The Great Spirit of all mankind, looked down upon; a mass of human beings, some gone to the "Traditional Happy Hunting Grounds of worthy Indians." Those who had escaped now had time to weigh, in after-thought, the myth of unrealities. (W. A. R., and C. A. Gildersleeve & Son, Wounded Knee Battleground Store, Wounded Knee, South Dakota.)

WYACONDA, Missouri
The town was named for the Wyaconda River, and is Sioux Indian meaning, "a place often visited by the great spirit." (6)

WYALUSING, Pennsylvania
Indian for "the place of the old man," or "good hunting grounds." It was settled in the early 1750's by members of the Susquehanna Company, a New England group which claimed most of the area by right of charter and Indian purchase. (4)

WYANDOTTE, Michigan
The site of Wyandotte was first occupied by the Wyandotte Indians, for whom it was named. After the Indians were driven westward, Major John Biddle, in 1818, obtained land in the area, which included the old Indian townsite, and established a farm. He later sold the farm to a company which established an Iron and Steel Company on the water here. From then on the town was on its way to the present city of over 43,000. (2)

WYNOT, Nebraska
This town was started in 1907. A few citizens were trying to think up a name for the new town. One said, "Why not name it – ?" another "Why not name it – ?" This situation kept up so long that an old German settler who had been taking it all in quietly finally exploded, "Vi not! Vi Not! Name it Vi Not!" So they named it Wynot, Nebraska. (1)

WYOCENA, Wisconsin
In south-central Wisconsin, this village has not only an unusual name, but had an unusual beginning. Major Elbert A. Dickason settled here in 1843. The area was still the home of the Menomonee, and a virgin, unspoiled land, cut through by the beautiful Duck Creek. He started farming here, raising some of the first wheat in the territory.

One night he had a dream that a village named Wyocena had sprung up upon his land. The next day he related his dream to his house guest, Benjamin Day. After talking it over, they both agreed that this was one dream that had true merit, so they set about to make it come true. And come true it did.

Today Wyocena is a thriving Wisconsin community, in Columbia County, with a 3rd class post office. The name Wyocena, although a name dreamed by Major Dickason, probably had its origin with the Menomonee of the area, though its meaning, if there is one, is unknown. The well-known phrase "We are such things as dreams are made of" has the town of Wyocena as living proof. (1)

WYOMISSING, Pennsylvania
In Berks County, the name is Indian and means "place of flats." (4)

WYTOPITLOCK, Maine
An Indian name? Not so! Settled in 1830, the town got its name in an intriguing manner. A family named Pitlock lived in this vicinity in a log cabin. Now Mr. Pitlock was a logger, as were all the settlers here, and while working in the wood one day he was killed. His wife and children lived on in the cabin for quite some time. Being an attractive widow, young men from the logging camp would say, "Guess I'll go out and see the Widow Pitlock." The phrase became so commonplace for the locale, that, when a town was established here, the residents just had to name it for the Widow Pitlock, or Wytopitlock, as it is known today. (1)

X-RAY, Texas
X-Ray, a ranching community in western Erath County, was settled before the Civil War and named for its location at a road intersection. A village developed about 1890, when Thurber coal mining was begun. X-Ray natural gas field was discovered in 1920. (3)

YACHATS, Oregon
In 1856 an Indian reservation for the Coo, Umpqua, Calapooya, Siuslaw and Alsea Tribes was established near the present-day Yachats. September 16, 1875, the reservation was closed, the Indians moved to Siletz Reservation, and the land was opened to settlement.

Shortly thereafter a village grew up at the confluence of the Yachats River and the Pacific Ocean, and was called Oceanview. Finally, in 1917, as the settlement grew, it was decided that the name Oceanview was too common, and on February 18, 1917, the name officially became Yachats. It is believed that the name was taken from a small group of Indians (probably a sub-tribe) called the Yahutes, and the name means "Dark waters under the mountain." When the sun comes up over the mountains behind the village, the name is quite appropriate as the mountain casts its shadow upon the waters.

Interesting to note, the first streets of Yachats were paved with shells from the numerous shell mounds left by the Indians. The Yachats vicinity, south to Ten Mile Creek, contains perhaps the greatest concentration of Indian shell mounds found anywhere on the West Coast. (1)

YAKIMA, Washington
Yakima, meaning "black bear," was named for an Indian tribe, and is located east of the Cascade Mountains in the south-central section. Fort Simcoe State Historical Site is a major tourist attraction here. (Office of Secretary of State, Olympia, Wash.)

YARD, Texas
Yard, Anderson County, on the Trinity River, was originally a part of Tennessee Colony. The first store in the community was kept by Bruce Gray, who is said to have named the settlement by including a request by a customer for a *yard* of cloth, on a list of names prepared for the post office department. It was short, so they picked it. (3)

YARDS, Virginia
Yards, Tazewell County, Virginia, had its beginning as a Railway Yard. It was called "The Yards," and the shipping point was "Flat Top Yards." When the post office was established here it was *shortened* to Yards. (1)

YEEHAW, Florida
A small cluster of buildings, the name that sounds like the braying of an ass, is in reality an Indian name and means "wolf." (6)

YELLOW BLUFF, Alabama
A town got its name from the steep, yellow clay walls (or bluff) near a landing situated on the Alabama River. The first post office was at the landing, with mail brought by boats from Montgomery, Selma, and Mobile. Mail was also brought by horseback from Pine Hill. On September 11, 1918, when the railroad arrived, the post office moved to the depot, and with it came the name "Yellow Bluff." (1)

YELLOW CREEK, Ohio
This small hamlet received its name from the little stream that flows nearby. The area was, for many years, the home of Logan, the Mingo chief (from West Virginia). It was here in 1774 that his sister and several friends were

killed by Americans under a Colonel Greathouse. It was this act that put Chief Logan back on the warpath against the white man. (6)

YELLOW HOUSE, Texas
Yellow House, in southern Lamb County, was named for the color of the clay in nearby Yellow House Canyon when the site became headquarters for a division of the X I T Ranch about 1880. The ranch windmill was a landmark for surveyors and cowboys. George W. Littlefield bought the Yellow House division of the X I T in 1901. (3)

Yellow Jacket, Colorado

YELLOW JACKET, Colorado
Yellow Jacket, located in Montezuma County, takes its name from Yellow Jacket Canyon, which was named for "Old Chief Yellowjacket, a mean old Skunk," who was chief of the Navajos. (1)

YELLOW PINE, Alabama
According to old-timers of the town, Yellow Pine got its name from the yellow pine that was milled here years ago. (1)

YELL SETTLEMENT, Texas
Yell Settlement, in Hays County, about twenty-two miles northwest of San Marcos, was settled in 1874 by Tom George, Elisha McCuistion, and Mordecai Yell. Yell was a circuit-riding Methodist minister for whom the settlement was named. (3)

YELLVILLE, Arkansas
Established around the 1850's, it was once known as Shawneetown, but was later named for Colonel Archibald Yell, a famous figure in Arkansas politics. During one of his campaigns he is said to have visited Shawneetown, named for an Indian village that had once occupied the site, and paid the residents $50 to rename the town after him. (6)

YESO, New Mexico
When the railroad built through here in 1906, the depot was built on a high hill. Many names were suggested for the site, but it was the old-time Mexican and Indian workers who came up with the most acceptable name, "El Yeso," Spanish for "The Gyp Rock." The locale here is primarily hard white rock, which goes deep into the earth.

When the post office was established, the Post Office Department, in its zeal for short, brief names, insisted that the "El" portion be dropped, and the name shortened to "Yeso." (1)

YORBA LINDA, California
What is now Yorba Linda was a part of the original Rancho Santa Ana, granted to José Antonio Yorba in the early 1800's. In 1888, a boom town called Carlton sprung up a short distance northwest of the present site of Yorba Linda, but failed for lack of water. Taking a lesson from this, the Janss Investment Company filed a map in 1908 and started the town of Yorba Linda in 1909, selling fruit ranches for $150 to $300 per acre with one share of water stock included with each acre.

In 1913, the community's most renowned citizen, Richard Nixon, was born.

The name Yorba Linda, which rolls off the tongue with such ease, is a combination of the family names "Yorba," and "Linda," which means "beautiful" in Spanish. (2)

YOUNG AMERICA, Indiana
This area was purchased from the Miamis about 1838–39. There were very few whites in the territory at that time. About 1855 a sawmill was hauled into a small clearing and set up. Young America was inscribed on the name plate, and someone suggested using it for a name of the lumber camp rather than Henryville which had been previously chosen. The town was platted as such December 30, 1863, and a post office established and named Young America, February 8, 1876. (1)

YOUNG HARRIS, Georgia
Located at the foothills of Brasstown Bald Mountain, the highest spot in

Georgia. First known by the name McTier, it was later changed to Young Harris in memory of Young Loften Gerdine Harris, founder of Young Harris College here, in 1884. (1)

YPSILANTI, Michigan

At the beginning of the nineteenth century this part of Michigan was still considered frontier country, peopled mainly by Indians and trappers. In 1809 a busy trading post existed on the Huron River some 35 miles west of civilization's outpost, Detroit. The post grew rapidly and by 1823 it was a sizable community known as Woodruff's Grove. When the U. S. Congress appropriated funds for the improvement of the Old Chicago Road, new settlers arrived to beat back the wilderness, build homes, and establish farms.

The settlement was chartered as a village in 1832. The following year it received its present name: Ypsilanti. This was America's way of recognizing the great Greek general of the 1820's, Demetrius Ypsilanti. He had gained worldwide fame as a result of his heroic stand against the Turks in the Alamo-like battle for Greek independence.

Interestingly enough, as a very young man Demetrius Ypsilanti was so inspired by the American struggle for independence that he had come to this continent and had actually fought in the Battle of Monmouth. (2)

YREKA, California

Legend and fact. First the legend: A drunken miner shooting up a bakery sign shot out the "B"; inverted, the sign now reads "YREKA." Accepted fact: The town was to be named in the Indian language after Mount Shasta, which was then called "Ieka." While the town was being chartered by the legislature, no one was certain of the Indian spelling so they spelled it as it sounded, and it came out Yreka. (2)

YUCAIPA, California

Named for the Yucaipa Valley, where the Serrano Indians lived until the first white invasion by Padres and soldiers, which occurred when Captain Juan Bautista de Anza traversed the San Bernadino Mountains to the north, followed by Padre Francisco Garces. Padre Garces was exploring, and it was he who discovered the San Bernardino Valley.

The Serrano Indians called their valley "Green Valley," because grain grew in abundance. Colonists who came in the early 1800's tried to imitate the gutteral Indian pronunciation of the name of the valley by writing "Ucipe" or "Yucaipe." The name finally evolved into "Yucaipa." The present town adopted the name and came into being around 1910. (Chamber of Commerce, Yucaipa Valley)

YUCCA, Texas

Yucca, a switch on the Texas and New Orleans Railroad in eastern Uvalde County, was established when the road was built in 1881 and named for the Spanish dagger plant found in the area. (3)

ZELIENOPLE. Pennsylvania

Zenienople's earliest known history began with habitation by the Delaware and Seneca Indians. In 1753, the area was claimed by the state of Virginia. By 1774, it was annexed by King George III, an action which was listed as one of the grievances in the Declaration of Independence. Baron Frederick William Detmar Basse, a German nobleman, purchased the area from the Philadelphia Land Company in 1802, and named the town after his daughter Zelie. (2)

ZEPHYR, Texas

Zephyr, in eastern Brown County, is said to have been named by surveyors who were caught, not by a zephyr, but by a blue norther (a cold, chilling wind out of the north), as they surveyed the original land grants. A school was organized about 1877, and the settlement became a station on the Gulf, Colorado, and Santa Fe Railroad in 1886. In 1903, the town was almost completely destroyed by another Zephyr—this one a cyclone—but it was later rebuilt. (3)

ZIGZAG, Oregon

Zigzag, a station of Rhododendron, and not too far from Government Camp, in Clackamas County, received its unusual name because of the zigzag manner in which the Salmon River passes it by, and from the equally unusual formation of the Hood Mountains.

Both the Barlow Trail and the Old Oregon Trail passed through this village at one time. (1)

ZIGZAG, Texas

Zigzag, so named because of the many turns of the road leading into it. It is a Medina County community seven miles west of Devine. In a fine farming section, the Zigzag settlement once had a post office, but it was later discontinued. (3)

ZIM, Minnesota

This small town, once a booming lumber camp, was named after a pioneer lumberman named Zimmerman, who was affectionately called "Zim." (1)